THE CREATIVITY QUESTION

D1196845

THE CREATIVITY

QUESTION

Edited by ALBERT ROTHENBERG

and CARL R. HAUSMAN

Duke University Press

Durham, N.C. · 1976

M. Anderson '77

Copyright © 1976 by Duke University Press

L.C.C. card no. 75–30132

I.S.B.N. (cloth ed.) 0–8223–0353-1

I.S.B.N. (paperbound ed.) 0–8223–0354-x

Printed in the United States of America
by Kingsport Press, Inc.

TO JULIA AND CAROLYN

CONTENTS

CHAPTER THREE · EXPLANATIONS 1: FORMS AND SCOPE

CHAPTER FOUR · EXPLANATIONS 2: SPECIAL TRENDS

Chapter Five · ALTERNATIVE APPROACHES

PREFACE

This book of readings can be traced to a twofold inception: chance and the convergence of two directed interests. Chance made possible the first meeting of the editors, a psychiatrist and a philosopher. The previous investigative interests of the editors were brought together because of this meeting. Although no claim is made that the overall result is a radical creation, both valuable and totally new, the combination of chance and directed interest does suggest two general characteristics that, to us, seem evident in creative processes: novelty or the unprecedented, and order, or control and design. A control or design present in the activity and an unexpected or unprecedented appearance of a phenomenon or an entity are two of the marks of creativity. These two features are central to the thinking that lies behind the general construction as well as the thread of discussions accompanying the selections we have included in this book.

In addition to this underlying focus on the combination of novelty and control, several other principles operated in our choices and organization of the selections. These principles are the product of the two professional or disciplinary perspectives of the editors. Although it might conceivably be of some interest to spell out our view of these perspectives in great detail, we believe that our views will be evident in what we say in the general introduction, in explanatory comments throughout the book, and in the selections from our own writings that are included. Moreover, each of us has discussed his perspective in other places.[1] We conceive philosophy in a somewhat traditional and general sense in distinction to some current and influential philosophical movements. Philosophy is a reflective, critical, and sustained development of our understanding of the widest possible range of experience into the most comprehensive and coherent view that it is possible to construct. Psychiatry, in the broadest sense, is an approach to amelioration of difficulties and discordances in human behavior and experience, an approach derived from systematic and empirically based information about both normal and abnormal psychological processes.

1. See especially Rothenberg, Albert. "The Iceman Changeth: Toward an Empirical Approach to Creativity," *Journal of the American Psychoanalytic Association*, 17:549–607, 1969; Hausman, Carl R. *A Discourse on Novelty and Creation*. The Hague: Nijhoff, 1975.

This brief account of our general perspectives should help the reader see why we have adopted the principles that underlie the organization of the book. Although these principles will be understood better following a reading of the Introduction, we shall sketch them here in anticipation of our more thorough discussion of the complex cluster of issues and points of view associated with the study of creativity.

The main body of selections falls into three general categories: description, explanation, and alternative approaches, in Chapters Two, Three, and Five respectively. These categories illustrate the major issues involved in approaches to creativity. The selections that appear under the category of description focus primarily on identifying significant features and stages or phases of creative processes. Those that fall under explanation are attempts to determine the conditions or factors responsible for creative activity; also, they are essentially geared toward predicting creative activity and its outcome. The third category covers selections in which the authors explore the possibility of understanding creativity in ways that do not require that creative acts be predicted or that all conditions for their occurrence be named.

Basically, the inquiry into creativity has not progressed in a clear continuous line of historical development. Recognizing that some chronology and historical development exists and is therefore of some interest, however, we have presented selections chronologically when this presentation does not interfere with the conceptual principle. We have also included a special chapter, Chapter Four, containing some recent examples of attempts to explain creativity and illustrating some special types of exploratory trends: creativity of women, brain research, synectics, extrasensory perception, behaviorism and creativity, and computer programming.

Since specific orientations to creativity can be traced to particular initiating thinkers and investigators, we have included a separate chapter, Chapter One, composed of seminal accounts. This chapter should serve both to illustrate the essential types of orientations toward understanding creativity, and to provide some developmental perspective. Selections from the following are included: Plato's writing on creativity as the foundation for two traditions, supernaturalism, which finds the source of creative acts in a superhuman power, and a tradition which rejects the hope of explaining creativity rationally; Aristotle's works as the foundation for both naturalism and rationalism, orientations in which creative acts are rationally explained as natural events or as consequences of universal and ultimate principles; Freud's work as the initiator of a clear-cut emphasis on fantasy and unconscious processes in creation; Galton's writings as seminal to a strong emphasis on genetic explanation within the naturalist tradition; Kant's work as an initiator of the type of alternative approach that emphasizes the self-determining and unpredictable aspects of the creative act rather than those aspects that are associated with antecedent conditions and prediction.

After the presentation of seminal accounts, the sequence of chapters in the book is intended to illustrate a progression and a transition in which studies of creativity focus less on description and more on explanation, and finally to highlight the challenge to explanation presented in the chapter on alternative approaches. We do not necessarily intend these alternative approaches to be the final word on creativity; we present them last so that the thoughtful sequential reader will appreciate the full significance of their orientations. Further explanations of the sequences and organization of selections will be found in the general introduction as well as in the introductions to each chapter. References and recommendations for further reading are included for each chapter.[2]

The editors wish to acknowledge their gratitude to all those who helped make this volume possible. Albert Rothenberg's aspect of the work was supported in part by two five-year Research Scientist Career Development Program Awards from the United States Public Health Service. The Estate of Gladys B. Ficke, Ralph F. Colin Executor, and the John Simon Guggenheim Memorial Foundation also provided time and support required to complete the book as it reached its final stages. Carl Hausman's contribution was supported by resources from the Central Fund for Research, The Pennsylvania State University. Also, two summer grants from the American Philosophical Society and the award of a sabbatical leave by The Pennsylvania State University, 1974–75, were essential to providing time needed to work on the volume at various stages of its construction.

Albert Rothenberg warmly acknowledges the man who most encouraged his interest in creativity during his college years, Henry A. Murray. Carl Hausman is grateful to all his teachers and colleagues who have provided encouragement and friendly criticism for the writing and study associated with the topic of this book. Both editors express appre-

2. For a complete bibliography of scientific writings on creativity, we refer the reader to: Rothenberg, A., and Greenberg, B. *The Index of Scientific Writings on Creativity: Creative Men and Women.* Hamden, Conn.: Archon Books, 1974; and Rothenberg, A., and Greenberg, B. *The Index of Scientific Writings on Creativity: General, 1566–1974.* Hamden, Conn.: Archon Books, 1976. A discussion of the philosophical antecedents of the traditions and perspectives on the problems of creativity, particularly as these are found in Plato, Aristotle, and Kant, appears in Hausman, *Discourse on Novelty and Creation,* pp. 2-17.

ciation to the students in our seminar on creativity given in the spring of
1971 at The Pennsylvania State University. The reactions of these students
to our interdisciplinary approach to "the creativity question" were helpful
to us in our decisions about how to organize this volume. And we thank
Georgia Goeters for her typing assistance and Marie LeDoux for her
crucial help with final typing, permissions correspondence, and organization. Finally, we wish to acknowledge the excellent assistance in editing
and proofreading rendered by Robert Cater.

THE CREATIVITY QUESTION

INTRODUCTION

THE CREATIVITY QUESTION

The search for knowledge about creativity is linked with magic, the demonic, and the divine, yet such knowledge is at the forefront of rational inquiry. Creativity is paradoxical and complex, and the most steadfast investigator is constantly beset with feelings of awe and a sense of mystery as he pursues his inquiry. Creativity encompasses the magical incantations and drawings of primitive man, the appearance of new forms in nature, and the evil genius of Faust. It is a human capacity but it seems to transcend human capacities. On the one hand, the investigator is lured and excited by a tantalizing paradox, and on the other, he is deterred by nagging doubts about whether he is naively trying to explore and rationalize an impenetrable aspect of human experience. To make matters more complicated, investigation is fraught with a host of concrete and theoretical problems. The empirical investigator constantly turns to creative persons for his data and he interrupts their work for lengthy interviews or myriad types of tests and experiments. The philosophical investigation of creativity raises issues about the creation of the world, free will versus determinism, and the basic nature of experience—issues that some consider fruitless and unanswerable. Yet there is a need for rational understanding of creativity that supersedes these doubts, irritations, and criticisms: creativity has direct pertinence to diverse types of disciplines and to the enhancement of humanistic goals in our technological and atomic age.

In psychiatry and psychology an understanding of creativity is of utmost and immediate importance. Pertaining quite directly to basic concepts of health and disease, insights into creativity would contribute significantly to the medical practice of psychiatry. Although there have been many advances in psychiatric knowledge during the past century, the basic concepts of mental health and illness are still notoriously confused and inconsistent. Certain types of behavior can be fairly readily classified as maladaptive or markedly deviant but these classifications have little relationship to any clear, positive concept of adaptive behavior or psychological health. Unlike those in the field of medicine, who describe health in terms of statistical norms and averages, psychiatrists have resisted equating the statistically frequent with the healthy. Although such rejection of the average as healthy or normal seems to be quite appropriate in the area of human behavior, psychiatrists have provided no alternative to the medical approach except some vague and implicit standard of ideal behavior. Consequently, by default, each psychiatric practitioner establishes his own personal, value-laden criteria of health with each of his patients. This problem is surely more than merely of theoretical significance. Without clear criteria for health as well as for disease, it is difficult to establish goals of treatment or to evaluate the effectiveness of the myriad forms of therapy that are practiced today. Since creativity is in the most definite sense a capacity of those specially talented human beings who contribute significantly to society and to life, it is an ideal form of behavior; consequently, it behooves us to try to understand creativity as specifically as possible in order to develop a clear notion of ideal, normal, and pathological. For example, is it appropriate to speak of creativity as a legitimate goal of therapy or as an aspect of health? Is the absence of creativity appropriately considered to be a manifestation of disease? Though many will rush forward with firm and ready answers, we submit that these questions can only be answered meaningfully when we know as much as possible about what creativity is.

For psychology the problem of creativity also pertains to questions about normal functioning, and it relates as well to current central concerns with motivation, cognitive functioning, psycholinguistics, and personality theory. Creativity involves unusual, seemingly deviant psychological processes that lead to highly positive outcomes. The processes of creation, particularly artistic creation, highlight issues about unconscious and conscious motivation, and creative thinking is a form of cognition with special relationships to learning, concept formation, and problem-solving. Literary creativity has much pertinence to psycholinguistics. An understanding of creativity must be incorporated in any account of motivation, cognition, linguistic functioning, or personality, and a clarification of the apparently aberrant but positive creative processes should shed light on more routine psychological functions.

In philosophy the acknowledgment of the possibility of radical creativity, i.e., creation in some sense *ex nihilo,* or out of nothing, has been central to the development of the relatively recent movement of existential philosophy. As an issue radical creativity is also important for another dominant contemporary movement, analytic philosophy. In opposing metaphysics, the analytic philosopher must come to grips in a critically important way with whether or not radical creation is meaningful. If it is considered meaningful, he needs to propose an appropriate analysis of the topic. If it is considered meaningless, then he should account for language referring to the appearance of new things. Anyone directing philosophical inquiry toward some form of comprehensive view must come to grips with the place of creativity in our experience.

Many other types of professionals, including educators, educational psychologists, business executives, and government personnel concerned with manpower, are interested in creativity in an immediate and pressing way, primarily in order to identify and nurture creative talent. Clearly a laudable aim, nurturing creativity could contribute greatly to the benefit of all mankind. How such a purpose could be advanced or whether it is in fact feasible to consider nurturance of creativity a realistic possibility depends entirely on an understanding of the phenomenon.

Traditionally, artists of all types have been concerned with exploring and imparting some understanding of the nature of their own creativity, both within their art and in public utterances; many artists and art critics believe that systematic exploration of creativity is crucially important to art and art criticism. And many modern artists consider the documentation of a creative process unfolding to be a central artistic goal. Artists' current special concern with creativity, we feel, lends particular support to our assertion that the investigation of creativity is at the forefront of rational inquiry. Artists are our most perceptive commentators on the human condition. The investigation of creativity is at the forefront of contemporary rational inquiry because it potentially sheds light on crucial areas in the specific fields of behavioral science and philosophy and, more deeply, because it concerns an issue related to man's survival: his understanding and improvement of himself and the world at a time when conventional means of understanding and betterment seem outmoded and ineffective.

Although highly important and pressing, the task of gaining knowledge about creativity is very difficult. In all its aspects, creativity is quite complex. Numerous and complicated methodological and conceptual problems arise. For one thing, the topic has generated a web of conflicting assumptions in which investigators all too readily become enmeshed. Empirical scientists studying creativity seem to be particularly caught in such a web. Traditionally, it has not seemed particularly necessary or fruitful for empirical scientists to concern themselves with basic assumptions about the scope and methodology of their particular subjects of study at every step along the way. Constantly raising such issues often serves to retard progress in inquiry. There have been times in the history of thought, however, when questioning basic assumptions has had far-reaching consequences. For instance, at one point psychologists questioned basic notions about causality and found it necessary to modify earlier assumptions. In keeping with Hume's thesis that causal connections can be understood only as invariant sequences, many psychologists substituted the notion of "correlation" for cause, believing that such a modification could avoid unfruitful speculation. Similarly, with regard to creativity, we believe it is crucially important for investigators from diverse disciplines to concern themselves with basic assumptions. This topic particularly demands that the investigator look at his presuppositions about continuities and regularities in nature, a matter to which we shall return throughout this book.

In identifying and organizing the material on this topic, we ourselves have made a basic assumption. We have taken for granted that there is some common pattern to diverse activities that are commonly and generally designated as "creative," i.e., activities that share the essential attributes of both *newness* and *value*. We have therefore included studies focusing on the genius and processes of creation in art, science, and other fields as well as those emphasizing a presumed capacity for creativity in everyone. Minimally, however, creativity consists of the capacity for, or state of, bringing something into being. And bringing something into being involves at least three separable components: an agent, a process, and a product. In surveying the literature, therefore, it will be useful to distinguish between three different foci of interest: the creative person, the creative process, and the created object. Although investigators of creativity do not always specify the particular focus or foci of their studies, it is helpful to bear these foci in mind because they influence method and conclusions. Some investigations are devoted exclusively to one of these three foci. For example, MacKinnon's, Barron's, and Helson's studies are focused on the personality attributes of architects, writers, and mathematicians, while Roe reports on the personality characteristics of scientists. Kris, Kubie, Wallas, Patrick, Crovitz, and Skinner focus almost exclusively on the creative process, and Morgan and Kant base their conclusions on the characteristics of the created object. Other investigators include more than one of these foci at the same time. For example, Lee discusses artists and the process of creating art, Ehrenzweig the work of art and the process of creating it, Rank the artist and the art product.

Frequently investigators are not aware that the data appropriate to one focus differ significantly from the data appropriate to another. The creative person does not necessarily use all his attributes and capacities during the creative process, for instance, and not all aspects of an art product are necessarily new and created. Much of art is imitation rather than creation. Working in an artistic field is not synonymous with being creative. Moreover, investigators are often not aware that there are both differences and interrelationships: conclusions about one set of data imply definite conclusions about the other two. If Oedipal conflicts or fear of death in creative persons lead directly to the production of art or to scientific creations, then nothing new occurs either in the creative process or the created product. Oedipal conflicts and fear of death are neither new nor unique: they exist in everyone. The problems produced by ignoring the distinctions and interrelationships among the components of creativity are legion. For instance, investigators must bear in mind that the three components are not equally susceptible to direct investigation. This is of special importance for the multidisciplinary perspectives of the studies contained in this volume because psychologists and psychiatrists generally have access to information about personality attributes, and the philosophical approach seems to pertain especially to considerations about the nature of the created object.

Another assumption pertains to the basic definition of creativity. As we said, we have assumed that creative activities and created products have the criterial attributes of newness and value. Newness or novelty, the appearance of intelligible attributes or experiences that are different from preceding attributes or experiences, is intrinsic to the concept of creation. Although the literal definition of the term "creation" does not necessarily include the attribute of value, i.e., intrinsic worth and/or pragmatic usefulness, the term is almost invariably used to convey value, either tacitly or explicitly. Value is required to differentiate between creations and merely eccentric or banal entities and experiences.

Traditionally, it has been assumed that special talent or genius is necessary to produce new and valuable entities. Nowadays, however, it is rather popular among professional researchers as well as nonprofessionals to insist that the potential for creativity exists in everyone. This increasingly common assumption seems to arise from a recognition of similarities between certain aspects of created products and various types of behavior or psychological processes — but, it should be emphasized, it is not based on a similarity of known facts about the creative *process* and other types of behavior or processes. Hence, since art creations seem spontaneous and increase our awareness of experience, the personality qualities of spontaneity and openness to experience — potential attributes of everyone — seem related to creativity. The assumption of a potential for creativity in everyone does not necessarily refer to the creation of tangible products; the proposal that everyone is capable of producing tangible creations is highly hypothetical and difficult to prove, especially in the absence of an understanding of the means whereby tangible creations are produced. Primarily the issue turns on what we expect creativity to contribute to experience. The particular locus of inquiry — where one begins and what one expects to gain — depends upon how broadly or narrowly creativity is conceived. If creativity is conceived as equivalent to the broad and general qualities of spontaneity and openness, then we may center our inquiry on creativity in everyone. If, on the other hand, creativity is conceived as requiring radical change, productive of far-reaching new value, then we should confine our study to special talent or genius.

Scope of Research and Inquiry

In spite of the complexity of the topic, progress has been made. The selections here cover a wide range representing diverse disciplines with diverse definitions and approaches to creativity. Some approach creativity as a capacity or state qualitatively limited to the genius or persons with special talent whereas others, especially Maslow, Rogers, and Gordon, define creativity or a type of creativity as potentially present in everyone. Kant asserts that genius, or creativity, is found in the arts but not in science; Galton, Lombroso, Roe, Guilford, Barron, Helson, Wallach and Kogan, and Torrance attempt to study genius and/or creativity in diverse areas including science, mathematics, jurisprudence, and politics as well as the activities of school children. Guilford, Crovitz, and Getzels and Csikszentmihalyi define creative thinking as a form of problem-solving. Bergson finds creativity in the flux of time and Maritain traces human creativity to God. To some extent, the diversity of definition reflects the diversity of purpose of the various types of investigators. Philosophers, by and large, are interested in creativity as related to a world view or as a topic in aesthetics and their discussions of creativity either constitute part of a total philosophy or imply one. Psychologists are interested in making predictions about creativity and in developing tests which identify creative talent. Educational psychologists, represented here by E. P. Torrance, have many of the same goals as other psychologists but they are also especially interested in nurturing and developing creativity. And W. J. J. Gordon, the management consultant, strongly emphasizes this latter aim. Psychoanalysts also have an interest in predicting and identifying creativity but are especially interested in relating the psychodynamics of the phenomenon to other issues in psychoanalytic theory and they frequently pay attention to the relationship between creativity and abnormal behavior.

Methods of investigation also differ, though less so than definitions and purposes. They include experiments such as those of Patrick, and Getzels and Csikszentmihalyi; psychological test procedures; statistical analyses; clinical descriptions; quasi-empirical speculations; deductive metaphysics; phenomenological descriptions; and introspective accounts. Interestingly, there is a fair degree of methodological overlap between some philosophical and psychoanalytic investigations: several studies of both types cite occasional empirical examples to support rather far-ranging speculations. Although psychoanalysts might challenge the philosophers' empiricism and philosophers might challenge the psychoanalysts' approach to speculation, in view of the similarity in method it is curious that so little interdisciplinary discourse has so far taken place. Stimulating such discourse is one of the major purposes of this book. At the other end of the methodological spectrum is the approach of psychologists such as Barron, MacKinnon, Helson, Roe, and Guilford, who have collected a good deal of empirical data with little or no explicit theory at the start.

With such diversity, there is bound to be a good deal of general disagreement and contradiction. But there are also specific controversies between certain authors on particular points: Schachtel criticizes Kris's notion of "regression in the service of the ego" as neglectful of the adaptive value of a capacity for "openness to the world." Beardsley requires rather drastic modifications of the teleological approach (exemplified here by the work of Blanshard) as well as of the determinists' attempt to explain creativity by antecedent causation; Ehrenzweig contradicts Kris's and Kubie's emphasis on the role of preconscious processes and reintroduces an earlier psychoanalytic emphasis on the Unconscious, albeit presenting a new formulation of unconscious functioning in art. Rather than discussing these important and suggestive disagreements here, we refer the reader to the selections themselves and postpone detailed discussion for another work. Let us instead look at some of the specific concepts and findings about creativity that emerge from the selections to follow to see what kind of contribution they make to our understanding.

What factors and processes are involved in creativity? Several of the authors emphasize and define specific mental attributes that enter into creation. Wallas and Patrick emphasize specific phases occurring in a fairly regular sequence and include a phase of incubation where creative work occurs outside of consciousness. Blanshard and Cannon, Ehrenzweig and Jung, as well as Freud and other psychoanalysts represented here also emphasize a process occurring outside of consciousness. These formulations of nonconscious processes in creativity differ in significant ways. Blanshard's subconscious functions in accord with a system of teleological necessity and does not have the specifically defined determining effect upon consciousness of the Freudian Unconscious. Cannon's process is extraconscious rather than unconscious and also differs from the psychoanalytic Unconscious in having no necessary determining effect upon consciousness. Jung emphasizes the autonomous complexes which unearth the Collective Unconscious. Like the Freudian Unconscious, Jung's Collective Unconscious does have a determining effect on consciousness in creation. In addition, the Collective Unconscious accounts for an audience's favorable response to a creation, particularly an artistic creation. In the study presented here, Freud emphasizes the role of fantasy in the production of literary works. For Freud, such fantasy is primarily a manifestation of preconscious thoughts and feelings; in his general theory, however, he also emphasizes the role of the Unconscious in creation. Kris supplements Freud's general formulations with a specific notion of "regression in the service of the ego" or ego-controlled regression. According to Kris, "regression in the service of the ego" is the specific means whereby preconscious and unconscious material appear in the creator's consciousness. Kubie's emphasis on preconscious processes is derived from both Freud and Kris. But unlike them, Kubie insists that preconscious processes alone produce creations. Coming from another type of background, the psychoanalytically oriented art teacher, Anton Ehrenzweig, emphasizes the role of the Unconscious in artistic creation. Ehrenzweig postulates a special process previously undescribed, however, which he calls "unconscious dedifferentiation." Since this process involves a specific kind of perception allowing for unconscious scanning, it is operative both in the artistic creative process and in the audience's appreciation of art.

Among the authors who tend to emphasize and describe conscious mental attributes or, more accurately, do not emphasize any processes outside of consciousness, formulations range from general to rather specific. Kant refers to the interplay of the faculties of imagination and understanding in the production of art, Poe to logic and deliberately controlled techniques, Coleridge to an active and constructive type of imagination,

Croce to intuition-expression, Collingwood to imagination as a synthesizing activity previous to discursive or relational thought, Beardsley to breaking old gestalts and forming new ones, Gordon to metaphorization. Schachtel formulates a specific type of perception as operative in the production of works of art, "allocentric perception." Involving an "openness to the world," this type of perception is characteristic of the most mature stage of human perceptual development. It is especially developed in the artist who uses this ability to stimulate "allocentric perception" in his audience.

Guilford, Mednick, and Getzels and Csikszentmihalyi also formulate specific attributes that operate either consciously or unconsciously and play a role in creative thinking in art and other areas. Guilford describes an intellectual factor of "divergent production," and Mednick the process of combining remote associations. "Divergent production" consists of providing alternate solutions to open-ended problems. Remotely related associations, according to Mednick, are combined to form creations through association by contiguity, serendipity, and mediation. Getzels and Csikszentmihalyi describe a "concern for discovery," a factor that dictates the artist's methods of working and contributes to the newness and value of the product.

Rothenberg defines a specific thought process operating in creation called "Janusian thinking," the capacity to conceive and utilize two or more opposite or contradictory ideas, concepts, or images *simultaneously*.[1] Although Rothenberg emphasizes that this process operates in consciousness, he also attempts to provide a link to previously mentioned formulations about nonconscious processes. Rothenberg states that "Janusian thinking" facilitates the unearthing of unconscious material through the use of the ego defense of negation. Negation takes account of what is unconscious and repressed without removing repression or necessarily promoting acceptance of the repressed material.

A wholly different type of attribute is the capacity for extrasensory perception, which is discussed by Krippner and Murphy. While formulations linking extrasensory perception, or the psi factor, to creativity have been very tentative, the phenomenon is not clearly related either to consciousness or unconscious operations. Moreover, there is little agreement among researchers in this area about whether the capacity for extrasensory perception is present in everyone or whether it is the special attribute of a particular few.

1. "Actively conceiving two or more opposite, contradictory, or antithetical ideas, concepts, or images *simultaneously*" (revised definition; see bibliography for Chapter Five).

Other authors tend to emphasize attributes of the whole person rather than mental attributes alone, and their formulations pertain to the personality of the creator, his motivations and conflicts, and his biological makeup. Rank, Lee, MacKinnon, Barron, Maslow, and Rogers formulate extensive pictures of the creative person and the nature of the motivation to create. They also attempt to account for some aspects of the creative process as well. Rank describes an artist type who is distinct from the neurotic type and who overcomes his fear of death by an act of will directed toward immortality. This artist type, in his ideal self, is representative of the collective ideology, and his expression of this ideal self accounts for his success with his audience. Lee describes an intense conflict in the artist between his dependence on his mother and his destructive impulses toward her generative organs, a conflict producing states of temporary depression which are overcome by an act of restitution in the creation of art. This act of restitution is an attempt to restore the organs destroyed in fantasy and a restitution or self-healing of the creator's own disabled and depressed state. Both MacKinnon and Barron describe many attributes of the creative person, including autonomy, a high degree of feminine orientation in males, intuition, an orientation to perception rather than judgment, flexibility, self-acceptance, and psychological richness and complexity. Barron emphasizes the paradoxical presence of high degrees of ego strength along with psychopathologic qualities in creative people and MacKinnon believes his overall findings demonstrate Rank's formulation of an artist personality type. Maslow and Rogers, both defining creativity very broadly, emphasize the personality attributes of openness to experience and Rogers further emphasizes the importance of a locus of evaluation within the person and the ability to toy with elements and concepts. To be sure, many psychoanalysts focusing primarily on mental attributes also describe whole-person characteristics, as their formulations pertain to a total personality theory. Thus, Kubie differentiates creativity from neurosis and Kris distinguishes the regression of the creative process from the regression found in schizophrenia. Freud points to the unhappiness and conflict of the daydreamer and of the writer who fashions his art from the material of daydreams.

Galton and Lombroso assert that there is a general biological factor in genius and, by implication, in creativity. Without specifying the nature of this factor or its operation in producing creations or works of genius, Galton asserts, and tries to prove, that special talent or genius in diverse areas is inherited. Interestingly, Galton's formulation relates to a root meaning of the word "genius" — to beget. It also coincides with the traditional and popular idea that geniuses are born, not made. Lombroso relates genius to insanity and follows the generally held psychiatric theory of his time that insanity is a form of degeneration. It has not generally been realized that Lombroso also constantly acknowledges the positive contributions of men of genius and differentiates between ordinary insanity and the insanity associated with genius. Consequently his position is in some ways in agreement with Barron's later finding of a high degree of psychopathology as well as ego strength in creative persons. Koestler is also interested in biological processes but, unlike Galton and Lombroso, he focuses on such processes as reproduction in order to derive a general formulation about creativity. His concept of bisociation—the combination of two self-consistent but habitually incompatible frames of reference—is meant to account for creations in all areas: in culture, societies, and nature as well as in individuals. Bogen and Bogen are concerned with the structure of the brain and presumably the biological factors underlying thought itself; they speculate that there is both a "propositional mind," primarily responsible for logical and linguistic functions, and an "appositional" mind, primarily responsible for nonrational and visiospatial functions. Creativity, in their view, results from the coordinated function of these two types of mind.

The factors and processes in creativity specified by the authors represented in this volume do not exhaustively cover the field. Many other important findings and formulations are to be found in the references listed in our bibliographies. We have summarized some of the main factors and processes indicated by major investigators and thinkers, primarily some specific formulations that emphasize certain common features in creativity. We shall discuss these common features and their significance later. First, however, we would like to raise an underlying issue about the investigation of creativity that pertains to the formulations just presented and clarifies the perspective of authors represented in our chapter on Alternative Approaches.

The Possibility of Explaining Creativity

Regardless of differences in orientation and specific approach, there are two basic concerns that undergird most, if not all, inquiries about creativity. Investigators and thinkers are generally concerned either with describing or with explaining. Although these concerns certainly overlap, they can be distinguished as guiding purposes.

If the researcher is interested primarily in describing creativity, he tries to find special characteristics or phases within creative activities. If he is systematic, he may use comparisons or controls to differentiate creative from noncreative or less creative activity. The information the researcher gathers may be derived from what the creator says, what biographers have found, or what systematic observation shows. A descriptive study always emphasizes observation rather than interpretation: the data for the study should consist only of observable behavior. Of course, as already suggested, there is the possibility—some would say the necessity—that interpretation and thus an explanatory element may be introduced into the description. The selection from Graham Wallas in Chapter Two illustrates this. His term, "incubation," intended as a description of a stage in creative processes, is drawn from the field of biology and conceptually includes far more than what can be specified at the observable level. "Incubation" refers to unobserved and unobservable operations within the creative process.

The point that descriptions may slip into interpretation is important not only because it enjoins us to be cautious about believing that our descriptions are pure, but also because it suggests the possibility that a description may actually be explanatory. An investigator purportedly using description may not only devote his attention to describing what actually occurs, he may also look for general kinds of occurrences linked to particular events. He may attempt to account for creativity by relating creative acts to general, lawful processes. Once he tries this, his descriptions include data arranged hierarchically from a conceptual point of view and he has pointed the way toward explanation. Skinner's presentation in Chapter Four and the work of C. W. Taylor, cited in the bibliographic sections of Chapters Two and Three, demonstrate a manifest use of description as a form of explanation. The aim of explaining is far more ambitious than the aim of describing only what appears in creative acts. But it is an aim that is present in all studies of creativity, either clearly espoused, or lurking behind as an implicit hope, or as an aim that is explicitly rejected on the grounds that it cannot be achieved.

In saying that the aim of explaining creativity may be hoped for or rejected, we are pointing to a fundamental issue underlying the various perspectives adopted in studies of creativity throughout the history of thought. That creativity is in some way explicable has been taken for granted by a long tradition of thinkers; but there is another tradition that challenges this assumption. And both traditions provide some kind of understanding of creativity. In order to bring this issue into focus, it will be helpful first to consider the kinds of explanation associated with the study of creativity. Selections in Chapters One, Three, and Four of this volume illustrate these.

Particular examples highlight some of the differences. The selections from Mednick and Guilford, for instance, bring one kind of explanation into sharp relief. Both investigators believe that it is possible to find conditions necessary for creating. Both attempt to identify specific capacities or ways of thinking that are invariably present in creative activity. They aim at determining the factors and combinations of factors that must be present before a creative act is achieved. If all such conditions could be correctly identified, we would have one kind of understanding of creativity. Somewhat different in orientation is Otto Rank. His interest in explaining creativity is directed toward finding motives that function in distinctive ways in the creative person. Hence, he explains creativity by referring to the creator's purposes. He says that the creator attempts to overcome a fear of death and achieve a kind of immortality through creativity. Blanshard's view of explanation contrasts even more sharply with Mednick's and Guilford's approach. Blanshard proposes that in order to explain creativity we need to find the general purposive complex of conditions that necessitates creative acts.

These examples suggest that the kind of understanding we seek depends upon the particular expectations we have. We may, like Guilford and Mednick, want to know about the conditions or factors leading to and responsible for the successful completion of a creative act. These factors may be causes, or necessary (and perhaps sufficient) conditions for creativity. Knowledge of these might then enable us to predict which persons will be creative. In contrast, we may, like Blanshard, want to identify a system of principles that permits us to see creative acts in a context of necessities. Knowledge of such a context would enable us to deduce the kinds of processes that are creative.

Expectations about explanation fall into two general types that may be called "genetic" and "teleological." We use the term "genetic" to suggest that, in wanting to explain, we may be searching for the genesis of an event or a thing. This type of explanation refers to antecedent conditions out of which the thing or event originates. It is important to emphasize that such antecedents must have been fully present or operative within the past time relevant to the thing to be explained. *Antecedent conditions must be present at the time they are supposed to function to produce their effect.* Guilford and Mednick set their sights on genetic explanation. Although Rank looks for purposes within the creative person's experiences, he too is concerned primarily with the genetic aspect of creative acts. The purposes he identifies are dynamic mechanisms within the creative personality, mechanisms that antedate any specific creative achievements. For all three of these writers, factors accounting for creativity serve essentially as a "push" rather than a "lure" for creation, i.e., genetic rather than teleological explanation.

If an explanation is teleological, it includes reference to future goals, or to conditions and states that either are only ideal or are to be actualized at some future time. Before the occurrence of the thing to be explained, such goals are not actual; they are possibilities. They are ideals yet to be realized. A complete explanation of this type would make all past, present, and future experience intelligible, because it would permit the deduction of all possible knowledge about all possible experience. Such an explanation would provide a set of necessary connections that include the potentialities of all things in experience and their future goals. And it would, of course, also require the occurrence of the thing to be explained. In its strongest version, then, teleology implies system and completeness. As complete, the system comprehends all intelligible phenomena. This type of explanation is more likely to be found in philosophical discourse, but it is represented, at least in part, in some psychiatric and psychological theories. Among the authors represented in this book, Schachtel proposes that personality develops toward certain ways of living and perceiving that are to be realized. When realized, these ways of living and perceiving are more fully present in certain types of persons. And Rank, though essentially focused on antecedents, looks for a typology based on goals.

Several intrinsic requirements are shared by the two types of explanation. Common to both is the implicit demand that connections be found among the pertinent phenomena and that these connections allow for the possibility of prediction. The connections may be logical or mathematical relationships, continuities within which phenomena occur, or simply regularities. In the least stringent interpretation, such connections are viewed as correlations. But even in this interpretation the connections must be repeatable so that predictions are possible. Thus if one can identify certain kinds of repeated circumstances and correlations in the past, these correlations are predictable. The strongest interpretation of these connections is that they are necessities. A teleological account may propose connections that are necessary, much like logical or mathematical deductions. Usually such an account is distinguished from one using empirical hypotheses that are confirmed only through predictable correlations. Yet even if the investigator aims at fitting phenomena to be explained into a teleological system, he seeks an explanation with predictive power. If the explanation were fully known, it would also allow for prediction because, through deduction, one could predict the phenomena occurring within the system.

Another distinction is required. In addition to adopting either a teleological or genetic type of explanation, investigators have also espoused at least one of three broad orientations, orientations based upon fundamental assumptions about the admissible content of explanations as well as appropriate methods for obtaining information. Terms used to refer to these inevitably distort and overlap, particularly when applied broadly. However, with this caution in mind, the three views may be referred to as naturalism, rationalism, and supernaturalism.

Although the term "naturalism" has been used in many different ways, it will here be restricted to the following: any view that all events, including mental processes, occur in an entirely lawful, empirical, and scientifically knowable universe. For the naturalist, whatever cannot be understood as occurring within the lawful framework of our universe is interpreted in one or more of the following three ways: (1) as an illusion, that is, as something appearing as unlawful because of our ignorance, which may be overcome through such achievements as better technology or more comprehensive theory; (2) as an unintelligible or arbitrary and recalcitrant deviation in the universe, not amenable to scientific knowledge; or (3) as meaningless and not a proper topic for scientific inquiry. It should be evident that the genetic explanations cited above are naturalistic, according to our use of the term. A teleologist also might be inclined toward naturalism, if he restricts knowledge to what is scientific and if he sees violations of known laws as illusory, or as due to ignorance.

If naturalism is assumed by an investigator hoping to explain creativity, he also must assume that creative acts and processes are intelligible in terms of lawful behavior. Such acts and processes must be predictable by virtue of the correlations of conditions and the type of results that permit us to generalize about creativity. Creative acts, then, are natural events that are just as intelligible as are all other events in nature. They occur as instances of natural processes. The tradition of naturalism with respect to the study of creativity can be traced primarily to Aristotle. Hence Aristotle is represented in this book as a thinker who is seminal to the naturalist tradition of thought about creativity.

The term "rationalism" refers to the attempt to explain phenomena in terms of a set of principles that specify a structure of relationships necessitating these phenomena. In contrast to naturalism, the rationalist explanation may include independently known principles, i.e., those not necessarily derived from specific empirical observation. Rationalism is most clearly represented in this book by authors using teleological explanation. Such a view is broader than naturalism in its aspirations, and it is generally considered to be nonempirical, or at least less empirical.

"Supernaturalism" requires that explanation identify a source or originating principle independent of natural processes. This source may be a fundamental principle or agency related to or internal to a rationalist system. It may be divine, e.g., a muse, God. In creativity inquiry, the supernatural tradition began primarily with Plato.

In summary, then, explanations may be primarily genetic or teleological and they may adopt a viewpoint of naturalism, rationalism, or supernaturalism. We have said, however, that the most fundamental difference in general approaches to creativity lies in the contrast between those who assume that creative acts can be explained and those who challenge this assumption. What, then, can be said about the challenge? In answering this question, it will be helpful to consider an objection that can be raised to all types of explanation. Almost all investigators who try to explain creativity agree that there is some distinction between the genuinely new or novel and the merely different. But explanation, whether naturalistic, rationalistic, or supernaturalistic, must exclude genuine novelty in the product. Explanation implies that a created product is necessitated either by antecedent causes or by possibilities to be realized in the future.

This objection points to a conflict between the aims of inquiry and the character of the phenomenon in question. Most of the major investigators included in this book assume that creativity can be explained. At the same time, they either claim or imply that creative processes yield novelty. Even some of the most empirically and rigorously designed genetic and naturalistic approaches, such as Mednick's, Guilford's, and MacKinnon's (illustrated in Chapter Three), all acknowledge newness in the products they consider to be creations. Given such acknowledgments, it is incumbent on these investigators to show how their explanations take account of new aspects in the creation. As the new aspects would not be in existence before the creative process took place, they could not be accounted for by reducing or tracing them to preformed conditions.

It might be objected here that our demand on these investigators who assume a genetic explanation—that they exhaustively trace the new aspects of a creation to antecedents—is too strong. Rather, the counterobjection asserts, they need only be *correlated* with antecedents. No prediction should be expected to cover all qualities that will be present in the predicted phenomenon. All that is required is the identification of factors, say, divergent production abilities, or some specified critical talent, or the will to achieve certain purposes. These factors need only be correlated with creative activity in order to serve as a basis for predicting that persons who manifest them will, under proper conditions, create.

In answering this counter-objection, we emphasize the following: if one could show that such general conditions are regularly related to and correlated with created results, the success of a genetic explanation based on these correlations would be determined by the predictive power of the findings, i.e., the degree to which prediction is complete and accurate. *But the degree to which predictive power is attained is also the degree to which the products of so-called creative processes would not be unprecedented, unexpected, and therefore new.* Those who insist that creative acts can in principle be predicted must reject the widely held opinion that, for created products—artistic, scientific, or whatever—it is the specific, subtle, uncommon qualities that are crucial for considering the product to be a creation. General properties of a product anticipated in such instances as Guilford's divergent result, or the achievement of Rank's artist whose purposes are known beforehand, do not show the product to be a creation. A product is a creation insofar as it manifests unprecedented specific qualities that are integral to a new specific value. If these specific qualities are not included explicitly in the prediction, then the prediction is incomplete and perhaps meaningless with respect to what is new.

Some of the writers in this volume who propose explanations acknowledge limits to explaining creativity. Freud, for example, refrains from relating psychodynamic factors to the qualitative aspects (the aesthetic form) of the work of art in the selection here, and elsewhere he emphatically states, "Before the problem of the creative artist, analysis must, alas, lay down its arms."[2] Similarly, Ehrenzweig sees a dilemma in the creative act. For him, the dilemma consists of the creator's need to select from an infinite range of alternatives without a predetermined criterion of choice. In the absence of this predetermined criterion, the result, in its created aspect, could not be predicted.

The general point we insist upon also applies to suggestions that a teleological system or formulations implying such a system explain creative activity. There, it is evident that the creative activity must, in some sense, be preformed within the system that purportedly explains creativ-

2. Freud, S. "Dostoevsky and Parricide" (1928), in Strachey, J. (ed.), *The Standard Edition of the Complete Psychological Works of Sigmund Freud*, Vol. 21. London: Hogarth Press 1961, p. 177.

ity. As Blanshard puts it, creative activity is controlled by an ideal order that provides fulfillment of the creative act. However, either this ideal order must be full in all its details, so that what appears as new is already necessitated within the system, or else the appearance of the new is unique with respect to the system, and thereby it eludes the system. If the teleologist is to maintain his hope of providing an explanation, he should presumably adopt the former alternative. The control of the system of creation would, therefore, be a completely detailed control. But in that case, the only way the teleologist could preserve newness or novelty in creation would be to insist that novelty is present in the finite consciousness of the creator who discovers what was already present within the ideal order. Whatever novelty there is, then, would be found within the creator's experience of discovering and in the surprise experienced by those who respond to his productions. Newness would lie in the creator's and the audience's awareness of discovering something in the product that is unprecedented in their experience. If novelty is interpreted in this manner, either of two alternatives is implied. One alternative is that the surprise of discovery is not included in the teleological system as a whole. An aspect of the experience of the creator, then, is left unexplained, because the *awareness* of novelty could not be required by the system. The other alternative is that the surprise of discovery does have its place in the system. In that case, nothing is new, not even the illusion that something is new.

To be sure, one might find the notion that nothing is new more palatable than the alternative insisting on radical newness. One may see advantages in proposing another definition of novelty in creation. For example, an investigator may insist that there is only a re-experiencing of original novelty or of diversified possibilities established in some cosmologically conceived origin. Alternatively, he might stipulate that novelty consists of elements from one context, such as an historical period or a specific culture, appearing in a different one. In other words, he might adopt the view that "there is nothing new under the sun." If he does so, however, it is necessary to be aware of the implications of his view.

Bergson, Peirce, Morgan, and Hausman in Chapter Five suggest some of the implications of the claim that "there is nothing new under the sun." Their arguments indicate that an alternative approach to understanding creative acts is necessary. All four insist that explanations cannot adequately accommodate spontaneity or newness. They share a position derived from an emphasis on the acceptance of evidence of variation and growth in the evolution of nature. In addition, each offers reasons for rejecting a deterministic world view and argues for a world view that is open to discontinuities and breaks within the complexes of regularities or causal relations partially constituting the world. Moreover, some writers, such as Bergson, Collingwood, and Croce, take the phenomenon of discontinuity even more directly into consideration. They offer positive accounts of creativity that meet different requirements from those assumed in the orientations of naturalism, rationalism, or supernaturalism. For these latter writers, explanation and understanding of creativity are not synonymous.

The Understanding and Investigation of Creativity

Bearing these objections and limitations in mind, what is the significance of the factors and processes in creativity already outlined and what kind of understanding can be obtained? If a composite picture of all the factors and processes mentioned earlier were constructed, assuming that all the formulations were to some degree correct, a fairly consistent pattern would emerge. Although the description of this pattern would be so general and broad as to be highly unsatisfactory for providing much understanding of creativity, it nevertheless is worth mentioning, because it concretely illustrates the issue in creativity research we would like to emphasize. Therefore, let us point out that almost all authors — possibly excepting E. A. Poe, who stresses straightforward logic, and Galton, who omits psychological considerations — emphasize special kinds of psychological factors and processes operative in creativity. Even those authors who relate creativity to problem-solving state that special *kinds* of problem-solving factors are involved in creative thinking. Furthermore, all of these psychological factors and processes are characterized by an unrestricted, unruled, "free" quality, as well as by a tendency to incorporate broad areas of experience. Even the authors who differ about the importance of pathological factors in relation to creativity are potentially united in recognizing that some form of deviation from norms or rules, either in behavior or thought, is present in the phenomenon.

As we suggested, this picture is broad indeed and it could quite justifiably be said that, as a general formulation, it adds little that a cursory consideration of creativity would not immediately suggest. A deeper enhancement of understanding lies, to be sure, in an extended and careful consideration of the specific factors and processes discussed and described by the authors included here. But consideration of both the composite picture and each of the specific factors catalogued points to an underlying issue: what has been formulated pertains only to the *necessary* conditions for creativity but not the *sufficient* condition or conditions. When both necessary and sufficient conditions are present, we speak of a cause. Only Galton's account could clearly be construed as a formulation of cause in this sense, but even if his account were correct it leaves out any clarification of the operation of creativity in human affairs, i.e., any specification of the kinds of processes and factors inherited by men and women of genius. Furthermore, in modern times, we have come to see that an exclusively hereditarian account of any human faculty or behavior is inadequate since the interaction between heredity and environment is highly complex and incompletely understood. Crovitz's proposal for computer-produced creative solutions implies a knowledge of cause, though Crovitz himself does not insist that human creative thinking necessarily proceeds as he describes.

Why have only necessary conditions been formulated? Have the methods of investigation been inadequate or, as we have suggested, is there something about the nature of the phenomenon being studied that precludes the finding of a sufficient condition? Rather than emphasizing only the objections and limitations we have outlined so far, we would like to answer this question affirmatively: yes, it is the essence of creativity to defy prediction and, furthermore, the phenomenon of creativity affirms the presence of discontinuity and spontaneity in the world.

In saying this about investigations already carried out, we want to emphasize that we are not merely stating that many investigations have had methodological and conceptual flaws, although these certainly exist. Many psychiatric and psychological investigators have shown a confusion about the distinctions and interrelationships among the foci of interest— persons, process, or product—and they have used unclear definitions of creativity, inadequately controlled experimental designs, or inappropriate testing procedures. Most commonly, they have ignored considerations pertaining to the achievement of value in creative activity, and in their experiments or speculations have paid little attention to this criterial attribute. For example, those who tacitly or explicitly equate the unusual or different (often the term "original" is used) with the creative forget that the merely different is often without value and that consequently such experiments or speculations may not pertain at all to creativity, the state or capacity that produces the valuable as well as the new. Philosophical investigators have erred primarily in an uncritical and unsystematic use of empirical evidence to derive general principles or to support various aspects of their overall speculations. By and large, they have tended to take at face value the testimonies and descriptions of creative persons about their creative experiences. As a general rule, human beings are seldom so carefully introspective or insightful about their own psychological processes to warrant taking any testimony about these processes at face value; there is no reason to believe that creators should be any better in this respect than other people. An artist's testimony about his experiences and approaches must be interpreted or evaluated rather than only taken literally in order to be used as evidence. There is, in fact, some reason to believe that creators' reports are *unreliable* accounts of actual experience since the public utterances of creative artists about themselves are often intended by the artist himself to enhance the corpus of his work or, at least, to be consistent with his artistic or literary image. Indeed, many creators who refuse to make any public statements about themselves or their creative experiences often say that such statements are already incorporated in the work itself and no further comment is required.

All of these flaws relate to the major point we are making, although they do not in themselves justify our stance. Creativity is not only complicated and difficult to study and understand, but it is radically different from other phenomena that can be explained in terms of cause. Basically, there is an unavoidable paradox: creations, when they appear, are in some way recognizable and familiar to us and, therefore, they must have something in common with antecedent experiences. However, creations, in the most complete sense, are also radically new and therefore, in some respect, unfamiliar. Their specific natures cannot be predicted from a knowledge of their antecedents. Nor can they be deduced from preformed ideal and future conditions proposed by teleologists. In this sense, creations are undetermined, both genetically and teleologically, and sufficient conditions for their appearance cannot *in principle* be provided. Creativity, therefore, cannot be explained according to any traditional model of explanation by cause or prediction. We maintain, however, that it can be made intelligible and our principle for providing intelligibility to the phenomenon is a recognition of the irreducible paradox: *Creativity is both determined and undetermined at the same time.*

Clearly, the investigation of such a paradoxical phenomenon requires a revolutionary approach. Traditional scientific investigation presupposes the possibility of establishing specific sufficient conditions for the phenomenon investigated, whether causes are expressed in terms of correlations, contiguities, or sequences. Philosophical investigation in itself is not generally oriented toward identifying specific causalities, i.e., particular empirical sequences. Our proposal for the revolutionary approach to investigation is based directly on our affirmation of the essential nature of creativity. In any appropriate investigation consideration must be taken of the simultaneously determined and undetermined factors in creativity.

Concretely, this suggestion need not be as baffling as it may at first appear. Empirical investigations should preferably be focused on the creative process and adopt a phenomenological approach, i.e., using as few preconceptions or biases as possible or, more realistically, having awareness and due understanding of the effects of preconceptions and biases. While the focus is on the creative process, the nature of the resulting product must also be taken into account: if the resulting product is a creation in its clearest sense, radically new and valuable, generalities about the creative process could not completely account for the new and discontinuous although they might account for certain aspects of the value. They might, for instance, partially explain the value attributed to a work of art in terms of a concordance between the creator's unconscious processes and those of his audience. Empirical investigation might also be focused profitably on the creative person using a phenomenological type of approach, but it should be emphasized that an exclusive focus on the person or agent runs the risk of stressing only the determined aspects of creation, because such an approach necessarily overlooks the break with antecedents that occurs during the act or process of creating. Only if the creative moment or moments are considered to be primarily a matter of the self-creation of the person and, following Maslow, a form of creativity is defined as a phenomenon occurring exclusively within the person, could this methodological limitation be avoided.

Basically, all empirical approaches, including the focus on the process, are aimed at specification of the necessary factors in creativity. Theories may develop that permit prediction on the basis of these necessary factors. Such predictions would refer to the context in which a creation occurs rather than to its exact content or nature. Many such necessary conditions are very little understood and investigation of the appearance of value, in such terms as the interaction between the creator and his audience, could be very fruitfully investigated. Investigation and fuller explication of the nature of nonradical novelty, such as what Lloyd Morgan calls recurrent novelty — the repetition of novelty that has previously occurred — or else another kind of novelty associated with the appearance of something familiar in a different context, also can provide further insight into some necessary or related factors in creativity.

While the empirical investigator would do well to bear in mind the paradoxical nature of the phenomenon he is studying, the philosopher also needs to pay attention to the paradox. Particularly if he is concerned with a metaphysics built on spontaneity and discontinuity, he must acknowledge the determined factors in creation. For example, the metaphysician needs to examine the role of the ideal and the actual in creation and the possibility of self-determinism or autonomous cause as an intelligible notion. There seems, moreover, to be a good deal of agreement among diverse types of investigators that the process of artistic creation involves personal and often conflictual elements within the artist as well as special types of free intuitive thinking that are not characteristic of ordinary conscious thought. Generally, such factors as personal conflict and intuition have been explained through reference to concepts of preconscious, extraconscious, or unconscious functioning. This type of functioning seems to be a necessary factor in creativity. The philosopher emphasizing discontinuity should take such a determining factor into consideration in developing a metaphysics that includes human consciousness or else he should find some alternate formulation to account for the role of factors such as psychological conflict and intuition in creation.

Up until now, we have discussed the model for a revolutionary approach to the investigation of creativity in terms of tasks related to the discrete orientations of empirical and philosophical investigation. We have done this for illustrative purposes only. Basically, the approach to investigation and understanding transcends disciplinary concerns and relates to the unique nature of creativity itself. All investigation and understanding of creativity requires attention to the paradox of determined together with undetermined aspects, and the most adequate general approach would involve resolutions, syntheses, or integrations of the polarity. We are not ourselves attempting to provide such a general integration here but merely suggesting some outlines for it. Concretely, the investigator of creativity must, at the least, alternate between the determined and undetermined aspects of the phenomenon: he bears in mind that explanations involving prediction do not account for the undetermined aspect of creation and that an exclusive emphasis on the undetermined aspect can retard fruitful inquiry. In studying the determined aspect of creativity, he tries to gain knowledge that enables him to make limited predictions, or he concerns himself with viewing creativity as part of an overall conceptual framework. In focusing on the undetermined aspect, he regards the phenomenon in its autonomy, independent of antecedent causal sequences and teleological conditions. He looks for unique features in creativity. This approach has an affirmative as well as a negative purpose. Negatively, it serves to remind us not to expect too much of explanation. Affirmatively, it sustains our recognition of novelty and the integration of newness and value in creation. An investigator of the undetermined aspect, for instance, would need to be inventive in introducing us to new terms and connections, or new ways of using terms and of describing connections appropriate to spontaneity and new value. Tender-minded as this approach may appear, we believe it is required in the study of creativity; it allows us to understand much of the adaptive behavior of man without reduction of the essence of his humanity. It affirms the presence of spontaneity and freedom in the world.

Chapter One

SEMINAL ACCOUNTS

Each of the five selections in this chapter is seminal to a particular orientation in creativity inquiry. The works of Plato, Aristotle, Kant, and Freud, of course, have had seminal influence in the entire intellectual tradition of Western civilization. Selections by these authors are of special interest, because, along with Galton, they have each set the stage in particular ways for future descriptions and explanations of creativity. Although none of these writers except Galton was concerned with developing a comprehensive theory about creativity, each indicated for the first time a definite approach to the phenomenon and the problems it generates.

Aristotle's discussion of art as a production of what is preformed and imposed on matter is seminal to both the naturalist and rationalist assumptions about explaining creativity described in the introductory chapter of this book. Plato's discussion of divine inspiration is seminal to both the supernaturalist orientation to explanation and the type of orientation we have characterized as an alternative approach, an approach that tends to emphasize the inexplicability of creativity. Kant stands between Aristotle and Plato. His discussion is seminal to alternative approaches both affirming the human source of the creative process and insisting on a self-generating principle that is basically unexplained. Also, since Kant may be considered the originator of the field of aesthetics, his work is seminal to all modern philosophical accounts of creativity in art.

Freud and Galton both have a naturalist and rationalist orientation to explanation, but they diverge with respect to their assumptions about the type of genetic factors accounting for creativity. Galton adopts an extreme form of genetic explanation in attempting to account for creativity through the antecedent biological mechanism of heredity. His work is therefore seminal for modern investigators seeking mechanisms that fully account for creativity (so-called "mechanistic" approaches). Freud also seeks antecedent factors in creativity, but he acknowledges the possibility that these cannot exhaustively explain the phenomenon. Most significant for creativity investigation is Freud's place as the originator of an emphasis on nonconscious human factors in the creative process.

Although the selections illustrate seminal accounts and are presented in chronological order, they do not indicate any clear historical development in the interpretation of creativity. More striking, in fact, is the divergence of thought and the distinctness of approach. Although there is some overlap in general ways, each author presents a unique interpretation.

Plato illustrates a nonnaturalist perspective preparing the way for the supernaturalist tradition because he argues for a source of creativity that is independent of natural and human resources. He poses the problem of explaining creativity and he suggests that rational explanation breaks down because the creator's knowledge and preestablished rules of procedure cannot fully account for his achievement. Thus Plato emphasizes inspiration and suggests that the creative artist is "out of his mind" during the creative process. This suggestion is the basis for a tradition of interpretation that makes inspiration crucial and which, in many instances, emphasizes either madness, altered consciousness, or mystery in the creative process. More recent and contemporary perspectives on the relation of madness or psychopathology to creativity are contained in the selections by Lombroso, Jung, Rank, Kris, and Kubie in Chapters Two and Three of this book. Plato refers also to the muse, a divine source for the creator's inspiration. This intellectual appeal to the divine is seminal to the supernatural tradition as well as to the viewpoint that creativity is basically a mystery. Maritain's account in Chapter Three is an example of a more recent supernaturalist orientation and the selections in Chapter Five, Alternative Approaches, all affirm the mystery of creativity to some degree.

Aristotle offers a way of understanding creative acts naturalistically. For him creative processes, like other natural and human processes, are explicable in terms of antecedent conditions. It is important to emphasize that Aristotle, unlike Plato, views the resources with which the artist begins as both necessary *and* sufficient to account for all that is found in the created product. Since Aristotle rejects any supernatural agency or mystery in creativity, his work is seminal to the rationalist as well as the naturalist tradition of interpretation. Many of the selections in subsequent chapters of this book follow in the spirit of the tradition initiated by Aristotle. Selections in Chapter Two, Descriptive Accounts, for instance, all show the influence of Aristotle's position, though some of the writers whose works are represented there resist being placed in a strict naturalistic category.

In the selection presented here Aristotle not only identifies and discusses natural productive processes, but he also refers to processes occurring spontaneously or by chance. Since spontaneous activities do not originate in natural conditions leading to anticipated results, it might be considered that Aristotle also stated a position relating to a nonnaturalistic alternative approach to creativity. Some readers might wonder why a selection from Aristotle's more extensive discussion of chance in the *Physics* is not included. After all, spontaneous activity leads to what is unexpected and unpredicted. If a creator produces something new and unexpected, then perhaps his creativity is a product of chance. This suggestion is provocative and important. It is not consistent, however, with the overall Aristotelian view that has been most influential on the investigation of creativity. For Aristotle, understanding concerns what occurs by nature rather than chance; he does not consider chance operative in the creation of art and could not be considered to have proposed an essentially nonnaturalistic approach.

Kant was the first writer on creativity to develop the distinction between radical creation and imitation. For Kant, creation of art is not only independent of prior procedures or rules, but it is independent of all conditions other than spontaneous activity made possible through faculties in the creator's consciousness. His position contrasts significantly with Plato's, because the latter asserts that creative activity is controlled by a source independent of the creator's consciousness. In another way, too, Kant differs from Plato, and from Aristotle as well. Both Plato and Aristotle view the art product as an imitation or a representation of a reality separate from the product. For Kant, the creator gives the rule to his work; he generates his style and the significance of the product in accordance with his freely functioning imagination. Hence the product does not imitate nature.

Although Kant does not look outside human activity for the control of the creative process, it should be emphasized that he belongs neither to the naturalist nor the rationalist tradition. He finds the locus of creativity in a unique and spontaneous act that introduces a leap in ordinary natural processes. If the genius makes the rules, then genius cannot be explained by rules (laws) that already exist.

Galton, like Kant, adopts the view that creativity is to be found in genius. However, in sharp contrast to Kant, Galton correlates genius with hereditary factors. In this respect, his work springs out of the general naturalistic tradition of Aristotle. And within this tradition, Galton's work illustrates a strand using a genetic type of explanation based on a mechanism or set of mechanisms. For Galton the mechanism of heredity is the cause of creativity. His view is seminal to a particular naturalistic approach followed by other investigators of genius and talent such as Cattell, Terman, and Cox (see Selected Bibliography for Chapter Two). Moreover, the presupposition that genius or talent is inherited is frequently adopted or implied by various types of biological and psychological accounts of creative persons and creative processes (see especially the Greenacre references in the Selected Bibliography for Chapter Three). The type of rigorously genetic explanation exemplified by Galton's work is also reflected in the recent selections by Skinner and Crovitz included in Chapter Four. Crovitz's presentation of a computer or machine procedure for creation is a prototype of the mechanistic or the machine-as-model form of explanation.

Freud's discussion of an aspect of the creative process in writers is naturalistic in its appeal to dynamic factors in the human psyche as necessary conditions of creative work. Although Freud is a naturalist in orientation, his naturalism is not as mechanistic as Galton's. With this, the first detailed exposition of the connections between the work of the creative artist and a generally occurring and distinctively psychological process, fantasy or day-dreaming, Freud not only crystallized the psychoanalytic perspective on creativity but spelled out some general psychological laws about fantasy. His work is seminal for the widely held modern view that fantasy is intrinsic to creative thinking. Interestingly, Freud's view is in some respects similar to Plato's nonnaturalism; he, like Plato, points to conditions that are independent of the individual consciousness of the creator. In a sense Freud replaces Plato's divinity or muse, which inspires the artist, with the individual Unconscious. Moreover, as we pointed out earlier, Freud has directly questioned whether psychoanalysis would ever solve the problem of the creative artist. In the selection here, he refrains from attempting to explain creativity fully and it could be said that he therefore essentially affirms the mystery, though he does not seem to believe that explanations will *necessarily* always elude the investigator. For Plato they must, for only if men become one with divinity can they fully understand the control of inspiration.

Plato, Kant, and Freud all share a view that creativity is to some degree puzzling. They believe that, like other noncreative types of activity, creative acts spring from some source or set of conditions. At the same time they recognize that creative processes are actually different from other kinds of processes: creative processes lead to products that do not seem directly traceable to antecedent conditions or the workings of established laws.

PLATO · Inspiration

[*This selection represents the only Platonic dialogue devoted in its entirety to the question of understanding the creative process in poetry. Other dialogues germane to creativity are* The Timaeus (*concerning the creation of the universe*), The Phaedrus, *and* The Symposium. *Passages in the latter two reinforce the suggestion in the selection here that creative ability is in some way a kind of divine madness. In addition, passages in* The Republic *and* The Laws *provide relatively extended discussions of the relation of art to knowledge and morality. Plato emphasizes the importance of inspiration from an external source and a state in which the creator is out of his senses; though he uses the term "madness," he does not seem to be describing the psychotic condition as currently defined.*]

Ion: Then what can be the reason, Socrates, for my behavior? When anyone discusses any other poet, I pay no attention, and can offer no remark of any value. I frankly doze. But whenever anyone mentions Homer, immediately I am awake, attentive, and full of things to say.

Socrates: The riddle is not hard to solve, my friend. No, it is plain to everyone that not from art [skill] and knowledge comes your power to speak concerning Homer. If it were art that gave you power, then you could speak about all the other poets as well. There is an art of poetry as a whole? Am I not right?

.   .   .   .

Socrates: I . . . will proceed to show you what . . . [the discussion] betokens. As I just now said, this gift you have of speaking well on Homer is not an art; it is a power divine, impelling you like the power in the

Source   *From Plato,* The Ion, *in Cooper, L. (trans.) and Hamilton, E., and Cairns, H. (eds.),* Plato: The Collected Dialogues, *pp. 218–221. New York: Pantheon Books (Bolligen Series), 1961. Reprinted from Lane Cooper (trans.):* Plato: Phaedrus, Ion, Gorgias *and* Symposium, *with passages from* The Republic *and* Laws. *Copyright, 1938, by Lane Cooper. Used by permission of Cornell University Press.*

stone Euripides called the magnet, which most call 'stone of Hereclea.' This stone does not simply attract the iron rings, just by themselves; it also imparts to the rings a force enabling them to do the same thing as the stone itself, that is, to attract another ring, so that sometimes a chain is formed, quite a long one, of iron rings, suspended from one another. For all of them, however, their power depends upon that loadstone. Just so the Muse. She first makes men inspired, and then through these inspired ones others share in the enthusiasm, and a chain is formed, for the epic poets, all the good ones, have their excellence, not from art, but are inspired, possessed, and thus they utter all these admirable poems. So is it also with the good lyric poets; as the worshiping Corybantes are not in their senses when they dance, so the lyric poets are not in their senses when they make these lovely lyric poems. No, when once they launch into harmony and rhythm, they are seized with the Bacchic transport, and are possessed—as the bacchants, when possessed, draw milk and honey from the rivers, but not when in their senses. So the spirit of the lyric poet works, according to their own report. For the poets tell us, don't they, that the melodies they bring us are gathered from rills that run with honey, out of glens and gardens of the Muses, and they bring them as the bees do honey, flying like the bees? And what they say is true, for a poet is a light and winged thing, and holy, and never able to compose until he has become inspired, and is beside himself, and reason is no longer in him. So long as he has this in his possession, no man is able to make poetry or to chant in prophecy. Therefore, since their making is not by art, when they utter many things and fine about the deeds of men, just as you do about Homer, but is by lot divine—therefore each is able to do well only that to which the Muse has impelled him—one to make dithyrambs, another panegyric odes, another choral songs, another epic poems, another iambs. In all the rest, each one of them is poor, for not by art do they utter these, but by power divine, since if it were by art that they knew how to treat one subject finely, they would know how to deal with all the others too. Herein lies the reason why the deity has bereft them of their senses, and uses them as ministers, along with soothsayers and godly seers; it is in order that we listeners may know that it is not they who utter these precious revelations while their mind is not within them, but that it is god himself who speaks, and through them becomes articulate to us. The most convincing evidence of this statement is offered by Tynnichus of Chalcis. He never composed a single poem worth recalling, save the song of praise which everyone repeats, well nigh the finest of all lyrical poems, and absolutely what he called it, an 'Invention of the Muses.' By this example above all, it seems to me, the god would show us, lest we doubt, that these lovely poems are not of man or human workmanship, but are divine and from the gods, and that the poets are nothing but interpreters of the gods, each one possessed by the divinity to whom he is in bondage. And to prove this, the deity on purpose sang the loveliest of all lyrics through the most miserable poet. Isn't it so, Ion? Don't you think that I am right?

ION: You are indeed, I vow! Socrates, your words in some way touch my very soul, and it does seem to me that by dispensation from above good poets convey to us these utterances of the gods.

ARISTOTLE · Creation As Making

[*In this selection Aristotle proposes a general account of art as a productive activity. Despite its fame and influence, Aristotle's* The Poetics *is not relevant here because it is not primarily concerned with the problem of explaining creativity but with stating techniques and analyzing the specific art form of the drama. Although Plato argues for the inexplicable, mysterious basis of creativity, Aristotle argues here that creative processes obey fully natural laws.*]

Of things that come to be, some come to be by nature, some by art, some spontaneously. Now everything that comes to be comes to be by the agency of something and from something and comes to be something. And the something which I say it comes to be may be found in any category; it may come to be either a 'this' or of some size or of some quality or somewhere.

Now natural comings to be are the comings to be of those things which come to be by nature; and that out of which they come to be is what we call matter; and that by which they come to be is something which exists naturally; and the something which they come to be is a man or a plant or one of the things of this kind, which we say are substances if anything is — all things produced either by nature or by art have matter; for each of them is capable both of being and of not being, and this capacity is the

SOURCE   *From Aristotle,* Metaphysics, *in Ross, W. D. (trans. and ed.),* The Oxford Translation of Aristotle, *Vol. 8, pp. 791–795. Oxford: Oxford University Press, 1928. Reprinted by permission of the Oxford University Press, Oxford.*

matter of each—and, in general, both that from which they are produced is nature, and the type according to which they are produced is nature (for that which is produced, e.g. a plant or an animal, has a nature), and so is that by which they are produced—the so-called 'formal' nature, which is specifically the same (though this is in another individual); for man begets man.

Thus, then, are natural products produced; all other productions are called 'makings'. And all makings proceed either from art or from a faculty or from thought. [ftnt. deleted] Some of them happen also spontaneously or by luck [ftnt. deleted] just as natural products sometimes do; for there also the same things sometimes are produced without seed as well as from seed. Concerning these cases, then, we must inquire later, [ftnt. deleted] but from art proceed the things of which the form is in the soul of the artist. (By form I mean the essence of each thing and its primary substance.) For even contraries have in a sense the same form; for the substance of a privation is the opposite substance, e.g. health is the substance of disease (for disease is the absence of health); and health is the formula in the soul or the knowledge of it. The healthy subject is produced as the result of the following train of thought:—since *this* is health, if the subject is to be healthy *this* must first be present, e.g. a uniform state of body, and if this is to be present, there must be heat; and the physician goes on thinking thus until he reduces the matter to a final something which he himself can produce. Then the process from this point onward, i.e. the process towards health, is called a 'making'. Therefore it follows that in a sense health comes from health and house from house, that with matter from that without matter; for the medical art and the building art are the form of health and of the house, and when I speak of substance without matter I mean the essence.

Of the productions or processes one part is called thinking and the other making—that which proceeds from the starting-point and the form is thinking, and that which proceeds from the final step of the thinking is making. And each of the other, intermediate, things is produced in the same way. I mean, for instance, if the subject is to be healthy his bodily state must be made uniform. What then does being made uniform imply? This or that. And this depends on his being made warm. What does this imply? Something else. And this something is present potentially; and what is present potentially is already in the physician's power.

The active principle then and the starting-point for the process of becoming healthy is, if it happens by art, the form in the soul, and if spontaneously, it is that, whatever it is, which starts the making, [ftnt. deleted] for the man who makes by art, as in healing the starting-point is perhaps the production of warmth (and this the physician produces by rubbing). Warmth in the body, then, is either a part of health or is followed (either directly or through several intermediate steps) by something similar which is a part of health; and this, viz. that which produces the part of health, is the limiting point [ftnt. deleted] and so too with a house (the stones are the limiting-point here) and in all other cases.

Therefore, as the saying goes, it is impossible that anything should be produced if there were nothing existing before. Obviously then some part of the result will pre-exist of necessity; for the matter is a part; for this is present in the process and it is this that becomes something. But is the matter an element even in the *formula?* We certainly describe in both ways [ftnt. deleted] what brazen circles are; we describe both the matter by saying it is brass, and the form by saying that it is such and such a figure; and figure is the proximate genus in which it is placed. The brazen circle, then, has its matter *in its formula.*

As for that out of which as matter they are produced, some things are said, when they have been produced, to be not that but 'thaten'; e.g. the statue is not gold but golden. And a healthy man is not said to be that from which he has come. The reason is that though a thing comes both from its privation and from its substratum, which we call its matter (e.g. what becomes healthy is both a man and an invalid), it is said to come rather from its privation (e.g. it is from an invalid rather than from a man that a healthy subject is produced). And so the healthy subject is not said to be an invalid, but to be a man, and the man is said to be healthy. But as for the things whose privation is obscure and nameless, e.g. in brass the privation of a particular shape or in bricks and timber the privation of arrangement as a house, the thing is thought to be produced *from* these materials, as in the former case the healthy man is produced *from* an invalid. And so, as . . . a thing is not said to be that from which it comes, here the statue is not said to be wood but is said by a verbal change to be wooden, not brass but brazen, not gold but golden, and the house is said to be not bricks but bricken (though we should not say without qualification, if we looked at the matter carefully, even that a statue is produced from wood or a house from bricks, because coming to be implies change in that from which a thing comes to be, and not permanence). It is for this reason, then, that we use this way of speaking.

Since anything which is produced is produced by something (and this I call the starting-point of the production), and from something (and let this be taken to be not the privation but the matter; for the meaning we

attach to this has already [ftnt. deleted] been explained), and since something is produced (and this is either a sphere or a circle or whatever else
it may chance to be), just as we do not make the substratum (the brass),
so we do not make the sphere, except incidentally, because the brazen
sphere is a sphere and we make the former. For to make a 'this' is to make
a 'this' out of the substratum in the full sense of the word. [ftnt. deleted]
(I mean that to make the brass round is not to make the round or the
sphere, but something else, i.e. to produce this form in something different from itself. For if we make the form, we must make it out of something
else; for this was assumed. [ftnt. deleted] E.g. we make a brazen sphere;
and that in the sense that out of this, which is brass, we make this other,
which is a sphere.) If, then, we also make the substratum itself, clearly we
shall make it in the same way, and the processes of making will regress
to infinity. Obviously then the form also, [ftnt. deleted] or whatever we
ought to call the shape present in the sensible thing, is not produced, nor
is there any production of it, nor is the essence produced; for this is that
which is made to be in something else either by art or by nature or by
some faculty. But that there is a *brazen sphere,* this we make. For we make it
out of brass and the sphere; we bring the form into this particular matter,
and the result is a brazen sphere. But if the essence of sphere in general is
to be produced, something must be produced out of something. For the
product will always have to be divisible, and one part must be this and
another that; I mean the one must be matter and the other form. If, then, a
sphere is 'the figure whose circumference is at all points equidistant from
the centre', part of this will be the medium in which the thing made will
be, and part will be in that medium, and the whole will be the thing produced, which corresponds to the brazen sphere. It is obvious, then, from
what has been said, that that which is spoken of as form or substance is
not produced, but the concrete thing which gets its name from this is
produced, and that in everything which is generated matter is present,
and one part of the thing is matter and the other form.

Is there, then, a sphere apart from the individual spheres or a house
apart from the bricks? Rather we may say that no 'this' would ever have
been coming to be, if this had been so, but that the 'form' means the 'such',
and is not a 'this'—a definite thing; but the artist makes, or the father
begets, a 'such' out of a 'this'; and when it has been begotten, it is a 'this
such'. [ftnt. deleted] And the whole 'this', Callias or Socrates, is analogous
to 'this brazen sphere', but man and animal to 'brazen sphere' in general.
Obviously, then, the cause which consists of the Forms (taken in the sense
in which some maintain the existence of the Forms, i.e. if they are some-

thing apart from the individuals) is useless, at least with regard to comings-to-be and to substances; and the Forms need not, for this reason at least, be self-subsistent substances. In some cases indeed it is even obvious that the begetter is of the same kind as the begotten (not, however, the *same* nor one in number, but in form), i.e. in the case of natural products (for man begets man), unless something happens contrary to nature, e.g. the production of a mule by a horse. (And even these cases are similar; for that which would be found to be common to horse and ass, the genus next above them, has not received a name, but it would doubtless be both, in fact something like a mule.) Obviously, therefore, it is quite unnecessary to set up a Form as a pattern (for we should have looked for Forms in these cases if in any; for these are substances if anything is so); the begetter is adequate to the making of the product and to the causing of the form in the matter. And when we have the whole, such and such a form in this flesh and in these bones, this is Callias or Socrates; and they are different in virtue of their matter (for that is different), but the same in form; for their form is indivisible. . . .

IMMANUEL KANT · Genius Gives the Rules

[*Kant's account emphasizes the unprecedented, spontaneous nature of the creative act or process; as the work of genius provides the rules for any activity, genius is a guiding and determining factor in itself. This selection from* The Critique of Judgment *comes from an extended argument designed to show the relationship of aesthetic experience — that of the creator as well as the observer — to other kinds of experience. Kant's emphasis on the importance of the aesthetic experience within a complete theory of man and nature served as a basis for future philosophies of art and for what today is known as the field of aesthetics. It is particularly important to appreciate the context of this selection in an architectonic of three volumes including* The Critique of Pure Reason *and* The Critique of Practical Reason. *In* The Critique of Pure Reason, *Kant clarifies understanding as a faculty that actively orders experience according to definite conceptual categories. He also explains that*

SOURCE From Kant, I., The Critique of Judgement, Meredith, J. C. (trans.), pp. 188–192, 197–200, 203–204. Oxford: Oxford University Press, 1952. Reprinted by permission of the Oxford University Press, Oxford.

imagination gives an initial unity to a field of sensation and perceptual experi-
ence. In The Critique of Practical Reason, *he proposes that reason, another*
function of the mind, postulates principles that are free with respect to natural
process and the faculty of understanding. In The Critique of Judgment, *he*
shows how the free mind is connected with understanding through imagination.]

Genius is the talent (or natural gift) which gives the rule to Art. Since
talent, as the innate productive faculty of the artist, belongs itself to Nature,
we may express the matter thus: *Genius* is the innate mental disposition
(*ingenium*) *through which* Nature gives the rule to Art.

Whatever may be thought of this definition, whether it is merely arbitrary or whether it is adequate to the concept that we are accustomed to
combine with the word *genius* (which is to be examined in the following
paragraphs), we can prove already beforehand that according to the signification of the word here adopted, beautiful arts must necessarily be
considered as arts of *genius*.

For every art presupposes rules by means of which in the first instance a
product, if it is to be called artistic, is represented as possible. But the
concept of beautiful art does not permit the judgment upon the beauty
of a product to be derived from any rule, which has a *concept* as its determining ground, and therefore has at its basis a concept of the way in
which the product is possible. Therefore, beautiful art cannot itself devise
the rule according to which it can bring about its product. But since at
the same time a product can never be called Art without some precedent
rule, Nature in the subject must (by the harmony of its faculties) give the
rule to Art; *i.e.* beautiful Art is only possible as a product of Genius.

We thus see (1) that genius is a *talent* for producing that for which no
definite rule can be given; it is not a mere aptitude for what can be learnt
by a rule. Hence *originality* must be its first property. (2) But since it also
can produce original nonsense, its products must be models, *i.e. exemplary*;
and they consequently ought not to spring from imitation, but must serve
as a standard or rule of judgment for others. (3) It cannot describe or
indicate scientifically how it brings about its products, but it gives the
rule just as nature does. Hence the author of a product for which he is
indebted to his genius does not know himself how he has come by his
Ideas; and he has not the power to devise the like at pleasure or in accordance with a plan, and to communicate it to others in precepts that will
enable them to produce similar products. (Hence it is probable that the
word genius is derived from *genius,* that peculiar guiding and guardian
spirit given to a man at his birth, from whose suggestion these original

Ideas proceed.) (4) Nature by the medium of genius does not prescribe rules to Science, but to Art; and to it only in so far as it is to be beautiful Art.

.   .   .   .

Every one is agreed that genius is entirely opposed to the *spirit of imitation*. Now since learning is nothing but imitation, it follows that the greatest ability and teachableness (capacity) regarded *quâ* teachableness, cannot avail for genius. Even if a man thinks or composes for himself, and does not merely take in what others have taught, even if he discovers many things in art and science, this is not the right ground for calling such a (perhaps great) *head,* a genius (as opposed to him who because he can only learn and imitate is called a *shallow-pate*). For even these things could be learned, they lie in the natural path of him who investigates and reflects according to rules; and they do not differ specifically from what can be acquired by industry through imitation. Thus we can readily learn all that *Newton* has set forth in his immortal work on the Principles of Natural Philosophy, however great a head was required to discover it; but we cannot learn to write spirited poetry, however express may be the precepts of the art and however excellent its models. The reason is that *Newton* could make all his steps, from the first elements of geometry to his own great and profound discoveries, intuitively plain and definite as regards consequence, not only to himself but to every one else. But a *Homer* or a *Wieland* cannot show how his Ideas, so rich in fancy and yet so full of thought, come together in his head, simply because he does not know and therefore cannot teach others. . . .

If now it is a natural gift which must prescribe its rule to art (as beautiful art), of what kind is this rule? It cannot be reduced to a formula and serve as a precept, for then the judgment upon the beautiful would be determinable according to concepts; but the rule must be abstracted from the fact, *i.e.* from the product, on which others may try their own talent by using it as a model, not to be *copied* but to be *imitated*. How this is possible is hard to explain. The Ideas of the artist excite like Ideas in his pupils if nature has endowed them with a like proportion of their mental powers. Hence models of beautiful art are the only means of handing down these Ideas to posterity. . . .

.   .   .   .

We say of certain products of which we expect that they should at least in part appear as beautiful art, they are without *spirit*[1]; although we find

1. [In English we would rather say "without *soul*"; but I prefer to translate *Geist* consistently by *spirit,* to avoid the confusion of it with *Seele.*]

nothing to blame in them on the score of taste. A poem may be very neat and elegant, but without spirit. A history may be exact and well arranged, but without spirit. A festal discourse may be solid and at the same time elaborate, but without spirit. Conversation is often not devoid of entertainment, but it is without spirit: even of a woman we say that she is pretty, an agreeable talker, and courteous, but without spirit. What then do we mean by spirit?

Spirit, in an æsthetical sense, is the name given to the animating principle of the mind. But that by means of which this principle animates the soul, the material which it applies to that [purpose], is what puts the mental powers purposively into swing, *i.e.* into such a play as maintains itself and strengthens the mental powers in their exercise.

Now I maintain that this principle is no other than the faculty of presenting *æsthetical Ideas*. And by an æsthetical Idea I understand that representation of the Imagination which occasions much thought, without, however, any definite thought, *i.e.* any *concept*, being capable of being adequate to it; it consequently cannot be completely compassed and made intelligible by language. — We easily see that it is the counterpart (pendant) of a *rational Idea*; which conversely is a concept to which no *intuition* (or representation of the Imagination) can be adequate.

The Imagination (as a productive faculty of cognition) is very powerful in creating another nature, as it were, out of the material that actual nature gives it. We entertain ourselves with it when experience becomes too commonplace, and by it we remould experience, always indeed in accordance with analogical laws, but yet also in accordance with principles which occupy a higher place in Reason (laws too which are just as natural to us as those by which Understanding comprehends empirical nature). Thus we feel our freedom from the law of association (which attaches to the empirical employment of Imagination), so that the material supplied to us by nature in accordance with this law can be worked up into something different which surpasses nature.

Such representations of the Imagination we may call *Ideas*, partly because they at least strive after something which lies beyond the bounds of experience, and so seek to approximate to a presentation of concepts of Reason (intellectual Ideas), thus giving to the latter the appearance of objective reality, — but especially because no concept can be fully adequate to them as internal intuitions. The poet ventures to realise to sense, rational Ideas of invisible beings, the kingdom of the blessed, hell, eternity, creation, etc.; or even if he deals with things of which there are examples in experience, — *e.g.* death, envy and all vices, also love, fame, and the like,—he tries, by means of Imagination, which emulates the play of Reason in its quest after a maximum, to go beyond the limits of experience and to present them to Sense with a completeness of which there is no example in nature. This is properly speaking the art of the poet, in which the faculty of æsthetical Ideas can manifest itself in its entire strength. But this faculty, considered in itself, is properly only a talent (of the Imagination).

If now we place under a concept a representation of the Imagination belonging to its presentation, but which occasions in itself more thought than can ever be comprehended in a definite concept, and which consequently æsthetically enlarges the concept itself in an unbounded fashion, the Imagination is here creative, and it brings the faculty of intellectual Ideas (the Reason) into movement; *i.e.* by a representation more thought (which indeed belongs to the concept of the object) is occasioned than can in it be grasped or made clear.

Those forms which do not constitute the presentation of a given concept itself but only, as approximate representations of the Imagination, express the consequences bound up with it and its relationship to other concepts, are called (æsthetical) *attributes* of an object, whose concept as a rational Idea cannot be adequately presented. Thus Jupiter's eagle with the lightning in its claws is an attribute of the mighty king of heaven, as the peacock is of his magnificent queen. They do not, like *logical attributes*, represent what lies in our concepts of the sublimity and majesty of creation, but something different, which gives occasion to the Imagination to spread itself over a number of kindred representations, that arouse more thought than can be expressed in a concept determined by words. They furnish as *æsthetical Idea,* which for that rational Idea takes the place of logical presentation; and thus as their proper office they enliven the mind by opening out to it the prospect into an illimitable field of kindred representations. But beautiful art does this not only in the case of painting or sculpture (in which the term "attribute" is commonly employed): poetry and rhetoric also get the spirit that animates their works simply from the æsthetical attributes of the object, which accompany the logical and stimulate the Imagination, so that it thinks more by their aid, although in an undeveloped way, than could be comprehended in a concept and therefore in a definite form of words. . . .

. . . .

In accordance with these suppositions genius is the exemplary originality of the natural gifts of a subject in the *free* employment of his cognitive faculties. In this way the product of a genius (as regards what is to be ascribed to genius and not to possible learning or schooling) is an example, not to be imitated (for then that which in it is genius and constitutes the spirit of the work would be lost), but to be followed, by another genius; whom it awakens to a feeling of his own originality and whom it stirs so to exercise his art in freedom from the constraint of rules, that thereby a new rule is gained for art, and thus his talent shows itself to be exemplary. But because a genius is a favourite of nature and must be regarded by us as a rare phenomenon, his example produces for other good heads a school, *i.e.* a methodical system of teaching according to rules, so far as these can be derived from the peculiarities of the products of his spirit. For such persons beautiful art is so far imitation, to which nature through the medium of a genius supplied the rule.

FRANCIS GALTON · Genius As Inherited

[*Galton was one of the most eminent scientists of the late nineteenth century. His work on the inheritance of genius is an attempt to extend Darwin's theory of evolution to the transmission of human faculties. These excerpts come from the earliest of his three works on the topic and show: his definition of terms, a sample from the section on poets illustrating the approach, a summary of results, and his overall conclusion. Though Galton includes as geniuses many varieties of eminent persons who would not generally be considered either geniuses or creative persons, a long series of studies on genius and heredity and on creativity and heredity have followed his work.*]

I propose to show . . . that a man's natural abilities are derived by inheritance, under exactly the same limitations as are the form and physical features of the whole organic world. Consequently, as it is easy, notwithstanding those limitations, to obtain by careful selection a permanent breed of dogs or horses gifted with peculiar powers of running, or of doing anything else, so it would be quite practicable to produce a highly-gifted race of men by judicious marriages during several consecutive generations. I shall show that social agencies of an ordinary character,

SOURCE   *From Galton, F., Hereditary Genius: An Inquiry into Its Laws and Consequences, pp. 1–4, 228–229, 316–318, 376. London: Macmillan and Co., 1869. Acknowledgment to Macmillan, London and Basingstoke.*

whose influences are little suspected, are at this moment working towards the degradation of human nature, and that others are working towards its improvement. I conclude that each generation has enormous power over the natural gifts of those that follow, and maintain that it is a duty we owe to humanity to investigate the range of that power, and to exercise it in a way that, without being unwise towards ourselves, shall be most advantageous to future inhabitants of the earth.

I am aware that my views, which were first published four years ago in *Macmillan's Magazine* (in June and August 1865), are in contradiction to general opinion; but the arguments I then used have been since accepted, to my great gratification, by many of the highest authorities on heredity. In reproducing them, as I now do, in a much more elaborate form, and on a greatly enlarged basis of induction, I feel assured that, inasmuch as what I then wrote was sufficient to earn the acceptance of Mr. Darwin ("Domestication of Plants and Animals," ii. 7), the increased amount of evidence submitted in the present volume is not likely to be gainsaid.

The general plan of my argument is to show that high reputation is a pretty accurate test of high ability; next, to discuss the relationships of a large body of fairly eminent men — namely, the Judges of England from 1660 to 1868, the Statesmen of the time of George III., and the Premiers during the last 100 years — and to obtain from these a general survey of the laws of heredity in respect to genius. Then I shall examine, in order, the kindred of the most illustrious Commanders, men of Literature and of Science, Poets, Painters, and Musicians, of whom history speaks. I shall also discuss the kindred of a certain selection of Divines and of modern Scholars. Then will follow a short chapter, by way of comparison, on the hereditary transmission of physical gifts, as deduced from the relationships of certain classes of Oarsmen and Wrestlers. Lastly, I shall collate my results, and draw conclusions.

It will be observed that I deal with more than one grade of ability. Those upon whom the greater part of my volume is occupied, and on whose kinships my argument is most securely based, have been generally reputed as endowed by nature with extraordinary genius. There are so few of these men that, although they are scattered throughout the whole historical period of human existence, their number does not amount to more than 400, and yet a considerable proportion of them will be found to be interrelated.

Another grade of ability with which I deal is that which includes numerous highly eminent, and all the illustrious names of modern English history, whose immediate descendants are living among us, whose histories are popularly known, and whose relationships may readily be traced by the help of biographical dictionaries, peerages, and similar books of reference.

A third and lower grade is that of the English Judges, massed together as a whole, for the purpose of the prefatory statistical inquiry of which I have already spoken. No one doubts that many of the ablest intellects of our race are to be found among the Judges; nevertheless the *average* ability of a Judge cannot be rated as equal to that of the lower of the two grades I have described.

.   .   .   .

I have taken little notice . . . of modern men of eminence who are not English, or at least well known to Englishmen. I feared, if I included large classes of foreigners, that I should make glaring errors. It requires a very great deal of labour to hunt out relationships, even with the facilities afforded to a countryman having access to persons acquainted with the various families; much more would it have been difficult to hunt out the kindred of foreigners. I should have especially liked to investigate the biographies of Italians and Jews, both of whom appear to be rich in families of high intellectual breeds. Germany and America are also full of interest. It is a little less so with respect to France, where the Revolution and the guillotine made sad havoc among the progeny of her abler races.

.   .   .   .

I have examined into the relationships of the following 56 poets. Of some of them — as of those of Ferdusi, Terence, and Sappho — there seems to exist no record at all, and my information is very scanty about many of the others. Nevertheless I find that the 20 poets whose names are printed in *italics*, have had eminent kinsfolk, and that some of the remainder afford minor proofs of herditary ability: thus the father of Burns and the mother of Schiller were far from mediocrity; Southey's aunt, Miss Tyler, was passionately fond of the theatre. We may fairly conclude that at least 40 per cent of the Poets have had eminently gifted relations.

List of Poets

Æschylus; Alfieri; Anacreon; *Ariosto; Aristophanes;* Beranger; Burns; *Byron;* Calderon; Campbell; Camoens; *Chaucer; Chenier; Coleridge; Corneille; Cowper;* Dante; *Dibdin; Dryden;* Euripides; Ferdusi; La Fontaine; *Goethe;* Goldoni; Gray; *Heine; Hook;* Horace; Ben Jonson; Juvenal; Keats; Lucretius; Metastasio; *Milman; Milton;* Molière; Moore; Oehlenschläger; Ovid; Petrarch; Plautus; Pope; Praed (but see Appendix); *Racine;* Sappho;

Schiller; Shakespeare; Shelley; Sophocles; Southey; Spenser; *Tasso*; Terence; *Vega*; Virgil; Wieland; *Wordsworth*.

Æschylus, great Greek tragedian; also highly renowned as a warrior, and all his family were distinguished for bravery. He began early to write, but was æt. 41 before he gained his first prize for a drama. He afterwards gained sixteen; *d*. æt. 69.

B. Cynægeirus distinguished himself so highly at Marathon, together with Æschylus, that their feats were commemorated by a descriptive painting.

B. Ameinas was noted as having commenced the attack on the Persian ships at Salamis.

[n.] Philocles was victorious over the "King of Œdipus" by Sophocles, but probably with a posthumous tragedy of Æschylus.

[a S.] Euphorion and Bion were said to have gained four victories with posthumous pieces of Æschylus. What may have been their share and that of Philocles in the completion of these plays is unknown; but at all events, from and by means of these persons arose what was called the tragic school of Æschylus, which continued for the space of 125 years.

Ariosto, Ludovico; author of the epic "Orlando Furioso," and of many excellent satires. He wrote dramas as a boy, and showed an early disposition for poetry, but was educated for the law, which he abandoned under an overpowering impulse towards literature. Never married; had two illegitimate sons.

B. Gabriel; a poet of some distinction. He finished the comedy of "La Scholastica," which his brother had left uncompleted at his death. He wrote several poems, and left a MS. volume of Latin verses, which were published posthumously.

N. Orazio was an intimate friend of Tasso. He wrote the "Argomenti," and other works.

Aristophanes, Greek comedian of the highest order; author of fifty-four comedies, of which only eleven have reached us. His genius showed itself so early, that his first play—and it won the second prize—was written when he was under the age prescribed by law for competitors. It was therefore submitted under a borrowed name.

3 S. His three sons—Philippus, Araros, and Nicostratus—were all poets of the middle comedy.

Byron, Lord. Very ill-educated at home; did not show genius when at Harrow; his "Hours of Idleness" were published æt. 19, and the

"English Bards and Scotch Reviewers," which made him famous,
æt. 21; *d.* æt 36.

[G.] Hon. Admiral Byron, circumnavigator; author of the "Narrative."

[F.] Captain Byron; imprudent and vicious.

[*f.*] Was strange, proud, passionate, and half-mad. "If ever there were a
case in which hereditary influences, arising out of impulse, passions,
and habits of life, could excuse eccentricities of character and extremes of conduct, this excuse must be pleaded for Byron, as having
descended from a line of ancestry distinguished on both sides by
everything calculated to destroy all harmony of character, all social
concord, all individual happiness." (Mrs. Ellis.)

s. Ada, Countess of Lovelace; had remarkable mathematical gifts.

.   .   .   .

Let us now bring our scattered results side to side, for the purpose of
comparison, and judge of the extent to which they corroborate one another,—how far they confirm the provisional calculations made in the
chapter on Judges from more scanty data, and where and why they
contrast.

The number of cases of hereditary genius analysed in the several chapters of my book, amounts to a large total. I have dealt with no less than
300 families containing between them nearly 1,000 eminent men, of whom
415 are illustrious, or, at all events, of such note as to deserve being printed
in black type at the head of a paragraph. If there be such a thing as a decided law of distribution of genius in families, it is sure to become
manifest when we deal statistically with so large a body of examples.

In comparing the results obtained from the different groups of eminent
men, it will be our most convenient course to compare the columns B of
the several tables. Column B gives the number of kinsmen in various
degrees, on the supposition that the number of families in the group to
which it refers is 100. All the entries under B have therefore the same
common measure, they are all *percentages*, and admit of direct intercom-
parison. I hope I have made myself quite clear: lest there should remain
any misapprehension, it is better to give an example. Thus, the families
of Divines are only 25 in number, and in those 25 families there are 7
eminent fathers, 9 brothers, and 10 sons; now in order to raise these numbers to percentages, 7, 9, and 10 must be multiplied by the number of
times that 25 goes into 100, namely by 4. They will then become 28, 36,
and 40, and will be found entered as such, in column B, p. 275; the parent
numbers 7, 9, 10, appearing in the same table in the column A.

In the following table, the columns B of all the different groups are printed side by side; I have, however, thrown Painters and Musicians into a single group of Artists, because their numbers were too small to make it worth while to consider them apart. Annexed to these is a column B calculated from the whole of the families put together, with the intention of giving a general average. . . .

	Separate Groups.								All groups together.		
Number of families, each containing more than one eminent man	85	39	27	33	43	20	28	25	300		
Total number of eminent men in all the families	262	130	89	119	148	57	97	75	977		
	Judges, p. 61.	Statesmen, p. 109.	Commanders, p. 148.	Literary, p. 171.	Scientific, p. 195.	Poets, p. 227.	Artists, pp. 238 and 249.	Divines, p. 275.	Illustrious and eminent men of all classes.		
	B.	B.	B.	B.	B.	B.	B.	B.	B.	...	...
Father	26	33	47	48	26	20	32	28	31	...	...
Brother	35	39	50	42	47	40	50	36	41	...	...
Son	36	49	31	51	60	45	89	40	48	...	...
Grandfather	15	28	16	24	14	5	7	20	17	...	...
Uncle	18	18	8	24	16	5	14	40	18	...	...
Nephew	19	18	35	24	23	30	18	4	22	...	...
Grandson	19	10	12	9	14	5	18	16	14	...	...
Great-grandfather	2	8	8	3	0	0	0	.4	3	...	...
Great-uncle	4	5	8	6	5	5	7	4	5	...	...
First cousin	11	21	20	18	16	0	1	8	13	...	...
Great-nephew	17	5	8	6	16	10	0	0	10	...	...
Great-grandson	6	0	0	3	7	0	0	0	3	...	...
All more remote	14	37	44	15	23	5	18	16	31	...	...

Nature teems with latent life, which man has large powers of evoking under the forms and to the extent which he desires. We must not permit ourselves to consider each human or other personality as something supernaturally added to the stock of nature, but rather as a segregation of what already existed, under a new shape, and as a regular consequence of previous conditions. Neither must we be misled by the word "individuality," because it appears from the many facts and arguments in this

book, that our personalities are not so independent as our self-consciousness leads us to believe. We may look upon each individual as something
not wholly detached from its parent source,—as a wave that has been
lifted and shaped by normal conditions in an unknown, illimitable ocean.
There is decidedly a solidarity as well as a separateness in all human, and
probably in all lives whatsoever; and this consideration goes far, as I
think, to establish an opinion that the constitution of the living Universe
is a pure theism, and that its form of activity is what may be described as
co-operative. It points to the conclusion that all life is single in its essence,
but various, ever varying, and inter-active in its manifestations, and that
men and all other living animals are active workers and sharers in a vastly
more extended system of cosmic action than any of ourselves, much less
of them, can possibly comprehend. It also suggests that they may contribute, more or less unconsciously, to the manifestation of a far higher life
than our own, somewhat as—I do not propose to push the metaphor too
far—the individual cells of one of the more complex animals contribute
to the manifestation of its higher order of personality.

SIGMUND FREUD · Creative Writers and Daydreaming

[*Except for some cursory remarks in the* Introductory Lectures on Psychoanalysis, The Interpretation of Dreams, Formulations on the Two Principles of Mental Functioning, *and the preface to Marie Bonaparte's* The Life
and Works of Edgar Allan Poe, *this selection represents Freud's only direct
formulation about the creative process and the only place where he spells
out in some detail specific processes and conditions that lead to the creation of
a particular type of art. The creative writer, he says, molds his own wish-ful-
filling fantasies into a form that is pleasing and attractive to others. Although
he has also applied psychoanalysis extensively to the biography of artists such
as DaVinci and Dostoevsky as well as to an understanding of art products and
humor, he himself did not consider these latter types of investigations to be
direct explications of the creative process.*]

SOURCE *From Freud, S.,* Creative Writers and Day-Dreaming *(1908), in Strachey, J. (ed.),*
The Standard Edition of the Complete Psychological Works of Sigmund Freud, *Vol. 9, pp.
143–144, 146–153. London: Hogarth Press, 1959. Reprinted by permission of Sigmund Freud Copy-
rights Ltd., The Institute of Psycho-Analysis, and the Hogarth Press Ltd. Also from Chapter IX, "The
Relation of the Poet to Day-Dreaming," from* Collected *Papers, Volume 4, edited by Ernest Jones,
M.D., authorized translation under the supervision of Joan Riviere, published by Basic Books,
Inc., by arrangement with The Hogarth Press Ltd. and The Institute of Psycho-Analysis, London.*

We laymen have always been intensely curious to know — like the Cardinal who put a similar question to Ariosto [ftnt. deleted] — from what sources that strange being, the creative writer, draws his material, and how he manages to make such an impression on us with it and to arouse in us emotions of which, perhaps, we had not even thought ourselves capable. . . .

. . . .

Should we not look for the first traces of imaginative activity as early as in childhood? The child's best-loved and most intense occupation is with his play or games. Might we not say that every child at play behaves like a creative writer, in that he creates a world of his own, or, rather, rearranges the things of his world in a new way which pleases him? It would be wrong to think he does not take that world seriously; on the contrary, he takes his play very seriously and he expends large amounts of emotion on it. The opposite of play is not what is serious but what is real. In spite of all the emotion with which he cathects his world of play, the child distinguishes it quite well from reality; and he likes to link his imagined objects and situations to the tangible and visible things of the real world. This linking is all that differentiates the child's 'play' from 'phantasying.'

The creative writer does the same as the child at play. He creates a world of phantasy which he takes very seriously — that is, which he invests with large amounts of emotion — while separating it sharply from reality. Language has preserved this relationship between children's play and poetic creation. It gives [in German] the name of 'Spiel' ['play'] to those forms of imaginative writing which require to be linked to tangible objects and which are capable of representation. It speaks of a 'Lustspiel' or 'Trauerspiel' ['comedy' or 'tragedy': literally, 'pleasure play' or 'mourning play'] and describes those who carry out the representation as 'Shauspieler' ['players': literally 'show-players']. The unreality of the writer's imaginative world, however, has very important consequences for the technique of his art; for many things which, if they were real, could give no enjoyment, can do so in the play of phantasy, and many excitements which, in themselves, are actually distressing, can become a source of pleasure for the hearers and spectators at the performance of a writer's work.

. . . .

A child's play is determined by wishes: in point of fact by a single wish — one that helps in his upbringing — the wish to be big and grown up. He is always playing at being 'grown up', and in his games he imitates what he knows about the lives of his elders. He has no reason to conceal this wish. With the adult, the case is different. On the one hand, he knows that he is expected not to go on playing or phantasying any longer, but to act in the real world; on the other hand, some of the wishes which give rise to his phantasies are of a kind which it is essential to conceal. Thus he is ashamed of his phantasies as being childish and as being unpermissible.

Let us now make ourselves acquainted with a few of the characteristics of phantasying. We may lay it down that a happy person never phantasies, only an unsatisfied one. The motive forces of phantasies are unsatisfied wishes, and every single phantasy is the fulfilment of a wish, a correction of unsatisfying reality. These motivating wishes vary according to the sex, character and circumstances of the person who is having the phantasy; but they fall naturally into two main groups. They are either ambitious wishes, which serve to elevate the subject's personality; or they are erotic ones. In young women the erotic wishes predominate almost exclusively, for their ambition is as a rule absorbed by erotic trends. In young men egoistic and ambitious wishes come to the fore clearly enough alongside of erotic ones. But we will not lay stress on the opposition between the two trends; we would rather emphasize the fact that they are often united. Just as, in many altar-pieces, the portrait of the donor is to be seen in a corner of the picture, so, in the majority of ambitious phantasies, we can discover in some corner or other the lady for whom the creator of the phantasy performs all his heroic deeds and at whose feet all his triumphs are laid. Here, as you see, there are strong enough motives for concealment; the well-brought-up young woman is only allowed a minimum of erotic desire, and the young man has to learn to suppress the excess of self-regard which he brings with him from the spoilt days of his childhood, so that he may find his place in a society which is full of other individuals making equally strong demands.

We must not suppose that the products of this imaginative activity — the various phantasies, castles in the air and daydreams — are stereotyped or unalterable. On the contrary, they fit themselves in to the subject's shifting impressions of life, change with every change in his situation, and receive from every fresh active impression what might be called a 'date-mark'. The relation of a phantasy to time is in general very important. We may say that it hovers, as it were, between three times — the three moments of time which our ideation involves. Mental work is linked to some current impression, some provoking occasion in the present which has been able to arouse one of the subject's major wishes. From there it harks back to a memory of an earlier experience (usually an infantile one) in which this wish was fulfilled; and it now creates a situation relating to the future which represents a fulfilment of the wish. What it thus creates is a day-dream or phantasy, which carries about it traces of its origin from the occasion which provoked it and from the memory. Thus past, present and future are strung together, as it were, on the thread of the wish that runs through them.

. . . .

I cannot pass over the relation of phantasies to dreams. Our dreams at night are nothing else than phantasies like these, as we can demonstrate from the interpretation of dreams. [ftnt. deleted] Language, in its un-rivalled wisdom, long ago decided the question of the essential nature of dreams by giving the name of 'day-dreams' to the airy creations of phan-tasy. If the meaning of our dreams usually remains obscure to us in spite of this pointer, it is because of the circumstance that at night there also arise in us wishes of which we are ashamed; these we must conceal from ourselves, and they have consequently been repressed, pushed into the unconscious. Repressed wishes of this sort and their derivatives are only allowed to come to expression in a very distorted form. When scientific work had succeeded in elucidating this factor of *dream-distortion*, it was no longer difficult to recognize that night-dreams are wish-fulfilments in just the same way as day-dreams — the phantasies which we all know so well.

[margin handwritten notes: distorted wishes concealing wishes — socially pressure judgement]

So much for phantasies. And now for the creative writer. May we really attempt to compare the imaginative writer with the 'dreamer in broad daylight', [ftnt. deleted] and his creations with day-dreams? Here we must begin by making an initial distinction. We must separate writers who, like the ancient authors of epics and tragedies, take over their material ready-made, from writers who seem to originate their own material. We will keep to the latter kind, and, for the purposes of our comparison, we will choose not the writers most highly esteemed by the critics, but the less pretentious authors of novels, romances and short stories, who never-theless have the widest and most eager circle of readers of both sexes. One feature above all cannot fail to strike us about the creations of these story-writers: each of them has a hero who is the centre of interest, for whom the writer tries to win our sympathy by every possible means and whom he seems to place under the protection of a special Providence. If, at the end of one chapter of my story, I leave the hero unconscious and bleeding from severe wounds, I am sure to find him at the beginning of the next being carefully nursed and on the way to recovery; and if the first volume closes with the ship he is in going down in a storm at sea, I am certain, at the opening of the second volume, to read of his miraculous rescue—a rescue without which the story could not proceed. The feeling of security with which I follow the hero through his perilous adventures is the same as the feeling with which a hero in real life throws himself into the water to save a drowning man or exposes himself to the enemy's fire in order to storm a battery. It is the true heroic feeling, which one of our best writers has expressed in an inimitable phrase: 'Nothing can happen to *me!'* [ftnt. deleted] It seems to me, however, that through this revealing characteristic of invulnerability we can immediately recognize His Majesty the Ego, the hero alike of every day-dream and of every story. [ftnt. deleted]

Other typical features of these egocentric stories point to the same kinship. The fact that all the women in the novel invariably fall in love with the hero can hardly be looked on as a portrayal of reality, but it is easily understood as a necessary constituent of a day-dream. The same is true of the fact that the other characters in the story are sharply divided into good and bad, in defiance of the variety of human characters that are to be observed in real life. The 'good' ones are the helpers, while the 'bad' ones are the enemies and rivals, of the ego which has become the hero of the story.

We are perfectly aware that very many imaginative writings are far removed from the model of the naïve day-dream; and yet I cannot suppress the suspicion that even the most extreme deviations from that model could be linked with it through an uninterrupted series of transitional cases. It has struck me that in many of what are known as 'psychological' novels only one person—once again the hero—is described from within. The author sits inside his mind, as it were, and looks at the other characters from outside. The psychological novel in general no doubt owes its special nature to the inclination of the modern writer to split up his ego, by self-observation, into many part-egos, and, in consequence, to personify the conflicting currents of his own mental life in several heroes. Certain novels, which might be described as 'eccentric', seem to stand in quite special contrast to the type of the day-dream. In these, the person who is introduced as the hero plays only a very small active part; he sees the actions and sufferings of other people pass before him like a spectator. Many of Zola's later works belong to this category. But I must point out that the psychological analysis of individuals who are not creative writers, and who diverge in some respects from the so-called norm, has shown us analogous variations of the day-dream, in which the ego contents itself with the role of spectator.

If our comparison of the imaginative writer with the day-dreamer, and of poetical creation with the day-dream, is to be of any value, it must, above all, show itself in some way or other fruitful. Let us, for instance, try to apply to these authors' works the thesis we laid down earlier concerning the relation between phantasy and the three periods of time and the wish which runs through them; and, with its help, let us try to study the connections that exist between the life of the writer and his works. No one has known, as a rule, what expectations to frame in approaching this problem; and often the connection has been thought of in much too simple terms. In the light of the insight we have gained from phantasies, we ought to expect the following state of affairs. A strong experience in the present awakens in the creative writer a memory of an earlier experience (usually belonging to his childhood) from which there now proceeds a wish which finds its fulfilment in the creative work. The work itself exhibits elements of the recent provoking occasion as well as of the old memory. [ftnt. deleted]

Do not be alarmed at the complexity of this formula. I suspect that in fact it will prove to be too exiguous a pattern. Nevertheless, it may contain a first approach to the true state of affairs; and, from some experiments I have made, I am inclined to think that this way of looking at creative writings may turn out not unfruitful. You will not forget that the stress it lays on childhood memories in the writer's life—a stress which may perhaps seem puzzling—is ultimately derived from the assumption that a piece of creative writing, like a day-dream, is a continuation of, and a substitute for, what was once the play of childhood.

We must not neglect, however, to go back to the kind of imaginative works which we have to recognize, not as original creations, but as the refashioning of ready-made and familiar material. . . . Even here, the writer keeps a certain amount of independence, which can express itself in the choice of material and in changes in it which are often quite extensive. In so far as the material is already at hand, however, it is derived from the popular treasure-house of myths, legends and fairy tales. The study of constructions of folk-psychology such as these is far from being complete, but it is extremely probable that myths, for instance, are distorted vestiges of the wishful phantasies of whole nations, the *secular dreams* of youthful humanity.

. . . by what means the creative writer achieves the emotional effects

in us that are aroused by his creations we have as yet not touched on . . .
at all. But I should like at least to point out to you the path that leads from
our discussion of phantasies to the problems of poetical effects.

. . . I have said . . . that the day-dreamer carefully conceals his phantasies
from other people because he feels he has reasons for being ashamed of
them. I should now add that even if he were to communicate them to us
he could give us no pleasure by his disclosures. Such phantasies, when we
learn them, repel us or at least leave us cold. But when a creative writer
presents his plays to us or tells us what we are inclined to take to be his
personal day-dreams, we experience a great pleasure, and one which probably arises from the confluence of many sources. How the writer accomplishes this is his innermost secret; the essential *ars poetica* lies in the technique of overcoming the feeling of repulsion in us which is undoubtedly
connected with the barriers that rise between each single ego and the
others. We can guess two of the methods used by this technique. The
writer softens the character of his egoistic day-dreams by altering and
disguising it, and he bribes us by the purely formal—that is, aesthetic—
yield of pleasure which he offers us in the presentation of his phantasies.
We give the name of an *incentive bonus*, or a *fore-pleasure*, to a yield of
pleasure such as this, which is offered to us so as to make possible the release of still greater pleasure arising from deeper psychical sources.
[ftnt. deleted] In my opinion, all the aesthetic pleasure which a creative
writer affords us has the character of a fore-pleasure of this kind, and our
actual enjoyment of an imaginative work proceeds from a liberation of
tensions in our minds. It may even be that not a little of this effect is due
to the writer's enabling us thenceforward to enjoy our own day-dreams
without self-reproach or shame. This brings us to the threshold of new,
interesting and complicated enquiries; but also, at least for the moment,
to the end of our discussion.

CHAPTER TWO

DESCRIPTIVE ACCOUNTS

The selections in this chapter are all, in a broad sense, descriptions of various aspects of the creative process or of creative capacities. With the exception of Lombroso, none of the authors attempts a theory of the nature of creativity. For the most part, these accounts document and define the phases and qualities of the creative process or the characteristics of creative persons. They range from Poe's specific account of how he wrote his famous poem, "The Raven," to the sweeping clinical descriptions of Lombroso. In different cases, the definition of creativity — the process or capacity of the personality to be described — varies.

The sequence begins with selections by three creators, the poets Poe and Coleridge and the scientist Cannon. Although many investigations of creativity begin with the invocation of a personal and purportedly "expert" testimony of a creator about his own creative experiences, we do not intend the selections from Poe, Coleridge, and Cannon to serve this purpose here. As stated in our Introduction, we do not consider the uninterpreted public testimonies of creators to be particularly valid sources of data. Furthermore, many collections of creators' testimonies are readily available and do not require republication in this volume (see Selected Bibliography for Chapter Two). The discussions by these particular creators are included along with other systematic descriptive accounts because they have attempted to step back from their personal experiences and to organize them into generalized categories. Coleridge approaches creation from the vantage point of a critic with personal experience of the process, and Poe writes as a literary critic of his own work and a self-designated "philosopher" in this account. Poe asserts that the poetic process is highly controlled and rational and Coleridge makes an important distinction between fancy as an organizer of given images and productive imagination as a spontaneous agency responsible for new syntheses of images. Walter B. Cannon, the great physiologist, attempts to develop generalizations about the experience of scientific discovery by reference to empirical studies and the experiences of other scientists in addition to his own. He traces the origin of scientific hunches to "extraconscious" sources, closely following Sherrington[1] in his definition of "extraconscious" rather than Freud. Freud's Unconscious differs from Cannon's formulation in that it exerts a specific determining influence on consciousness, i.e., by virtue of being hidden, unconscious factors influence and determine behavior to a greater extent than conscious factors.

Wallas's account of the phases of preparation, incubation, illumination, and verification in creative thinking has been widely used and accepted as a description by authors of psychology textbooks, investigators in cognitive psychology, and by philosophers, critics, and biographers. In view of that wide acceptance, we also have included in this section Patrick's seminal experimental study of Wallas's phases of creative thought. Patrick's study is not a description in itself but it is a controlled exploration attempting to validate a description. Though she claims to have established Wallas's phases, a careful consideration of methods — which omits an evaluation of the quality or newness of the completed work — raises doubts about the conclusions drawn. A later study similar to Patrick's was carried out by Eindhoven and Vinacke (see Selected Bibliography for this chapter) and they concluded that there was no evidence for Wallas's phases.

It may be surprising to some to find Lombroso's famous account of the relationship between genius and insanity in a section on description, since this account clearly sets out to ascertain that creativity or genius is a form of physical degeneration. We have purposely included this selection here in order to highlight the close relationship between description and explanation. Descriptions are invariably based on presuppositions and assumptions; usually, such presuppositions and assumptions tacitly, if not explicitly, point to some kind of explanation. Although Lombroso clearly has an explicit theory about the nature of genius or creativity, his approach primarily illustrates the classical method of clinical description: documentation and cataloguing of cases. It therefore serves to illustrate some of the pitfalls and advantages of clinical description as a source of evidence. The research of C. W. Taylor (cited in the Selected Bibliography, p. 355) on identifying or describing characteristics of the creative person is an example of a descriptive approach explicitly concerned with explanation and prediction. The characteristics Taylor identifies and describes by such means as a "Biographical Inventory" will, he believes, provide

1. Sherrington, C. *Man on His Nature*. New York: Macmillan, 1941.

a basis for predicting the persons who will be successfully creative. These characteristics, therefore, would also be responsible for creativity.

The majority of selections included in this chapter are descriptions of the creative process. Lombroso's and Maslow's accounts differ from the others in this section because they primarily provide descriptions of the creative person. Although Lombroso nowhere uses the term "creativity" specifically, his presentation pertains to a definition of creativity as a quality or capacity of special and unique persons in society, men and women of genius. Maslow, on the other hand, specifically attempts to construct a broader definition of the creative person, and he discusses and describes two types: the self-actualizing creative person and the special talent creative person. Maslow's assertion that the potentiality for self-actualizing creativity exists in everyone is based on clinical observations sharply differing from those of Lombroso. Rogers's attempt at a theory of creativity, appearing in the last chapter of this book, is based on observations similar to Maslow's and also assumes a potentiality for creativity in everyone.

EDGAR ALLAN POE · Creation As Craft

[*Poe, the poet and short story writer, here describes a specific experience of literary creation. He emphasizes purely rational, conscious factors as playing the chief, or only, role in his creation of the famous poem, "The Raven." Though many critics and literary persons have questioned the truth or accuracy of this account, as a testimonial of a creative person it presents a unique emphasis on the craft of writing and a repudiation of the importance of inspiration.*]

Charles Dickens, in a note now lying before me, alluding to an examination I once made of the mechanism of "Barnaby Rudge," says—"By the way, are you aware that Godwin wrote his 'Caleb Williams' backwards? He first involved his hero in a web of difficulties, forming the second volume, and then, for the first, cast about him for some mode of accounting for what had been done."

SOURCE *From Poe, E. A., "The Philosophy of Composition,"* Graham's Magazine of Literature and Art, *April 1846, Vol. 28, No. 4, pp. 163–164.*

I cannot think this the *precise* mode of procedure on the part of Godwin — and indeed what he himself acknowledges, is not altogether in accordance with Mr. Dickens' idea — but the author of "Caleb Williams" was too good an artist not to perceive the advantage derivable from at least a somewhat similar process. Nothing is more clear than that every plot, worth the name, must be elaborated to its *dénouement* before any thing be attempted with the pen. It is only with the *dénouement* constantly in view that we can give a plot its indispensable air of consequence, or causation, by making the incidents, and especially the tone at all points, tend to the development of the intention.

There is a radical error, I think, in the usual mode of constructing a story. Either history affords a thesis — or one is suggested by an incident of the day — or, at best, the author sets himself to work in the combination of striking events to form merely the basis of his narrative — designing, generally, to fill in with description, dialogue, or autorial comment, whatever crevices of fact, or action, may, from page to page, render themselves apparent.

I prefer commencing with the consideration of an *effect*. Keeping originality *always* in view — for he is false to himself who ventures to dispense with so obvious and so easily attainable a source of interest — I say to myself, in the first place, "Of the innumerable effects, or impressions, of which the heart, the intellect, or (more generally) the soul is susceptible, what one shall I, on the present occasion, select?" Having chosen a novel, first, and secondly a vivid effect, I consider whether it can best be wrought by incident or tone — whether by ordinary incidents and peculiar tone, or the converse, or by peculiarity both of incident and tone — afterward looking about me (or rather within) for such combinations of event, or tone, as shall best aid me in the construction of the effect.

I have often thought how interesting a magazine paper might be written by any author who would — that is to say, who could — detail, step by step, the processes by which any one of his compositions attained its ultimate point of completion. Why such a paper has never been given to the world, I am much at a loss to say — but, perhaps, the autorial vanity has had more to do with the omission than any one other cause. Most writers — poets in especial — prefer having it understood that they compose by a species of fine frenzy — an ecstatic intuition — and would positively shudder at letting the public take a peep behind the scenes, at the elaborate and vacillating crudities of thought — at the true purposes seized only at the last moment — at the innumerable glimpses of idea that arrived not at the maturity of full view — at the fully matured fancies discarded in despair as unmanageable — at the cautious selections and rejections — at the painful erasures and interpolations—in a word, at the wheels and pinions—the tackle for scene-shifting—the stepladders and demon-traps—the cock's feathers, the red paint and the black patches, which, in ninety-nine cases out of the hundred, constitute the properties of the literary *histrio*.

I am aware, on the other hand, that the case is by no means common, in which an author is at all in condition to retrace the steps by which his conclusions have been attained. In general, suggestions, having arisen pell-mell, are pursued and forgotten in a similar manner.

For my own part, I have neither sympathy with the repugnance alluded to, nor, at any time, the least difficulty in recalling to mind the progressive steps of any of my compositions; and, since the interest of an analysis, or reconstruction, such as I have considered a *desideratum*, is quite independent of any real or fancied interest in the thing analyzed, it will not be regarded as a breach of decorum on my part to show the *modus operandi* by which some one of my own works was put together. I select "The Raven," as the most generally known. It is my design to render it manifest that no one point in its composition is referrible either to accident or intuition—that the work proceeded, step by step, to its completion with the precision and rigid consequence of a mathematical problem.

Let us dismiss, as irrelevant to the poem *per se*, the circumstance—or say the necessity—which, in the first place, gave rise to the intention of composing *a* poem that should suit at once the popular and the critical taste.

We commence, then, with this intention.

The initial consideration was that of extent. If any literary work is too long to be read at one sitting, we must be content to dispense with the immensely important effect derivable from unity of impression—for, if two sittings be required, the affairs of the world interfere, and every thing like totality is at once destroyed. But since, *ceteris paribus*, no poet can afford to dispense with *any thing* that may advance his design, it but remains to be seen whether there is, in extent, any advantage to counterbalance the loss of unity which attends it. Here I say no, at once. What we term a long poem is, in fact, merely a succession of brief ones—that is to say, of brief poetical effects. It is needless to demonstrate that a poem is such, only inasmuch as it intensely excites, by elevating, the soul; and all intense excitements are, through a psychal necessity, brief. For this reason, at least one half of the "Paradise Lost" is essentially prose—a succession of poetical excitements interspersed, *inevitably*, with corresponding depressions—the whole being deprived, through the extremeness of its length, of the vastly important artistic element, totality, or unity, of effect.

It appears evident, then, that there is a distinct limit, as regards length, to all works of literary art—the limit of a single sitting—and that, although in certain classes of prose composition, such as "Robinson Crusoe" (demanding no unity), this limit may be advantageously overpassed, it can never properly be overpassed in a poem. Within this limit, the extent of a poem may be made to bear mathematical relation to its merit—in other words, to the excitement or elevation—again in other words, to the degree of the true poetical effect which it is capable of inducing; for it is clear that the brevity must be in direct ratio of the intensity of the intended effect:—this, with one proviso—that a certain degree of duration is absolutely requisite for the production of any effect at all.

Holding in view these considerations, as well as that degree of excitement which I deemed not above the popular, while not below the critical, taste, I reached at once what I conceived the proper *length* for my intended poem—a length of about one hundred lines. It is, in fact, a hundred and eight.

My next thought concerned the choice of an impression, or effect, to be conveyed: and here I may as well observe that, throughout the construction, I kept steadily in view the design of rendering the work *universally* appreciable. I should be carried too far out of my immediate topic were I to demonstrate a point upon which I have repeatedly insisted, and which, with the poetical, stands not in the slightest need of demonstration—the point, I mean, that Beauty is the sole legitimate province of the poem. A few words, however, in elucidation of my real meaning, which some of my friends have evinced a disposition to misrepresent. That pleasure which is at once the most intense, the most elevating, and the most pure, is, I believe, found in the contemplation of the beautiful. When, indeed, men speak of Beauty, they mean, precisely, not a quality, as is supposed, but an effect—they refer, in short, just to that intense and pure elevation of *soul—not* of intellect, or of heart—upon which I have commented, and which is experienced in consequence of contemplating "the beautiful." Now I designate Beauty as the province of the poem, merely because it is an obvious rule of Art that effects should be made to spring from direct causes—that objects should be attained through means best adapted for their attainment—no one as yet having been weak enough to deny that the peculiar elevation alluded to, is *most readily* attained in the poem. Now the object, Truth, or the satisfaction of the intellect, and the object Passion, or the excitement of the heart, are, although attainable, to a certain extent, in poetry, far more readily attainable in prose. Truth, in fact, demands a precision, and Passion, a *homeliness* (the truly passionate will comprehend me) which are absolutely antagonistic

to that Beauty which, I maintain, is the excitement, or pleasurable elevation, of the soul. It by no means follows from any thing here said, that
passion, or even truth, may not be introduced, and even profitably introduced, into a poem—for they may serve in elucidation, or aid the general effect, as do discords in music, by contrast—but the true artist will
always contrive, first, to tone them into proper subservience to the predominant aim, and, secondly, to enveil them, as far as possible, in that
Beauty which is the atmosphere and the essence of the poem.

Regarding, then, Beauty as my province, my next question referred to
the *tone* of its highest manifestation—and all experience has shown that
this tone is one of *sadness*. . . .

SAMUEL TAYLOR COLERIDGE · Fancy and Imagination

[*Coleridge here explicitly concentrates on a theoretical interpretation of the
relationships among mental functions and the production of poetry. He draws
a clear distinction between fancy and constructive imagining. His rather well-
known account of his own poetic process in the preface to* Kubla Khan *contrasts with the theory presented here in suggesting that at least some aspects
of his control of the process were outside his own consciousness. As a poet and
as a critic, Coleridge helped to crystallize the tradition in poetry and criticism,
starting in the nineteenth century and extending into modern times, that holds
individual originality in high esteem.*]

The imagination . . . I consider either as primary, or secondary. The
primary imagination I hold to be the living power and prime agent of all
human perception, and as a repetition in the finite mind of the eternal act
of creation in the infinite I AM. The secondary I consider as an echo of the
former, co-existing with the conscious will, yet still as identical with the
primary in the kind of its agency, and differing only in degree, and in the
mode of its operation. It dissolves, diffuses, dissipates, in order to re-
create; or where this process is rendered impossible, yet still, at all events,

Source   *From Coleridge, S. T.,* Biographia Literaria: or Biographical Sketches of My Liter-
ary Life and Opinions, *Vol. 1, pp. 144, 150–151. London: Rest Fenner, 1817. Edition by John
Shawcross, Oxford: Oxford University Press, 1907. Reprinted by permission of Oxford University
Press.*

it struggles to idealize and to unify. It is essentially *vital*, even as all objects (as objects) are essentially fixed and dead.

Fancy, on the contrary, has no other counters to play with, but fixities and definites. The Fancy is indeed no other than a mode of memory emancipated from the order of time and space; and blended with, and modified by that empirical phenomenon of the will, which we express by the word choice. But equally with the ordinary memory, it must receive all its materials ready made from the law of association.

Whatever more than this, I shall think it fit to declare concerning the powers and privileges of the imagination in the present work, will be found in the Critical Essay on the uses of the Supernatural in poetry and the principles that regulate its introduction: which the reader will find prefixed to the poem of The Ancient Mariner.

.   .   .   .

My own conclusions of the nature of poetry, in the strictest use of the word, have been in part anticipated in the preceding disquisition on the fancy and imagination. What is poetry? is so nearly the same question with, what is a poet? that the answer to the one is involved in the solution of the other. For it is a distinction resulting from the poetic genius itself, which sustains and modifies the images, thoughts, and emotions of the poet's own mind. The poet, described in ideal perfection, brings the whole soul of man into activity, with the subordination of its faculties to each other, according to their relative worth and dignity. He diffuses a tone and spirit of unity, that blends, and (as it were) fuses, each into each, by that synthetic and magical power to which we have exclusively appropriated the name of imagination. This power, first put in action by the will and understanding, and retained under their irremissive, though gentle and unnoticed, control (*laxis effertur habenis*) reveals itself in the balance or reconciliation of opposite or discordant qualities: of sameness, with difference; of the general, with the concrete; the idea, with the image; the individual, with the representative; the sense of novelty and freshness, with old and familiar objects; a more than usual state of emotion, with more than usual order; judgment ever awake and steady self-possession, with enthusiasm and feeling profound or vehement; and while it blends and harmonizes the natural and the artificial, still subordinates art to nature; the manner to the matter; and our admiration of the poet to our sympathy with the poetry.

.   .   .   .

Finally, good sense is the body of poetic genius, fancy its drapery, motion its life, and imagination the soul that is every where, and in each; and forms all into one graceful and intelligent whole.

WALTER BRADFORD CANNON · The Role of Hunches in Scientific Thought

[*Cannon's physiological theories of homeostasis and of the "flight and fight" syndrome were important and creative scientific achievements. In this selection, he emphasizes the role of sudden leaps of thought and of inspiratory experiences in scientific discovery and scientific creation. Cannon's presentation is a relatively rare instance of a scientist's report of his own experience along with an interpretation of that experience. Though he emphasizes the importance of hunches in certain aspects of the scientific approach, Cannon otherwise subscribes to the use of stepwise inductive and deductive thinking.*]

How do investigators obtain insight into ways of possible progress toward acquiring new knowledge? Do they sit down and think intensively about the existing status and what the next move shall be or do they count upon revelation for hints and clairvoyance? Evidence indicates that reliance has been placed on both methods.

From the years of my youth the unearned assistance of sudden and unpredicted insight has been common. While a student in high school I was occasionally puzzled by "originals" in algebra, the solution of which was not at all clear when I went to sleep at night. As I awoke in the morning the proper procedures were immediately evident and the answers were quickly obtained. On an occasion I was handed a complicated toy which was out of order and would not operate. I examined the mechanism carefully but did not see how the defect might be corrected. I resorted to sleep for a solution of the problem. At daybreak the corrective manipulation appeared thoroughly understandable, and I promptly set the contraption going.

As a matter of routine I have long trusted unconscious processes to serve me—for example, when I have had to prepare a public address. I would gather points for the address and write them down in a rough outline. Within the next few nights I would have sudden spells of awakening, with an onrush of illustrative instances, pertinent phrases, and fresh ideas related to those already listed. Paper and pencil at hand permitted the capture of these fleeting thoughts before they faded into oblivion. The process has been so common and so reliable for me that I have supposed that it was at the service of everyone. But evidence indicates that it is not.

An illuminating inquiry into the nature of the flash of ideas and the

SOURCE *From Cannon, W. B., "The Role of Hunches," The Way of an Investigator, pp. 57–67. Copyright 1945 by W. W. Norton & Company, Inc., New York. Copyright renewed 1972 by Bradford Cannon. Reprinted by permission.*

extent of its occurrence among scientific men was reported by Platt and Baker[1] in 1931. They called the phenomenon a "hunch," a word meaning originally a push or sudden thrust. In ordinary experience it means the quick gleam of a suggestion that flares unexpectedly as the answer to a difficult question or as the explanation of a puzzle. They defined the scientific hunch as "a unifying or clarifying idea which springs into consciousness as a solution to a problem in which we are intensely interested."

In their inquiry into the appearance of hunches among chemists they received answers from 232 correspondents. Assistance from a scientific revelation or a hunch in the solution of an important problem was reported by 33 per cent; 50 per cent reported that they had such assistance occasionally; and only 17 per cent, never. Professor W. D. Bancroft, the Cornell University chemist, tells of talking to four fellow chemists regarding aid from hunches and finding that to three of them the experience was commonplace. The fourth did not understand what was meant by the reference and testified that he had never had the feeling of an inspiration, had never had an idea come to him unexpectedly from some strange "outside" realm. He had worked consciously for all his results and what was described by the others meant nothing to him.

In typical cases a hunch appears after long study and springs into consciousness at a time when the investigator is not working on his problem. It arises from a wide knowledge of facts, but it is essentially a leap of the imagination, for it reaches forth into the range of possibilities. It results from a spontaneous process of creative thought. Noteworthy in the statistics given by Platt and Baker is the evidence that having hunches was not unknown to 83 per cent of the chemists who replied to the questionnaire. This high percentage raises the query as to whether the advantage of receiving sudden and unexpected insight might not be cultivated and thus possessed by all.

According to my experience a period of wakefulness at night has often been the most profitable time in the twenty-four hours. This is the only credit I know that can be awarded to insomnia. As an example of an idea which came to me in one such illuminating moment, I will describe a device that was used in the laboratory to obtain an automatically written record of the clotting of blood. It consisted of a very light lever with the long arm ending in a writing point. The long arm was not quite counterweighted by a fixed load on the short arm, but when in addition a small

1. W. Platt and R. A. Baker, "The Relation of the Scientific 'Hunch' to Research," *Journal of Chemical Education*, VIII (1931), 1969–2002.

wire was hung on the end of the short arm it slightly overbalanced the other side. The wire was so arranged that it dipped into a small glass tube containing a few drops of blood freshly taken from the running stream in an artery. A check on the long arm prevented the heavier short arm from falling. When the check was lifted, however, the short arm fell and the wire descended into the blood as the writing point rose and wrote a record. This showed that the blood had not clotted. The check was then restored; a minute later it was again lifted and again a record was written. The process was repeated thus at regular intervals. As soon as the blood clotted it supported the light wire and, now, when the check was raised, the heavier long arm did not rise and the fact that the blood had turned to a jelly was registered on the recording surface. All this was presented to me as a complete mechanism in a brief period of insight when I awoke in the night.

Another example I may cite was the interpretation of the significance of bodily changes which occur in great emotional excitement, such as fear and rage. These changes—the more rapid pulse, the deeper breathing, the increase of sugar in the blood, the secretion from the adrenal glands— were very diverse and seemed unrelated. Then, one wakeful night, after a considerable collection of these changes had been disclosed, the idea flashed through my mind that they could be nicely integrated if conceived as bodily preparations for supreme effort in flight or in fighting. Further investigation added to the collection and confirmed the general scheme suggested by the hunch.

A highly interesting instance of the appearance of a hunch with im portant consequences has been told by Otto Loewi, formerly professor of pharmacology at the University of Graz. The incident is related to the first demonstration of a chemical agent liberated at the end of nerves and, as already mentioned, acting as an intermediary between the impulses which sweep along a nerve and the structures they control. Many years ago T. R. Elliott, while a student at Cambridge, England, had suggested that the reason why adrenaline, when injected into the body or applied to an absorbing surface, mimics the action of sympathetic nerves, might be because these special nerves, when active, discharge adrenaline at their terminals. Thus there would be no essential difference between the effects of adrenaline delivered by the streaming blood and adrenaline serving as a chemical deputy for the arriving impulses. Later, H. H. Dale had proved that the substance, acetylcholine, could mimic the action of such nerves as the vagus, which can cause among other effects a slower beating of the heart. There was no proof, however, that in any condition nerves actually produce their effects by means of a chemical mediator. The crucial problem was that of demonstrating whether the idea was correct or not.

One night, after falling asleep over a trifling novel, Dr. Loewi awoke possessed by a brilliant idea. He reached to the table beside his bed, picked up a piece of paper and a pencil, and jotted down a few notes. On awakening next morning he was aware of having had an inspiration in the night and he turned to the paper for a reminder. To his consternation he could not make anything of the scrawl he found on it. He went to his laboratory, hoping that sense would come to what he had written if he were surrounded by familiar apparatus. In spite of frequently withdrawing the paper from his pocket and studying it earnestly, he gained no insight. At the end of the day, still filled with the belief that he had had a very precious revelation the night before, he went to sleep. To his great joy he again awoke in the darkness with the same flash of insight which had inspired him the night before. This time he carefully recorded it before going to sleep again. The next day he went to his laboratory and in one of the neatest, simplest and most definite experiments in the history of biology brought proof of the chemical mediation of nerve impulses. He prepared two frog hearts which were kept beating by means of a salt solution. He stimulated the vagus nerve of one of the hearts, thus causing it to stop beating. He then removed the salt solution from this heart and applied it to the other one. To his great satisfaction the solution had the same effect on the second heart as vagus stimulation had had on the first one: the pulsating muscle was brought to a standstill. This was the beginning of a host of investigations in many countries throughout the world on chemical intermediation, not only between nerves and the muscles and the glands they affect but also between nervous elements themselves.

In the lives of scientists there are numerous instances of the value of hunches. Helmholtz, the great German physicist and physiologist, when near the end of his life, told of the way in which the most important of his ideas had occurred to him. After investigating a problem "in all directions," he testified, "happy ideas come unexpectedly without effort like an inspiration. So far as I am concerned, they have never come to me when my mind was fatigued or when I was at my working table." Rest was necessary for the appearance of the original ideas and they occurred as a rule in the morning after a night's sleep.

For years during which Darwin was accumulating great numbers of facts he saw no general meaning in them, but felt that they had some great significance which he had not yet perceived. Then, suddenly, the flash of vision came. In his brief autobiography he writes, "I can remember the very spot in the road, whilst in my carriage, when to my joy, the solution occurred to me." Thereafter, with vast toil in the arrangement of facts and in careful exposition, he framed his statement of the theory of biological evolution.

.   .   .   .

There has been much discussion of what lies back of the experience of having hunches. They have been ascribed to the operations of the "sub-conscious mind." This expression seems to me to be a confusion of terms, for it involves the concept that a mind exists of which we are not con-scious. I am aware that in psychology this view has been held. Indeed, one psychologist with whom I discussed the matter declared that wherever nerves co-ordinate the activity of muscles, a mind is present. I told him that the nerve net in the wall of the intestine brings about a contraction of muscles above a stimulated point and a relaxation below it so that a mass within the tract is moved onward. This is co-ordinated action, and I asked him whether he would ascribe a mind to the intestine. His reply was, "Undoubtedly." The attitude thus expressed was extreme. It may be taken, however, as a basis for criticizing the assumption that there is a mind wherever nervous activity goes on, when in fact there is no evidence to support the notion. Numerous highly complex responses which can be evoked from the spinal cord and many nice adjustments made by the part of the brain that manages our normal balance and posture are wholly unconscious. There is no indication whatever that anything which we recognize as a mind is associated with these nervous activities.

To me as a physiologist, mind and consciousness seem to be equivalent, and the evidence appears to be strong that mind or consciousness is as-sociated with a limited but shifting area of integrated activity in the cor-tex of the brain. The physiologist assumes that, underlying the awareness of events as it shifts from moment to moment, there are correlated proc-esses in the enormously complicated mesh of nervous connections in the thin cortical layer. Such activities could go on, however, in other parts of the cortex and at the time be unrelated to the conscious states. They would be similar in character to the activities associated with consciousness, but would be extraconscious. Our knowledge of the association between mental states and nervous impulses in the brain is still so meager that we often resort to analogy to illustrate our meaning. The operation going on in an industry under the immediate supervision of the director is like the cerebral processes to which we pay attention; but meanwhile in other parts of the industrial plant important work is proceeding which the direc-tor at the moment does not see. Thus also with extraconscious processes.

By using the term "extraconscious processes" to define unrecognized operations which occur during attention to urgent affairs or during sleep, the notion of a subconscious mind or subconsciousness can be avoided.

The question arises as to what conditions are favorable and what unfavorable for the appearance of hunches. Among the unfavorable conditions are mental and physical fatigue, petty irritations, noise, worry over domestic or financial matters, states of depression, and strong emotions. Other unfavorable conditions include being driven to work under pressure and being interrupted or feeling that there may be interruption at any time, as in the demands of administrative duties.

Among the favorable conditions is a great interest in the problem to be solved, a clear definition of this problem, and an eager desire for its solution. A large store of related information already acquired is another prerequisite. The greater the number of facts which are pertinent to the urgent problem and which can be combined in novel ways for explaining the puzzle it presents, the more likely is the puzzle to be solved. The relative facts should be systematically organized; indeed it is better to have a small number of facts well co-ordinated than a great mass of incongruous data. A sense of well-being and a feeling of freedom are other advantageous circumstances. R. S. Woodworth in his *Psychology* has listed as conditions favoring invention a good physical state, a fresh mind, mastery of the subject, striving for a result, confidence, enterprise, willingness to take a chance, eagerness for action, and readiness to break away from routine. A helpful atmosphere for the appearance of a hunch is produced by discussing the problem with other investigators and by reading articles pertinent to it and also pertinent to methods useful for its solution.

The foregoing considerations reveal that the occurrence of a scientific hunch is closely related to antecedent preparations, and that its value is dependent on subsequent activities directed toward testing its validity. . . .

.   .   .   .

Different criteria for classifying scientists engaged in experimental studies have been suggested. Bancroft has proposed two groups: the guessers and the accumulators. The guessers are men who work with use of theories and hypotheses; the accumulators are mainly collectors of facts — often using, to be sure, ingenious and delicate methods in order to learn new facts. According to Platt and Baker the chemists who reported that their ideas came to them consciously were of the accumulator type. Many of them, indeed, declared that the idea of the hunch was quite distasteful. The replies from other chemists indicated that they were typical guessers. It is probable that an inquiry would show that the guessers are usually the revealers of new directions for future research and that hunches are highly significant in their scientific life. Although accumulators and those who may be designated as "gleaners" may not originate novel enterprises, they perform important functions in filling the gaps which may have been left by the more enterprising and bolder spirits.

Some readers may be surprised by the testimony that important advances in science are commonly the result of sudden revelations—really, unearned grants of insight—instead of being the product of prolonged and assiduous thinking. The hunch is not alone in giving the investigator an inviting opportunity to use his talents . . . he is favored at times by the good fortune of happy accidents. Neither the bounties from insight nor the bounties from chance, however, relieve the investigator from the necessity of hard labor, for the suggestion which is presented from either source still has to pass the rigorous test of critical proving before it can be admitted to the realm of truth.

GRAHAM WALLAS · Stages in the Creative Process

[*Wallas describes four phases or stages in creative thinking: preparation, incubation, illumination, and verification. Though derived from his own introspection and scattered observations rather than systematic empirical observation, Wallas's phases have been widely accepted by theorists and investigators of creativity.*]

We can . . . take a single achievement of thought—the making of a new generalization or invention, or the poetical expression of a new idea—and ask how it was brought about. We can then roughly dissect out a continuous process, with a beginning and a middle and an end of its own. Helmholtz, for instance, the great German physicist, speaking in 1891 at a banquet on his seventieth birthday, described the way in which his most important new thoughts had come to him. He said that after previous investigation of the problem "in all directions . . . happy ideas come unexpectedly without effort, like an inspiration. So far as I am concerned,

SOURCE *"Stages of Control," from* The Art of Thought *by Graham Wallas, copyright, 1926, by Harcourt Brace Jovanovich, Inc.; copyright, 1954, by May Graham Wallas. Reprinted by permission of the publishers. Pp. 79–83, 85–87, 93–95.*

they have never come to me when my mind was fatigued, or when I was at my working table. . . . They came particularly readily during the slow ascent of wooded hills on a sunny day." [ftnt. deleted] Helmholtz here gives us three stages in the formation of a new thought. The first in time I shall call Preparation, the stage during which the problem was "investigated . . . in all directions"; the second is the stage during which he was not consciously thinking about the problem, which I shall call Incubation; the third, consisting of the appearance of the "happy idea" together with the psychological events which immediately preceded and accompanied that appearance, I shall call Illumination.

And I shall add a fourth stage, of Verification, which Helmholtz does not here mention. Henri Poincaré, for instance, in the book *Science and Method*, . . . describes in vivid detail the successive stages of two of his great mathematical discoveries. Both of them came to him after a period of Incubation (due in one case to his military service as a reservist, and in the other case to a journey), during which no conscious mathematical thinking was done, but, as Poincaré believed, much unconscious mental exploration took place. In both cases Incubation was preceded by a Preparation stage of hard, conscious, systematic, and fruitless analysis of the problem. In both cases the final idea came to him "with the same characteristics of conciseness, suddenness, and immediate certainty." . . . Each was followed by a period of Verification, in which both the validity of the idea was tested, and the idea itself was reduced to exact form. "It never happens," says Poincaré, in his description of the Verification stage, "that unconscious work supplies *ready-made* the result of a lengthy calculation in which we have only to apply fixed rules. . . . All that we can hope from these inspirations, which are the fruit of unconscious work, is to obtain points of departure for such calculations. As for the calculations themselves, they must be made in the second period of conscious work which follows the inspiration, and in which the results of the inspiration are verified and the consequences deduced. The rules of these calculations are strict and complicated; they demand discipline, attention, will, and consequently, consciousness." . . . In the daily stream of thought these four different stages constantly overlap each other as we explore different problems. An economist reading a Blue Book, a physiologist watching an experiment, or a businessman going through his morning's letters, may at the same time be "incubating" on a problem which he proposed to himself a few days ago, be accumulating knowledge in "preparation" for a second problem, and be "verifying" his conclusions on a third problem. Even in exploring the same problem, the mind may be unconsciously incubating on one aspect of it, while it is consciously employed in preparing for or verifying another aspect. And it must always be remembered that much very important thinking, done for instance by a poet exploring his own memories, or by a man trying to see clearly his emotional relation to his country or his party, resembles musical composition in that the stages leading to success are not very easily fitted into a "problem and solution" scheme. Yet, even when success in thought means the creation of something felt to be beautiful and true rather than the solution of a prescribed problem, the four stages of Preparation, Incubation, Illumination, and the Verification of the final result can generally be distinguished from each other.

. . . .

The educated man has, again, learnt, and can, in the Preparation stage, voluntarily or habitually follow out, rules as to the order in which he shall direct his attention to the successive elements in a problem. . . .

. . . .

. . . the thinker . . . will often (particularly if he is working on the very complex material of the social sciences) have several kindred problems in his mind, on all of which the voluntary work of preparation has been, or is being done, and for any of which, at the Illumination stage, a solution may present itself.

The fourth stage, of Verification, closely resembles the first stage, of Preparation. It is normally, as Poincaré points out, fully conscious, and men have worked out much the same series of mathematical and logical rules for controlling Verification by conscious effort as those which are used in the control of Preparation.

There remain the second and third stages, Incubation and Illumination. The Incubation stage covers two different things, of which the first is the negative fact that during Incubation we do not voluntarily or consciously think on a particular problem, and the second is the positive fact that a series of unconscious and involuntary (or foreconscious and forevoluntary) mental events may take place during that period. It is the first fact about Incubation which I shall now discuss, leaving the second fact—of subconscious thought during Incubation, and the relation of such thought to Illumination—to be more fully discussed in connection with the Illumination stage. Voluntary abstention from conscious thought on any particular problem may, itself, take two forms: the period of abstention may be spent either in conscious mental work on other problems, or in a relaxation from all conscious mental work. The first kind of Incubation economizes time, and is therefore often the better. We can often get more result in the same time by beginning several problems in succession, and voluntarily leaving them unfinished while we turn to others, than by finishing our work on each problem at one sitting. A well-known academic psychologist, for instance, who was also a preacher, told me that he found by experience that his Sunday sermon was much better if he posed the problem on Monday, than if he did so later in the week, although he might give the same number of hours of conscious work to it in each case. It seems to be a tradition among practising barristers to put off any consideration of each brief to the latest possible moment before they have to deal with it, and to forget the whole matter as rapidly as possible after dealing with it. This fact may help to explain a certain want of depth which has often been noticed in the typical lawyer-statesman, and which may be due to his conscious thought not being sufficiently extended and enriched by subconscious thought.

. . . .

. . . I shall now discuss the much more difficult question of the degree to which our will can influence the less controllable stage which I have called Illumination. Helmholtz and Poincaré, in the passages which I quoted above, both speak of the appearance of a new idea as instantaneous and unexpected. If we so define the Illumination stage as to restrict it to this instantaneous "flash," it is obvious that we cannot influence it by a direct effort of will; because we can only bring our will to bear upon psychological events which last for an appreciable time. On the other hand, the final "flash," or "click" . . . is the culmination of a successful train of association, which may have lasted for an appreciable time, and which has probably been preceded by a series of tentative and unsuccessful trains. The series of unsuccessful trains of association may last for periods varying from a few seconds to several hours. H. Poincaré, who describes the tentative and unsuccessful trains as being, in his case, almost entirely unconscious, believed that they occupied a considerable proportion of the whole Incubation stage. "We might," he wrote, "say that the conscious work, [i.e., what I have called the Preparation stage], proved more fruitful because it was interrupted [by the Incubation stage], and that the rest restored freshness to the mind. But it is more probable that the rest was occupied with unconscious work, and that the result of this work was afterwards revealed." [ftnt. deleted]

Different thinkers, and the same thinkers at different times, must, of course, vary greatly as to the time occupied by their unsuccessful trains of association; and the same variation must exist in the duration of the final and successful train of association. Sometimes the successful train seems to consist of a single leap of association, or of successive leaps which are so rapid as to be almost instantaneous. Hobbes's "Roman penny" train of association occurred between two remarks in an ordinary conversation, and Hobbes . . . ends his description of it with the words, "and all this in a moment of time, for thought is quick." [ref. deleted] Hobbes himself was probably an exceptionally rapid thinker, and Aubrey may have been quoting Hobbes's own phrase when he says that Hobbes used to take out his note-book "as soon as a thought darted." [ftnt. deleted]

CATHERINE PATRICK · Creative Thought in Artists

[Patrick offers the first systematic attempt to confirm Wallas's suggestions about distinct and definable stages in the creative process. Asking persons involved in creative writing, drawing, and scientific problem-solving to describe their thoughts while working, she sought to observe the creative process as directly as possible. Her works thus represent a landmark attempt to carry out psychological experiments on creativity. This selection comes from one of a number of reports of her studies; it does not include reference to her later work with scientists showing results similar to those reported here.]

The problem is to study as directly as possible the process of creative thought in sketching pictures. Artists have consented to sketch pictures under experimental conditions, and for purposes of comparison non-artists have also performed the task of drawing under the same conditions.

.   .   .   .

In a previous study by the present author [see references in Selected Bibliography] creative thought in poets was studied. The poets composed poems, talking aloud during the process. An analysis of the reports shows that there are four stages of creative thought, preparation, incubation, illumination, and revision or verification. . . .

.   .   .   .

One hundred subjects took part in this experiment and were divided into two groups, an "experimental group" of 50 artists and a "control group" of the same number of non-artists.

SOURCE From Patrick, C., "Creative Thought in Artists," Journal of Psychology, 1937, Vol. 4, pp. 35–40, 51–54, 66–67. Reprinted by permission of The Journal Press, Provincetown, Mass.

The terms "experimental" and "control groups" are not strictly correct as applied to our procedure. At the outset, the experimental factor was conceived to be "previous practise in making pictures," and the question was what difference this experimental factor would make in the process of drawing a sketch. Our "control group" can be thought of as furnishing a norm. The work amounts to a comparison between two groups.

The experimental group was composed only of artists of ability, whose work has appeared in the better exhibits. . . .

The control group was composed of 50 persons who were not doing any art work and had never done any, except possibly as school assignments. If they had only done a little art work at school ten or twenty years ago and had not done any since, it was considered that the effect of such small training would be negligible. A variety of occupations was represented. There were psychology students, secretaries, teachers, economists, biologists, nurses, engineers, lawyers, librarians, and home-makers.

Several cities and various sections of the country were represented in the selection of subjects for both groups. One of the cities was in the middle west, another in the east, and a third in the south.

The two groups were equated on the basis of the vocabulary test taken from the Thorndike CAVD Intelligence Test. This measure of vocabulary ability was the closest one to intelligence that could be obtained, for it would have been impossible to get the cooperation of artists in taking a regular intelligence test. Since there is a high correlation between vocabulary and intelligence tests, it was thought that this would give a good index of general ability. . . .

Twenty-one of the artists were men as compared with 23 of the controls. The groups were thus approximately equated as to the distribution of the sexes.

The groups were approximately equated as to age. The ages could only be estimated, for no direct information was available on that point. The average estimated age for the experimental group was 34 years as compared with 29 for the controls, a difference of 5 years. The median was 30 for the artists compared with 30 years for the controls. We did not think it was necessary to have the distribution of ages exactly the same in both groups, for all of the subjects were mature adults. It has been shown that vocabulary ability does not change much after reaching maturity until old age.

The subjects were all of the white race. Thus the two groups were equated in sex, age, and race, and in vocabulary ability, which is closely related to intelligence. They differed in that the experimental group was composed of artists of ability, while the control group was composed of those who had not done art work, except to a negligible degree. The differences that have come out in this experiment can be attributed to the greater ability of the artists to create pictures.

. . . .

For this type of experiment it was necessary to have an individual interview with each subject. The experimenter made a personal call on each artist at his or her studio or home. It was thought that the artist would be able to create a picture more naturally there than in a laboratory where the situation is more or less artificial. Almost all of the interviews were held in the afternoon, which was found to be the most convenient time for the subjects.

The first part of the interview consisted of a preliminary conversation, the chief purpose of which was to enable the artist to become accustomed to talking aloud, while the experimenter recorded what he said in shorthand. [ftnt. deleted] Also it served the purpose of getting some of the information for the questionnaire on methods of work. The nature of this conversation varied from person to person, and its duration from fifteen minutes to an hour, depending on whether the artist talked more or less at ease.

When the artist had become accustomed to the situation, he was presented with a poem and asked to draw a picture about it or whatever it suggested. The poem was a selection from Milton's "L'Allegro" and was chosen because of the variety of images which it contained. . . .

. . . .

A record was kept of everything that was spoken and drawn from the moment of presenting the poem until the subject announced that the picture was finished, and needed no more revision. The subject was then asked the remaining questions on the questionnaire about methods of work, which he had not answered in the preliminary conversation. . . .

. . . .

(a). *Stages of Thought.* As we examine the results of this experiment we find evidence of four stages of thought, to which we shall apply the terms *preparation, incubation, illumination,* and *verification.* Helmholtz . . . had used the first three terms, and Wallas . . . and Poincaré . . . used all four. [refs. deleted]

In order to investigate the first one, *preparation,* when the subject is receiving various ideas, we have measured the number of thought changes that occur in each quarter. We find that three-fourths of the thought changes occur in the first quarter for both groups. This substantiates the theory that there first comes a period of preparation.

To present evidence that this leads to *incubation,* or the second stage, we have noted those cases in which the idea of the poem appeared earlier in the report, after which the subject talked of various things, and then this original idea reappeared as the subject of the poem. This is the fact in four-fifths of the cases in both groups. Our data are in accord with the hypothesis that preparation leads to incubation.

The stage of *illumination*, in making a picture, would be the period at which the general shapes of the objects were first sketched. For both groups we find that the general shapes of three-fourths of the objects were first sketched in the second and third quarters, with more in the second. This bears out the statement that illumination or formulation of thought follows preparation and incubation.

The fourth stage, *verification* or revision, is easily identified. We find that three-fourths of the instances of revision occur in the third and fourth quarters, with more in the last quarter, in both groups. Revision thus constitutes the final stage.

We will now discuss the characteristics of these four stages of thought more in detail. First comes *preparation*, when the subject is assembling or receiving new ideas. During this time the associations shift rapidly. Preparation is a time when the creative thinker is receiving or gathering his raw material.

Incubation follows preparation, although it may accompany it. We quote below some of the statements regarding incubation which were obtained from the artists by aid of our questionnaire:

> "I almost always carry an idea around a while in my mind before I start to work. It keeps coming back several times while I am doing other things, and I can work it out later. Sometimes I lose it if I don't work on it. In coming back it changes, and sometimes improves as it comes back. If I don't grab it I may get something different."

> "I incubate an idea for periods of two or three weeks. It may be for a month or more when I am not working on it. I think now of making a picture of Coconut Grove as it used to look, and I have been incubating that two years. Then I get to feel like I want to paint. I keep vaguely thinking of something like it to do. I am thinking now of a still life. This afternoon I may start on it. The idea recurs while I am doing other things, as I have thought of a still life for two or three weeks now. I think of the roundness of the fruit, and shapes against the glass bottle. It recurs in color, so when I am ready to paint I know what I want to do and do it very rapidly. A complicated thing becomes simple by thinking about it. I noticed

a tree and did not think about it and before I knew it, I had all sorts of information for making it."

"I usually carry an idea around in my mind. I see the picture completely in my mind before I paint. It recurs from time to time and lasts a couple of weeks. I know the color scheme before I start and get a model to fit that."

"I incubate a planned thing and other types of pictures more than a landscape, which I see. I draw a landscape from life but do not incubate it. I find a thing to interpret not as seen but as the effect of light, etc. One must put over to the observer what one sees. Often I incubate an idea and it keeps recurring, as I saw children in the north end of town and the idea stayed with me until painted a while later."

"I incubate an idea, as color and movement might interest me. It lasts a week only. It grows more intense till finished."

"I often carry an idea around for several weeks before I make a picture though sometimes longer. I got ideas in Santa Fe last summer to do now. The ideas recur from time to time while I am occupied with other things."

From the data of the questionnaire, we find that the artists generally incubate an idea, which may be accompanied by a feeling. It is often only partly formulated into what would constitute a mental picture and is but vaguely expressed. Most of them gave the report that incubation consisted of an idea which kept recurring over a period of time ranging from a few minutes to several years.

From the data of the questionnaire and reports obtained under the conditions of this experiment incubation can be defined as follows: A mood or idea is being incubated when it involuntarily repeats itself with more or less modification during a period when the subject is also thinking of other topics. According to Poincaré [ref. deleted] this modification is due to the working of the subconscious mind. Helmholtz [ref. deleted] states that the modification is due to the overcoming of fatigue and the handling of material better. Similarly Woodworth [ref. deleted] writes that "in the preparatory period the necessary cues have been assembled along with much irrelevant material, which is an interference." With lapse of time when the individual makes a fresh attack the whole matter is clear.

Illumination follows incubation. This is seen from the data of the questionnaire where the idea is incubated before it is sketched. The essential structure is completed at one sitting although it may be revised later. In the period of illumination, when the artist first sketches a picture, he is generally in an emotional state. On the other hand, there are a fifth of the artists who state that they very rarely sketch a picture with an emotional feeling. They usually work in a cold, detached, objective state. Thus an artist is often emotionally stirred up at the time of sketching a picture, but it is not necessary or essential that he be so.

While most of them say that portions of a picture generally come more spontaneously and automatically than other parts, yet a fourth of them assert that there is no difference between the parts, which occur with the same difficulty. Thus illumination occurs when the idea, which has been incubating, becomes definitely related to a specific goal. It is the period when a picture is first sketched.

The idea, which is obtained in illumination, must be elaborated and revised during the last stage of verification. We find that this stage occurs in almost all of the pictures drawn in this experiment. Although there is revision, the essential structure is seldom changed.

These four stages, which can be distinguished in creative thought, may overlap. Incubation often occurs along with preparation, and revision may begin during the period of illumination. In the stage of preparation, while the subject is still receiving new ideas, one idea may be incubated and recur from time to time. Also revision of objects may start before all of them are sketched.

overlap

.   .   .   .

A previous experiment, similar to this one, was performed on poets. [ftnt. deleted] The method was the same, except that the poet was shown a picture of a landscape and asked to write a poem about it. He similarly talked aloud all the time that he was doing it, and the experimenter recorded all that was said in shorthand.

We will now compare the results of the two experiments in those respects where such a comparison is possible.

In the first place, we find that both poets and artists, as well as the two control groups, all exhibit the four stages of thought. Over half of the thought changes of all groups occur in the first quarter of the process, indicating that there is first a stage of preparation, when associations are shifting.

The second stage, incubation, is present in all four groups. It is found in over two-thirds of the cases of each.

The third stage, illumination, is likewise found in all four groups. In writing poetry, it is found in the first formulation of lines. In drawing pictures, as pointed out above, it is present when the general shapes of objects are first drawn. In all four groups, we find that over two-thirds of the first writing of lines or drawing of objects occurs in the second and third quarters, which indicates that illumination follows preparation and incubation.

The fourth stage, revision or verification, appears in all four groups. An instance of revision for a poet would be changing a word or line to extend the meaning, the partial or total re-reading of the poem, and changing words or lines to fit the meter. For all four groups, over three-fourths of the instances of revision occur in the third and fourth quarters with most in the last quarter, which indicates revision follows the other three stages.

When the data are treated a little differently, using the percentage of subjects showing "most" instances in each quarter, we find the same results. About three-fourths of the subjects of all four groups show most thought changes in the first quarter, about three-fourths show most instances which indicate illumination in the second and third quarters, and over half show most instances which indicate revision in the last quarter.

CESARE LOMBROSO · Genius and Insanity

[*Lombroso, a late nineteenth-century psychiatrist, approached his study relating genius to insanity from the point of view of the biological theories of human behavior current in his time. Degeneration of the brain was then widely considered to be the cause of abnormal functioning. Though Lombroso appreciated the accomplishments of genius, his concept of the insane consisted of any deviations from ordinary or average behavior, a concept not shared by modern psychiatry. Many psychiatrists today would consider his clinical descriptions to pertain to mild aberrations and psychoneurotic patterns rather than psychotic or insane ones alone.[1] The selection here only represents the first part of Lombroso's extensively documented description of deviant behavior in men of genius and does not include his discussion of the importance of meteorological conditions, race, and heredity, as well as the relative lack of importance of social conditions, in producing genius. While arguing that genius was closely allied with insanity, Lombroso eventually concluded that the insanity of genius was a special type.*]

SOURCE   From Lombroso, C., The Man of Genius, pp. 5–10, 13–19, 21–22, 24–26, 32–33, 35–37. London: Charles Scribner's Sons, 1895.
    1. Lombroso uses the term "neurosis" as equivalent to insanity.

The paradox that confounds genius with neurosis, however cruel and sad it may seem, is found to be not devoid of solid foundation when examined from various points of view which have escaped even recent observers.

A theory, which has for some years flourished in the psychiatric world, admits that a large proportion of mental and physical affections are the result of degeneration, of the action, that is, of heredity in the children of the inebriate, the syphilitic, the insane, the consumptive, &c.; or of accidental causes, such as lesions of the head or the action of mercury, which profoundly change the tissues, perpetuate neuroses or other diseases in the patient, and, which is worse, aggravate them in his descendants, until the march of degeneration, constantly growing more rapid and fatal, is only stopped by complete idiocy or sterility.

Alienists have noted certain characters which very frequently, though not constantly, accompany these fatal degenerations. Such are, on the moral side, apathy, loss of moral sense, frequent tendencies to impulsiveness or doubt, psychical inequalities owing to the excess of some faculty (memory, æsthetic taste, &c.) or defect of other qualities (calculation, for example), exaggerated mutism or verbosity, morbid vanity, excessive originality, and excessive pre-occupation with self, the tendency to put mystical interpretations on the simplest facts, the abuse of symbolism and of special words which are used as an almost exclusive mode of expression. Such, on the physical side, are prominent ears, deficiency of beard, irregularity of teeth, excessive asymmetry of face and head, which may be very large or very small, sexual precocity, smallness or disproportion of the body, lefthandedness, stammering, rickets, phthisis, excessive fecundity, neutralized afterwards by abortions or complete sterility, with constant aggravation of abnormalities in the children.[1]

Without doubt many alienists have here fallen into exaggerations, especially when they have sought to deduce degeneration from a single fact. But, taken on the whole, the theory is irrefutable; every day brings fresh applications and confirmations. Among the most curious are those supplied by recent studies on genius. The signs of degeneration in men of genius they show are sometimes more numerous than in the insane. Let us examine them.

Height. First of all it is necessary to remark the frequency of physical signs of degeneration, only masqued by the vivacity of the countenance

1. Magnan, *Annales Médicopsych.*, 1887; Déjerine, *L'Hérédité dans les Maladies Mentales*, 1886; Ireland, *The Blot upon the Brain*, 1885.

and the prestige of reputation, which distracts us from giving them due importance.

The simplest of these, which struck our ancestors and has passed into a proverb, is the smallness of the body.

Famous for short stature as well as for genius were: Horace (*lepidissimum homunculum dicebat Augustus*), Philopœmen, Narses, Alexander (*Magnus Alexander corpore parvus erat*), Aristotle, Plato, Epicurus, Chrysippus, Laertes, Archimedes, Diogenes, Attila, Epictetus, who was accustomed to say, "Who am I? A little man." Among moderns one may name, Erasmus, Socinus, Linnæus, Lipsius, Gibbon, Spinoza, Haüy, Montaigne, Mezeray, Lalande, Gray, John Hunter (5ft. 2in.), Mozart, Beethoven, Goldsmith, Hogarth, Thomas Moore, Thomas Campbell, Wilberforce, Heine, Meissonnier, Charles Lamb, Beccaria, Maria Edgeworth, Balzac, De Quincey, William Blake (who was scarcely five feet in height), Browning, Ibsen, George Eliot, Thiers, Mrs. Browning, Louis Blanc, Mendelssohn, Swinburne, Van Does (called the Drum, because he was not any taller than a drum), Peter van Laer (called the Puppet). . . .

Among great men of tall stature I only know Volta, Goethe, Petrarch, Schiller, D'Azeglio, Helmholtz, Foscolo, Charlemagne, Bismarck, Moltke, Monti, Mirabeau, Dumas *perè*, Schopenhauer, Lamartine, Voltaire, Peter the Great, Washington, Dr. Johnson, Sterne, Arago, Flaubert, Carlyle, Tourgueneff, Tennyson, Whitman.

Rickets. Agesilaus, Tyrtæus, Æsop, Giotto, Aristomenes, Crates, Galba, Brunelleschi, Magliabecchi, Parini, Scarron, Pope, Leopardi, Talleyrand, Scott, Owen, Gibbon, Byron, Dati, Baldini, Moses Mendelssohn, Flaxman, Hooke, were all either rachitic, lame, hunch-backed, or club-footed.

Pallor. This has been called the colour of great men. . . . It was ascertained by Marro[2] that this is one of the most frequent signs of degeneration in the morally insane.

Emaciation. The law of the conservation of energy which rules the whole organic world, explains to us other frequent abnormalities, such as precocious greyness and baldness, leanness of the body, and weakness of sexual and muscular activity, which characterize the insane, and are also frequently found among great thinkers. Lecamus[3] has said that the greatest geniuses have the slenderest bodies. Cæsar feared the lean face of Cassius. Demosthenes, Aristotle, Cicero, Giotto, St. Bernard, Erasmus,

2. *I Caratteri dei Delinquenti*, 1886, Turin.
3. *Méd. de l' Esprit*, ii.

Salmasius, Kepler, Sterne, Walter Scott, John Howard, D'Alembert, Fénelon, Boileau, Milton, Pascal, Napoleon, were all extremely thin in the flower of their age.

Others were weak and sickly in childhood; such were Demosthenes, Bacon, Descartes, Newton, Locke, Adam Smith, Boyle, Pope, Flaxman, Nelson, Haller, Körner, Pascal, Wren, Alfieri, Renan.

. . . .

Physiognomy. Mind, a celebrated painter of cats, had a cretin-like physiognomy. So also had Socrates, Skoda, Rembrandt, Dostoieffsky, Magliabecchi, Pope, Carlyle, Darwin, and, among modern Italians, Schiaparelli, who holds so high a rank in mathematics.

Cranium and Brain. Lesions of the head and brain are very frequent among men of genius. . . .

. . . .

The capacity of the skull in men of genius, as is natural, is above the average, by which it approaches what is found in insanity. (De Quatrefages noted that the greatest degree of macrocephaly was found in a lunatic, the next in a man of genius.) . . .

. . . .

Stammering. Men of genius frequently stammer. I will mention: Aristotle, Æsop, Demosthenes, Alcibiades, Cato of Utica, Virgil, Manzoni, Erasmus, Malherbe, C. Lamb, Turenne, Erasmus and Charles Darwin, Moses Mendelssohn, Charles V., Romiti, Cardan, Tartaglia.

Lefthandedness. Many have been left-handed. Such were: Tiberius, Sebastian del Piombo, Michelangelo, Fléchier, Nigra, Buhl, Raphael of Montelupo, Bertillon. Leonardo da Vinci sketched rapidly with his left hand any figures which struck him, and only employed the right hand for those which were the mature result of his contemplation; for this reason his friends were persuaded that he only wrote with the left hand.[4] Mancinism or leftsidedness is to-day regarded as a character of atavism and degeneration.[5]

Sterility. Many great men have remained bachelors; others, although married, have had no children. . . .

Croker, in his edition of *Boswell,* remarks that all the great English poets had no posterity. He names Shakespeare, Ben Jonson, Milton, Otway,

4. Gallichon in *Gazette des Beaux Arts,* 1867.
5. Lombroso, *Sul Mancinismo motorio e sensorio nei sani e negli alienati,* 1885, Turin.

Dryden, Rowe, Addison, Pope, Swift, Gay, Johnson, Goldsmith, Cowper. Hobbes, Camden, and many others, avoided marriage in order to have more time to devote to study. . . .

Unlikeness to Parents. Nearly all men of genius have differed as much from their fathers as from their mothers (Foscolo, Michelangelo, Giotto, Haydn, &c.). That is one of the marks of degeneration. . . .

Precocity. Another character common to genius and to insanity, especially moral insanity, is precocity. Dante, when nine years of age, wrote a sonnet to Beatrice; Tasso wrote verses at ten. . . .

This precocity is morbid and atavistic; it may be observed among all savages. The proverb, "A man who has genius at five is mad at fifteen" is often verified in asylums.[6] The children of the insane are often precocious. Savage knew an insane woman whose children could play classical music before the age of six, and other children who at a tender age displayed the passions of grown men. Among the children of the insane are often revealed aptitudes and tastes—chiefly for music, the arts, and mathematics—which are not usually found in other children.

Delayed Development. Delay in the development of genius may be explained, as Beard remarks, by the absence of circumstances favourable to its blossoming, and by the ignorance of teachers and parents who see mental obtusity, or even idiocy, where there is only the distraction or amnesia of genius. . . .

.   .   .   .

Misoneism. The men who create new worlds are as much enemies of novelty as ordinary persons and children. They display extraordinary energy in rejecting the discoveries of others; whether it is that the saturation, so to say, of their brains prevents any new absorption, or that they have acquired a special sensibility, alert only to their own ideas, and refractory to the ideas of others. . . .

Vagabondage. Love of wandering is frequent among men of genius. I will mention only Heine, Alfieri, Byron, Giordano Bruno, Leopardi, Tasso, Goldsmith, Sterne, Gautier, Musset, Lenau. . . .

Unconsciousness and Instinctiveness. The coincidence of genius and insanity enables us to understand the astonishing unconsciousness, instantaneousness and intermittence of the creations of genius, whence its great resemblance to epilepsy, the importance of which we shall see later,

6. Savage, *Moral Insanity,* 1886.

and whence also a distinction between genius and talent. "Talent," says Jürgen-Meyer,[7] "knows itself; it knows how and why it has reached a given theory; it is not so with genius, which is ignorant of the how and the why. Nothing is so involuntary as the conception of genius.". . .

. . . .

Somnambulism. Bettinelli wrote: "Poetry may almost be called a dream which is accomplished in the presence of reason, which floats above it with open eyes." This definition is the more exact since many poets have composed their poems in a dream or half-dream. . . .

Genius in Inspiration. It is very true that nothing so much resembles a person attacked by madness as a man of genius when meditating and moulding his conceptions. . . . According to Réveillé-Parise, the man of genius exhibits a small contracted pulse, pale, cold skin, a hot, feverish head, brilliant, wild, injected eyes. After the moment of composition it often happens that the author himself no longer understands what he wrote a short time before. . . .

. . . .

Contrast, Intermittence, Double Personality. When the moment of inspiration is over, the man of genius becomes an ordinary man, if he does not descend lower; in the same way personal inequality, or, according to modern terminology, double, or even contrary, personality, is . . . one of the characters of genius. . . .

"If there are two such different men in you," said his mistress to Alfred de Musset, "could you not, when the bad one rises, be content to forget the good one?"[8] Musset himself confesses that, with respect to her, he gave way to attacks of brutal anger and contempt, alternating with fits of extravagant affection; "an exaltation carried to excess made me treat my mistress like an idol, like a divinity. A quarter of an hour after having insulted her I was at her knees; I left off accusing her to ask her pardon; and passed from jesting to tears."

Stupidity. The doubling of personality, the amnesia and the misoneism so common among men of science, are the key to the innumerable stupidities which intrude into their writings. . . .

Hyperæsthesia. If we seek, with the aid of autobiographies, the differences which separate a man of genius from an ordinary man, we find that

7. *Genie und Talent.*
8. *Confessions d'un Enfant du Siècle*, pp. 218, 251.

they consist in very great part in an exquisite, and sometimes perverted, sensibility.

.   .   .   .

On account of this exaggerated and concentrated sensibility, it becomes very difficult to persuade or dissuade either men of genius or the insane. In them the roots of error, as well as those of truth, fix themselves more deeply and multiplexly than in other men, for whom opinion is a habit, an affair of fashion, or of circumstance. Hence the slight utility of moral treatment as applied to the insane; hence also the frequent fallibility of genius.

.   .   .   .

Paræsthesia. To the exhaustion and excessive concentration of sensibility must be attributed all those strange acts showing apparent or intermittent anæsthesia, and analgesia, which are to be found among men of genius as well as among the insane. Socrates presented a photoparæsthesia which enabled him to gaze at the sun for a considerable time without experiencing any discomfort. The Goncourts, Flaubert, Darwin had a kind of musical daltonism.

Amnesia. Forgetfulness is another of the characters of genius. . . .

.   .   .   .

Originality. Hagen notes that originality is the quality that distinguishes genius from talent.[9] And Jürgen-Meyer: "The imagination of talent reproduces the stated fact; the inspiration of genius makes it anew. The first disengages or repeats; the second invents or creates. Talent aims at a point which appears difficult to reach; genius aims at a point which no one perceives. The novelty, it must be understood, resides not in the elements, but in their shock." . . .

Genius divines facts before completely knowing them; thus Goethe described Italy very well before knowing it; and Schiller, the land and people of Switzerland without having been there. And it is on account of those divinations which all precede common observation, and because genius, occupied with lofty researches, does not possess the habits of the many, and because, like the lunatic and unlike the man of talent, he is often disordered, the man of genius is scorned and misunderstood. . . .

.   .   .   .

Originality, though usually of an aimless kind, is observed with some frequency among the insane . . . and especially among those inclined to

9. *Ueber die Verwandtschaft des Genies mit dem Irrsinn*, 1887.

literature. They sometimes reach the divinations of genius: thus Bernardi, at the Florence Asylum in 1520, wished to show the existence of language among apes.[10]

. . . .

Fondness for Special Words. This originality causes men of genius, as well as the insane, to create special words, marked with their own imprint, unintelligible to others, but to which they attach extraordinary significance and importance. . . .

10. Delepierre, *Histoire Littéraire des fous*, Paris, 1860.

ABRAHAM H. MASLOW · Creativity in Self-Actualizing People

[*Maslow's primary interest is in psychological concepts of normality hinging on the notion of self-actualization. Here he differentiates between creativity associated with great tangible achievements and the potential for creativity and self-actualization in everyone. Maslow was highly influenced by existentialism and was the founder of the humanist psychology movement. His concept of the "peak experience," touched on here, has influenced many investigators of so-called "altered states of consciousness."*]

I first had to change my ideas about creativity as soon as I began studying people who were positively healthy, highly evolved and matured, self-actualizing. I had first to give up my stereotyped notion that health, genius, talent and productivity were synonymous. A fair proportion of my subjects, though healthy and creative in a special sense that I am going to describe, were *not* productive in the ordinary sense, nor did they have great talent or genius, nor were they poets, composers, inventors, artists or creative intellectuals. It was also obvious that some of the greatest talents of mankind were certainly not psychologically healthy people, Wagner, for example, or Van Gogh or Byron. Some were and some weren't, it was clear. I very soon had to come to the conclusion that great talent

Source   From Maslow, A. H., "Creativity in Self-Actualizing People," Toward a Psychology of Being, *pp. 135–141, 143, 145. Copyright 1968 2nd ed. by Van Nostrand Reinhold Company, New York. Reprinted by permission.*

was not only more or less independent of goodness or health of character but also that we know little about it. For instance, there is some evidence that great musical talent and mathematical talent are more inherited than acquired [ref. deleted]. It seemed clear then that health and special talent were separate variables, maybe only slightly correlated, maybe not. We may as well admit at the beginning that psychology knows very little about special talent of the genius type. I shall say nothing more about it, confining myself instead to that more widespread kind of creativeness which is the universal heritage of every human being that is born, and which seems to co-vary with psychological health.

Furthermore, I soon discovered that I had, like most other people, been thinking of creativeness in terms of products, and secondly, I had unconsciously confined creativeness to certain conventional areas only of human endeavor, unconsciously assuming that *any* painter, *any* poet, *any* composer was leading a creative life. Theorists, artists, scientists, inventors, writers could be creative. Nobody else could be. Unconsciously I had assumed that creativeness was the prerogative solely of certain professionals.

But these expectations were broken up by various of my subjects. For instance, one woman, uneducated, poor, a full-time housewife and mother, did none of these conventionally creative things and yet was a marvellous cook, mother, wife and homemaker. With little money, her home was somehow always beautiful. She was a perfect hostess. Her meals were banquets. Her taste in linens, silver, glass, crockery and furniture was impeccable. She was in all these areas original, novel, ingenious, unexpected, inventive. I just *had* to call her creative. I learned from her and others like her that a first-rate soup is more creative than a second-rate painting, and that, generally, cooking or parenthood or making a home could be creative while poetry need not be; it could be uncreative.

. . . .

In other words, I learned to apply the word "creative" (and also the word "esthetic") not only to products but also to people in a characterological way, and to activities, processes, and attitudes. And furthermore, I had come to apply the word "creative" to many products other than the standard and conventionally accepted poems, theories, novels, experiments or paintings.

The consequence was that I found it necessary to distinguish "special talent creativeness" from "self-actualizing (SA) creativeness" which sprang much more directly from the personality, and which showed itself widely in the ordinary affairs of life, for instance, in a certain kind of humor. It looked like a tendency to do *anything* creatively: e.g., house-keeping, teaching, etc. Frequently, it appeared that an essential aspect of SA creativeness was a special kind of perceptiveness that is exemplified by the child in the fable who saw that the king had no clothes on (this too contradicts the notion of creativity as products). Such people can see the fresh, the raw, the concrete, the idiographic, as well as the generic, the abstract, the rubricized, the categorized and the classified. Consequently, they live far more in the real world of nature than in the verbalized world of concepts, abstractions, expectations, beliefs and stereotypes that most people confuse with the real world [ref. deleted]. This is well expressed in Rogers' phrase "openness to experience" [ref. deleted].

All my subjects were relatively more spontaneous and expressive than average people. They were more "natural" and less controlled and in-hibited in their behavior, which seemed to flow out more easily and freely and with less blocking and self-criticism. This ability to express ideas and impulses without strangulation and without fear of ridicule turned out to be an essential aspect of SA creativeness. Rogers has used the excellent phrase, "fully functioning person," to describe this aspect of health [ref. deleted].

Another observation was that SA creativeness was in many respects like the creativeness of *all* happy and secure children. It was spontaneous, effortless, innocent, easy, a kind of freedom from stereotypes and cliches. And again it seemed to be made up largely of "innocent" freedom of perception, and "innocent," uninhibited spontaneity and expressiveness. Almost any child can perceive more freely, without a priori expectations about what ought to be there, what must be there, or what has always been there. And almost any child can compose a song or a poem or a dance or a painting or a play or a game on the spur of the moment, without planning or previous intent.

.   .   .   .

In any case, this all sounds as if we are dealing with a fundamental characteristic, inherent in human nature, a potentiality given to all or most human beings at birth, which most often is lost or buried or in-hibited as the person gets enculturated.

My subjects were different from the average person in another charac-teristic that makes creativity more likely. SA people are relatively un-frightened by the unknown, the mysterious, the puzzling, and often are positively attracted by it, i.e., selectively pick it out to puzzle over, to meditate on and to be absorbed with. I quote from my description [ref. deleted]: "They do not neglect the unknown, or deny it, or run away from it, or try to make believe it is really known, nor do they organize, dichotomize, or rubricize it prematurely. They do not cling to the familiar, nor is their quest for the truth a catastrophic need for certainty, safety, definiteness, and order, such as we see in an exaggerated form in Goldstein's brain-injured or in the compulsive-obsessive neurotic. They can be, when the total objective situation calls for it, comfortably disorderly, sloppy, anarchic, chaotic, vague, doubtful, uncertain, indefinite, approximate, inexact, or inaccurate (all at certain moments in science, art, or life in general, quite desirable).

"Thus it comes about that doubt, tentativeness, uncertainty, with the consequent necessity for abeyance of decision, which is for most a torture, can be for some a pleasantly stimulating challenge, a high spot in life rather than a low."

One observation I made has puzzled me for many years but it begins to fall into place now. It was what I described as the resolution of dichotomies in self-actualizing people. Briefly stated, I found that I had to see differently many oppositions and polarities that all psychologists had taken for granted as straight line continua. For instance, to take the first dichotomy that I had trouble with, I couldn't decide whether my subjects were selfish or unselfish. (Observe how spontaneously we fall into an either-or, here. The more of one, the less of the other, is the implication of the style in which I put the question.) But I was forced by sheer pressure of fact to give up this Aristotelian style of logic. My subjects were very unselfish in one sense and very selfish in another sense. And the two fused together, not like incompatibles, but rather in a sensible, dynamic unity or synthesis very much like what Fromm has described in his classical paper on healthy selfishness [ref. deleted]. My subjects had put opposites together in such a way as to make me realize that regarding selfishness and unselfishness as contradictory and mutually exclusive is itself characteristic of a lower level of personality development. So also in my subjects were many other dichotomies resolved into unities, cognition vs. conation (heart vs. head, wish vs. fact) became cognition "structured with" conation as instinct and reason came to the same conclusions. Duty became pleasure, and pleasure merged with duty. The distinction between work and play became shadowy. How could selfish hedonism be opposed to altruism, when altruism became selfishly pleasurable? These most mature of all people were also strongly childlike. These same people, the strongest egos ever described and the most definitely individual, were also precisely the ones who could be most easily ego-less, self-transcending, and problem-centered [ref. deleted].

But this is precisely what the great artist does. He is able to bring together clashing colors, forms that fight each other, dissonances of all kinds, into a unity. And this is also what the great theorist does when he puts puzzling and inconsistent facts together so that we can see that they really belong together. And so also for the great statesman, the great therapist, the great philosopher, the great parent, the great inventor. They are all integrators, able to bring separates and even opposites together into unity.

We speak here of the ability to integrate and of the play back and forth between integration within the person, and his ability to integrate whatever it is he is doing in the world. To the extent that creativeness is constructive, synthesizing, unifying, and integrative, to that extent does it depend in part on the inner integration of the person.

In trying to figure out why all this was so, it seemed to me that much of it could be traced back to the relative absence of fear in my subjects. They were certainly less enculturated; that is, they seemed to be less afraid of what other people would say or demand or laugh at. They had less need of other people and therefore, depending on them less, could be less afraid of them and less hostile against them. Perhaps more important, however, was their lack of fear of their own insides, of their own impulses, emotions, thoughts. They were more self-accepting than the average. This approval and acceptance of their deeper selves then made it more possible to perceive bravely the real nature of the world and also made their behavior more spontaneous (less controlled, less inhibited, less planned, less "willed" and designed). They were less afraid of their own thoughts even when they were "nutty" or silly or crazy. They were less afraid of being laughed at or of being disapproved of. They could let themselves be flooded by emotion. In contrast, average and neurotic people wall off fear, much that lies within themselves. They control, they inhibit, they repress, and they suppress. They disapprove of their deeper selves and expect that others do, too.

What I am saying in effect is that the creativity of my subjects seemed to be an epiphenomenon of their greater wholeness and integration, which is what self-acceptance implies. The civil war within the average person between the forces of the inner depths and the forces of defense and control seems to have been resolved in my subjects and they are less split. As a consequence, more of themselves is available for use, for enjoyment and for creative purposes. They waste less of their time and energy protecting themselves against themselves.

. . . what we know of peak-experiences supports and enriches these conclusions. These too are integrated and integrating experiences which are to some extent, isomorphic with integration in the perceived world. In these experiences also, we find increased openness to experience, and increased spontaneity and expressiveness. Also, since one aspect of this integration within the person is the acceptance and greater availability of our deeper selves, these deep roots of creativeness [ref. deleted] become more available for use.

. . . .

The kind of creativeness I have been trying to sketch out is best exemplified by the improvisation, as in jazz or in childlike paintings, rather than by the work of art designated as "great."

In the first place, the great work needs great talent which, as we have seen, turned out to be irrelevant for our concern. In the second place, the great work needs not only the flash, the inspiration, the peak-experience; it also needs hard work, long training, unrelenting criticism, perfectionistic standards. In other words, succeeding upon the spontaneous is the deliberate; succeeding upon total acceptance comes criticism; succeeding upon intuition comes rigorous thought; succeeding upon daring comes caution; succeeding upon fantasy and imagination comes reality testing. Now come the questions, "Is it true?" "Will it be understood by the other?" "Is its structure sound?" "Does it stand the test of logic?" "How will it do in the world?" "Can I prove it?" Now come the comparisons, the judgments, the evaluations, the cold, calculating morning-after thoughts, the selections and the rejections.

. . . .

To summarize, SA creativeness stresses first the personality rather than its achievements, considering these achievements to be epiphenomena emitted by the personality and therefore secondary to it. It stresses characterological qualities like boldness, courage, freedom, spontaneity, perspicuity, integration, self-acceptance, all of which make possible the kind of generalized SA creativeness, which expresses itself in the creative life, or the creative attitude, or the creative person. I have also stressed the expressive or Being quality of SA creativeness rather than its problem-solving or product-making quality. SA creativeness is "emitted," or radiated, and hits all of life, regardless of problems, just as a cheerful person "emits" cheerfulness without purpose or design or even consciousness. It is emitted like sunshine; it spreads all over the place; it makes some things grow (which are growable) and is wasted on rocks and other ungrowable things.

Finally, I am quite aware that I have been trying to break up widely accepted concepts of creativity without being able to offer in exchange a nice, clearly defined, clean-cut substitute concept. SA creativeness is hard to define because sometimes it seems to be synonymous with health itself, as Moustakas [ref. deleted] has suggested. And since self-actualization or health must ultimately be defined as the coming to pass of the fullest humanness, or as the "Being" of the person, it is as if SA creativity were almost synonymous with, or a *sine qua non* aspect of, or a defining characteristic of, essential humanness.

SA creativity = essential humanness.

CHAPTER THREE

EXPLANATIONS 1: FORMS AND SCOPE

As might be expected, the studies in this chapter come primarily from scientists or applied scientists, specifically psychologists and psycho-analysts. It is the task of science to explain and to predict, and all of the scientific authors in this section approach the problem of creativity with that job in mind, either implicitly or explicitly. All set out some specific explanation of creativity, as a whole or in part, or else they present an approach that will result in a specific explanation. Although usually mind-ful of the particular theoretical perspective behind their explanations, there is little explicit concern with whether the explanations are basically genetic or teleological (according to the definitions we proposed in our Introduction). By and large the scientists here present genetic types of explanations.

The philosophical writings in this section—those of Blanshard and Maritain—pay some attention to the basic kind of explanation offered as well as suggesting a particular solution. Blanshard proposes a teleological explanation of creative thought and, in other portions of the work from which our selection is taken, he criticizes associationism—for him the cardinal example of the genetic explanation in psychology. Maritain offers a rich and poetic account, from his own philosophical and psycho-logical perspective, of the functions of conscious and preconscious com-ponents within creative experience in poetry. While Maritain believes he overcomes problems connected both with genetic and teleological types of explanation, his final appeal, like Plato's, is to a source more fundamental than any completely human agency. For Maritain, a supra-human agency is the ultimate origin of creativity—a solution that some would consider a type of genetic and teleological explanation combined.

We have organized the selections in this chapter according to disci-plinary or theoretical approach as well as according to the type of explanation, genetic or teleological. Disciplinary or theoretical approaches are grouped together as follows: the philosophical selections from Blanshard and Maritain are first, followed by the selection from the novelist-biographer, Arthur Koestler; next come the group of psychoanalysts, from Rank through Ehrenzweig;[1] the final portion of the section, starting with Schachtel,[2] consists of selections from the work of general psychologists. The second principle of organization is that teleological explanations precede genetic ones: in this chapter, the first selection by Blanshard illustrates the extreme teleological position and the last selection by Mednick is at the other extreme because it illustrates the purely genetic type of explanation of associationism. Within the grouping of each disciplinary approach the same principle of sequence is followed; the teleological explanations or those with teleological elements precede the genetic. Thus the explanations by Rank, Jung, and Kris, all of which emphasize a purpose or goal to some degree, come before Lee, Kubie, and Ehrenzweig. Schachtel's theory, which derives from Gestalt psychology primarily and is therefore teleological, begins the psychologists' section. Following Schachtel is Getzels's and Csikszentmihalyi's study of "concern for discovery," a goal developing within the creative process itself. Chronological sequence is only followed within the subgroupings formed in accordance with the two organizational principles.

We have primarily adopted conceptual rather than chronological principles of organization because there has been no clear chronological development of explanatory accounts of creativity. Although many of the explanations relate to each other in some respect, they do not directly build upon one another. In a broad historical sense, the psychoanalytic interest in creativity antedates the interest of the general psychologists included here. In fact, it is fair to say that the upsurge of scientific interest in creativity in this century began with the psychoanalysts who first became interested in art and artistic creation because of their wider concern with the phenomena of motivation, affect, and irrational id processes. Art and artistic creation, the early psychoanalysts believed,

---

1. Strictly speaking, neither Jung nor Rank should be called psychoanalysts as both eventually diverged from Freudian psychoanalysis, particularly Jung, who founded an alternate theory of "analytic psychology." Also, Ehrenzweig was an art teacher by profession rather than a psychoanalyst. But all of these writers are close enough to the dynamic psychoanalytic approach to warrant their loose categorization as psychoanalysts.

2. Schachtel is a member of the William Alanson White Institute of Psychiatry, Psychology and Psychoanalysis. Although he is technically a so-called "nonmedical psychoanalyst," the theory represented in the selection here is strongly influenced by Gestalt psychology and warrants his placement with the authors in general psychology rather than the more exclusively psychoanalytic ones.

manifested such phenomena in high degree. In more recent times the psychoanalytic perspective has shifted to a more general emphasis on ego processes rather than id processes and this shift is reflected in the works of Lee, Kris, and Kubie represented here as well as some other psychoanalytic authors not included: Beres, Rosen, Rose, Muensterberger, Modell, Noy, and both Bergler and Greenacre to a lesser degree (see references in Selected Bibliography). Since creativity was from the first considered to involve the ego defense of sublimation, despite its alleged roots in the id, it would not be correct to say that a clear-cut chronological development in creativity theory has occurred; primarily there has been some increased tendency to emphasize ego rather than id processes and there has been some refinement in the formulation of the type of ego processes involved. An important shift seems to be that few psychoanalytic authors today refer specifically to the ego defense of sublimation in artistic creativity, but they attempt to describe alternate types of ego functioning.

The beginning of the modern interest in creativity by general psychologists is usually dated to a 1950 presidential address to the American Psychological Association by J. P. Guilford (see reference in Selected Bibliography) in which he eloquently emphasized the need for research in this area. Although some of the ensuing psychological research has involved the testing of some psychoanalytic explanations (see the Wild and Pine references as studies of "regression in the service of the ego" in Selected Bibliography) and an incorporation of psychoanalytic perspectives, the general psychological approach to creativity has largely been based on factor or trait psychology as exemplified in the work of Guilford (more recently, information theory), Torrance, Wallach and Kogan, Getzels and Csikszentmihalyi, Barron, MacKinnon (more recently Rankian theory), or on associationism as in the case of Mednick. Though the philosophical interest in creativity antedated that of both psychoanalysis and general psychology, the philosophical explanations included here seem to have had little influence on the scientists and to have been little influenced by them in turn. However, there are some scientists included here who have undoubtedly been influenced by philosophical perspectives, e.g., Rank, Jung, Barron, Mednick, and Getzels and Csikszentmihalyi. Such influence is direct, relating primarily to basic presuppositions that guide the scientist's approach to his topic.

The selections included are intended to represent the explanatory accounts of major investigators of creativity. Barron and MacKinnon, working in direct collaboration, have collected the largest body of psychological data about contemporary creative persons to this date. While Torrance's and Wallach's and Kogan's work are largely based on Guilford's theory and findings, Torrance's study on identifying and fostering creativity and Wallach's and Kogan's research on creativity and intelligence are themselves extensive and influential. Moreover, since they are concentrated primarily on school milieu and children, their studies exemplify the important interest and research efforts of child and educational psychologists in the field. Among the psychoanalysts, Kubie's work on creativity is only incidental to his wide-ranging interest in a variety of clinical and theoretical problems in psychoanalysis. His theory, however, represents a specific extension and development of Kris's formulation of the role of preconscious process in creation and it has received a good deal of professional and lay interest.

Two issues in creativity research have generated a large number of studies which unfortunately could not be included here. In addition to Wallach and Kogan, many investigators, including Getzels, Jackson, Csikszentmihalyi, and Barron, have paid a good deal of attention to the relationship between creativity and intelligence. Taylor, a major proponent of creativity research, as well as Sprecher, Ghiselin, and MacKinnon, have paid attention to developing criteria for defining creativity operationally and identifying creative persons. Although the general trend of research results about the relationship between creativity and intelligence point to the same type of lack of correlation described by Wallach and Kogan here—i.e., very high intelligence and creativity are not necessarily positively related, though a somewhat elevated level of intelligence seems crucial—the matter is still in much dispute. Studies pertaining to the criteria for creativity and the identification of creative persons are important for researchers trying to develop empirical approaches and, as mentioned in the previous chapter, they have been used as predictive tools. However, since the work of most of these investigators is cited over and over in this book and since the researches in creativity and intelligence as well as criteria for creativity are only indirectly geared toward explanation, we have only included here a recent description of the now classical work of Wallach and Kogan as an example of the former type of research. Ultimately space considerations dictate a good portion of any selection process and the fascinating longitudinal studies of persons of high intelligence carried out by Terman (see Selected Bibliography for Chapter One) and his associates which only indirectly pertain to creativity are unfortunately also not included.

Many disagreements exist among the investigators included in this chapter. Except for Schachtel, who explicitly criticizes Kris, most of these disagreements are implicit or are not specifically alluded to in the selections. One of the disagreements not mentioned and needing some clarification is that between Ehrenzweig and Kubie, Ehrenzweig differing explicitly with Kubie in a later portion of the book containing the material included here. Ehrenzweig emphasizes unconscious "dedifferentiation" and criticizes Kubie's emphasis on preconscious processes. This disagreement is a fairly basic one and it also leads Ehrenzweig to call for a modification of the psychoanalytic theory of the nature of primary process. However, lest there be some confusion about the difference, it should be mentioned that Ehrenzweig's definition of preconscious processes is much narrower than Kubie's. Ehrenzweig limits the content of the preconscious to thoughts and perceptions that are immediately out of awareness and can relatively easily be brought into consciousness. This formulation of the preconscious differs from that of Kubie, and of Freud and Kris as well, all of whom postulate a defensive barrier between the preconscious and conscious systems. And the difference in formulation undoubtedly influences the sharpness of Ehrenzweig's disagreement with these other psychoanalysts.

Although Koestler stands alone as a novelist, biographer, and self-educated scientist, his work is of a scope to warrant inclusion here. His explanation is in many ways genetic in type with teleological elements.

BRAND BLANSHARD · The Teleology of the Creative Act

[*Blanshard discusses the creative process in the context of an extensive work devoted to a total theory of thinking. His defense of teleology depends upon this analysis. He argues that creative processes develop according to the requirements of a teleological order that operates in nonconscious as well as conscious mental activity. The creator's innovation constitutes the achievement of an end, an end exhibiting an inner necessity. This inner necessity fits the teleological structure of thought. This selection follows a detailed challenge to associationism in his book and is succeeded by a development of his view of the role of the subconscious in invention.*]

SOURCE *From Blanshard, B., The Nature of Thought, Vol. 2, pp. 130–135, 144–146, 148, 155–156, 162, 164–165. Atlantic Highlands, N.J.: Humanities Press, 1964. Reprinted by permission.*

. . . We are now to look more narrowly at the leap of suggestion or invention. Perhaps if we run over again the steps that are taken by reflection before it comes to the leap, we shall be able to follow its movement more clearly.

The movement begins, we saw, with a collision, a collision between a system or order already present in the mind and some fragment that ought to be included in this and yet remains outside it. . . .

. . . Since our account here diverges from that of the well-known chapter by James, it will perhaps be well to have his view before us. According to James there are two chief factors in reasoning, namely, sagacity and inference, whose part in the process may be described as follows. We are confronted, let us say, with some problem demanding solution, perhaps a very simple practical problem—how shall I get this door open? perhaps some sweeping one of theory such as, Why do the planets remain in their orbits? For the solution of such problems not all the circumstances before us are of equal value, some being of no account and some essential. It is in the selection of the essential ones that the first factor, sagacity, comes in. When the door refuses to open, for example, the reflective man, instead of beating it or tearing at it, as an animal might do, looks for the place where it catches, and having discovered this, holds the solution in his hands, for he knows that by lifting the door so as to remove the friction he can get it open. Once his sagacity takes control of his eye, he is on the way to his conclusion. . . .

. . . It is plain that in the work of invention sagacity is by far the more significant factor. The second factor no doubt is necessary, and its work at times is extraordinarily difficult, as is seen in Newton's development of a new branch of mathematics in order to calculate what would follow from his hypothesis of gravitation. But more commonly the elaboration of a new insight, once it has been arrived at, is relatively easy; what is hard is to hit upon the essential circumstance that carries the solution with it. Here it is that the ordinary man is most helpless. When the idea of a force pulling the planets toward the sun, and apples toward the earth, has once been pointed out to him, he has not the slightest difficulty in seeing its pertinence; indeed it seems so obvious that he wonders why the discovery should have been so difficult. But the power to hit upon it by himself is precisely what he lacks, and what marks the true discoverer. Can we follow the path of such discoverers in the finding of the essential? The more nearly we can do so, the nearer we shall come to the secret of invention.

Let us first hear what James has to say on the point.

'*How are characters extracted,*' he asks, '*and why does it require the advent of a genius in many cases before the fitting character is brought to light?* Why cannot anybody reason as well as anybody else? Why does it need a Newton to notice the law of the squares, a Darwin to notice the survival of the fittest?' His answer is that such discoveries require a remarkable eye for resemblances. 'This answers the question why Darwin and Newton had to be waited for so long. The flash of similarity between an apple and the moon, between the rivalry for food in nature and the rivalry for man's selection, was too recondite to have occurred to any but exceptional minds. *Genius, then,* as has been already said, *is identical with the possession of similar association to an extreme degree.*' And he quotes Bain in support: 'This I count the leading fact of genius. I consider it quite impossible to afford any explanation of intellectual originality except on the supposition of unusual energy on this point. [ftnt. deleted]

. . . Admirable so far as it goes; but surely inventive genius is more than this. What is here described as genius might be madness. A madman contemplating a door, or standing on the deck of a boat where he can wonder about the pointer, may be a bubbling fountain of analogies. Doors resemble all manner of things, from walls to geometrical figures; a ferryboat's pointer is equally like a lead pencil, a crayon, and a telegraph pole. If 'genius is identical with similar association in an extreme degree', such a man should qualify. Yet something more is obviously necessary. And this something more is the *control of analogy by the conditions of the problem.* . . .

. . . That analogy is of great aid in reflection is beyond question, and we shall soon examine its service more closely. What we must insist on, however, is that it is perfectly useless, because wanton and random, except as the agent of an implicit system seeking completion by means of it. If this is mysterious, it is at least far less mysterious than the right suggestion's popping out at us from a heterogeneous crowd of similes; indeed to anyone not obsessed by the notion that thought is a mechanical process, the idea of such control is as natural as it is necessary. . . .

. . . The achievement of new insight through the completion of the fragmentary, a completion carried out under the control of an inner necessity and within a system that in neatness and abstractness is poles apart from the mathematical, might be illustrated in countless cases. I shall take one that happens to be at hand. In a book I was reading recently I found an exclamation of admiring wonder at the way in which Shakespeare, after the harrowing series of mischances, deceptions, and murders that threatens to carry *Othello* to an insupportable close, contrives to set all right again with the Moor's magnificent speech at the end:

> 'Speak of me as I am; nothing extenuate,
> Nor set down aught in malice: then must you speak
> Of one that loved not wisely, but too well;
> Of one not easily jealous, but, being wrought,
> Perplex'd in the extreme; of one whose hand,
> Like the base Indian, threw a pearl away
> Richer than all his tribe.'

and so on to the gorgeous and tragic close. If the dramatist had kept to the abstract, there were many possibilities open to him when he composed this speech. And it would seem to follow from the theory adopted by James and many other psychologists,[1] that the author's genius, consisting in a prodigal power of analogy, did actually array before him a range of alternative endings from which he went on to make his choice. One may be fairly confident that nothing of the sort occurred. It is far more likely that as the drama moved to its close in Shakespeare's mind, only one possibility presented itself, with no alternatives at all. He wrote what he did for the same reason that we, in reading or hearing it, find it satisfying, namely that with the given dramatic situation in mind he 'could no other'. He had carried his hero from a height where nobility, courage and strength made him an object of love and honour, to a depth where nothing seemed left of him but a murderer mad with jealousy. But the descent has been gradual, and at the end the initial picture is obscured. How could the extent of the appalling tragedy be brought home, and the reader reconciled to it? To such a question in the abstract, there may be many alternative answers, but is there not something a little inept in supposing that such a writer would either propound himself this question or make a list of the abstract solutions of it? Even if he did both, any answer would be worthless until specified in terms of the concrete situation. He might conclude, for example, that a satisfying whole would be achieved if the hero could appear again to us in all his old strength and honour and blot out with his own hand the thing he had become, and Shakespeare does give us this. But so far we have nothing but the bare skeleton that would be revealed

---

1. 'Just as a new voluntary movement is "discovered" by means of selection in an over-production of movements, so in an exactly similar way, new reasoning always proceeds by the method of *selection in an over-production of acts thought of.'* — Rignano, *Psychology of Reasoning*, 91–2. Italics in text.

by reflective analysis. And for all Poe's famous and curious views on the philosophy of composition, it is clear that this is not the way in which the mind of the artist works. What Shakespeare actually gives us is something completely organic with what has gone before, a speech in which we feel in every syllable what Stuart Sherman would have called 'the formative pressure of the tone and structure of the entire work'. Given the character of Othello, his prevailing mood, his habits of speech, the situation in which he was placed, and given the need to round out the whole in accordance with the implicit demands of the aesthetic ideal, there was only one course for the Moor to take; and that he did. It is precisely because the deeper we go into Shakespeare's better work, the less fortuitous do such things seem, that we give him superlative praise. He was so true an artist and so great an inventor because he succeeded, as perhaps no one else has succeeded, first in entering with full measure and variety of feeling into the situation before him, and secondly in giving it a development that is free and satisfying because it remains, in every detail, under the control of aesthetic necessity. [ftnt. deleted]

. . . At its best, then, creative thought is not a tentative groping, but a straightforward march. But where the problems are at all difficult, it must be admitted that the conditions are seldom present which make this march possible. As Whewell said, 'to try wrong guesses is, with most persons, the only way to hit upon right ones'. And here it is that analogy comes in. It is the chief and constant resource for thought that is imperfectly in command of its matter. If the mind cannot solve its problem in terms dictated by the situation itself, it will try to solve it in terms of some other but similar situation. . . .

. . . Here then is an answer to our puzzle. To the criticism that analogy is the key to invention and yet that we could not select the analogy unless we had the key already, we reply with a distinction. We do have the key to the outer door; analogy does not supply this; it is only when prior insight has produced it and turned it in the lock that analogy can begin to work. On the other hand we do *not* have the key to the inner door where the specific solution is hiding, and here it is that analogy, through mere unguided simian play, may find for us the further key. But does this answer wholly satisfy? In the main it is both true and instructive, but we must admit that it is unsatisfactory in the same way that the dilemma it answers was unsatisfactory. The inventor would find it hard to discover in his somewhat nebulous musing anything corresponding to these explicit and hard distinctions. He may bow to the logician's insistence that he must either know a certain connection or not know it. But he could reply that he is curiously uncertain as to what he does know and what he doesn't, that he sometimes succeeds in solving problems without ever reaching clearness on this point, and that when success does come, he would often find it hard to tell whether analogy had played a part in it or not. We are all familiar with this state of mind. When, in virtue of something we have seen, we conclude 'X is timid' or 'X is a southern European', are we clear whether our result has come from analogy, and if it has, what its basis is? Yet we reach the conclusion somehow. And so, sometimes, of more original thinkers on matters of greater weight. How can any definite conclusion issue from what is so vague?

The answer is that we may lay hold of a connection and that it may work within our minds without ever becoming explicit. Long ago, in our study of perceptual thought, we found instances of this. A physician, for example, walked along a hospital ward, his eye fell on a child in one of the beds who had presented a difficult case, and he remarked, 'That child has pus in the abdomen'. When asked how he knew, he was unable to answer convincingly; but that he had made more than a lucky guess was attested by the fact that his 'lucky guesses' were continual. [ftnt. deleted] What more was involved? It was the implicit grasp of a general connection between certain appearances now before him and their hidden cause. No earlier case that is similar may have come explicitly to mind, and even if it did, the point of identity might have been veiled. Yet below the level of explicitness identity was at work. Somewhere, probably, the doctor had observed a case of pus in the abdomen, and in the case now before him certain features of the earlier case were repeated. At that time an ill-defined connection impressed itself on his mind between the diseased condition and these other accompanying features, and when these turned up again, the connected character itself was reinstated. What effected the reinstatement was an identity that from first to last may have lain buried out of sight.

·   ·   ·   ·   ·   ·   ·   ·   ·   ·   ·   ·   ·   ·   ·

. . . Thus invention is the emergence in the mind of novelty under the control of system. A connection between A and B such that the changes $A^1, A^2 . . .$, on the one side are responded to by changes $B^1, B^2 . . .$, on the other is already a system; and in a discovery like Darwin's, where, in the fully developed thought, each side had thousands of members, it may

itself have a high complexity. But probably the system at work in invention is never merely a connection of simples, a form of A operating alone
to redintegrate a form of B. The leap of suggestion is actually made from
a far broader base; the datum from which the physician passes to his di-
agnosis is a complex state which includes flushes, temperatures, pulse-
rates, and perhaps much else, which all converge upon his theory. Nor
must it be forgotten that this complex base, already a partial system, is itself a sub-system in an enormously wider system, namely, the nature and
laws of the organism as represented, for the most part implicitly, in the
physician's knowledge. We have seen long ago how comprehensive such
an apperceptive mass may be, and how powerful is the control it may exert
from behind the scenes on the processes of explicit thought. What primarily acts to produce suggestion is a sub-system that is relatively small,
but this acts with the co operation of innumerable moulding pressures
from this larger background.

. . . Of two minds engaged with the same problem and possessing, so
far as may be seen, the same data, one catches the essential cue and the
other does not; why? Because, it is said, one is more intelligent than the
other. Now what we really mean by this is not some perverse cleverness
or fertility that goes off in dazzling disregard of fact; we mean the sort of
thinking that is under control by the necessities of the case. So far as the
analogies are random and heterogeneous, thought is adrift on the tide of
association. So far as they become less random and heterogeneous we can
see necessity taking the helm. And when it does take the helm, why does
it steer the course it does? We can only answer as before. That the universal connection hit upon should be the right one; that Newton, contemplating planets and apples, should light on the concept of 'falling' as leading to the force he was in search of; that Darwin should select from men
and race-horses the feature essential to improvement of type; that the
suggestion should come to Leverrier of an undiscovered star; that Shakespeare should be carried, with or without analogies, to the last speech of
Othello—all these are explicable in one way only, namely that the ideal
order which their thought is attempting to realize has so far come to the
birth in them. The matter, as they brood over it, begins to take shape in
their minds, part throws out lines to part, and hidden affinities come to
light, not because they so order it, but because they have succeeded beyond the measure of most men in surrendering to a necessity that is at
once within them and beyond them. . . .

JACQUES MARITAIN · Creative Intuition in Art and Poetry

[*Maritain does not offer a scientific explanation as do most of the authors in this chapter. Nor does he, as a philosopher, aim at a fully naturalistic, rational explanation. Yet Maritain does point toward a source that ultimately accounts for creativity: suprahuman agency. Though springing from an inner spontaneity in the poet's mind, the spontaneous power of the creative act depends ultimately on divine power. The book from which this selection is taken is important as a sensitive and rich example of Thomistic philosophy directed specifically toward the topic of creativity.*]

. . . Is there . . . any truly philosophical solution to the debate of reason and poetry; is it possible to show that, in spite of all, poetry and the intellect are of the same race and blood, and call to one another; and that poetry not only requires artistic or technical reason with regard to the particular ways of making, but, much more profoundly, depends on intuitive reason with regard to poetry's own essence and to the very touch of madness it involves? The truth of the matter is neither in the Surrealist inferno, nor in the Platonic heaven. I think that what we have to do is to make the Platonic Muse descend into the soul of man, where she is no longer Muse but creative intuition; and Platonic inspiration descend into the intellect united with imagination, where inspiration from above the soul becomes inspiration from above conceptual reason, that is, poetic experience.

This is the very subject of this book. Here I should like only to outline the general philosophical framework needed for our considerations — in other words, to establish a first preliminary thesis, which paves the way for our further research, and which deals with the existence in us of a spiritual — not animal — unconscious activity.

It is difficult to speak of this problem without discussing a whole philosophy of man. We risk, moreover, being misled by the words we use. I would observe especially that the word *unconscious*, as I use it, does not necessarily mean a purely unconscious activity. It means most often an activity which is *principally* unconscious, but the point of which emerges into consciousness. Poetic intuition, for instance, is born in the unconscious, but it emerges from it; the poet is not unaware of this intuition,

SOURCE *From* Creative Intuition in Art and Poetry, *by Jacques Maritain, no. 1, The A. W. Mellon Lectures in the Fine Arts, Bollingen Series XXXV (copyright 1953 by the Trustees of the National Gallery of Art, Washington, D.C.), reprinted by permission of Princeton University Press: selections from pp. 90–100.*

on the contrary it is his most precious light and the primary rule of his virtue of art. But he is aware of it *sur le rebord de l'inconscient*, as Bergson would have said, on the edge of the unconscious.

My contention, then, is that everything depends, in the issue we are discussing, on the recognition of the existence of a spiritual unconscious, or rather, preconscious, of which Plato and the ancient wise men were well aware, and the disregard of which in favor of the Freudian unconscious alone is a sign of the dullness of our times. There are two kinds of unconscious, two great domains of psychological activity screened from the grasp of consciousness: the preconscious of the spirit in its living springs, and the unconscious of blood and flesh, instincts, tendencies, complexes, repressed images and desires, traumatic memories, as constituting a closed or autonomous dynamic whole. I would like to designate the first kind of unconscious by the name of *spiritual* or, for the sake of Plato, *musical* unconscious or preconscious; and the second by the name of *automatic* unconscious or *deaf* unconscious—deaf to the intellect, and structured into a world of its own apart from the intellect; we might also say, in quite a general sense, leaving aside any particular theory, *Freudian unconscious*. [ftnt. deleted]

These two kinds of unconscious life are in intimate connection and ceaseless communication with one another; in concrete existence they ordinarily interfere or intermingle in a greater or less degree; and, I think, never—except in some rare instances of supreme spiritual purification—does the spiritual unconscious operate without the other being involved, be it to a very small extent. But they are essentially distinct and thoroughly different in nature.

.   .   .   .

It is enough to think of the ordinary and everyday functioning of intelligence, in so far as intelligence is really in activity, and of the way in which ideas arise in our minds, and every genuine intellectual grasping, or every new discovery, [ftnt. deleted] is brought about; it is enough to think of the way in which our free decisions, when they are really free, are made, especially those decisions which commit our entire life [ftnt. deleted]—to realize that there exists a deep nonconscious world of activity, for the intellect and the will, from which the acts and fruits of human consciousness and the clear perceptions of the mind emerge, and that the universe of concepts, logical connections, rational discursus and rational deliberation, in which the activity of the intellect takes definite form and shape, is preceded by the hidden workings of an immense and primal preconscious life. Such a life develops in night, but in a night which is translucid and fertile, and resembles that primeval diffused light which was created first, before God made, as the Genesis puts it, "lights in the firmament of heaven to divide the day from the night" so as to be "for signs, and for seasons, and for days and years."

Reason does not only consist of its conscious logical tools and manifestations, nor does the will consist only of its deliberate conscious determinations. Far beneath the sunlit surface thronged with explicit concepts and judgments, words and expressed resolutions or movements of the will, are the sources of knowledge and creativity, of love and suprasensuous desires, hidden in the primordial translucid night of the intimate vitality of the soul. Thus it is that we must recognize the existence of an unconscious or preconscious which pertains to the spiritual powers of the human soul and to the inner abyss of personal freedom, and of the personal thirst and striving for knowing and seeing, grasping and expressing: a spiritual or musical unconscious which is specifically different from the automatic or deaf unconscious. [ftnt. deleted]

. . . .

. . . Before finishing, I should like to propose some philosophical elucidation of a little more technical nature. The notion of the psychological unconscious was made into a self-contradictory enigma by Descartes, who defined the soul by the very act of self-consciousness. Thus we must be grateful to Freud and his predecessors for having obliged philosophers to acknowledge the existence of unconscious thought and unconscious psychological activity.

. . . .

The intellect, as perennial philosophy sees it, is spiritual and, thus, distinct in essence from the senses. Yet, according to the Aristotelian saying, nothing is to be found in the intellect which does not come from the senses. Then it is necessary to explain how a certain spiritual content, which will be seen and expressed in an abstract concept, can be drawn from the senses, that is, the phantasms and images gathered and refined in the internal sensitive powers, and originating in sensation. It is under the pressure of this necessity that Aristotle was obliged to posit the existence of a merely active and perpetually active intellectual energy, νοῦς ποιητικός, the intellect agent, let us say the Illuminating Intellect, which permeates the images with its pure and purely activating spiritual light and actuates or awakens the potential intelligibility which is contained in them. Aristotle, moreover, added few and sometimes ambiguous indications about the Illuminating Intellect, which he only described as superior in nature to everything in man, so that the Arab philosophers thought that it was *separate,* and consequently one and the same for all men. The Schoolmen anterior to Thomas Aquinas also held it to be separate, and identified it with God's intellect. It was the work of St. Thomas to show and insist that, because the human person is an ontologically perfect or fully equipped agent, master of his actions, the Illuminating Intellect cannot be separate, but must be an inherent part of each individual's soul and intellectual structure, an inner spiritual light which is a participation in the uncreated divine light, but which is in every man, through its pure spirituality ceaselessly in act, the primal quickening source of all his intellectual activity.

.   .   .   .

. . . There are two things in this structure of our intellectual activity which play an essential role: the Illuminating Intellect and the intelligible germ or impressed pattern. And philosophical reflection is able to establish, through the logical necessities of reasoning, the fact of their existence, but they totally escape experience and consciousness.

On the one hand, our intellect is fecundated by intelligible germs on which all the formation of ideas depends. And it draws from them, and produces within itself, through the most vital process, its own living fruits, its concepts and ideas. But it knows nothing either of these germs it receives within or of the very process through which it produces its concepts. Only the concepts are known. And even as regards the concepts, they cause the object seen in them to be known, but they themselves are not directly known; they are not known through their essence, they are known only through a reflective return of the intellect upon its own operations; and this kind of reflective grasping can possibly not occur. There can exist unconscious acts of thought and unconscious ideas.

On the other hand, and this is the fundamental point for me, we possess in ourselves the Illuminating Intellect, a spiritual sun [ftnt. deleted] ceaselessly radiating, which activates everything in intelligence, and whose light causes all our ideas to arise in us, and whose energy permeates every operation of our mind. And this primal source of light cannot be seen by us; it remains concealed in the unconscious of the spirit.

Furthermore, it illuminates with its spiritual light the images from which our concepts are drawn. And this very process of illumination is unknown to us, it takes place in the unconscious; and often these very images, without which there is no thought, remain also unconscious or scarcely perceived in the process, at least for the most part.

Thus it is that we know (not always, to be sure!) what we are thinking, but we don't know how we are thinking; and that before being formed and expressed in concepts and judgments, intellectual knowledge is at first a beginning of insight, still unformulated, a kind of many-eyed cloud which is born from the impact of the light of the Illuminating Intellect on the world of images, and which is but a humble and trembling inchoation, yet invaluable, tending toward an intelligible content to be grasped.

I have insisted upon these considerations because they deal with the intellect, with reason itself, taken in the full scope of its life within us. They enable us to see how the notion of a spiritual unconscious or preconscious is philosophically grounded. I have suggested calling it, also, musical unconscious, for, being one with the root activity of reason, it contains from the start a germ of melody. In these remarks, on the other hand, we have considered the spiritual unconscious from the general point of view of the structure of the intellect, and with regard to the abstractive function of intelligence and to the birth of ideas. It was not a question of poetry. It was even a question of the origin and formation of the instruments of that conceptual, logical, discursive knowledge with which poetry is on bad terms. Well, if there is in the spiritual unconscious a nonconceptual or preconceptual activity of the intellect even with regard to the birth of the concepts, we can with greater reason assume that such a new conceptual activity of the intellect, such a nonrational activity of reason in the spiritual unconscious, plays an essential part in the genesis of poetry and poetic inspiration. Thus a place is prepared in the highest parts of the soul, in the primeval translucid night where intelligence stirs the images under the light of the Illuminating Intellect, for the separate Muse of Plato to descend into man, and dwell within him, and become a part of our spiritual organism.

ARTHUR KOESTLER · Bisociation in Creation

[*Koestler proposes that creations result from the association of two self-consistent but habitually incompatible frames of reference in the physical, psychological, or social world. His book* The Act of Creation *is a massive study rich in examples and careful speculation based upon psychological and biological theories as well as upon his own personal experience with literary*

SOURCE *Reprinted with permission of Macmillan Publishing Co., Inc. from* The Act of Creation *by Arthur Koestler. Copyright* © *Arthur Koestler, 1964. Also reprinted by permission of A. D. Peters and Company Limited. Pp. 32–33, 35–36, 657–660.*

creation as a novelist and biographer. Koestler uses a wide variety of examples,
and he incorporates ideas from different fields. These excerpts illustrate the
central thrust of his view.]

Some of the stories that follow, including the first, I owe to my late
friend John von Neumann, who had all the makings of a humorist: he
was a mathematical genius and he came from Budapest.

> Two women meet while shopping at the supermarket in the
> Bronx. One looks cheerful, the other depressed. The cheerful one
> inquires:
>   'What's eating you?'
>   'Nothing's eating me.'
>   'Death in the family?'
>   'No, God forbid!'
>   'Worried about money?'
>   'No . . . nothing like that.'
>   'Trouble with the kids?'
>   'Well, if you must know, it's my little Jimmy.'
>   'What's wrong with him, then?'
>   'Nothing is wrong. His teacher said he must see a psychiatrist.'
>   Pause. 'Well, well, what's wrong with seeing a psychiatrist?'
>   'Nothing is wrong. The psychiatrist said he's got an Oedipus
> complex.'
>   Pause. 'Well, well, Oedipus or Shmoedipus, I wouldn't worry so
> long as he's a good boy and loves his mamma.'

The next one is quoted in Freud's essay on the comic.

> Chamfort tells a story of a Marquis at the court of Louis XIV who,
> on entering his wife's boudoir and finding her in the arms of a
> Bishop, walked calmly to the window and went through the mo-
> tions of blessing the people in the street.
>   'What are you doing?' cried the anguished wife.
>   'Monseigneur is performing my functions,' replied the Marquis,
> 'so I am performing his.'

Both stories, though apparently quite different and in their origin more
than a century apart, follow in fact the same pattern. The Chamfort anecdote concerns adultery; let us compare it with a tragic treatment of that
subject—say, in the Moor of Venice. In the tragedy the tension increases
until the climax is reached: Othello smothers Desdemona; then it ebbs

away in a gradual catharsis, as (to quote Aristotle) 'horror and pity accomplish the purgation of the emotions'. . . .

In the Chamfort anecdote, too, the tension mounts as the story progresses, but it never reaches its expected climax. The ascending curve is brought to an abrupt end by the Marquis' unexpected reaction, which debunks our dramatic expectations; it comes like a bolt out of the blue, which, so to speak, decapitates the logical development of the situation. The narrative acted as a channel directing the flow of emotion; when the channel is punctured the emotion gushes out like a liquid through a burst pipe; the tension is suddenly relieved and exploded in laughter. . . .

.   .   .   .

I said that this effect was brought about by the Marquis' unexpected reaction. However, unexpectedness alone is not enough to produce a comic effect. The crucial point about the Marquis' behaviour is that it is both unexpected and perfectly logical — but of a logic not usually applied to this type of situation. It is the logic of the division of labour, the *quid pro quo*, the give and take; but our expectation was that the Marquis' actions would be governed by a different logic or code of behaviour. It is the clash of the two mutually incompatible codes, or associative contexts, which explodes the tension.

In the Oedipus story we find a similar clash. The cheerful woman's statement is ruled by the logic of common sense: if Jimmy is a good boy and loves his mamma there can't be much wrong. But in the context of Freudian psychiatry the relationship to the mother carries entirely different associations.

The pattern underlying both stories is *the perceiving of a situation or idea, L, in two self-consistent but habitually incompatible frames of reference, M_1 and M_2* Fig[ure 1]. The event L, in which the two intersect, is made to vibrate simultaneously on two different wavelengths, as it were. While this unusual situation lasts, L is not merely linked to one associative context, but *bisociated* with two.

I have coined the term 'bisociation' in order to make a distinction between the routine skills of thinking on a single 'plane', as it were, and the creative act, which, as I shall try to show, always operates on more than one plane. The former may be called single-minded, the latter a double-minded, transitory state of unstable equilibrium where the balance of both emotion and thought is disturbed. . . .

.   .   .   .

I hope I have laid sufficient emphasis on the fact that originality must be measured on subjective scales and that any self-taught novelty is a minor

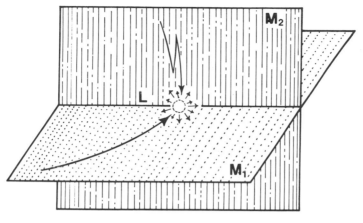

Figure [1]

bisociative act. This taken for granted, let me recapitulate the criteria which distinguish bisociative originality from associative routine.

The first criterion was the previous independence of the mental skills or universes of discourse which are transformed and integrated into the novel synthesis of the creative act. The student solving the train-bird problem is entitled to shout Eureka because his mathematical skills are so poorly integrated (or so easily dislocated) that the act of 'hooking them together' appears to him a novel discovery. The more unlikely or 'far-fetched' the mediating matrix M_2 — i.e. the more independent from M_1 — the more unexpected and impressive the achievement. The creative act could be described as the highest form of learning because of the high improbability (or anti-chance probability) of the solution.

If we now turn from subjective originality to discoveries which are new in actual fact, we again find the previous independence of the components that went into the 'good combination' to be a measure of achievement. Historically speaking, the frames of reference of magnetism and electricity, of physics and chemistry, of corpuscles and waves, developed separately and independently, both in the individual and the collective mind, until the frontiers broke down. And this breakdown was not caused by establishing gradual, tentative connections between individual members of the separate matrices, but by the amalgamation of two realms as wholes, and the integration of the laws of both realms into a unified code of greater universality. Multiple discoveries and priority disputes do not diminish the objective, historical novelty produced by these major bisociative events—they merely prove that the time was ripe for that particular synthesis.

Minor, subjective bisociative processes do occur on all levels, and are the main vehicle of untutored learning. But objective novelty comes into being only when subjective originality operates on the highest level of the hierarchies of existing knowledge.

The discoveries of yesterday are the truisms of tomorrow, because we can add to our knowledge but cannot subtract from it. When two frames of reference have become integrated into one it becomes difficult to imagine that previously they existed separately. The synthesis looks deceptively self-evident, and does not betray the imaginative effort it needed to put its component parts together. In this respect the artist gets a better deal than the scientist. The changes of style in the representative arts, the discoveries which altered our frames of perception, stand out as great landmarks for all to see. The true creativity of the innovator in the arts is more dramatically evident and more easily distinguished from the routine of the mere practitioner than in the sciences, because art (and humour) operate primarily through the transitory *juxtaposition* of matrices, whereas science achieves their permanent integration into a cumulative and hierarchic order. Laurence Olivier in Hamlet is perceived as Olivier and as Hamlet at the same time; but when the curtain goes down, the two personae separate again, and do not become amalgamated into a higher unit which is later combined with others into still higher units.

A further criterion of the creative act was that it involves several *levels of consciousness*. In problem-solving pre- and extra-conscious guidance makes itself increasingly felt as the difficulty increases; but in the truly creative act both in science and art, underground levels of the hierarchy which are normally inhibited in the waking state play a decisive part. It is perhaps significant that the German word for the Creator is *Schöpfer*, and for creating *schöpfen*—'to scoop' in the sense of drawing water in buckets from a well. The Creator is thus visualized as creating the world out of His own depth, and the creative mind with a small *c* is supposed to apply a similar procedure. But whatever the inner sources on which the Lord of Genesis drew while his spirit hovered over the dark waters, in the case of humble mortals the sources are in the phylogenetically and ontogenetically older, underground layers of his mind. He can only reach them through a temporary regression to earlier, more primitive, less specialized levels of mentation, through a *reculer pour mieux sauter*. In this respect the creative act parallels the process of biological regeneration—the liberation of genetic potentials normally under restraint, through the de-differentiation of damaged tissues. Thus the creative process involves levels of the mind separated by a much wider span than in any other mental activity—except in pathological states, which represent a *reculer sans sauter*. The emotional manifestations of the Eureka act—sudden illumination followed by abreaction and catharsis—also testify to its subconscious origins; they are to some extent comparable to the cathartic effects of the analyst's method of bringing 'repressed complexes' into the patient's consciousness.

The re-structuring of mental organization effected by the new discovery implies that the creative act has a revolutionary or *destructive* side. The path of history is strewn with its victims: the discarded isms of art, the epicycles and phlogistons of science.

Associative skills, on the other hand, even of the sophisticated kind which require a high degree of concentration, do not display the above features. Their biological equivalents are the activities of the organism while in a state of dynamic equilibrium with the environment—as distinct from the more spectacular manifestations of its regenerative potentials. The skills of reasoning rely on habit, governed by well-established rules of the game; the 'reasonable person'—used as a standard norm in English common law—is level-headed instead of multi-level-headed; adaptive and not destructive; an enlightened conservative, not a revolutionary; willing to learn under proper guidance, but unable to be guided by his dreams.

The main distinguishing features of associative and bisociative thought may now be summed up, somewhat brutally, as follows:

Habit	*Originality*
Association within the confines of a given matrix	Bisociation of independent matrices
Guidance by pre-conscious or extra-conscious processes	Guidance by sub-conscious processes normally under restraint
Dynamic equilibrium	Activation of regenerative potentials
Rigid to flexible variations on a theme	Super-flexibility (*reculer pour mieux sauter*)
Repetitiveness	Novelty
Conservative	Destructive-Constructive

And thus we are back where we left off in the first book; the circle is closed.

OTTO RANK · Life and Creation

[*Although he was one of Freud's early followers, Rank had deviated from the mainstream of the psychoanalytic movement by the time this excerpt was written. His formulation of a personality typology distinguishing between an artist type, a neurotic type, and an adaptive type is one of the foundations of his own psychoanalytic position. For Rank, the artist was always inevitably in conflict with society but, in the end, his type of mental development was really an ideal that all might strive for. In placing the artist apart, Rank deviated rather markedly from the psychoanalytic trends of his time. Although Freud did not equate artistic activity and neurosis, many other psychoanalysts of the time did so. Aside from his work on art, Rank is also known for an emphasis on the importance of Will, birth trauma, and separation anxiety in human experience. Further formulations about the nature of art and the artist, including the development of the idea that male creators are motivated by jealousy of female procreation, are found throughout the corpus of his writings listed in the Selected Bibliography for this chapter.*]

. . . In spite of all "unconsciousness" in artistic production (a point to which we shall return later), there can be no doubt that the modern individualist type of artist is characterized by a higher degree of consciousness than his earlier prototype: the consciousness not only of his creative work and his artist's mission, but also of his own personality and its productiveness. If, as it should seem, the instinctive will-to-art (Riegl), which creates abstract forms, has in this last stage of artistic development become a conscious will-to-art in the artist, yet the actual process which leads a man to become an artist is usually one of which the individual is not conscious. In other words, the act which we have described as the artist's self-appointment as such is in itself a spontaneous expression of the creative impulse, of which the first manifestation is simply the forming of the personality itself. Needless to say, this purely internal process does not suffice to make an artist, let alone a genius, for, as Lange-Eichbaum has said, only the community, one's contemporaries, or posterity can do that. Yet the self-labelling and self-training of an artist is the indispensable basis of all creative work, and without it general recognition could never arise. The artist's lifelong work on his own productive personality appears to run through definite phases, and his art develops in proportion to the

SOURCE *From* Art and Artist, *by Otto Rank, translated by Charles Francis Atkinson. Copyright 1932 and renewed 1960 by Alfred A. Knopf, Inc. Reprinted by permission of Alfred A. Knopf, Inc. Pp. 37–42, 47–49, 59–60.*

success of these phases. In the case of great artists the process is reflected in the fact that they had either a principal or a favourite work, at which they laboured all their lives (Goethe's *Faust*, Rodin's *Porte d'enfer*, Michelangelo's Tomb of Julius, and so on), or a favourite theme, which they never relinquished and which came to be a distinct representation of themselves (as, for example, Rembrandt's self-portraits).

On the other hand, this process of the artist's self-forming and self-training is closely bound up with his life and his experiences. In studying this fundamental problem of the relation between living and creating in an artist, we are therefore again aware of the reciprocal influence of these two spheres. All the psychography and pathography (with its primary concern to explain the one through the other) must remain unsatisfactory as long as the creative impulse, which finds expression equally in experience and in productiveness, is not recognized as the basis of both. For, as I already showed in my essay on Schiller (written in 1905), creativeness lies equally at the root of artistic production and of life experience.[1] That is to say, lived experience can only be understood as the expression of volitional creative impulse, and in this the two spheres of artistic production and actual experience meet and overlap. Then, too, the creative impulse itself is manifested first and chiefly in the personality, which, being thus perpetually made over, produces art-work and experience in the same way. To draw the distinction quite drastically between this new standpoint and earlier ones, one might put it that the artist does not create from his own experience (as Goethe, for instance, so definitely appears to do), but almost in spite of it. For the creative impulse in the artist, springing from the tendency to immortalize himself, is so powerful that he is always seeking to protect himself against the transient experience, which eats up his ego. The artist takes refuge, with all *his own* experience only from the life of *actuality*, which for him spells mortality and decay, whereas the experience to which he has given shape imposes itself on him as a creation, which he in fact seeks to turn into a work. And although the whole artist-psychology may seem to be centred on the "experience," this itself can be explained only through the creative impulse—which attempts to turn ephemeral life into personal immortality. In creation the artist tries to immortalize his mortal life. He desires to transform death into life, as it were, though actually he transforms life into death. For not only does the created work not go on living; it is, in a sense, dead; both as regards the material, which renders it almost inorganic, and also spiritually

1. *Das Inzest-Motiv in Dichtung und Sage*. . . . I found the same conception later in Simmel's *Goethe* (Berlin, 1913).

and psychologically, in that it no longer has any significance for its creator, once he has produced it. He therefore again takes refuge in life, and again forms experiences, which for their part represent only mortality — and it is precisely because they are mortal that he wishes to immortalize them in his work.

The first step towards understanding this mutual relation between life and work in the artist is to gain a clear idea of the psychological significance of the two phenomena. This is only possible, however, on the basis of a constructive psychology of personality, reaching beyond the psychoanalytical conception, which is a therapeutic ideology resting on the biological sex-impulse. We have come to see that another factor must be reckoned with besides the original biological duality of impulse and inhibition in man; this is the psychological factor *par excellence*, the individual will, which manifests itself both negatively as a controlling element, and positively as the urge to create. This creator-impulse is not, therefore, sexuality, as Freud assumed, but expresses the antisexual tendency in human beings, which we may describe as the deliberate control of the impulsive life. To put it more precisely, I see the creator-impulse as the life impulse made to serve the individual will. When psychoanalysis speaks of a sublimated sexual impulse in creative art, meaning thereby the impulse diverted from its purely biological function and directed towards higher ends, the question as to what diverted and what directed is just being dismissed with an allusion to repression. But repression is a negative factor, which might divert, but never direct. And so the further question remains to be answered: what, originally, led to such repression? As we know, the answer to this question was outward deprivation; but that again suggests a merely negative check, and I, for my part, am of opinion that (at any rate from a certain definite point of individual development) positively willed control takes the place of negative inhibition, and that it is the masterful use of the sexual impulse in the service of this individual will which produces the sublimation.

But even more important for us than these psychological distinctions is the basic problem of why this inhibition occurs at all, and what the deliberate control of the vital impulse means to the individual. Here, again, in opposition to the Freudian conception of an external threat as the cause of the inhibition, I suggest that the internal threatening of the individual through the sexual impulse of the species is at the root of all conflict. Side by side with this self-imposed internal check, which is taken to be what prevents or lessens the development of fear, there stands the will as a positive factor. The various controls which it exercises enable the impulses to work themselves out partially without the individual's falling completely under their influence or having to check them completely by too drastic repression. Thus in the fully developed individual we have to reckon with the triad Impluse-Fear-Will, and it is the dynamic relationship between these factors that determines either the attitude at a given moment or—when equilibrium is established—the type. Unsatisfactory as it may be to express these dynamic processes in terms like "type," it remains the only method of carrying an intelligible idea of them—always assuming that the inevitable simplification in this is not lost sight of. If we compare the neurotic with the productive type, it is evident that the former suffers from an excessive check on his impulsive life, and, according to whether this neurotic checking of the instincts is effected through fear or through will, the picture presented is one of fear-neurosis or compulsion-neurosis. With the productive type the will dominates, and exercises a far-reaching control over (but not check upon) the instincts, which are pressed into service to bring about creatively a social relief of fear. Finally, the instincts appear relatively unchecked in the so-called psychopathic subject, in whom the will affirms the impulse instead of controlling it. In this type—to which the criminal belongs—we have, contrary to appearances, to do with *weak*-willed people, people who are subjected to their instinctive impulses; the neurotic, on the other hand, is generally regarded as the weak-willed type, but wrongly so, for his strong will is exercised upon himself and, indeed, in the main repressively so it does not show itself.

And here we reach the essential point of difference between the productive type who creates and the thwarted neurotic; what is more, it is also the point from which we get back to our individual artist-type. Both are distinguished fundamentally from the average type, who accepts himself as he is, by their tendency to exercise their volition in reshaping themselves. There is, however, this difference: that the neurotic, in this voluntary remaking of his ego, does not get beyond the destructive preliminary work and is therefore unable to detach the whole creative process from his own person and transfer it to an ideological abstraction. The productive artist also begins (as a satisfactory psychological understanding of the "will-to-style" has obliged us to conclude) with that re-creation of himself which results in an ideologically constructed ego; this ego is then in a position to shift the creative will-power from his own person to ideological representations of that person and thus to render it objective. It must be admitted that this process is in a measure limited to within the individual himself, and that not only in its constructive, but also in its destructive, aspects. This explains why hardly any productive work[2] gets through without morbid crises of a "neurotic" nature; it also explains why the relation between productivity and illness has so far been unrecognized or misinterpreted, as, for instance, in Lombroso's theory of the insanity of genius. Today this theory appears to us as the precipitate left by the old endeavours to explain genius on rational-psychological lines, which treated such features as depart from the normal as "pathological." However much in the Italian psychiatrist's theory is an exaggeration of the materialism of nineteenth-century science, yet undeniably it had a startling success, and this I attribute to the fact that genius itself, in its endeavour to differentiate itself from the average, has probably dramatized its pathological features also. But the psychologist should beware of deducing from this apparent factor any conclusions as to the production or total personality, without taking into account the feeling of guilt arising from the creative process itself; for this is capable of engendering a feeling of inferiority as a secondary result, even though the primary result may be a conviction of superiority. As I have said elsewhere, the fundamental problem is *individual difference*, which the ego is inclined to interpret as inferiority unless it can be proved by achievement to be superiority.

.   .   .   .

If the impulse to create productively is explicable only by the conception of immortality, the question of the experience-problem of the neurotic has its source in failure of the impulse to perpetuate, which results in fear, but is also probably conditioned by it. There is (as I have shown) a double sort of fear: on the one hand the fear of life which aims at avoidance or postponement of death, and on the other the fear of death which underlies the desire for immortality. According to the compromise which men make between these two poles of fear, and the predominance of one or the other form, there will be various dynamic solutions of this conflict, which hardly permit of description by type-labelling. For, in practice, both in the neurotic and in the productive type—the freely producing and the thwarted—all the forces are brought into play, though with varying accentuation and periodical balancing of values. In general, a strong preponderance of the fear of life will lead rather to neurotic repression, and the fear of death to production—that is, perpetuation in the work produced. But the fear of life, from which we all suffer, conditions the problem of experience in the productive type as in other people, just as the fear of death whips up the neurotic's constructive powers. The individual whose life is braked is led thereby to flee from experience, because he

2. This applies, not only to most writers, but also, as Wilhelm Ostwald for one has convincingly proved, to the scientific creative type (*Grosse Männer*; Leipzig, 1909).

fears that he will become completely absorbed in it — which would mean death — and so is bound up with fear. Unlike the productive type, who strives to be deathless through his work, the neurotic does not seek immortality in any clearly defined sense, but in primitive fashion as a naïve saving or accumulation of actual life. But even the individualist artist-type must sacrifice both life and experience to make art out of them. Thus we see that what the artist needs for true creative art in addition to his technique and a definite ideology is life in one form or another; and the two artist-types differ essentially in the source from which they take this life that is so essential to production. The Classical type, who is possibly poorer within, but nearer to life, and himself more vital, takes it from without: that is, he creates immortal work from mortal life without necessarily having first transformed it into personal experience as is the case with the Romantic. For, to the Romantic, experience of his own appears to be an essential preliminary to productivity, although he does not use this experience for the enrichment of his own personality, but to economize the personal experiences, the burden of which he would fain escape. Thus the one artist-type constantly makes use of other life than his own — in fact, nature — for the purpose of creating, while the other can create only by perpetually sacrificing his own life. This essential difference of attitude to the fundamental problem of life throws a psychological light on the contrast in styles of various periods in art. Whatever æsthetic designation may be applied to this contrast, from the spiritual point of view the work of the Classicist, more or less naturalistic, artist is essentially *partial*, and the work of the Romantic, produced from within, *total*.[9] This totality-type spends itself perpetually in creative work without absorbing very much of life, while the partial type has continually to absorb life so that he may throw it off again in his work. It is an egoistical artist-type of this order that Ibsen has described in so masterly a fashion. He needs, as it were, for each work that he builds, a sacrifice which is buried alive to ensure a permanent existence to the structure, but also to save the artist from having to give himself. The frequent occasions when a great work of art has been created in the reaction following upon the death of a close relation seem to me to realize those favourable cases for this type of artist in which he can dispense with the killing of the building's

3. These types, evolved from a study of psychological dynamics (see my *Die Analyse des Analytikers*), are, as I have since discovered, accepted as the essential key-concepts of all polar contrasts of style by P. Frankl in his *Entwicklungsphasen der neueren Baukunst*. True, Frankl's work is not merely limited to architecture, but more narrowly still to the contrast in style between Renaissance and Baroque. We shall presently see, however ("*Schönheit und Wahrheit*"), that this contrast between totality and partiality is a general spiritual distinction between the Classical-naturalistic and primitive-abstract styles.

victim because that victim has died a natural death and has subsequently, to all appearances, had a monument piously erected to him.[4]

.   .   .   .

. . . In the life of many an artist [the relation to the opposite sex] is a disturbing factor, one of the deepest sources of conflict, indeed, when it tends to force or beguile him into closer touch with life than is necessary or even advantageous to his production. To make a woman his Muse, or to name her as such, therefore, often amounts to transforming a hindrance into a helper—a compromise which is usually in the interest of productiveness, but renders no service to life. Here, again, everything naturally depends on the artist's dynamic type and his specific conflict over life and production. There are artists for whom even a feminine Muse represents nothing but a potential homosexual relation; for they see in her not so much the woman as a comrade of like outlook and like aims, who could equally well—and possibly better—be replaced by a male friendship. On the other hand, there is an artist-type which is totally unable to produce at all without the biological complement of the other sex and indeed depends directly on the sexual life for its stimulus. For the type which is creative in and by means of sexual abstinence has its opposite in another type which, strange to say, is not only not exhausted by the sexual act but is definitely stimulated to create thereby. Schulte-Vaerting has described this type as the "sexual superman," but it seems to me rather that here too some hidden mechanism of fleeing from life is involved, which impels the artist from biological mortality to individual immortality in production after he has paid his tribute to sexuality.

4. Shakespere's *Hamlet* and Mozart's *Don Juan* are familiar examples of the reaction after a father's death, while Wagner's *Lohengrin* followed on the death of the composer's mother. These works are supreme examples of artists negotiating with the problem of the Beyond. To these instances may be added Ibsen's epilogue *When We Dead Awake;* here the death is that of the artist himself.

CARL G. JUNG · On the Relation of Analytic Psychology to Poetic Art

[Jung describes an autonomous creative complex that is separate from the complexes rooted in psychopathology. Although he attempts a limited ex-

SOURCE   From Jung, C. G., "On the Relation of Analytical Psychology to Poetic Art," Baynes, H. G. (trans.), British Journal of Medical Psychology, 1923, Vol. 3, pp. 219, 225, 226, 227–231. Copyright 1923 by the British Psychological Society. Reprinted by permission.

planatory account of the creative process in the excerpt presented here, it should be emphasized that elsewhere he emphatically said, "Any reaction to stimulus may be causally explained; but the creative act, which is the absolute antithesis of mere reaction will forever elude the human understanding."[1] Therefore, he, like many of the writers in the last chapter of this book, also affirms an antirationalist approach to creativity that affirms mystery. The basic tenet of Jung's approach to art is that archetypal themes of the Collective Unconscious, the historically constant and universal Unconscious of the human race, are transformed in some way by the artist. Though not specifying how the artist accomplishes this, except through the autonomous complexes described here, Jung's basic tenet is intended to account for the universal appeal of art.]

Before analytical psychology can do justice to the work of art, it must entirely rid itself of medical prejudice, for the art work is not a morbidity, and demands, therefore, a wholly different orientation from the medical. The physician must naturally seek the prime cause of a sickness in order to eradicate it, if possible, by the roots, but just as naturally must the psychologist adopt an entirely contrary attitude towards the work of art. He will not raise the question, which for the art-work is quite superfluous, as to its undoubted general antecedents, its basic human determinants, but he will enquire into the meaning of the work, and will be concerned with its preconditions only in so far as they are necessary for the understanding of its meaning. Personal causality has as much and as little to do with the work of art, as has the soil with the plant that springs from it. Doubtless we may learn to understand some peculiarities of the plant by becoming familiar with the character of its habitat. And for the botanist this is, in fact, an important component of his knowledge. But nobody will maintain that therewith all the essentials relating to the plant itself have been recognised. The personal orientation which is demanded by the problem of personal causality, is out of place in the presence of the work of art, just because the work of art is not a human being, but is essentially supra-personal. It is a thing which has no personality, hence for it the personal is no criterion. Indeed the especial significance of the genuine art-work lies in the fact, that it has successfully rid itself of the restraints and blind alleys of the personal and breathes an air infinitely remote from the short-winded perishableness of the merely personal.

. . . .

But, you may ask, what contribution can analytical psychology make to the root-problem of artistic "creation," *i.e.* the mystery of the creative

1. Jung, C. G. *"Psychology and Literature,"* in Modern Man in Search of a Soul. *New York: Harcourt, Brace, 1933, p. 177.*

energy? . . . Since "no creative mind can penetrate the inner soul of Nature," you will surely not expect the impossible from our psychology, namely, a valid explanation of that great mystery of life, which we immediately feel in the creative impulse. Like every other science, psychology has only a modest contribution to make towards the better and deeper understanding of the phenomena of life, but it is no nearer than its sisters to absolute knowledge.

.   .   .   .

. . . I [have] described the work existing *in statu nascendi* as an autonomous complex. The concept is used merely to distinguish all those psychic formations which, at first, are developed quite unconsciously, and only from the moment when they attain threshold-value are able to break through into consciousness. The association which they then make with consciousness has not the importance of an assimilation, but rather of a perception; which means to say, that the autonomous complex, although certainly perceived, cannot be subjected to conscious control, whether in the form of inhibition or of voluntary reproduction. The autonomy of the complex reveals itself in the fact, that it appears or vanishes when and in such guise as accords with its own indwelling tendency; it is independent of the option of consciousness. The creative complex shares this peculiarity with every other autonomous complex. It is, moreover, at this point that the possibility of an analogy with morbid psychic processes presents itself, for the latter class (and mental disorders in particular) are especially distinguished by the appearance of autonomous complexes. The divine frenzy of the artist has a perilously real relation to morbid states without being identical with them. The analogy consists in the presence of an autonomous complex. The fact of such a presence, however, proves nothing either for or against the morbid hypothesis, since normal men also submit either temporarily or permanently to the tyranny of autonomous complexes. This fact is simply one of the normal peculiarities of the psyche, and for a man to be unaware of the existence of an autonomous complex merely betrays a higher degree of unconsciousness. For instance, every typical attitude, that is to a certain extent differentiated, shows a tendency to become an autonomous complex, and in the majority of cases actually becomes one. Every instinct too has more or less the character of an autonomous complex. In itself, therefore, there is nothing morbid in an autonomous complex, only its stored-up energy and disturbing appearance on the scene involve suffering and illness.

How does an autonomous complex arise? From some cause or another — a closer investigation of which would at this point lead us too far afield — a hitherto unconscious region of the psyche is thrown into activity; this activation brings about a certain development and extension through the inclusion of related associations. The energy employed in this operation is naturally withdrawn from consciousness, unless the latter prefers to identify itself with the complex. But where this is not the case there results, what Janet has termed an "abaissement du niveau mental." The intensity of conscious interests and activities gradually fades, whereupon, either an apathetic inactivity — a condition very common with artists — or a regressive development of the conscious functions takes place, *i.e.* a descent to their infantile and archaic pre-stages, hence something akin to a degeneration. The "parties inférieures des fonctions" force themselves to the front, the instinctive rather than the ethical, the naïvely infantile instead of the deliberated and mature, the unadapted in place of the adapted. This also is shown in the lives of many artists. From the energy thus withdrawn from the conscious control of the personality the autonomous complex develops.

But in what does the autonomous creative complex consist? Of this we can know next to nothing so long as the completed work offers us no insight into its foundations. The work gives us a finished picture in the widest sense. This picture is accessible to analysis, just in so far as we are able to appreciate it as a *symbol*. But in so far as we are not able to discover any symbolic value in it, we have thereby ascertained that, for us at least, it means no more than it obviously says — in other words: so far as we are concerned it is no more than it seems. I use the word "seems," because it is conceivable that our own bias forbids any wider appreciation of it. At all events in the latter case we can find no motive and no point of attack for analysis. In the former case, however, a phrase of Gerhart Hauptmann will come to our minds almost with the force of an axiom: "Poetry means the distant echo of the primitive word behind our veil of words." Translated into psychological language, our first question would run: to which primordial image of the collective unconscious can we trace the image we see developed in the work of art?

This question demands elucidation in more than one respect. As I have already observed, the case here assumed is that of a symbolical art-work, a work, therefore, whose source is not to be found in the *personal unconscious* of the author, but in that sphere of unconscious mythology whose primordial images are the common heritage of mankind. Accordingly, I have termed this sphere the *collective unconscious*, thereby distinguishing it from a personal unconscious, which I regard as the totality of those psychic processes and contents which in themselves are not only acces-

sible to consciousness, but would often be conscious were they not subjected to repression as a result of incompatibility, and, therefore, artificially
suppressed beneath the threshold of consciousness. From this sphere
also art receives tributaries, dark and turbid though they be, and when
paramount they make the work of art more a symptomatic than a symbolical product. This kind of art might conceivably be left without injury or
regret, to the Freudian purgative method.

In contrast to the personal unconscious which is, in a sense, a relatively
superficial stratum immediately below the threshold of consciousness,
the collective unconscious is under normal conditions quite incapable of
consciousness, and hence by no analytical technique can it be brought
to conscious recollection, being neither repressed nor forgotten. In itself,
the collective unconscious cannot be said to exist at all; that is to say, it
is nothing but a possibility, that possibility, in fact, which from primordial
time has found expression in the definite form of mnemic images or ana-
tomical structure. It is inherited in the structure of the brain. It does not
yield inborn ideas, but inborn possibilities of ideas, which also set definite
bounds to the most daring phantasy. It provides categories of phantasy-
activity, ideas *a priori*, as it were, the existence of which cannot be determined without experience. In finished or shaped material it appears only
as the regulative principle of its shaping, *i.e.* only through the conclusion
derived *a posteriori* from the perfected work of art are we able to reconstruct the primitive foundation of the primordial image. The primordial
image or archetype is a figure, whether it be daemon, man, or process,
which repeats itself in the course of history, wherever creative phantasy
is freely manifested. Essentially, therefore, it is a mythological figure. If we
subject these images to a closer investigation, we discover that they are,
in a sense, the formulated resultants of countless typical experiences of
our ancestors. They are, as it were, the psychic residua of numberless
experiences of the same type. They depict millions of individual experiences in the average, presenting a kind of picture of the psychic life, distributed and projected into the manifold shapes of the mythological
pandemonium. These mythological forms, however, are in themselves
themes of creative phantasy that still await their translation into conceptual language, of which as yet there exist only laborious beginnings. Such
concepts, for the most part still to be created, could provide us with an
abstract, scientific understanding of the unconscious processes which
are the roots of the primordial images. Each of these images contains a
piece of human psychology and human destiny, a relic of suffering and
delight which has happened countless times in our ancestral story, and,

on the average, follows ever the same course. It is like a deeply graven river-bed in the soul, in which the waters of life, that had spread hitherto with groping and uncertain course over wide but shallow surfaces, suddenly become a mighty river, just when that particular concatenation of circumstances comes about which from immemorial time has contributed to the realisation of the primordial image. The moment when the mythological situation appears is always characterised by a peculiar emotional intensity; it is as though chords in us were touched which had never resounded before, or as though forces were unchained of whose existence we had never dreamed. The struggle for adaptation is a laborious matter, because we have constantly to be dealing with individuals, *i.e.* atypical conditions. It is no wonder then, that at the moment when a typical situation occurs, either we are suddenly aware of a quite extraordinary release, as though transported, or we are seized upon as by an overwhelming power. At such moments we are no longer individuals, but the race, the voice of all mankind resounds in us. The individual man, therefore, is never able to use his powers to their fullest range, unless there comes to his aid one of those collective presentations we call ideals, which liberates in his soul all the hidden forces of instinct, to which the ordinary conscious will can alone never gain access. The most effective ideals are always more or less transparent variants of the archetype. This is very noticeable in the fact, that such ideals have so great a liability to allegorisation, *e.g.* the motherland as the mother, wherein of course the allegory contributes not the smallest motive-power, which finds its source in the symbolic value of the motherland-idea. The corresponding archetype in this case is the so-called "participation mystique" of the primitive with the soil on which he dwells, and which alone holds the spirit of his ancestors. Exile spells misery.

Every relation to the archetype, whether through experience or the mere spoken word, is "stirring," *i.e.* it is effective, it calls up a stronger voice than our own. The man who speaks with primordial images speaks with a thousand tongues, he entrances and overpowers, while at the same time he uplifts the idea he is trying to express above the occasional and the transitory into the sphere of the ever-existing; he exalts personal destiny into the destiny of mankind, thus evoking all those beneficent forces which have enabled mankind to find rescue from every hazard and to outlive the longest night.

That is the secret of effective art. The creative process, in so far as we are able to follow it at all, consists in an unconscious animation of the archetype, and in a development and shaping of this image till the work is completed. The shaping of the primordial image is, as it were, a translation into the language of the present, thus enabling every man to be stirred again by the deepest springs of life which would otherwise be closed to him. Therein lies the social importance of art; it is constantly at work educating the spirit of the age, since it brings to birth those forms of which the age stands most in need. Recoiling from the unsatisfying present the yearning of the artist reaches out to that primordial image in the unconscious which is best fitted to compensate the insufficiency and one-sidedness of the spirit of the age. This image it seizes; and while raising it from deepest unconsciousness brings it into relation with conscious values, thereby transforming its shape, until it can be accepted by contemporary man in accordance with his powers.

The nature of the work of art permits conclusions about the character of the period from which it sprang. What was the significance of Realism and Naturalism to their age? What was the meaning of Romanticism or Hellenism? They were tendencies of art which brought to the surface that unconscious element of which the contemporary mental atmosphere had most need. The artist as educator of his time—that is a subject about which much might be said to-day.

People and times, like individual men, have their peculiar tendencies or attitudes. The very word "attitude" betrays the necessary one-sidedness which every definite tendency postulates. Where direction is, there must also be exclusion. But exclusion means, that such and such psychic elements which could participate in life are denied their right to live through incompatibility with the general attitude. The normal man can endure the general tendency without injury; hence, it is the man of the by-streets and alley-ways who, unlike the normal man, cannot travel the broad high-way, who will be the first to discover those elements which lie hidden from the main streets and which await participation in life.

The artist's relative lack of adaptation becomes his real advantage, for it enables him to keep aloof from the main streets the better to follow his own yearning and to find that thing which the others unwittingly passed by. Thus, as in the case of the single individual whose one-sided conscious attitude is corrected by unconscious reactions towards self-regulation, art also represents a process of mental self-regulation in the life of nations and epochs.

I am aware that I have only been able to give certain intuitive perceptions, and these only in the barest outlines. But I may perhaps hope, that what I have been obliged to omit, namely, the concrete application to poetic works, has been furnished by your own thoughts, thus giving flesh and blood to my abstract intellectual frame.

HARRY B. LEE · Unconscious Processes in the Artist

[*Lee was one of the first Freudian psychoanalysts to take sharp issue with the concept of sublimation, the defensive conversion of id impulses, as responsible for the production of art. His argument against sublimation is presented in another portion of the article from which this selection is taken. Lee's proposal that the act of creation was an act of restitution oriented toward overcoming hostile fantasies and depression was an early attempt at emphasizing the overcoming of disabilities through creating. This type of formulation has been adopted by more recent theorists, such as Niederland (see Selected Bibliography for this chapter), who view creation as a symbolic attempt at overcoming physical or psychological defects and diseases. In addition to his formulation of the psychodynamics of creativity presented here, Lee has extensively reviewed and analyzed theories of aesthetics and creativity as well as formulated a theory of the psychology of the aesthetic response in the works listed in the Selected Bibliography for this chapter.*]

. . . ordinarily the artist must deal chiefly with two types of tension — namely a dread of the loss of love from the maternal representative in conscience, and the unconscious fear that his generative function is damaged. These tensions are markedly increased, and in addition an unconscious need for punishment is activated, whenever thwarting excites his rage inordinately. He succeeds in liquidating moderate increases in these tensions by exploiting further his environmental reservoirs of love and reassurance; particularly does he draw closer to his substitute mother, towards whom he now resolves guilt by ingratiating himself through making reparations of various kinds, generally with small gifts, artistic favors, or sexual intercourse. Somewhat greater increases in these tensions are accommodated with the addition of unconsciously arranged minor sufferings, such as by loss of sleep, overwork and financial difficulty. In fact, the artist's tendencies to ease his conscience by making reparation, and by self-punishment are some of his most distinguishing characteristics. The reparations he attempts at these times are very often in identification with some æsthetic activity or interest of his father which in childhood he construed to be valued by the mother as wooing. [ftnt. deleted] Perhaps atonement by reparation is readily available to the artist because as a child he had a devoted, easily forgiving, and loving mother [ftnt. deleted] who facilitated his resolution of guilt in this way.

Source From Lee, H. B., "A Theory Concerning Free Creation in the Inventive Arts," Psychiatry, 1940, Vol. 3, pp. 283–286, 288–292. Copyright 1940 by Psychiatry. Reprinted by special permission of The William Alanson White Psychiatric Foundation, Inc. and H. B. Lee.

Over-responsive to the gratification of his defensive needs to be loved and praised, the artist is at the same time extremely sensitive to thwarting of these needs; this sensitivity, and his self-absorption during the frequent melancholy moods which overtake him, help to isolate him from life, and result in the picture of loneliness he ordinarily presents. Thwarting becomes for him an insupportably excessive stimulus for several reasons: any disturbance in the flow of reassurance from relationships with people threatens with failure the efficient repression of his unconscious dreads that he is not loved by conscience and that his generative organs are damaged; the capacities of his ego for repression, and for reactively altering itself in order to counteract destructive tendencies due to thwarting, have already been taxed; and a relatively small thwarting tends to become an excessive stimulus also from the fact that it reactivates deeply repressed hatred of the mother due to her original thwarting of his erotic demands and his self-esteem during the Œdipal period. Accordingly, any moderate frustration of the artist's system of defense needs is received as a humiliating blow, and is over-reacted to with rage whose repression overtaxes the already extensive reaction-formations erected against destructive impulses; the portion of the ego thus weakened through the undermining of its reaction-formations by an acute access of intense rage suffers a regression and re-cathects earlier positions of the libido. The larger, dominant portions of the ego and super-ego do not regress even though the conflict has been introverted. In this partial narcissistic regression, the artist's relation to his thwarter is now the more ambivalent relationship of partial love with incorporation. In phantasy, he has attacked the thwarter whom he hates, whose love he urgently needs, and whom he now possesses, *but only intraphysically, and in a damaged form.* The artist's guilt over hostility is experienced particularly towards the maternal representative in conscience because his impulse to attack is regarded unconsciously as the equivalent of an attack upon the maternal reproductive function, or upon some member thereof. He becomes acutely depressed since he feels himself no longer loved by conscience which, instead, even proceeds to treat him as cruelly as he had wished to treat the thwarter. In addition, he has suffered an acute inflation of self-regarding needs due to the loss of the love of the thwarter, and of the maternal side of conscience; also, because his usual identification with the damaged object through his sense of guilt has now been vastly extended. *The free artist's presenting sense of guilt is due to secondary hostility, and does not derive from unconscious incestuous sexual phantasies* as has been formulated by Freud, and repeated by Rank, Stekel, Abraham, Sachs and others.

When the unconscious tendencies of the artist are observed clinically, his ordinary difficulties in working, lengthy inhibitions of inspired work, peculiar attitudes to punctuality and to money, odd sense of humor, childish caprice and playfulness, penury, Bohemianism, flamboyance, impulsiveness, frequent despondent mood, moments of irascibility, extreme sensitiveness, paranoid tendencies, imperfect sense of reality, lackadaisical habits, isolation, self-absorption, spirituality, asceticism, and other "temperamental" traits commonly perceived as his characteristics are all seen to derive either from his special self-regarding and mother-ingratiating needs, from a limited satisfaction of these defense needs, or from mental depression sequel to rage upon some thwarting of their gratification. The reactive traits which comprise an important contribution to the artist's character are found to be not especially stable since they are often infiltrated with hostility which requires concealment; for example, his life as a whole is actually anything but orderly in time or space, yet through numerous unimportant, but to him magically significant, ceremonials of orderliness or cleanliness he impresses himself and others with denials of his unconscious tendencies towards destructiveness.

The artist's melancholy disposition has been commented upon in descriptions of his personality at least since the time of Aristotle who remarked that genius is allied to melancholy. The poet partly recognizes this in himself when he writes:

> The Poet, gentle creature that he is
> Hath, like the lover, his unruly times;
> His fits when he is neither sick nor well,
> Though no distress be near him but his own
> Unmanageable thoughts.
> [Wordsworth's *Prelude*, Book I]

The artist's depression, its recurrent nature, and its symptoms of suffering and inhibition, are not recognized [ftnt. deleted] as such by the artist or his friends who regard them as an "æsthetic retreat" or the due expressions of a temperamental, because gifted, nature; or else they attribute his depressive hebetude and despondency to external circumstances such as overwork or a presumed organic illness; neither are they recognized as attacks of depression by psychologists who dismiss his brooding and inability to work in classification of periods of artistic brooding, æsthetic reverie, contemplation, "musing," "incubation," or "germination."

When the artist is seized with a *mobile depression*, [ftnt. deleted] he strives to isolate himself from people and his usual recreations since he feels despondent, irritable, and intellectually foggy. Speech and movement are retarded. He believes that his creative ability has come to an end, and that there will never again be any joy in it; the world has lost its sheen, and its people do not look good to him, neither do his past works; he feels sad, and things seem to have lost some of their feeling of being quite real. He is extremely irritable towards those who come his way or try to claim his attention at these times. Unable to focus his thought in reading, if he succeeds in forcing his interest to it, the most he can tolerate is to browse among mystical or religious writings and poetry. From time to time, his gloomy phantasies take on a paranoid coloring, calling up in review particularly those past situations in which he believed himself to have been taken advantage of, humiliated, or badly treated in other ways. He finds that he is unable to begin new work, or to conclude that which he had begun. Sometimes he attempts to flee his unhappiness by a change of physical environment, usually by a vacation trip alone, and to some secluded spot where he will not be too comfortable physically; or by his seizing upon some expedient for permanently shutting the thwarter from his life.

During the periods when he is only very mildly depressed, the artist produces works which are not inspired, which he finds it laborious to produce, and which he judges to be artificial, mediocre, and "not right." Often the most he can force his attention to is the routine filling-in of some repetitive design, and the copying or contemplation of his past works. If he completes a direct or varied copy of his past work, even though others may find much beauty in the copy, he feels that it is lacking in its most essential ingredients—the beautiful formalization and originality with which spirit and vision have fired his freely created work.

If the artist should attempt to work during his more severe depressions—and he does so in the hope of thus forcibly overcoming his sadness and hebetude—he finds that he is unable to concentrate his interest upon the project or to gain satisfaction from his efforts. At such times he becomes obsessed with grave doubts about his artistic ability, and fears that he has finally lost it; panicky with the belief that he has permanently lost his creative power, he struggles to recapture it, and to escape his suffering as well, through instituting changes in his physical environment or physical changes in himself. He busies himself with cleaning his implements, or in putting his usually disorderly workshop into scrupulous order, and he may attempt to re-create the environmental setting of past inspired moments, even to ritualizing some part of these to which, unconsciously, he then attaches a magical value, [ftnt. deleted] or he may move his workshop a short distance, or to another "climate," in the hope that a radical external change will result in a *renaissance* which will recapture for him the capacity to create. He might take to liquor in excess, or to other drugs, in order to achieve a state of mental excitement similar to the ecstasy attendant upon his past experiences of inspirational enthusiasm; [ftnt. deleted] sometimes he will attempt by sheer force to regain confidence in his ability as, for example, by turning to the use of violently bright colors in painting, or to the noisy exertion of carving marble.

. . . .

Inspiration is an unconscious mental process dictated by the dynamic needs and quantitative relationship which comprise the emergency situation described, and intended to relieve it. It consists of an effort to achieve in fancy, and of oneself, the restitution to life and organic integrity of the particular person towards whom the artist had allowed himself to experience again the impulse to destroy; the motive for doing so resides in the great need to render oneself again *persona grata* with the maternal root of conscience. Inspiration delivers the ego from a considerable portion of the remaining—optimum of—guilt, and eases particularly its inflated ordinary tensions by a fancied restoration of the destroyed-person-contained in the-creature-self in a significantly undamaged, perfect and beautiful form. It is the ego's testimony to conscience that its creature portion has reformed, pity having been restored, and a plea that it deserves to be redeemed from *limbo* for good behavior. The energy spared from the need to suffer was utilized by the ego to rehabilitate its forsaken reaction-formations against hostility; the regenerated and idealized creature-portion of itself is now employed to ingratiate the entire ego with the maternal representative in conscience; this is achieved through exhibiting to conscience impressive identifications with the mother's wishes for her child's renunciation [ftnt. deleted] of living by the pleasure-principle in regard to excretory pleasure, and of destructiveness and dependence; thus, in the artist's reprogression, the dominant-share-of-the ego-*as mother* now re-enacts towards the erring-portion-of-itself-*as-child*, and in introverted form, a piece of the history of its learning process during early childhood; [ftnt. deleted] it heals itself in recapitulating and parading before conscience the history of its mother-praised infantile progression from early anal sadistic stages to later anal sadistic stages, and thence to early genital stages. [ftnt. deleted] In this sense only is the artist correct when he describes his creativeness with the analogy of parturition.

Inspiration eventuates successfully [ftnt. deleted] only when this reprogressive achievement of the ego has re-formed its creature portion so that it deserves to sue for redemption; now sufficiently ingratiated with the maternal representative in conscience to regain some of its favor and approval, the ego's experience of inspiration brings with it feelings of beatitude, inner security, an infantile measure of omnipotence, restored "vision," and a sense of freed energy; an additional quantity of energy devoted to the work of suffering and to repression of the acutely inflated ordinary tensions is thus spared to the ego which now re-invests it in the impoverished reality-testing and motor functions, and at late anal and early genital levels. *Ec-stasy* indicates the ego's emergence from the *stasis* of depression; in this it resembles the manic phase of manic-depressive psychosis, from which it differs chiefly in the degree of ambivalence. When inspiration occurs, the artist says that he has finally achieved the elusive "vision" [ftnt. deleted] he had been trying to capture for a long time; and, seized with an overwhelming, restless eagerness, he is compelled by still great defense needs to exploit further, now in creativeness, the success of his inspired avenue of relief; he does so by transforming the real with his inspired conception, *viz.* in accordance with the less ambivalent style of feeling with which, in childhood, he had related himself to his mother and others during the later pre-genital stages. In this way, creation dramatizes inspiration; and the *opus* consists of a votive and magically significant token offering of himself to conscience as re-formed, [ftnt. deleted] guiltless and quite loveable. This is free inventive creation, and the artist needs to be active in it not from any motive derived from potential external valuations of the *opus*, but because of an inner compulsion to real-ize in a fragment of the world outside, *i.e.*, in the medium, [ftnt. deleted] a magical re-creation in symbol of the destroyed-thwarter-as-restored-and-loved. Creation is not only a step beyond inspiration in the artist's task of freeing himself further from excessive guilt and anxieties, and an effort to cling to the beatific exaltation which comes to him with forgiveness and being loved by conscience, but, more significantly, *it is the next step in a series of re-progressive unconscious processes whose function is to restore the withdrawn fuller cathexis of an outer world which can now include the thwarter-as-friend.* Inspiration had restored the thwarter to life and organic integrity, but only in phantasy; the creation of art repeats this symbolic restoration by materializing it with *finesse,* [ftnt. deleted] and with the significance of homeopathic magic, in a crude fragment of the real world.

The thwarter restored as undamaged friend, the self reborn loveable and undamaged, and the mother's regenerative function renewed intact, are all celebrated in symbol with the work of transforming a sample of the real world—the real, and inanimate [dead], medium—with formal brilliance. Now the artist can revive his actual relationship to the thwarter and others with the interest he had invested in them prior to its withdrawal by introversion. The transcription of the inspired conception into an art product occurs in a manner which inspirits the medium with the same psychic achievements as were accomplished imaginally by inspiration, but now with much greater gain to the synthetic functioning of the ego; for the inspired artist, having tasted again some love and approval from conscience, proceeds hurriedly to exploit not only the gains to be achieved from the creative dramatization of inspiration, but also whatever potentialities the medium offers for the further successful discharge of guilt and inflated ordinary tensions. Thus, the task of the artist in creating becomes the materialization of his inspired conception with such exquisite craftsmanship, originality, [ftnt. deleted] beautiful formalization, and savour of renewed spirituality as will witness to conscience his mastery of the creature portion of himself in his mastery of the difficulties of the medium as well as in his loving treatment thereof. [ftnt. deleted] Accordingly, in the perfect use of an imperfect, crude, or difficult medium, the creative work is done lovingly and with magically beautiful vision; *the artist truly addresses his Muse as well as the medium of his choice with a loving homage;* he exploits the material by planting there his vision, and then through penetrating it with spirit; [ftnt. deleted] in this intercourse, he achieves from the medium, and from his struggle with the difficulties and limitations it offers, responses which revise with ever more beautiful forms the inspired vision he has already planted there. He achieves, momentarily, the illusion that his creation lives, [ftnt. deleted] and feels that he, too, lives fully and joyfully only during the enthusiasm of his creative moods; for, during these fugitive moments, in reformation of himself and in his re-form of a sample of the outside world, he has magically re-created his infantile self in the image of the ideals of his mother for him, [ftnt. deleted] and has recaptured intensely the gratification of being loved by the maternal representative in conscience as he was by his mother in childhood. [ftnt. deleted]

The free creation of art thus enshrines, materialized in a real form, the symbolic restitution to the world outside, as intact, undamaged, perfect, and beautiful in form, of the psychic representations of the destroyed person—the generative function of the mother—and the self; and it constitutes an earnest tender of assurances to conscience that now in reality, as well as imaginally, the thwarter will be treated as a friend; inspiration had promised the same, but only imaginally, as a testimony of good intentions, and at a time when fuller object-relationship was still restricted at the command of conscience, and impossible because of the introversion of interest.

It is, therefore, understandable why, in the despair of the emergency described, the artist must entreat the maternal representative in conscience, that is, he turns again to the loving, forgiving, and teaching mother of his childhood for urgently needed approval and assistance, *i.e.*, he "invokes his Muse." It is no matter of indifference that the ancients spoke of inspiration as being of divine origin; and that they regularly invoked a feminine Muse. The Muse is, of course, none other than the idealized mother of the artist's childhood days, the one who first led out his interest to cope with painful reality, and for whose love he had embraced the doubtful gratification of eating vegetables, and relinquished his excretory pleasures; for whose forgiveness he struggled to control rage and to renounce destructive tendencies; who in his own ancient days taught him to transform babble into disciplined song and talk, and un coördinated movement into ordered gesture, walk, play, and dance; whose love and approval he gained *in doing these well*, [ftnt. deleted] and whom he now owns as the maternal representative in conscience. . . .

The occurrence of the special type of imagination we call inspiration denotes that the artist is transcending a partial regression through successfully conceiving an ideal and magical resurrection of the person he had destroyed in fancy. The artist has turned creator in order to rehabilitate the creature portion of himself in accordance with the ideals of his Muse,—the mother *imago*. The destructive tendency now repudiated, pity and piety are restored; *laborare est orare* is particularly true for the creating artist. The sermons which the sculptor finds in stones and "bodies forth" are the ones his recovered spirituality has already hidden there, and animated for him. [ftnt. deleted] The disciplined recording of the imagined resurrection in some plastic language, and with loving homage, *i.e.*, with art, is the next step of the introverted artist toward recovering a fuller investment of the real with interest. His projection of interest to the medium transfigures it with the same inner harmony and spirituality as in inspiration he had transfigured himself; and he proceeds to regenerate himself in transforming this dead fragment of the real world, the medium, in identification with the discipline of certain fundamental dictates of society as to what constitutes acceptable form; [ftnt. deleted] these disciplines, the arts and sciences, are regarded as feminine and maternal. Thus, successful creation yields additional increments of energy spared from tasks of defense, and furnishes the bridge to reality over which interest can again flow outwards; at first with superrational treatment of the medium in some novel consonance with these dictates of a maternal discipline in order to transform it with formalized beauty which is personally significant as magical; [ftnt deleted] and later redirected into friendship for the mother-substitute and the thwarter, who are invested with interest as projected personifications of the loving maternal representative in conscience, and of the redeemed creature portion of himself. Thus ends the artist's cycle of mobile depression; in formal materialization he reanimated both thwarter and self, and recaptured what is most essential to his disposition: the gratification of being loved by a mother-substitute in the same narcissistic ways as he was by conscience in inspired creation, and by his mother—or her imago—during early childhood. [ftnt. deleted]

Free creativeness restores the artist to his former mental integrity, replaces at his command energies which he had short-circuited from the outer world to himself during a mobile depression, and returns him to his former level of adjustment to reality. The economic gains from the creative mental processes described lie in their efficacy for palliating quickly, once the optimum of guilt is attained, the pain endured through suffering and from a greatly extended identification with the damaged object; in affording ec-stasy to the despondent artist—the acute pleasure of winning again forgiveness, approval, and love from the maternal root of conscience, as well as of recapturing an experience of infantile magical omnipotence, [ftnt. deleted] and in relating him again to a salutary reality. [ftnt. deleted]

ERNST KRIS · On Preconscious Mental Processes

[*Kris's concept "regression in the service of the ego" as developed here is very widely accepted among psychoanalysts as a partial explanation of the creative process. Although he does not actually use the term "regression in the service of the ego" in this particular selection, his references to ego-controlled regression relate to that concept. In emphasizing the role of fantasy and*

SOURCE From Kris, E., "On Preconscious Mental Processes," Psychoanalytic Explorations in Art, pp. 303, 310–318. New York: International Universities Press, Inc., 1952. Reprinted by permission.

preconscious functioning, Kris took a principle from Freud's work on Jokes
and the Unconscious *(see Selected Bibliography for Chapter One) and
developed it into a full theory of creativity. As an art historian as well as a
psychoanalyst, Kris attempts to emphasize some of the adaptive aspects of
creativity and he distinguishes regression in the creative process from the
regression connected to psychotic states. His concept of regression as a phenomenon that includes sleep and sexual orgasm is very broad and his overall
formulation is a shift from a previously exclusive emphasis on the unconscious
roots of creativity by many early psychoanalysts. Another important article
spelling out his conception of the functioning of ego-controlled regression in
creation is "On Inspiration." Kris's interest in creativity was part of his general
interest in developing and extending psychoanalytic ego psychology. Along
with Hartmann, Lowenstein, Anna Freud, and Erikson, Kris has been one of the
most prominent psychoanalytic ego psychology theorists to date.*]

In recent psychoanalytic writings preconscious mental processes
are rarely mentioned, even when fundamentals are discussed [ref. de-
leted]. . . .

. . . .

It is a strange fact that, in spite of all varieties of clinical experience
which throw light on preconscious mental processes, the main source
of reference for many of these processes should have remained for almost
thirty years a book of the Belgian psychologist Varendonck, entitled *The
Psychology of Daydreams* (1921) which reports a great variety of self-
observed thought processes. [ftnt. deleted] . . .

. . . .

The first and up to now only relevant critical evaluation of Varendonck's
book, from the psychoanalytic point of view, is Freud's introduction to it
(1921). It has rarely, if ever, been quoted, and in the German translation
of Varendonck's book it was not fully reproduced. In studying ". . . the
mode of thought activity to which one abandons oneself during the state
of distraction and into which we readily pass before sleep and upon
incomplete awakening . . ." Varendonck has rendered a valuable service.
While Freud appreciates confirmation found for his views on the psychology of dreams and "defective acts," he sharply opposes Varendonck's
central thesis. Freud asserts that there is no difference between preconscious and conscious mental processes. What Varendonck calls day-
dreaming does not owe its peculiarities to ". . . the circumstance that it
proceeds mostly preconsciously. . . . For that reason I think it is advisable,
when establishing a distinction between the different modes of thought

activity not to utilize the relation to consciousness in the first instance."
Freud suggests that one should distinguish in daydreams, as well as in
the chain of thoughts studied by Varendonck, freely wandering fantastic
thinking as opposed to intentionally directed reflection, since it is known
"that even strictly directed reflection may be achieved without the co-
öperation of consciousness."

If we take this distinction as our starting point and remember that the
economic and structural approach, the study of cathexes and ego function,
has proved its value in discussing problems in the psychology of preconscious mental processes, we are easily led to one area of deliberation.
The ego, we assume, has two kinds of bound energy at its disposal:
neutralized energy, and libido and aggression in their nonneutralized
form [ref. deleted]. Fantastic, freely wandering thought processes tend to
discharge more libido and aggression and less neutralized energy; pur-
poseful reflection and solving problems, more neutralized energy. In
fantasy, the processes of the ego are largely in the service of the id. Not
only the id, however, is involved. Naturally, the superego and "narcissistic" strivings play their part. The content of freely wandering fantasies
is extended over the pleasure-unpleasure continuum; hence the probability that in this kind of process, the discharge of nonneutralized libido
and aggression will be maximized. In reflective thinking the contrary is
likely. Reflective thinking, according to Freud (problem solving, as we
would prefer to say), serves to a higher degree the autonomous ego interests. Discharge of libido and aggression is therefore likely to be mini-
mized, and that of neutralized ego energy to be of greater relevance.
[ftnt. deleted]

We now turn to a brief discussion of the second continuum of preconscious thought processes, that which extends between logical verbali-
zation and fantastic imagery; the hypnagogic fantasies to which Freud
refers in the passage quoted above, some of Varendonck's wandering
fantasies, and fantasies of the more fanciful patients in psychoanalysis
designate the area of the phenomena in question. We are clearly dealing
with problems of ego regression.

The very fact that such phenomena of ego regression are infinitely more
frequent in fantasy than in deliberative preconscious processes suggests
that in fantasy the discharge of libido and aggression may have in general
a greater proximity to the id—to mobile energy discharges. The id, as it
were, intrudes upon ego functions.

Topographically, ego regression (primitivization of ego functions)
occurs not only when the ego is weak—in sleep, in falling asleep, in fan-

tasy, in intoxication, and in the psychoses—but also during many types of creative processes. This suggested to me years ago that the ego may use the primary process and not be only overwhelmed by it. [ftnt. deleted] This idea was rooted in Freud's explanation of wit [ref. deleted] according to which a preconscious thought "is entrusted for a moment to unconscious elaboration," and seemed to account for a variety of creative or other inventive processes. However, the problem of ego regression during creative processes represents only a special problem in a more general area. The general assumption is that under certain conditions the ego regulates regression, and that the integrative functions of the ego include voluntary and temporary withdrawal of cathexis from one area or another to regain improved control [ref. deleted]. Our theory of sleep is based upon the assumption of such a withdrawal of cathexis. Sexual functions presuppose similar regressive patterns, and the inability to such suspension of ego control constitutes one of the well-known symptoms of obsessional, compulsive characters.

The clinical observation of creators and the study of introspective reports of experiences during creative activity tend to show that we are faced with a shift in the cathexis of certain ego functions. Thus a frequent distinction is made between an inspirational and an "elaborational" phase in creation. [ftnt. deleted] The inspirational phase is characterized by the facility with which id impulses, or their closer derivatives, are received. One might say that countercathectic energies to some extent are withdrawn, and added to the speed, force, or intensity with which the preconscious thoughts are formed. During the "elaborational" phase, the countercathectic barrier may be reinforced, work proceeds slowly, cathexis is directed to other ego functions such as reality testing, formulation, or general purposes of communication. Alternations between the two phases may be rapid, oscillating, or distributed over long stretches of time.

In ascribing to the ego the control of regression in terms of shifts in the cathexis of ego functions, which can be related to or pitted against each other in various ways, we gain a frame of reference that might in the present tentative state of our knowledge prove useful in various ways. Consider, for example, the shift of cathexis between the ego function of perception (the system Pcpt) and preconscious thought. The individual, immersed in preconscious thought, takes less notice of his environment. Idle fantasies are given such a pejorative description as decrease of attention or, with Freud, of being distracted by fantasy. At this point we seem to gain a further and improved understanding of one problem. It is generally assumed that preconscious thought processes become conscious by hypercathexis. We now realize that there are various degrees of hypercathexis. If energy is diverted from the perceiving function of the ego to fantasy, this in itself may not lead to consciousness but simply to an intensification of the preconscious process. Emergence into consciousness would still be dependent on other conditions.

The automatic functions of the ego are commonly considered to include a special kind of preconscious processes which become conscious only in the case of danger or under other special requirements [ref. deleted]. Consciousness in these instances is no guarantee of improved function; on the contrary, automatic (habit) responses in driving automobiles or the use of tools, for instance, seem to have undoubted advantages. Similarly, the shift from consciousness to preconsciousness may account for the experience of clarification that occurs when after intense concentration the solution to an insoluble problem suddenly presents itself following a period of rest. Briefly, we suggest that the hypercathexis of preconscious mental activity with some quantity of energy withdrawn from the object world to the ego—from the system Pcpt to preconscious thinking—accounts for some of the extraordinary achievements of mentation. [ftnt. deleted]

. . . .

The appropriateness of describing thought processes in terms of cathexis and discharge is further supported if we turn to some reactions of individuals upon becoming conscious of their preconscious fantasies or of the result of their preconscious productive deliberation. [ftnt. deleted]

The privileges of fantasy are manifold. When fantasy has taken us far afield we do not as a rule experience shame or guilt—shame, for instance, for having arrogated some of the properties of infantile omnipotence, guilt because the fantasy may have been ruthless and antisocial. Patients may feel ashamed or guilty in reporting such fantasies, although they did not feel so while they were engaged in them or when they recalled them. There is a feeling of not being responsible for one's fantasies.

Tentatively, we assume that in preoccupation with fantasy the ego withdraws cathexis from some functions of the superego. Our knowledge does not permit us to be more specific. One gains the impression that while the ego ideal loses its importance for the individual the punitive tendencies of the superego are enforced [ftnt. deleted] in some for whom self-punitive measures are part of the fantasy. In others the hypercathexis of the ego ideal is predominant, while the function of critical self-observation seems reduced.

The absolution from guilt for fantasy is complete if the fantasy one follows is not one's own. This accounts for the role of the bard in primitive society and, in part, for the function of fiction, drama, etc., in our society. Opportunity for discharge or catharsis is guiltlessly borrowed. A close study of the phenomenology of the subjective experiences connected with fantasy, autogenous or borrowed, tends to confirm the opinion that feelings of relief (temporary or protracted), or of saturation (and final disgust), can all easily be explained by well-known psychodynamics.

A feeling of relief and discharge, similar to that provided by fantasy, can also be gained when the successful solution of a problem has been achieved—when a piece of preconscious deliberation has come to a satisfactory conscious conclusion. The indisputable satisfaction which attends the solution of a problem is usually described in terms of the gratification of a sense of mastery, feelings of triumph from achievements related to ego interests [ref. deleted], feelings of self-esteem which reduce intrapsychic tension as between superego and ego, etc. It seems useful to consider in addition the possibility that the solution of problems—including all areas of creativity—affords pleasure through the discharge of neutral energy used in the pursuit of creative thinking. [ftnt. deleted] This consideration is new neither in psychoanalysis nor elsewhere in psychology. It is frequently referred to as functional pleasure. [ftnt. deleted] When Freud's interest was still close to the investigation of the psychology of thinking, he stated in *Wit and Its Relation to the Unconscious*: "When our psychic apparatus does not actually act in search of some urgently needed gratifications we let this apparatus itself work for pleasure gain. *We attempt to gain pleasure from its very activity.*" There can be little doubt that the activity to which Freud refers is chiefly the discharge of quantities of neutralized energy. An elaboration of this theory seemed to lead to improved understanding of aesthetic experience. [ftnt. deleted]

The gradual steps in the slow maturation of solving a problem sometimes extend over years. There is a considerable similarity or analogy between some aspects of this problem of thought formation and the problem of preconscious lapses. A solution once found may be forgotten, return after some time and be fitted into its frame of reference, or it may never again be recaptured. Undoubtedly combinations of all psychodynamic factors may interact to produce such results; and yet such forgetting, such selectivity of memory may be due also to a lack of integration necessary for the solution of the problem.

The appropriate material for the study of these phenomena is the history of science, and what Gestalt psychology can contribute has recently been tested in describing the development of Einstein's theory [see Wertheimer, Selected Bibliography for this chapter].

Freud's recently published *Aus den Anfängen der Psychoanalyse* provides an opportunity to study some of these problems in relation to psychoanalysis itself. This book consists of a series of intimate letters, notes, essays, and drafts written by Freud between 1887 and 1902. During these years Freud reports to a correspondent the emergence of new ideas and their subsequent slipping away, also, about premonitions of hypotheses to come, and a large set of related phenomena. In 1895 Freud became aware of the main psychological mechanism of dream formation and established a link between the dream mechanism and symptom formation. But his theory of symptom formation was then incomplete and in large part unusable, and the link between the two was dropped. For two years Freud forgot that he had once seen this connection, and he treated dream and neurosis as disconnected and alternative fields of his interest until in 1897 he temporarily reëstablished the connection, forgot it again, and only one year later fully established it, experiencing what in fact was a rediscovery, as a great and triumphant revelation. It took three years to safeguard this finding against lapses of memory, as it was only at the end of this period that the theory was integrated, infantile sexuality was discovered, and the problem of regression made accessible to closer investigation.

Examples of this kind indicate that only when the ego has completed its synthetic function by eliminating contradiction within the theory are the parts of the theory protected against slipping from conscious awareness. We may now revise and amplify the conditions required to eliminate the countercathexis between preconsciousness and consciousness. To the two conditions stated—ego syntonicity and full cathexis with neutral energy as prerequisites and consequences of integration [ftnt. deleted]— we now add that ego syntonicity consists not only of freedom from conflict in the intersystemic sense (id and superego), but also in the intrasystemic sense [ref. deleted] in relation to the various ego functions. In solving problems, the feeling of fitting propositions together satisfies the requirement of the synthetic function; critical examination of the context satisfies the requirements of reality testing in an extended sense. [ftnt. deleted]

Prob. solving [handwritten marginal note]

To return from this detour to the central question of reactions to the reaching of awareness of preconscious thought processes, let me repeat that normally there is an absence of reactions. In many instances of both fantasy and creativity, discharge and satisfaction can be experienced.

The mere feeling of relief is more manifest in fantasy, a mixture of relief and satisfaction more evident in creativity and solving problems. But there are instances in which these same experiences appear in a special form, in which the feeling exists that awareness comes from the outside world. This is obviously true of hallucinations, but it is also true of revelation or inspiration. [ftnt. deleted] In revelation or inspiration a preconscious thought is attributed to an outside agent from which it has been passively received. The literal and the attenuated meanings of the term form a continuum; we speak of inspiration also when a percept stimulates thought. Newton, who attributed the discovery of the law of gravity to the observation of a falling apple, is an instance. The perception there acted as a factor precipitating previously organized preconscious ideas waiting for the stimulus. [ftnt. deleted]

Why do creators of all kinds so often prefer to attribute their achievements to the influence of such external agents as chance, fate, or a divine providence? One motivation is avoidance of the wrath and envy of the gods; but there are other more significant and deeper motivations. The feeling of full control and discharge of tension in the state of becoming aware of significant ideas or achievements mobilizes deep layers of the personality. In the case of ecstatic revelation the hallucinatory character of the experience is manifest.

We believe that in the process of becoming conscious the preconsciously prepared thought is sexualized, which accounts for the experiences accompanying revelation. Id energies suddenly combine with ego energies, mobile with bound and neutralized cathexes, to produce the unique experience of inspiration which is felt to reach consciousness from the outside. Unconscious fantasies at work in some specific instances of these experiences can be reconstructed, and [elsewhere I have] tried to demonstrate the variety of experiences that are derived from the repressed fantasy of being impregnated and particularly of incorporating the paternal phallus. It has since become plausible that additional fantasies are involved. The feeling of triumph and release from tension remind the individual of a phase in his development in which passivity was a precondition of total gratification, and in which the hallucinated wish fulfillment became reality: the period of nursing. We find here another approach to the full intensity of believing and its relation to infantile omniscience as described by Lewin: the analytic process and the insight it produces can be experienced in terms of an archaic wish fulfillment. Changes in cathexis during the working of the psychic apparatus tend, I suggest, to be generally experienced in terms of such an archetype. The maturing of thought, the entry into awareness from preconsciousness to consciousness tend to be experienced as derived from outside, as passively received, not as actively produced. The tendency toward passive reception takes various shapes and forms, appears under the guise of various modalities, but the subjective experience remains one of reception. When, after the completion of his theory of dreams, Freud was urged to publish his theories of sexuality, he answered to his urging friend: "If the theory of sexuality comes, I will listen to it."

This relationship between creativity and passivity exemplifies once more one of the leading theses of this presentation: the integrative functions of the ego include self-regulated regression and permit a combination of the most daring intellectual activity with the experience of passive receptiveness.

LAWRENCE S. KUBIE · Creation and Neurosis

[*Although Kubie's direct work on creativity is limited to the book from which this selection is taken, his contention that neurosis interferes with creativity is based on his extensions of psychoanalytic theory and his broad clinical experience. In elaborating Kris's emphasis on preconscious functioning in creativity and asserting that the Preconscious alone is responsible for creation, Kubie completely rejects the previous psychoanalytic emphasis on the Unconscious.*]

I am not going to contrast normal men with neurotic men, or normal cultures with neurotic cultures. I want to characterize merely the essential differences between a *single normal and a single psychopathological act or moment of human life.* It is important to keep this sharply circumscribed purpose in mind; because until we can agree on a characterization of what constitutes the essential psychopathology of a single psychological event, we will hardly be able to agree upon what constitutes psychopathology in a total personality, or in any group of individuals which we call a society or a culture, or in the relation of psychopathology to creativity.

There is not a single thing which a human being can do or feel, or think,

SOURCE   From Kubie, L. S., Neurotic Distortion of the Creative Process, *pp.* 19–21, 137–143. *Lawrence, Kans.: University of Kansas Press, 1958. Copyright 1958 by the University of Kansas Press. Reprinted by permission.*

whether it is eating or sleeping or drinking or fighting or killing or hating or loving or grieving or exulting or working or playing or painting or inventing, which cannot be either sick or well. Furthermore, to which category any act belongs will depend not upon conformity to any cultural norm; not on the frequency of the act in any society (since statistical frequency of colds or dental caries has nothing to do with whether they are sick or well); not on whether an act, feeling, or thought seems superficially to be sensible or foolish, useful or valueless, constructive or destructive. Nor does the distinction depend upon any such legal artifice as whether the individual knows the difference between right or wrong: since the psychotic and the criminal may have as clear judgments on moral issues as any clergyman. The measure of health is flexibility, the freedom to learn through experience, the freedom to change with changing internal and external circumstances, to be influenced by reasonable argument, admonitions, exhortation, and the appeal to emotions; the freedom to respond appropriately to the stimulus of reward and punishment, and especially the freedom to cease when sated. The essence of normality is flexibility in all of these vital ways. The essence of illness is the freezing of behavior into unalterable and insatiable patterns. It is this which characterizes every manifestation of psychopathology, whether in impulse, purpose, act, thought, or feeling. As I have said elsewhere [ref. deleted), "Whether or not a behavioral event is free to change depends *not* upon the quality of the act itself, nor upon its individual or social consequences, but upon the nature of the constellation of processes that have produced it. Any moment of behavior is neurotic *if the processes that set it in motion predetermine its automatic repetition*, and this irrespective of the situation or the social or personal values or consequences of the act." Whenever psychological processes predetermine the tendency automatically to repeat, they are psychopathological. This applies to the businessman, artisan, or laborer, to the scientist or artist, and to everything each of them does. In the next section we will discuss what configuration of processes can predetermine the automatic repetition of behavior; since these are the storm centers of dreams and of illness to which the creative process is vulnerable.

(1) It . . . [is] my thesis that a type of mental function, which we call technically "the preconscious system," is the essential implement of all creative activity; and that unless preconscious processes can flow freely there can be no true creativity.

(2) Preconscious processes, however, never operate alone. They are under the continuous and often conflicting and distorting or obstructing influence of two other concurrent systems of symbolic functions, each of which is relatively anchored and rigid. Together the three systems constitute a spectrum with certain continuities, and at least one partial but critical discontinuity.

At one pole are the symbolic processes which we speak of as *conscious*, meaning thereby that the relation between the symbol and what it represents is intact, with the result that in this area we know most of what each symbol connotes. (We can never know *all*.)

At the other pole are the symbolic processes which we call unconscious, by which we mean that although the symbol is conscious, most of what it stands for is both unknown and inaccessible except by special methods of exploration.

(3) Conscious symbolic processes are the tool by which we communicate the bare bones of meaning to one another, by which we re-examine critically our own thinking, by which we group multiple fragments of experience into unified patterns of comparable or overlapping experiences, condense different units, rearrange them in logical or chronological categories, and build abstractions from them.

It is important to realize that without symbolic functions on the conscious level, human psychological functions would be limited to the sensory and emotional recall of fragments of past experiences. At their most vivid, these would be approximately analogous to the phenomena of the "phantom limb" (in which the sensory impressions of prior experiences are condensed and vividly relived): analogous also to the re-experiencing of confused or vaguely overlapping fragments of visual or olfactory or auditory perceptions out of the past, in dreamlike hypnagogic reveries.

Conscious symbolic processes have their primary roots in perceptions of past external and internal experiences; but evolve through generalizations into abstractions and their symbolic representations into the coded signals which we call words. This gives them their anchorage in reality, which is essential to the major function of the conscious system. Yet at the same time this automatically limits the free imaginative play of conscious symbolic processes.

On the other hand, it is also relevant to point out that without the verbal and symbolic condensations of speech, most of us would in all probability have a much richer sensory and affective recall of past events, both within the body and without. If verbal short cuts were eliminated, our everyday memories would be imprecise; but they could have the pseudo-hallucinatory vividness of hypnagogic reveries. In some respects they would be like the violent affects which can persist after dreams, even when the dreams themselves are obliterated. . . . Thus we pay a price for the superimposition of conscious symbolic function over our more primitive sensory Gestalts, and especially when the conscious symbol is a word. This price is the attenuation of the capacity to relive past experiences as vividly as though they were recurring in the present. In this sense, thinking-back verbally is a smoke screen for that true remembering which is an affectively charged re-living.

Only poets, novelists, painters and musicians are, in varying degrees and in a fragmentary way, exceptions to this rule. Certainly in all art forms, but particularly in the plastic arts and music, where the symbolic process comes closer to the nonverbal symbolic tools of the dream, there is an effort to reactivate and revivify the sensory and emotionalized (or "gut") components of past experience [ref. deleted].

(4) At the other pole are what we call unconscious symbolic processes. Here the essential fact is that the relationship of the symbol to what it represents is impaired, distorted, or actually lost (or as we say "repressed"). Furthermore, this repression cannot be lifted by any simple act of will. The iron curtain between the symbol and all that it represents cannot be penetrated; and we cannot become conscious of the symbolic meanings without special techniques, such as psychoanalysis, hypnosis, certain drugs, electrical processes, various chemical changes, etc. In other words, within the *unconscious system* the true connotations of the symbol are inaccessible even on need to our most intent, deliberate, conscious self-inspection. Moreover in the unconscious system this relationship cannot be altered by any influences until and unless it is brought out into the open. The symbol is to its *unconscious* root like a delegate who has been sent to the conference table to "negotiate," but with secret orders never to modify his position. He pretends to interchange with those who sit around the table; but his secret orders are unalterable and his ultimate position will be precisely what it was at the beginning. Similarly within the unconscious system the relationship of symbols to what they represent is impervious to conscious or preconscious experiences, with the result that it is, if anything, even more fixed and rigid than is the relation of the symbol to what it stands for in the conscious system.

The influence of this rigidity can be observed in the stereotyped repetitiousness of form and content in the works of the musician, of the artist, of the writer, and of the scientist. How often is it said that a man has painted the same painting over and over again, written the same poem, told the same story, composed the same music, ground the same scientific ax? Were it not for this fact, it would be impossible for the specialist in the arts to recognize a man's paintings from their technique and content, or his music without having been told who the composer was. It is the artist's unconscious which leaves a personal signature on his work as on his handwriting; and like a fingerprint left by a thief in the night, it is unmodifiable and therefore *non-creative*. This accounts also for the man who produces one play, one book, one poem, one painting, one piece of first-rate scientific work.

All of this is the price we pay whenever unconscious processes hold the upper hand in the dynamic unstable equilibrium among the CS, PCS, UCS systems during our creative efforts. The dread which haunts every creative person that this fate may be his is a product of some measure of imprecise insight into the fact that the creative potential of his preconscious processes will be captured, imprisoned, nullified, sterilized, and stereotyped by his own unconscious, i.e., by that very unconscious which paradoxically he defends desperately against any therapeutic intrusion or modification.

(5) Whence then comes our creative function? To answer this we have to stop for a moment to indicate what we mean by creativity. Clearly, by the creative process we mean the capacity to find new and unexpected connections, to voyage freely over the seas, to happen on America as we seek new routes to India, to find new relationships in time and space, and thus new meanings. Or to put it in another way, it means working freely with conscious and preconscious metaphor, with slang, puns, overlapping meanings, and figures of speech, with vague similarities, with the reminiscent recollections evoked by some minute ingredients of experience, establishing links to something else which in other respects may be quite different. It is free in the sense that it is not anchored either to the pedestrian realities of our conscious symbolic processes, or to the rigid symbolic relationships of the unconscious areas of the personality.

This is precisely why the free play of preconscious symbolic processes is vital for all creative productivity. Preconscious psychological functions stand on the fringes of consciousness. Here the meaning of the symbol is essentially analogic, yet relatively transparent, although it may be obfuscated in varying degrees for artistic purposes, as in the more obscure realms of modern art, modern verse, and modern music. Yet preconscious processes involve much more than all of this. They are also the most important economizing device which implements our thinking operations.

The price that we pay for traditional educational methods is that they either tie our preconscious symbolic processes prematurely to precise realities, or leave them to the mercy of distorting influences which arise around areas of unresolved unconscious conflict.

Together all of this carries the implication that the ad hoc postulate that there is a separate and special mechanism known as the sublimation of unconscious processes may not be needed to explain creativity, and may actually be misleading. This concept was formulated as an effort to explain creativity in relation to neurotic conflicts *before* the role of the preconscious system, its speed, its versatility, its brilliance, and its vulnerability were fully appreciated. The concept of sublimation, natural though it may have been, is based on inaccurate assumptions about the energetics of psychological processes [ref. deleted]. Furthermore the concept carries the impossible connotation that unconscious conflicts can be resolved if they can be expressed in socially valuable forms instead of in useless or destructive forms. Yet no compulsive work drive has ever healed itself through working, however successfully.

These considerations lead to a few conclusions:

(1) Neurosis corrupts, mars, distorts, and blocks creativeness in every field.

(2) No one need fear that getting well will cause an atrophy of his creative drive.

(3) This illusory fear rests on the erroneous assumption that it is that which is unconscious in us which makes us creative, whereas in fact the unconscious is our straitjacket, rendering us as stereotyped and as sterile and as repetitive as is the neurosis itself.

(4) Where unconscious influences play a dominant role the creative process in science or art becomes almost identical with the neurotic process—merely transmuting unconscious conflicts into some socially and artistically acceptable symbolic form.

(5) The goal to seek is to free preconscious processes from the distortions and obstructions interposed by unconscious processes and from the pedestrian limitations of conscious processes. The unconscious can spur it on. The conscious can criticize and correct and evaluate. But creativity is a product of preconscious activity. This is the challenge which confronts the education of the future.

ANTON EHRENZWEIG · Unconscious Scanning and Dedifferentiation in Artistic Perception

[*Although an art teacher by profession, Ehrenzweig has brought extensive knowledge of Gestalt psychology and psychoanalysis to bear on the understanding of art and the creative process, first in the book* The Psychoanalysis of Artistic Vision and Hearing *and, more recently, in the book from which this selection on unconscious scanning is taken. Arguing that traditional Gestalt formulations do not fully account for artistic perception, Ehrenzweig also reintroduces an emphasis on the psychoanalytic Unconscious in art. To do this, he postulates a new principle of dedifferentiation, a form of unconscious functioning that is more basic than any particular formal operation such as the mechanisms of primary process thinking.*]

What is common to all examples of dedifferentiation is their freedom from having to make a choice. While the conscious gestalt principle enforces the selection of a definite gestalt as a figure, the multi-dimensional attention of which Paul Klee speaks can embrace both figure and ground. While vertical attention has to select a single melody, horizontal attention can comprise all polyphonic voices without choosing between them. Undifferentiated perception can grasp in a single undivided act of comprehension data that to conscious perception would be incompatible. I have elsewhere called these mutually exclusive constellations the '. . . or-or . . .' structure of the primary process. Serial structure would be a better term. While surface vision is disjunctive, low-level vision is conjunctive and serial. What appears ambiguous, multi-evocative or open-ended on a conscious level becomes a single serial structure with quite firm boundaries on an unconscious level. Because of its wider sweep low-level vision can serve as the precision instrument for scanning far-flung structures offering a great number of choices. Such structures recur regularly in any creative search.

The superior efficiency of unconscious vision in scanning the total visual field has been confirmed by experiments in subliminal vision. 'Subliminal' is only another word for unconscious, differently named only because we are still reluctant to concede a truly unconscious quality to imagery that has become inaccessible because of its undifferentiated

SOURCE *From Ehrenzweig, A.,* The Hidden Order of Art, *pp. 32–33, 35–38, 42, 45–46. Berkeley: University of California Press, 1967. Reprinted by permission of George Weidenfeld and Nicolson/Arthur Barker Limited/World University Library.*

structure alone. It is possible to speak of a purely formal 'structural' repression which gives an unconscious quality to split-second tachistoscopic exposures and to the totally invisible subliminal images. When the still visible split-second exposure in tachistoscopic experiments is cut down below a critical threshold, the image disappears and the screen remains empty. The New York psycho-analyst, Charles Fisher [ref. deleted], presented Rubin's double profiles . . . subliminally and asked his observers to make drawings by free association. (In this way he used the same shortcut to the unconscious which Freud used after he had abandoned hypnosis as a means of tapping the unconscious.) The drawings produced a significant number of images where two objects faced each other in the manner of the double profiles. Obviously the split-second exposure had sufficed for subliminal vision to pick up the positive and negative shape simultaneously. Unconscious vision is thus proved to be capable of scanning serial structures and gathering more information than a conscious scrutiny lasting a hundred times longer. With impartial acuity subliminal vision registers details irrespective of whether they belong to the figure or to the ground. It tends to reverse the conscious preference for the figure and pays more attention to textural and background elements. Such displacement of emphasis is, of course, characteristic of the primary process. Subliminal images often enter subsequent dreams and display full-blown traits of condensation, displacement, representation by the opposite, fragmentation, duplication and other techniques of the primary process. But this again does not make it chaotic. Once dedifferentiation has been achieved, the wider serial structure of low-level images willingly accommodates and indeed contains from the outset many such possible variations of the originally selected gestalt constellation. What matters in our context is the fact that the undifferentiated structure of unconscious (subliminal) vision is far from being weakly structured or chaotic as first impressions suggest, but displays the scanning powers that are superior to conscious vision.

. . . let us . . . pursue the smooth functioning of the creative ego and observe its fruitful alternation between differentiated and undifferentiated modes of functioning. Any creative search, whether for a new image or idea, involves the scrutiny of an often astronomical number of possibilities. The correct choice between them cannot be made by a conscious weighing up of each single possibility cropping up during the search; if attempted it would only lead us astray. A creative search resembles a maze with many nodal points. . . . From each of these points many possible pathways radiate in all directions leading to further crossroads where a new network of high- and by-ways comes into view. Each choice is equally crucial for further progress. The choice would be easy if we could command an aerial view of the entire network of nodal points and radiating pathways still lying ahead. This is never the case. If we could map out the entire way ahead, no further search would be needed. As it is, the creative thinker has to make a decision about his route without having the full information needed for his choice. This dilemma belongs to the essence of creativity. The structure of a mathematical problem is a neat example. The creative thinker has to scrutinize it without any hope of a really clear view. Let us say an algebraic equation has to be transformed by a number of consecutive steps until it assumes a form that can be accepted as the solution of some unsolved problem. Each possible transformation opens up an unlimited number of new transformations, some fruitful, some ending in blind alleys. Admittedly, strict rules exist that govern algebraic transformations; but they do not say which of the possible transformations will prove fertile in the end. In order to judge the fruitfulness of each new step one has somehow to anticipate the entire route ahead. But a clear view is not possible, if only because of the great number of mutually exclusive possibilities. They add up to typical serial structures that overflow the narrow focus of normal attention. This means that the creative mathematician, as in any truly original problem in art and science, has to make correct decisions without having the full information needed for them. The mathematician, Hadamard [ref. deleted], who became interested in the psychology of mathematical thought, emphatically states that any attempt at visualizing the way ahead clearly only leads astray; the decision must be left to the unconscious. This demand implies my hypothesis that unconscious visualization is better equipped for scanning the complex serial structure of a new mathematical argument. Hadamard admits that the student cannot start by blotting out his conscious attention. He has first to learn the conscious rules governing mathematical transformations and he will check each step according to these rules. But at a certain point, which has to do with the awakening of creativity, he has to abandon precise visualization. Instead of concentrating on each single step he has to reach out and grasp the total structure of the argument as compared with any other possible structure. He has to visualize syncretistically the total structure though he cannot look sufficiently far ahead to see clearly the detailed choices and decisions awaiting him. In Wittgenstein's words: his view must be comprehensive though not clear in detail. Hadamard, like Poincaré before him, states categorically that it is necessary to cloud one's consciousness in order to make the right decision. But, of course, conscious vagueness is not enough if it does not lead to a shift of attention to unfocused low-level vision.

An excessive need for clear visualization is prompted by the schizoid dissociation of ego functions. It is characteristic of a rigid uncreative personality who cannot let go his hold on the surface functions. Ironically, academic teaching usually puts a premium on the precise visualization of the working process and its result. A good craftsman in any sphere of learning is exalted for his full control of the working process. He is supposed to see the way ahead with clarity and choose the most direct route to a desired result. For the beginner such ambitions are praiseworthy. But they become nonsense and a nuisance as soon as the craftsman has to solve a new truly original task. There he can only have comprehensive, but not clearly detailed view, in the manner of the mysterious syncretistic vision which can be precise in grasping a total structure the components of which are interchangeable.

. . . unconscious scanning — in contrast to conscious thought which needs closed gestalt patterns — can handle 'open' structures with blurred frontiers which will be drawn with proper precision only in the unknowable future. The lawgiver has to use words in just this way. He has to anticipate usages of his legal terms that might become necessary through social and economic developments in the unforeseeable future. The architect, in designing a serviceable building, also has to anticipate a number of possible uses for the building that are partly determined by unknowable future factors. In short these open forms are able to absorb genuine 'accidents' that fall wholly outside any kind of rational planning. Tentative scientific terms, good laws and good buildings are only 'defined' by subsequent use. Yet in all these cases — the logical use of words, the formulation of legal statutes, the design of buildings — the creative thinker has to grasp in a flash the total function of his work as distinct from its more detailed uses. Playing the creative game well is all that is needed. Precise visualization or worse still a straining of one's attention to see crystal-clearness where there is in fact none, will only produce wrong or unusable results.

. . . Academic teaching is wont to put a premium on powers of precise visualization, not only in the arts, but also in music or in science, and certainly also in logic. . . . I would explain this insistent demand for precision in academic teaching as a defensive secondary process in a psychoanalytic sense; the slighted surface faculties try to suppress unconscious scanning in order to retain full control of the working process. The necessary blurring of conscious focusing is felt as a danger and a threat of total chaos. This fear may be only another aspect of the more general misunderstanding of unconscious participation in creative work. . . . Wittgenstein's acceptance of vagueness in everyday language is often misunderstood as the advocacy of vague, woolly thinking. Hadamard's recommended procedure in the use of diagrams in geometry displaces the emphasis from important features to insignificant details. How easily could this advice be construed as encouragement of chaos! The displacement of proper emphasis is a typical primary-process technique. It is not easy for dry academicians to accept that syncretistic primary-process techniques rather than analytic clarity of detail are needed by the creative thinker to control the vast complexities of his work. Nor will my argument convince them.

ERNEST G. SCHACHTEL · Perceptual Modes and Creation

[*Although Schachtel's view of creativity is known primarily as a sharp critique of Kris's concept "regression in the service of the ego," it stands on its own as an example of a developmental cognitive approach related to Gestalt psychology. Schachtel views the development of the individual in terms of a progression from autocentric perception in childhood to allocentric perception in adulthood. In this selection Schachtel's definitions of autocentric and allocentric perception are presented first and then followed by his discussion of creative perception.*]

. . . an analysis of sensory experience reveals two basic modes of relatedness between perceiver and environment which are akin to, yet different from, Freud's two principles of mental functioning, the pleasure and the reality principle. A shift in the relative importance of these two perceptual modes characterizes the ontogenetic development of human perception, and the vicissitudes of their later transformation and development are closely linked with the psychic growth and maturation of man.

SOURCE *Excerpts from* Metamorphosis: On the Development of Affect, Perception, Attention, and Memory, *by Ernest G. Schachtel,* © *1959 by Basic Books, Inc., Publishers, New York, pp. 82–84, 237–238, 240–246, 248. Reprinted by permission.*

I shall designate these two basic modes of perceptual relatedness as the subject-centered, or *autocentric*, and the object-centered, or *allocentric*, mode of perception. The main differences between the autocentric and allocentric modes of perception are these: In the autocentric mode there is little or no objectification; the emphasis is on how and what the person feels; there is a close relation, amounting to a fusion, between sensory quality and pleasure or unpleasure feelings, and the perceiver reacts primarily to something impinging on him (although sometimes he may have brought about the impingement, for example by taking food into his mouth). In the allocentric mode there is objectification; the emphasis is on what the object [ftnt. deleted] is like; there is either no relation or a less pronounced or less direct relation between perceived sensory qualities and pleasure-unpleasure feelings — that is, such feelings are usually absent or less pronounced or of a different quality; the perceiver usually approaches or turns to the object actively and in doing so either opens himself toward it receptively or, figuratively or literally, takes hold of it, tries to "grasp" it.

The distinction between these two basic perceptual modes both differentiates between and cuts across the different senses. It cuts across them in this way: developmentally the autocentric mode holds almost exclusive sway at the beginning of life in all the senses of the newborn, and later the allocentric (higher) senses can and do function also in the autocentric mode, while the autocentric (lower) senses are capable of a very limited degree of allocentricity. Our distinction differentiates between the senses in that the higher, or allocentric, senses usually function predominantly in the allocentric mode and are the only ones capable of full-fledged allocentric functioning, while the lower, or autocentric, senses always function predominantly in the autocentric mode and are not capable of real allocentric perception.

. . . .

The phylogenesis of perception is characterized by the increasing amount, variety, and enrichment of sensory experience. It culminates in man's allocentric mode of perception, in which independently existing objects are perceived (objectification). Because of man's openness toward the world the number of possible objects of human perception and the variety of their aspects are infinite and inexhaustible. To what extent man realizes his potentiality of allocentric perception depends on the stage he reaches in his ontogenetic development. During this development he explores, in the playful encounters of childhood, an expanding environment and an increasing variety of object aspects in exercising his growing sensory-motor capacities. While part of this exploration takes place in the spontaneous and immediate encounter with the objects, an important part consists in the increasing acquaintance with their meaning in the culture. Such learning on the one hand enriches the object world of the growing child to a degree which could never be reached by an isolated individual. On the other hand, it also increasingly supplants the child's original approach to the objects and, especially in our time, entails the danger of *closing* his openness toward the world and of reducing all experience to the perception of such preformed clichés and "angles" as make up the world of "reality" seen by the family, peer group, and society in which he grows up. The perspective from which objects are perceived may narrow to "what they are there for" and "how one deals with them." Nature may no longer be seen as the mother of all living creatures including man, but may become an enemy to be conquered or a mere object to be exploited and used. Other people, too, may be seen from a similar viewpoint, the viewpoint of secondary autocentricity.

Where the perspective of secondary autocentricity becomes the only one and dominates all perception, allocentric as well as primary autocentric perception tend to stagnate and atrophy. In our time this stagnation tends to take the form of an alienation of man from the objects and from his own sensory capacities. The danger of this alienation is that man's dulled senses may no longer encounter the objects themselves but only what he expects and already knows about them, the labels formed by his society. The closed world of this perspective ceases to hold any wonder. Everything has its label, and if one does not know it the experts will tell him.

.   .   .   .

. . . Only if the concept of intelligence is restricted to mean adaptation to the status quo is it more intelligent to be done quickly with anything new. But if man's highest capacity is that of allocentric interest to which the world never becomes a closed book, then the greater intelligence may be that which does not quickly dispose of or deal with an object but wonders at it and does not tire easily of contemplating and exploring it even if to others it may be the most familiar thing imaginable.

In such perception the glance dwells on the frontiers of human experience and becomes creative, revealing hitherto unknown vistas. It has been compared with the child's glance when it is said that the artist [ftnt. deleted] and the wise man resemble a child. The resemblance consists in the freshness, spontaneity, interest, and openness with which the object is approached and reacted to. Just as these qualities and attitudes in the child are the prerequisite of expansion and progress in the encounter with the world, so they are in the adult. They make the encounter creative, be it in the sense of growth and enlargement of personal experience, or in the sense of enabling the artist or the scientist to add to the scope of human experience. Such openness toward and interest in the object is part of the phenomenon of creative experience which takes place in the whole human being with all his capacities and reactions even though one or the other may play a more dominant role in any particular act of creative experience. Thus, what we have seen in studying the ontogenetic development and the nature of allocentric perception can be of help in clarifying the nature of creative experience. [ftnt. deleted]

The problem of *creative experience* is essentially the same for all the human capacities such as perception, thought, feeling, and motor activity, comprising, in the widest sense, not only the hand that moves the brush in painting or manipulates the object to be explored or to be fashioned, but also the eye, the head, the body that approach the object from different angles, etc. It is the problem of the open encounter of the total person with the world, that is, with some part of the world. Of the different aspects of allocentric perception the *openness in turning toward* the object is the most basic and important one; the fullest interest in an object is possible only if the person opens himself fully toward as many object aspects as possible, that is, optimally toward the totality of the object.

The openness toward the object in creative experience is apparent both in the motivation for the encounter and in the way in which the encounter takes place. The main *motivation* at the root of creative experience is man's need to relate to the world around him, a need which, as we have seen, becomes particularly strong and striking when urgent physical needs such as for food and rest have been stilled. This need is apparent in the young child's interest in all the objects around him, in his ever renewed exploration of and play with them. It is equally apparent in the artist's lifelong effort to grasp and render something which he has envisaged in his encounter with the world, in the scientist's wonder about the nature of the object with which he is concerned, and in the interest in the objects around him of every person who has not succumbed to stagnation in a closed autocentric or sociocentric world. They all have in common the fact that they do not remain in a closed, familiar, labeled world but that they want to go beyond embeddedness in the familiar and in the routine, and to relate to another object, or to the same one more fully, or from another angle, anew, afresh. In such acts of relatedness man finds both the world and himself. This does not imply that other needs may not also play a role in and color or codetermine the creative experience. It only means that without the basic need to relate to the world, without openness toward the world, the experience will not enlarge, deepen, and make more alive the person's relation to the world, that is, will not be creative.

The *quality* of the encounter that leads to creative experience consists primarily in the openness during the encounter and in the repeated and varied approaches to the object, in the free and open play of attention, thought, feeling, perception, etc. In this free play the person experiences the object in its manifold relations to himself and also tentatively tries out, as it were, a great variety of relations between the object thus approached and other objects, ideas, experiences, feelings, objects of imagination, etc. In characterizing this activity as play I do not mean that it is playful rather than serious, but that it is not bound by rigorous rules or by conventional schemata of memory, thought, or perception. It may at times be playful, too; but that is not its main characteristic. It resembles the child's free play in his encounter with the world where playfulness, too, is not the main feature but the openness, the intensity of the interest, the repeated and varied approaches, which range all the way from the grave and serious, the absorbing and tantalizing, to the playful and the fleeting.

In the earliest stages of infancy the play of the child with the objects of the environment is at first limited to and determined by what happens to impinge on his senses. Later on it increasingly expands as the child can turn actively from one object to another. From then on it may at times range freely, at other times be focused more on a particular object, idea, feeling. In such focusing, relations may be established between the specific object and others that have been encountered in ranging more widely. In the creative process the person usually focuses more and more sharply on a particular area or object. As he approaches it from various angles in the tentative play of thought, senses, and motor behavior, he also connects it with other experiences. His relatedness to the object is intensified and he becomes more open to its different aspects and possible links.

What has been learned in such unfettered and open intercourse with the world may enlarge unnoticeably and gradually the person's experience and contribute to his growth, or it may crystallize suddenly in an insight, or in a new vision of something that seemed long familiar, or in an "inspiration." But it is truly assimilated and becomes consciously and freely available to the person only if it is either fashioned into an objective work, as in artistic or literary creation, or is otherwise elaborated by connecting it with, and making it part of, the conscious total life and experience of the person. This usually is a more laborious process than either the long incubation period of the many encounters between person and object or the subsequent flash of insight, vision, or inspiration. Both the period of immersion in the ever renewed encounters and the period of articulating and connecting the experiences won in the free play of the varied approaches are essential for the growth and expansion of the person's relation to the world through creative experience.

In Freud's work and in post-Freudian ego psychology, especially in the work of Kris, the view is expressed that such experience, especially as it leads to artistic creation, is always the product of a *repressed libidinal or aggressive impulse* and of a *regression* to infantile modes of thought or experience, to the primary process, albeit in the service of the ego. Freud considered it probable that the artist has a constitutionally given "looseness of repression"[1] and he ascribed certain "achievements of special perfection" to the temporary removal of the repression of an unconscious impulse which, for the particular occasion, becomes ego-syntonic and manifests "a resistance in the face of opposition similar to that of obsessional symptoms."[2]

This resistance in the face of all opposition, it seems to me, is the resistance not of an Id drive but of the conviction of the truth of artistic or scientific creation in the face of the opposition by the shared autocentricity of conventional perception and thought. Such truth is more likely to be encountered by the person who has continued and expanded the child's openness toward the world on the adult level and whose sensory and intellectual capacities have not entirely succumbed to the pressure of the accepted way in which everyone perceives the "realistic" world of the conventions of the day, the era, and the society. Just as the amnesia for early childhood is not due primarily to the repression of forbidden sexual impulses but to the transformation of the total manner of perceiving and thinking, [ftnt. deleted] so the unseeingness which in all of us, in varying degrees, stands in the way of a more creative vision is due more often to the encroachment of an already labeled world upon our spontaneous sensory and intellectual capacities than to the repression of a libidinal impulse.

Freud assumed that the artist suffers from too strong drives in craving honor, power, wealth, fame and to be loved by women and that, since he does not have the means of obtaining these satisfactions, he turns his back on reality and tries to obtain them in his phantasies, which, if he is worldly successful with his creations, in the end will get him what he

1. *Lockerheit der Verdrängungen*, S. Freud, "Vorlesungen zur Einführung in die Psychoanalyse," *Gesammelte Werke* (Imago Publishing Co., London, 1940), Vol. XI, pp. 390–391.
2. S. Freud, "The Unconscious," *Collected Papers* (Basic Books, New York, 1959), Vol. IV, p. 127.

originally wanted.[3] While these drives may play a role in an artist just as well as in a businessman or in anybody else, they are in no way specific for the artist nor are they unusually strong in all artists. However, what *is* essential for the artist is that he experiences and expresses more precisely, and without being blindfolded by the sociocentric view, what happens in his encounter with the world or some aspect of it. His need to relate to the world must not be channeled as completely by the conventional patterns and schemata of his culture as is the case for most people in our time, so that his senses, his sensibilities, and his mind can be more open, more innocent, like the child who, in Andersen's tale, saw and said that the emperor was naked and did not have the beautiful clothes that everybody else had persuaded himself to see or, at least, to profess having seen. Thus, the "looseness of repression" of which Freud speaks has to do more with the artist's vision not being fettered and molded completely by the conventional views, with his being more open toward the world and himself, than with the looseness of the repression of any particular libidinal impulse.

Kris makes the additional point that in the genesis of the work of art a *regression to primary-process thought* takes place. Unlike the regression in dreams or in pathological cases, it is controlled by, and in the service of, the ego. According to him, it is this regression which permits the discharge of the repressed impulses mentioned by Freud. The regression to primary-process thought takes place, according to Kris, both in fantastic, free-wandering thought processes and in creative processes, in the former under a condition of ego weakness, in the latter in the service of the ego.[4] But the seeming similarity emphasized by Kris is deceptive, and regression to primary-process thought is not typical of the creative process.

Primary-process thought uses freely displaceable cathexes in the unrestrained tendency toward full discharge of the tension of id drives by the path of (phantasied or hallucinated) wish fulfillment, that is, in the service of the striving to return to a tensionless state. [ftnt. deleted] There are daydreams, reveries, and idly wandering thoughts which are correctly or approximately described by the concept of primary-process thought. What the early stages of the creative process have in common with such reveries is mainly the fact that they, too, wander freely without being bound by the rules and properties of the accepted, conventional, familiar everyday world. In this free wandering they center, however, on the ob-

3. *Gesammelte Werke*, Vol. XI, p. 390.
4. Ernst Kris, "On Preconscious Mental Processes," in David Rapaport, *Organization and Pathology of Thought* (Columbia University Press, New York, 1951), pp. 474–493, especially 485–491.

ject, idea, problem which is the focus of the creative endeavor. What distinguishes the creative process from regression to primary-process thought is that the freedom of the approach is due not to a drive discharge function but to the openness in the encounter with the object of the creative labor.

This openness means that the sensibilities of the person, his mind and his senses, are more freely receptive, less tied to fixed anticipations and sets, and that the object is approached in different ways, from different angles, and not with any fixed purpose to use it for the satisfaction of a particular need, or the testing of one particular expectation or possibility. It seems likely that greater mobility of cathexis is found not only in mental processes serving primarily the discharge of an id drive but also in the described free play of all one's faculties in the open encounter with the world. In the latter case the function of the mobile cathexis is not primarily the discharge of an id drive in order to abolish tension but, on the contrary, the contact with a manifold, inexhaustible reality and the steeping of the person in many different aspects of the world, which takes place by means of thoughts and phantasies as well as by the play of the senses and the motor functions. Of course, the discharge of drive tension and the striving to make contact with some aspect of reality may also occur in the same train of phantasy or freely wandering thought. There may be constant transitions from one to the other, so that at one moment one may predominate, at the next the other.

The relatively undirected, freely wandering play of perception, thought, phantasy thus is not necessarily regressive but can be and often is progressive. Developmentally, the tendency to mere drive discharge and the tendency to relate to the world in many-sided sensory-motor-affective-thinking contacts move in opposite directions: the former tends to decrease, the latter to play an increasingly important role during early childhood. The free play of senses and mind in the open encounter with the world is capable of continued development as more and more aspects of the world are assimilated, while thought serving primarily discharge of tension is indeed in the service of the regressive tendency to abolish the encounter with reality and return to a state of rest and satiation.

.   .   .   .

While man's openness toward the world is clearly apparent in the child's wonder at the many objects in his environment and in his encounters, in which he discovers ever new aspects of the world, in most people the stress of life and the patterns of their culture and social group soon stifle the eager, youthful quest and close the once open mind so that it will encounter only the same, familiar objects. To their knowledgeable "realism" the suggestion of a different approach may appear unrealistic, or a regression to childish modes of behavior, or useless for the serious business of adaptation to reality as they know it. Even if they allow for the possibility of a different view of the world such allowance may be a mere word or thought without weight and substance.

Yet, in contrast to the animals, man is capable of continued growth and development throughout his life if he succeeds in remaining open to the world and capable of allocentric interest. Such openness is the basis of progress and of creative achievement in individual life as well as in the history of mankind.

On the one hand, man lives always in the world of the objects-of-use, in the perspective of secondary autocentricity. He could not exist without this perspective. In providing for his needs the objects-of-use perspective largely replaces the instinct-organization of the animals. But if man ceases to develop the allocentric mode of perception, if he loses that openness of senses and mind which transcends the object-of-use perspective and enables him to relate to others and to the world for the sake of the relationship itself, then his development stagnates in the closed world of secondary autocentricity, and the ontogenetic trend of development toward objectification and allocentric interest comes to a standstill. The basic difference between animal and human mental organization, man's openness toward the world, can be increasingly realized only if man retains and develops the allocentric mode of perception, the first appearance of which is the most important step in the development of perception in the growing child.

JACOB W. GETZELS and MIHALY CSIKSZENTMIHALYI · Concern for Discovery in the Creative Process

[*Getzels is widely known for his groundbreaking work on* Creativity and Intelligence *in collaboration with Phillip Jackson. In recent years he has concentrated on an extensive study of art students at the School of the Art*

SOURCE   From Getzels, J. W., and Csikszentmihalyi, M., "The Creative Artist as an Explorer," published by permission of Transaction, Inc. from Human Intelligence, Hunt, J. McV., Ed. Copyright © 1972, by Transaction, Inc. Pp. 182–183, 187–192.

Institute of Chicago in collaboration with Csikszentmihalyi, a long-time re-
searcher on creativity. The experiment summarized here is one of a series and
it illustrates an unusually thorough approach to the creative process in which
an evaluation of the created product is included. In their full report of the
experiment (see Selected Bibliography, p. 359: Csikszentmihalyi, M., and
Getzels, J. W., 1973), the authors also present evidence, based on interviews
and detailed observations, of the continual interest in exploring and making
discoveries throughout the course of the creative process by their more creative
subjects.]

What do we know about creativity . . . ? So far, most of the answers
have been indirect. Researchers have concentrated on describing creativity
in terms of the common personality characteristics the creative person
possesses: Is he outgoing, or introverted? Is he easygoing, or tense? Are
his values the same as those of most people, or different? The answers to
questions of this sort have helped us develop at least a fragmentary and
tentative model of what the creative man is like. But they told us almost
nothing about what he does when he is creating — what actually happens
when he sits down at the piano, or the typewriter or the sketch pad.

We have now begun to find some of the answers, specifically for the
artist, by observing him in the act of creation. We studied 200 young
artists who were, for the most part, still students at one of the leading art
schools in the country. Some of them were already winning prizes in
competitive shows, exhibiting in professional galleries, or supporting
themselves on the proceeds of their illustrating skills. (We felt that our
subjects deserved to be called "artists" because of their success in an art
school of the highest professional standards and for their perseverance in
pursuit of an artistic career, sometimes at considerable personal sacrifice.)

.   .   .   .

We arranged to have 31 male fine arts students prepare a drawing under
realistic studio conditions. We furnished a number of objects to be drawn;
the artist could select as many or as few as he wanted and arrange them
according to his own preference before beginning to draw. A detailed
account of the artist's behavior was kept, both before he began to draw
and while he was actually working at the easel. After the drawing was
completed, a prolonged interview was held to reconstruct as closely as
possible, the conscious mental process of which the artist had been aware
while engaged in the experiment. Of the great amount of information
collected by these methods, we want to focus here on three very simple
points observed for each artist before he began to draw:

☐ the number of objects picked up and examined;
☐ the extent to which he either chose to draw the same objects that everyone else did, or chose more unusual ones;
☐ the extent to which he explored the objects by stroking, weighing, moving their parts, etc.

Now, what was all this supposed to show? We were, of course, looking for something in particular. Our point of view was to conceive of creativity as a special kind of problem-solving process. Problems can be classified according to answers to the following six questions: Has the problem ever been formulated before by the problem-solver? By anyone else? Is the correct method of solution known to the problem-solver? To anyone else? Is the correct solution itself known to the problem-solver? To anyone else? There are certain problems for which the answer is "no" to all six questions. That is, they have never been formulated before, and, once formulated, there is no available method for their solution, nor is there a single correct answer to be reached. It is the formulation and solution of these problems that requires creativity. Actually, these are only potential problems, since they do not exist as problems until someone formulates them as such. Thus, in the case of this special sort of problem, the central question becomes "How are new problems discovered?" rather than the more usual question "How are existing problems solved?" The first step in creative activity involves the discovery, or formulation, of the problem itself.

Returning to our drawing experiment, we can now see why the artist's pre-drawing behavior was important. In picking up, manipulating, exploring and rearranging the objects to be drawn, the artist was trying to formulate an artistic problem. He might pose a problem in form by exploring how the intricate convolutions of a carburetor are related to the equally intricate rhythms of a bunch of grapes. He might formulate a problem of texture by placing a smooth steel shaft next to a battered baseball glove; or he might pose a problem of color—for example, how to give a relatively monochromatic drawing color variation—by choosing all his objects in a limited yellow-brown color range. Or he might formulate a problem of spatial relationship by rearranging several objects with little textural or color interest—say, three optical lenses in an unusual, apparently unbalanced or asymmetrical pattern. More likely, his problem would be a complex one, involving some combination of these basic elements of form, texture, color and spatial relationship. And of course the drawings were problematic on a meta-visual dimension as well. One artist, for instance, drew a solitary white sphere in one corner of the paper, and a congeries of other objects in the opposite corner. In the interview he disclosed that on one level the drawing tried to resolve the feeling of loneliness when confronted with a group of people.

As the artist drew, photographs were quietly taken of the drawing as it developed on the paper. The students were not required to stick to the problem as originally formulated; they were allowed to alter or rearrange the objects as they went along, or ignore the objects altogether if, after the beginning, a more interesting problem developed within the confines of the drawing itself. The only requirement we placed on the drawings was that they should satisfy the students' own standards. The completed drawings were then reviewed by a group of established, well-known painters; this panel of experts judged the students' work to be generally of high professional quality.

Now to relate creativity to the drawing process. If creativity lies in the artist's ability to discover and formulate a fresh problem, then his behavior in manipulating, exploring and selecting the elements of his problem — in this case, the objects to be drawn — should have been closely related to the creativity displayed in his finished drawing. This we found to be true. The drawings rated most original and artistically most valuable by the panel of established painters were the ones produced by students who had handled the most objects, explored the objects they handled most closely, and selected the most unusual objects to work with during the pre-drawing, problem-formulating period. These students were not necessarily the ones with the greatest technical skill or "craftsmanship" as rated by the same judges. Here, in what we have labelled "discovery-oriented behavior," seemed to lie a key to the creative process. We interpreted this and similar behavior observed during the execution of the drawing itself as the outward manifestations of a specific cognitive attitude, "concern for discovery." The meaning we inferred from our observations was supported by the interview statements, which revealed that the artist himself was consciously pursuing discovery as opposed to, for instance, expression of feeling or reproduction of beauty alone. This concern with discovery set apart those who were interested in formulating and solving new artistic problems from those who were content merely to apply their technical skill to familiar problems capable of more or less pat solutions.

The most skillful drawings, then, were not always the most original. We are all familiar with this distinction. Contemporary painters have stressed the idea that technical skill without a fresh approach, a new vision, is tedious and dead. Both originality and technical skill are de-

Table 1. Correlations Between Discovery Process Variables at the Stage of Problem Formulation and Evaluation of the Artistic Products by Five Artist-Critics (N = 31)

Process Variables	Dimensions of Evaluation		
	Over-all Aesthetic Value (Total 5 Raters)	Originality (Total 5 Raters)	Craftsmanship (Total 5 Raters)
Problem Formulation			
A. Number of objects examined	.48d	.52d	.16
B. Unusualness of objects chosen	.35a	.42c	.22
C. Exploration of objects	.44c	.58e	.34a
Total (ABC)	.40b	.54d	.28
Level of significance = a p < .05 b p < .025 c p < .01 d p < .005 e p < .0005			

sirable, but without the former there is no progress, there can be no change, whether in the field of art, or of science and technology.

By directly observing the artists' exploratory actions as they worked out new relationships between the problematic elements of their drawings, we learned that such activities may be quite reliable predictors of the creativity displayed in the finished product. And as usual, a research finding poses a further question: Is this process of measurable discovery also involved in the wider range of human creativity, in the more memorable "fruits of originality"?

ANNE ROE · Psychological Approaches to Creativity in Science

[Roe is one of the pioneers of modern psychology in the study of the relationship between personality and occupation. She has studied painters, biologists, anthropologists, and physical scientists primarily through the use of projective testing techniques and has collected a good deal of data about per-

SOURCE From Roe, A., "Psychological Approaches to Creativity in Science." Reprinted by permission of New York University Press from Essays on Creativity in the Sciences, edited by M. A. Coler and H. K. Hughes, © New York University 1963, pp. 153–154, 166–172, 177–182.

sonality attributes of persons in these fields. In presenting the following excerpt of her own and others' findings about the personality attributes of scientists, we include her beginning formulation separating the creative process from its final elaboration in the product. Her position that the process is not necessarily identified by the adequacy or uniqueness of the final product differs sharply from that of other authors in this volume and it has some bearing on her conclusion that the creative process is not unique to a few individuals with specific capacities.]

Many discussions of creativity and the creative process would have been clarified if a careful distinction had been made between the process itself and the product or result of the process. The process itself, that is, *what goes on within the individual,* is not directly related to any value which may—then, at some future time, or never—be placed upon the product. It is not related to the absolute uniqueness of the product or even to its adequacy. There are artistic productions and scientific theories which were rejected when they were first offered, only to be acclaimed by later generations; there are others which were acclaimed and have since been rejected; but the process within the individual was as creative in one instance as in the other. Similarly, the discoveries a child makes may be true creations even though many other persons have made them before him.

Such specifications as that of Stein, who defines a creative product as "a novel work that is accepted as tenable or useful or satisfying by a group at some point in time," [ref. deleted] focus upon the social acceptability of the product rather than upon the process. They do, in fact, refer to a particular subclass of results of a more general process, although admittedly to the subclass in which our chief interest resides. This seems to be the most general use of the term "creative" and will be followed here, except that the phrase "creative *process*" will carry no implication regarding the social usefulness or absolute novelty of the results.

The total gamut of scientific thinking includes both the creative process, that is, discovery or invention, and the verification, elaboration, and systematization of the new product. These stages are not always neatly distinguishable; in developing a hypothesis, for example, invention and some verification may alternate rapidly until it finally takes shape and is ready for formal test. We are here concerned primarily with the process itself, with discovery and invention, rather than with its final elaboration.

.   .   .   .

Intelligence. Numerous studies of undergraduate and graduate students in science have indicated that high general intelligence is characteristic of them.[6, Bloom 22,26] A few studies of scientists themselves have also shown this to be the case.[5,20,24]

Studies utilizing traditional factors of intelligence—verbal, quantitative, and spatial—have brought out differences between fields, although a high level of all of these factors is characteristic of most.[4,9,17,19] In general, social scientists and the more theoretically oriented of the physical and biological scientists are relatively higher on verbal tests than experimental physicists or engineers. On the other hand, these latter groups are relatively higher on quantitative tests, along with the theoretical physicists. Tests of spatial and mechanical factors have given rather conflicting results.

The relationship of general intelligence (or any of these factors) to creativity is another matter, however. It seems now to be the consensus that while a relatively high—perhaps about IQ 120—minimum level of intelligence is needed for scientific contributions, either inventive or elaborative, beyond that level other factors are of more importance, and possession of that or higher intelligence is by no means evidence of high creative potential.

Guilford and others have conducted investigations of the relation of aptitude to nonaptitude factors with particular reference to creativity, finding very low correlations between them.[7]

Getzels and Jackson identified a group of high school students in the top 20 percent of their like-sexed age peers on creativity measures but not in the top 20 percent on IQ measures and another group in the top 20 percent on IQ but not on creativity measures. They found that the scholastic achievement of the high creatives was as superior to the generality as was that of the high intelligents.[23] Torrance, in eight partial replications of this study with elementary school, high school, and graduate students, found the same results in six groups. In the other two, the high intelligents had better scholastic records, but in these two schools there was both a somewhat more normal distribution of talent and a greater emphasis in the teaching on traditional, memory-oriented procedures.[25] The implications of these findings for our selection procedures for scholarships and so forth are important and obvious.

Getzels and Jackson interpret their results in the light of Guilford's findings on the difference between divergent and convergent modes of thinking. (Divergent thinking is defined as "generation of information from given information, where the emphasis is upon variety of output from the same source." Convergent thinking is defined as "generation of information from given information, where the emphasis is upon achieving unique or conventionally accepted or best outcomes.") The work by Guilford and Merrifield on the structure of intellect has resulted in a conception of intelligence as factorially much more complex than previous studies had indicated, and they now propose a cubic model, the dimensions referring to *Operations*, with five classes, such as *cognition* and *memory*; *Products*, with six classes, such as *relations* and *transformations*; and *Contents* with four classes, such as *semantic* and *symbolic*. That is, five kinds of operations may be performed on four classes of contents to result in six kinds of products. Fifty-three of the 120 factors indicated by the model have been identified and corresponding tests constructed. It is Guilford's belief that not all of these factors are involved in creative thinking, but that some are of particular importance. These are the abilities in the general category of divergent thinking—fluency, adaptive and spontaneous flexibility, originality, and elaboration—and those in the transformation layer, involving changes in existing or known information or in its use. He points out, however, that "the weight to be given to any factors in connection with particular instances or classes of invention is a matter of empirical investigation."[8]

There are no replications of Guilford's work and no other studies of the structure of intellect which are remotely comparable to his in extent, complexity, and sophistication. The sheer number of factors involved is rather staggering in its implications for genetic interpretation, for any kind of selection, and like possibilities. Since Guilford has now succeeded in pulling the whole together into a well-conceptualized structure, it may well receive considerably more general acceptance. Guilford's tests were developed to coincide with hypotheses regarding the nature of the creative process, but as yet there have been no studies which could demonstrate whether or not creative persons are in fact consistently high in the tests believed to be related to creativity. Allen, Guilford, and Merrifield have reported a study of the opinions of thirty-five research scientists and engineers and of fifty nonscientists regarding the relative importance for scientific work of twenty-eight of these factors. The subjects were given nontechnical definitions of each factor, with an example of the mental activity believed involved, and asked to rank them for their importance to the creative scientist. Rank correlation was .87. The scientists themselves rated factors in the product category of transformations highest, particularly the redefinition factors, which are also in the convergent-production category. Divergent-production factors were not ranked as high as the authors had expected.[1]

Imagery. Studies of imagery are out of style at the present time among psychologists, but there is evidence in one study of rather sharp differences in preferred types of imagery. Biologists and experimental physicists seem to rely quite heavily upon visual imagery, which may be of a very elaborate sort. Theoretical physicists and social scientists tend to use auditory-verbal imagery predominantly. All groups studied reported a considerable amount of imageless thinking, particularly at crucial points.[16]

Some recent studies on the electroencephalograph and imagery have shown a relationship between the amount of alpha rhythm present and the extent to which visual imagery is used during thought. It is suggested that these differences are related to differences in verbal, as opposed to practical, intelligence.[13]

Gray-Walters, in a personal communication, suggests that there may be a relationship between variability of brain rhythms and the amount of creativity manifested by the individual, but this has not been tested experimentally. It is a most intriguing suggestion, and if it can be demonstrated, would open many possibilities.

Bartlett, in a discussion of the relationship between visual imagery and thought, suggests that visualists probably use more images than are really necessary. Perhaps some may be irrelevant to the immediate purpose and yet spark new discoveries. This could be thought of as a special variety of preconscious thought.[3]

Interests, Values, and Types. Interest tests, such as those of Strong and Kuder, show rather clear differences between scientists and nonscientists and among scientists of different specialties. Most of the studies with interest inventories on tests have been made with students. These are reviewed in Super and Bachrach and summarized as follows:

> The literature on scientific interest shows that this type of interest develops relatively early in life, that extremes of socio-economic status tend to inhibit or prevent the development of interests which are appropriate to scientific aptitudes, that scientific interest is characterized initially by interest in concrete things or activities and is relatively stable, that successful science students show interest profiles similar to those of successful workers in science fields, that the various fields of science have distinctive but related interests, and that the interests, while not predictive of success in these fields, are predictive of occupational choice and stability.[21]

Highly creative men tend to get high scores on femininity scales, and highly creative women on masculinity scales. Such men are more sensitive than most and have higher aesthetic interests; such women are more interested in things and ideas than other women. Highly creative groups tend to get relatively high scores on both theoretic and aesthetic values.

MacKinnon has reported that the Myer-Briggs Type Indicator [ref. deleted] differentiates sharply between creative and noncreative groups with respect to sensation vs. intuitive attitudes. On this test, 75 percent of the general population show a preference for sensation, but 100 percent of architects, 100 percent of mathematicians, 93 percent of research scientists, and 90 percent of writers in their creative groups showed a preference for intuition.[12]

Personality. A number of fairly recent studies using different techniques, different samplings, and having somewhat different purposes have attacked the problem of the personality characteristics of creative scientists, in contrast to those of the generality or to such groups as scholars or administrators.[2,5,12,18, McClelland 22] It is quite striking, then, that there is almost no conflict in the results. While most of the studies are not directly comparable to any of the others, the psychological interpretations are in close accord or dovetail very satisfactorily. These are summarized under general groups of characteristics below.

Creative persons are unusually open to experience. They are particularly observant and often see things in unusual ways. They are extremely curious. Their willingness to see what is there applies to perceptions of self as well as to the outside world, making it possible for them to admit unconventional thoughts, accept and reconcile apparent opposites, and be tolerant of ambiguities. [ref. deleted] Disorder does not too greatly dismay them, but they like to be able to resolve it. They prefer complexity and manage to come to an aesthetic ordering of experience.

They are highly independent in judgment, thought, and action, and they need and assume autonomy. They are willing to take a calculated risk, provided that more than chance is involved and that people are not involved. They are self-reliant and not subject to group standards and control. This may lead to unconventional behavior as well as to originality and unconventionality of thought. They do not accept authority on its own terms. This originality and unconventionality do not make for the stereotype of "adjustment," for organization men, or for all-American boys. One of the most disturbing aspects of the Getzels and Jackson study[23] and of other studies of Torrance[25] are the findings that the highly creative are definitely not preferred by their teachers or their peers and that sanctions are frequently invoked against them, though admittedly they often provoke them. Jex and Merrill found that the ability to get high scores on ingenuity tests was antagonistic to whatever is involved in high ratings of teachers by supervisors or principals. [ref. deleted]

They are high, but perhaps not extremely high, in ego strength, and their superegos are not compulsive. They are capable of considerable discipline and of great perseverance. They tend to be rather dominant.

They are markedly preoccupied with things and ideas and not with people. (This applies to some social scientists, though not to most.) They dislike emotionally toned preoccupations outside of their own field.

They are not gregarious or talkative. (This also does not apply to social scientists.) They are especially sensitive to interpersonal aggression and have marked distaste for interpersonal controversy in any form. They prefer to deal with disturbing instinctual drives by repressing them or avoiding situations which arouse them.

Their notable persistence indicates the presence of strong motivation, but analysis of the sources has not progressed very far. This is one of the most important factors contributing to the production of a scientist, and it must vary from one scientist to another. There has been considerable discussion of the probability of "neurotic" sources. I am sure that the motivation has a neurotic basis in many instances; I am equally sure that it need not always have, but this negative is much harder to document. Kubie has stated,

> [Not only does] a scientist's ability to endure the prolonged frustration and uncertainties of scientific research depend on neurotic components in his personality (both masked and overt), but also there are significant relationships between masked neurotic components in the personality of an apparently normal scientist, and such things as (a) the field of work which he chooses; (b) the problems within that field which he chooses to investigate; (c) the clarity with which he habitually uses his native capacity for logical thinking; (d) the ways in which he attacks scientific problems; (e) the scientific causes which he espouses; (f) the controversies in which he becomes entangled and how he fights; and (g) the joy or sorrow which he derived from the work itself and also from his ultimate success or failure. Thus over the intervening years I have seen men of imagination and erudition whose scientific lives were nonetheless baffled and unproductive, and also men with lesser gifts who seemed to function freely, creatively, and productively; scientists who were happy in spite of failure, and others who became depressed in spite of acknowledged and recognized success.[10,11]

Many have successfully extrapolated a personal problem into a problem to be studied scientifically. I see no cause for dismay in this—in fact, it seems to me to be one of the major inventions of the species.

There has been some discussion of the possible deleterious effects for creativity if psychotherapy modifies a neurotic structure that may be involved in an individual instance. It seems to be the general opinion that creativity is more likely to be enhanced by successful therapy than not. [refs. deleted]

. . . .

. . . it would appear that [the creative] process is not unique to a few individuals possessing only one or a limited number of specific capacities. Rather, it would seem that this is one of the ways in which humans interact with their environment, perhaps the most intricate way of all. It would appear to be a form of behavior of which all normal humans are capable to some degree, but one which is clearly manifested more often and more effectively by some persons than by others and more easily under some circumstances than under others. Such sources of variation as are known to us have been discussed. But what is the process itself?

Certainly it is akin to other modes of thought—indeed to speak of different modes of thought is probably marking off arbitrary boundaries on a natural continuum. This is a necessary procedure in analysis, however, and it introduces serious difficulties only when the categories become conceptually reified. [ref. deleted] The creative process is probably closest to problem solving, but it differs from it in a number of ways. In problem solving, the immediate goal is a specific one, and logical and orderly modes of approach are appropriate—if not always used. In the creative process there is no such clear goal as a rule, and illogical modes of thought are common. Newell, Shaw, and Simon consider that "creative activity appears simply to be a special class of problem-solving activity characterized by novelty, unconventionality, persistence, and difficulty in problem formulation."[14] A major differentiation is the extent of the involvement of the whole person; in the creative process this is very great, and noncognitive and emotional elements loom large, but they are a barrier to effective problem solving. (The whole range of scientific thinking embraces both of these, of course, but we are here concerned with discovery and invention rather than with elaboration.)

Some studies of the process have analyzed it into a series of more or less discrete steps, but perhaps more advance can be made if it is considered as essentially a single action. Among artists, scientists, and others for whom creative production is a way of life, it emerges from a background of absorption in a topic and begins in a state of "imaginative muddled suspense." As Ghiselin has put it, "the first stirrings and advances of even the most strictly intellectual creative achievements appear to be realized primarily in sensory or passional terms, or in both."[22] There seems to be a vague sort of manipulative play with incommunicable entities — visual, muscular, rarely if at all verbal — in this stage. There is no known technique for speeding up or calling forth the coalescence of all this into a new configuration. It usually comes without an immediate voluntary effort and almost invariably during a moment of dispersed attention, but conscious efforts to disperse attention to permit or facilitate this resolution have not been successful. Too intensive a concentration of conscious attention upon the problem seems to prevent that recourse to the depths of the person that is required. The apprehension of this new configuration, often called the moment of insight, typically comes suddenly and quite completely, although not necessarily so. The experience of insight may be a profoundly moving one, with a sense of great self-realization and intense aesthetic gratification. It is usually accompanied by feelings of certainty which may or may not prove to be valid. In science, insights must be subjected to verification.

Since the activities preceding the emergence of this new configuration are largely not fully conscious, study of them directly is remarkably difficult. Psychoanalytic theory distinguishes between primary and secondary processes of thinking and assigns the inventive phase largely to the primary process, elaboration and verification to the secondary process. Primary-process thinking is nonlogical, and makes use of such mechanisms as are common in dreaming — condensation, displacement, symbolization, and so on. When such ideas first arise in consciousness, they may take various forms — fragments of words or visual images, schematic patterns, a sense of relationship. The secondary process is logical and rational and under voluntary control.[15]

The very creative person is one who can permit himself indulgence in the primitive modes of thought of the primary process, and who has the ability to return easily to rational thought. Persons who are able to do this, who come up with many original ideas, may not also be equally interested in, or capable of, the disciplined and critical procedures required for logical development or evaluation of their ideas. They are "idea men," leaving the sometimes slow and laborious procedures of verification to others. There are also those whose chief contributions in science — and these contributions can be major — are seldom tinged by primary-process activities, but who have spent great effort and much time on the arduous work of elaboration. Finally, there are those who are capable of both to a high degree. These are very few and very precious.

If it is true, however, as I believe, that there is real creative potential in all human beings and that our cultural institutions, rooted in ancient misconceptions of the nature of man and his place in the universe, are enormously more effective in repressing it than encouraging it, our problem is not just to find the people who have somehow been able to resist these pressures. It is also to find ways to change the cultural climate.

References

1. Allen, M. S., Guilford, J. P., and Merrifield, P. R. *Rep. Psychol. Lab.*, **25** (1960).
2. Barron, F. "Originality in Relation to Personality and Intellect," *Journal of Personality*, 25:730–42 (1957).
3. Bartlett, R. J. "Does the Psychogalvanic Phenomenon Indicate Emotion?" *British Journal of Psychology*, **18**:23 (1927).
4. Castore, G. R. *A Screening and Selection Battery for Prospective Physicists and Chemical Engineers.* Unpublished doctoral dissertation. Pennsylvania State College, 1948.
5. Cattell, R. B., and Drevdahl, J. E. "A Comparison of the Personality Profile (16 P. F.) of Eminent Researchers with that of Eminent Teachers and Administrators, and of the General Population," *British Journal of Psychology*, **46**:248–61 (1955).
6. Cole, C. C., Jr. *Encouraging Scientific Talent.* College Entrance Examination Board (mimeographed), 1955.
7. Guilford, J. P., Christensen, P. R., Frick, J. W., and Merrifield, P. R. *Rep. Psychol. Lab.*, **20** (1957).
8. Guilford, J. P., and Merrifield, P. R. *Rep. Psychol. Lab.*, **24** (1960).
9. Harmon, L. R. *Ability Patterns in Seven Science Fields.* Technical Report No. 10, Washington: National Research Council, 1955.
10. Kubie, L. S. "Some Unsolved Problems of the Scientific Career," *American Scientist*, **41**:596–613 (1953).
11. ———. "Some Unsolved Problems of the Scientific Career II," *American Scientist*, **42**:104–12 (1954).
12. MacKinnon, D. W. Colloquium on Problems and Responsibilities of U.S. Colleges in the Research for Talented Students, College Entrance Examination Board, New York, N.Y. (1959).
13. Mundy-Castle, A. C. "Electrophysicological Correlates of Intelligence," *Journal of Personality*, **26**:184–99 (1958).
14. Newell, A., Shaw, J. C., and Simon, H. A. *The Processes of Creative Thinking.* Santa Monica, Calif.: Rand Corporation, 1958.
15. Rapaport, D. *Organization and Pathology of Thought.* New York: Columbia University Press, 1951.
16. Roe, A. "A Study of Imagery in Research Scientists," *Journal of Personality*, **19**:459–70 (1951).
17. ———. "A Psychologist Examines 64 Eminent Scientists," *Scientific American*, **187** (5):21–25 (1952).
18. ———. *The Making of a Scientist.* New York: Dodd, Mead & Co., 1952.
19. Schultz, M., and Angoff, W. H. Educational Testing Service Research Bulletin RB, 54–15 (May 25, 1954).
20. Smith, M. "Eminent Men," *Scientific Monthly*, **48**:554–62 (1939).
21. Super, D., and Bachrach, P. *Scientific Careers and Vocational Development Theory.* New York: Teachers College, Columbia University, 1957.
22. Taylor, C. W. (ed.) *The 1955 University of Utah Research Conference on the Identification of Creative Scientific Talent.* Salt Lake City: University of Utah Press, 1956. Includes Bloom, S.,

"Report on Creativity Research at the University of Utah," p. 182; McClelland, D. C., "The Calculated Risk: An Aspect of Scientific Performance," p. 96.

23. Taylor, C. W. (ed.) *The Third (1959) University of Utah Research Conference on the Identification of Creative Scientific Talent.* Salt Lake City: University of Utah Press, 1959. Includes: Getzels, J. W., and Jackson, P. W., "The Highly Intelligent and the Highly Creative Adolescent: A Summary of Some Research Findings"; Guilford, J. P., "Intellectual Resources and Their Value as Seen by Creative Scientists," p. 128; Smith, W. R., "Favorable and Unfavorable Working Conditions Reported by Scientists at Two Research Centers," p. 250; Sprecher, T. B., "A Proposal for Identifying the Meaning of Creativity," p. 29; Sprecher, T. B. (Chairman) Committee Report on Criteria of Creativity; Taylor, C. M., and Ghiselin, B., "Analyses of Multiple Criteria of Creativity and Productivity of Scientists," p. 5.

24. Terman, L. M. "Scientists and Non-Scientists in a Group of 800 Gifted Men," *Psychological Monographs,* **68** (No. 7, 1954).

25. Torrance, E. P. Research Memo BER–60–18. Bureau of Educational Research, College of Education, University of Minnesota (1960).

26. Wolfle, D., and Oxtoby, T. "Distributions of Ability of Students Specializing in Different Fields," *Science,* **116**:311–14 (1952).

DONALD W. MacKINNON · Architects, Personality Types, and Creativity

[*MacKinnon used an extensively cross-checked set of criteria to select a relatively large number of creative American architects for personality study at the Institute of Personality Assessment and Research at the University of California at Berkeley. The following selection is his most recent article about the results of this research, a report in which he also attempts an overall theoretical formulation for the first time. This formulation is based on Otto Rank's character typology. Other results are touched on in the Barron selection in this volume and in earlier articles by MacKinnon listed in the Selected Bibliography for this chapter.*]

. . . it is hard to realize that when a few years ago I turned my attention to the problem of creativity I did so without once thinking of the implications of Rankian theory for the work I was about to undertake. . . .

It was only after all of the data had been collected and I had spent long hours pondering their meaning that suddenly I was struck by a congruence between what I had actually done in designing the experiment

SOURCE From MacKinnon, D. W., "Personality and the Realization of Creative Potential," *American Psychologist,* 1965, *Vol. 20, pp. 273–281. Copyright 1965 by the American Psychological Association. Reprinted by permission of publisher and author.*

and in selecting the samples for study and what I would have done had I recalled at the time what Rank had written about the development of creative potential and individuality.

. . . .

The major relevance of Rank's theories for our study of creative persons is to be found in his conceptualization of three stages or phases in man's winning his own individuality and in realizing his own creative potential. Rank writes of these sometimes as stages or phases of development, sometimes as three types of persons which like all typological descriptions presuppose that the types are never fully actualized. When formulated as types they were labeled by Rank as the adapted type, the neurotic type, and the creative type. He also referred to them as the average or normal man, the conflicted or neurotic person, and the artist or man of will and deed.

The first unconscious — or should I say preconscious? — congruence between Rank's typology and the study which I shall report was the decision in studying creativity in architects to draw three samples from the profession, hopefully differing in the degree to which they had maximized and realized their creative potential.

But first, why should architects be chosen as the profession to be studied? It seemed to me, and to my collaborator in this research, Wallace B. Hall, that architects might as a group reveal that which is most characteristic of the creative person. If an architect's designs are to give delight, the architect must be an artist; if they are to be technologically sound and efficiently planned he must also be something of a scientist, at least an applied scientist or engineer. Yet clearly if one has any knowledge of architects and their practice, one realizes that it does not suffice that an architect be at one and the same time artist and scientist if he is to be highly creative in the practice of his profession. He must also to some extent be businessman, lawyer, advertiser, author-journalist, psychiatrist, educator, and psychologist (MacKinnon, 1962b).

To obtain our first sample of highly creative architects we asked five professors of architecture at the University of California, Berkeley, each working independently, to nominate the 40 most outstandingly creative architects in the country.

Had there been perfect agreement among the nominators, each would have mentioned the same 40. All told they gave us 86 names. Of these 86, 13 were nominated by all five panel members, 9 were nominated by four, 11 were nominated by three, 13 by two, while 40 were individual nominations by a single panel member. Subsequently, each panel member rated the creativity of those not nominated by him originally, provided he knew them well enough to do so.

On the basis of the mean rating of their creativeness and the summary statements as to why each had been nominated, which the panel members had also given us, the architects were listed in the order in which we would invite them to participate in the study. Our hope had been to win the cooperation of the first 40 whom we invited, but to get 40 acceptances we had to write 64 architects.

The 40 who accepted our invitation came to Berkeley in groups of 10, where they were subjects of an intensive assessment. But what of the 24 who declined our invitation to be studied? Are they more or less creative than the 40 who were willing to be assessed, or indistinguishable from them in their level of creativeness? When the nominating panel's mean ratings of creativity of each of the 64 architects were converted to standard scores, and the means for the 24 versus the 40 were compared, they were found to be identical: 50.0 ($SD = 9.9$) for the 24 not assessed as against 50.1 ($SD = 9.5$) for the 40 assessed architects.

We can make no claim to have studied the most creative architects in the country. We are assured, however, that the 40 whom we did assess, and to whom I shall hereafter refer as Architects I, are as a group indistinguishable in the level of their creativeness from the 24 who declined to be studied.

But to have limited our study to the assessment of 40 architects, each of whom was recognized as highly creative, would not have permitted us to say anything with confidence about the personality correlates of creativity. For the distinguishing characteristics of this sample — and there were many that we found — might well have nothing to do with their creativeness. Obviously the design of our study required that the profession of architecture be widely sampled beyond the assessed 40 Architects I, in order to discover whether and to what extent the traits of creative architects are characteristic of architects in general or peculiar to those who are highly creative.

To this end the *Directory of Architects* published in 1955 was searched in order to select two additional samples of architects both of which would match with respect to age and geographic location of practice the assessed sample of 40. The first of the supplementary samples, which I shall call Architects II, is composed of 43 architects, each of whom met the additional requirement that he had had at least 2 years of work experience and association with one of the 64 originally nominated and invited creative architects. The other additional sample, which I shall label Architects III, is composed of 41 architects, none of whom had ever worked with any of the nominated creative architects.

Architects I, II, and III were selected in this manner in hopes of tapping a range of creative talent sufficiently wide to be fairly representative of the profession as a whole. To determine whether or not we had succeeded, ratings on a 7-point scale of the creativity of all 124 architects were obtained from six groups of architects and architectural experts: the 5 members of the original nominating panel at the University of California, 19 professors of architecture distributed nationwide, 6 editors of the major American architectural journals, 32 Architects I, 36 Architects II, and 28 Architects III. The mean ratings of creativity for the three groups are: for Architects I, 5.46; for Architects II, 4.25; and for Architects III, 3.54. The differences are in the expected direction and are statistically highly significant ($p < .001$). In other words, the three groups do indeed represent significantly different levels of creativeness (MacKinnon, 1962b). At the same time, however, it must be noted that the three samples show an overlap in their judged creativity; they are not discontinuous groups, but, combined, approximate a normal distribution of judged creativeness ranging from a low of 1.9 to a high of 6.5 on a 7-point rating scale (MacKinnon, 1963).

In view of the approximately normal distribution of the rated creativity for the total sample of 124 architects, and with the further evidence that Architects I, II, and III do indeed represent significantly different levels of creativity, we have examined our data by two major means: (a) computing the correlations between the external judgments of the creativeness of our 124 architects and their scores on a multiplicity of traits, and (b) comparing differences of mean scores among Architects I, II, and III on these same assessed variables.

I must first point out, however, that our data are not so extensive for Architects II and III as for Architects I. Where the latter experienced a 3-day-long assessment, the former groups, working independently and at home, spent about 6 or 7 hours completing a selection of tests, questionnaires, and inventories from our total assessment battery. Under these conditions some tests, notably tests of intelligence and timed tests, could not be administered to Architects II and III.

Having recruited for study three groups of architects which, as it turned out, are discriminably different with respect to their mean level of actualized and manifest creativeness, the question I wish now to raise is whether and to what extent the traits and characteristics of Architects I, II, and III correspond to, and in that sense confirm, the qualities attributed by Rank to his three stages or types of personality structure and creative development or, on the other hand, fail to do so.

This is neither the time nor the place to attempt a full explication of Rank's theories. Instead I shall limit myself to a brief discussion of those aspects of his thought about which one must be reasonably clear if one is to understand his ideas about the constructive formation of personality and creative development.

Rank sees man as moving through life from the trauma of birth to the trauma of death. The character of this journey and the nature of the personality which develops en route are shaped and determined in large measure by the interaction and varying strengths of man's two basic and opposed fears: the fear of life and the fear of death.

The fear of life is basically the fear of separation, experienced first as the primal anxiety of the birth trauma which separates the infant from the mother, the womb, the wholeness of which it was formerly a part. The fear of life drives a person backward to earlier states of symbiotic union, symbolized as union with the mother, as well as to later stages of dependence on other persons and groups of persons more powerful than the self. The fear of life is the fear of having to stand alone and be alone, the fear of partialization and differentiation of oneself from the collectivity, the fear of standing out from the mass, the fear of all that living one's own life entails, the fear of true independence, the fear of becoming oneself and of being oneself.

But the life fear, the fear of separation and independence, is opposed by the fear of death, the fear of union and dependence, which makes one afraid of all that the life fear drives one toward—for symbiotic union is experienced as a sort of death, a regression, a return to the womb, a loss of individuality, indeed a loss of life itself.

Thus, Rank sees man as characterized by a basic ambitendency: driven by life fear to union with others, to relationships of symbiosis and dependence, to losing oneself and one's identity in the collectivity—and, on the other hand, driven by death fear to an assertion of oneself and one's individuality, to a separation of oneself from others, to independence and uniqueness. And Rank takes as a measure of the development of a person the extent to which he achieves a constructive integration of these conflicting trends.

Central to this theory of development of the person are Rank's concepts of will and guilt. Will is, for him, the integrative power of the personality as a whole, "a positive guiding organization and integration of the self which utilizes creatively, as well as inhibits and controls the instinctual drives [1945, p. 112]." It is first experienced by the child negatively as counterwill—as resistance to the restraints, demands, frustrations which he experiences from the parents because of his very dependence upon them. But the assertion of his counterwill against their will causes him to experience feelings of guilt, since he is still bound to them by dependence upon them, identification with them, love and gratitude for them.

If, in this process of separation in which the will of the parents is opposed by the child's counterwill and self-assertion, the parents accept the child as a more or less separate individual, granting him autonomy and opportunity to assert his own will, the child moves healthily toward the attainment of a secure sense of self and the expression of positive will in selecting, organizing, modifying, and recreating his own experiences. Being accepted by the parents as separate and different from them, the child does not feel separated from them in the sense of being rejected by them but has the experience of separating himself from them through exercising his own will, and consequently he wins for himself some measure of individuality.

Not all children in the expression of their counterwill experience so fortunate a fate. Not accepted by their parents as separate and different, they experience their will as a source of continuing guilt rather than of growing ego strength. They feel rejected, and thus are not able through an exercise of positive will to achieve for themselves that measure of separation which is the prerequisite for individuality.

Though every child experiences some measure of counterwill, there are many, Rank believes, who quite early are able so to identify their will with that of their parents as to be spared the pain of developing their own will further, and of developing the guilt which comes from striving for separation. Those who thus easily adapt to the will of their parents may later also find it easy to adapt to the will of society and to incorporate within themselves its dictates and its norms. Such a person, who now wills what he was earlier compelled to will, represents what Rank calls the adapted type. Rank sees this as a type of adjustment which often is established relatively early in the life of an individual, and one beyond which Rank's "normal, average man" never goes.

For such a person there is no strong drive toward individuation and also no conflict over conformance to the social norms. Such an adjustment guarantees a relatively harmonious working of the personality. Rank does not think of such a person as consciously conforming for the sake of expediency, but as naturally conforming to society because he never seriously thought of doing anything else. He is largely one with his surroundings and feels himself to be a part of them. Munroe (1955) has suggested that the adapted type's "relations with his society are reminiscent of the symbiotic relationship between person and environment which prevailed in the womb. They represent the first and easiest solution of the problem set by birth [p. 585]."[1]

The adapted type's form of adjustment, according to Rank (1945), "permits fewer possibilities of conflict but also fewer creative possibilities of any kind. . . . He has the consciousness of individuality but at the same time the feeling of likeness, of unity, which makes the relation to the outer world pleasant [p. 264]." [ftnt. deleted]

The next step or phase on the road to the development of individuality and the realization of creative potential is characterized, as Rank (1945) sees it, "by the feeling of division in the personality, through the disunity of will and counter-will, which means a struggle (moral) against the compulsion of the outer world as well as an inner conflict between the two wills [p. 264; see Footnote 3]." At this level of development the person strikes out on his own and attempts to form goals, ideals, and moral and ethical standards other than the socially sanctioned ones. He begins to take new attitudes towards himself and towards the world. There are here possibilities of development not achieved at the first level. If they are realized the person moves to the third level of creative and productive functioning, becoming the creative type. But if they are not realized, due to the inability of the person on this second level to resolve his conflicts, he remains stuck there plagued by self-criticism and feelings of guilt and inferiority.

Unlike the first type who "accepts reality with its demands and so adjusts his own individuality that he perceives and can accept himself as part of reality [Rank, 1945, p. 266]," the second type is conflicted in the sense that his own separateness is great enough to preclude his complete union with society, yet not sufficiently developed to permit him to win through to a creative expression of his own individuality. He is, in Rank's phrase, "a conflicted and neurotic man" whose creative potential is, however, greater than that of the average man.

Rank (1945) describes the third and highest level of development as "characterized by a unified working together of the three fully developed powers, the will, the counter-will, and the ideal formation born from the conflict between them which itself has become a goal-setting, goal-seeking force. Here the human being . . . is again at one with himself; what he

1. From Ruth L. Munroe, *Schools of Psychoanalytic Thought,* copyright 1955 by Holt, Rinehart and Winston, Incorporated.

does, he does fully and completely in harmony with all his powers and his ideals [p. 264; see Footnote 3]." Rank calls him variously the artist, the man of will and deed, the creative type.

The correspondences, if any are to be found, between our three samples of architects and Rank's three stages of the development of individuality would, I think we would agree, be expected to be found between Architects I and the creative type, the artist or man of will and deed; between Architects II and the conflicted or neurotic type; and between Architects III and the adapted type, the normal or average man.

The areas or domains in which we might search for differences between our three samples, and correspondences between them and the Rankian types, are several. I shall limit myself, however, to a discussion of three: (a) the nature of the individual's socialization and his interpersonal behavior, (b) the level of richness or complexity of his psychological development, and (c) the degree of personal soundness or psychological health which he manifests.

The presentation of such a complex body of data as we have collected poses a difficult problem of communication in a lecture like this. In the interest of obtaining as much simplicity and clarity as possible I shall, in reporting differences between groups, not present any actual mean scores. I shall instead merely indicate the nature of the differences, discussing, however, unless otherwise indicated, only differences that are significant at or beyond the .05 level of confidence.

The first domain in which one might expect to find differences between our three samples and the Rankian types is, as I have suggested, the area of socialization and interpersonal behavior. The most socialized, and consequently the least individualized, of Rank's three types is the adapted man. His adjustment to society, his incorporation of its norms within himself, and his identification with his surroundings is the most complete.

On the Heilbrun keys (Gough & Heilbrun, 1965) of the Adjective Check List (Gough, 1961), which measure several of the needs first conceptualized by Murray (1938), Architects III (the least creative group) score higher than Architects I (the most creative) on abasement, affiliation, deference, endurance, intraception, and nurturance—and on all of these dimensions the mean scores of Architects II are intermediate between the higher scores of Architects III and the lower scores of Architects I.

It is the other way around, though, on the scales measuring aggression and autonomy. On these dimensions the most creative group scores significantly higher than Architects II, who, in turn, score higher than Architects III.

Since the California Psychological Inventory (CPI; Gough, 1957a) was expressly developed to measure significant dimensions of interpersonal behavior, one would also expect the three groups of architects to reveal differences on this instrument congruent with the Rankian differentiations, and indeed they do. On every one of the Class II scales of the Inventory, scales designed to measure various aspects of socialization, Architects III earn higher mean scores than the highly creative Architects I. That is, they score higher on Socialization (So), Responsibility (Re), Self-Control (Sc), Tolerance (To), Good Impression (Gi), and Communality (Cm). And it is of interest to note that the mean scores of Architects II on all of these scales are intermediate between the higher scores of Architects III and the lower scores of Architects I, though the differences between the mean scores of Architects II and Architects III, and of Architects II and Architects I, are not significant.

On the Fundamental Interpersonal Relations Orientations-Behavior questionnaire (FIRO-B; Schutz, 1958), the greater socialization of the least creative Architects III is further demonstrated. On scales which measure the expressed desire to include others in one's activities (E^I), the expressed desire to be included in others' activities (W^I), as well as the expressed desire to be controlled by others, Architects III score higher than Architects I. The order is reversed, however, on the scale that measures the expressed desire to control others (E^C): There the most creative Architects I score higher than Architects II, and Architects II in turn higher than Architects III.

Something of the intermediate, ambitendent, conflicted nature of Architects II, congruent with the Rankian description of the second type, is likewise revealed by their scores on the FIRO-B. While they differ from Architects III in revealing less desire to include others in their activities, they are not distinguishable from them in the desire to be, themselves, included in others' activities. Similarly, while Architects II do not differ from Architects III in their desire to be controlled by others, they do differ from them in showing more desire to control others.

With respect to the number of organizations to which they belong, Architects I differ from both Architects II and Architects III in belonging to fewer social groups. Though on this measure of social belongingness Architects II do differ from Architects I, they do not differ from Architects I on an Institute of Personality Assessment and Research (IPAR) scale which measures independence (Barron, 1953c). On this scale, however, Architects I score as significantly more independent than Architects III. The obverse is revealed on the Vassar scale of social integration (Webster, Freedman,

& Heist, 1962), with Architects III showing, in accordance with expectation, a greater measure of social integration than do Architects I.

An examination of the Q values of items, sorted first to describe themselves in their architectural practice and second to describe the ideal architect, reveals differences among the three groups that confirm and elaborate the picture already obtained.

Architects I see, as most characteristic of themselves and of the ideal architect, some inner artistic standard of excellence and a sensitive appreciation of the fittingness of architectural solutions to that standard.

Architects II apparently place more stress upon the efficient execution of architecture, seeing as most saliently characteristic of the ideal the possession of that intellective ability, "strong powers of spatial visualization," which clearly is so crucial to the effective practice of architecture.

Architects III, unlike both Architects I and Architects II, choose as most characteristic of the ideal architect not the meeting of one's own standard but rather the standard of the profession. Once again they show that strong sense of responsibility to the group, rather than to themselves or to some inner ideal of perfection which is uniquely theirs (MacKinnon, 1963).

In summary, in the domains of socialization and interpersonal behavior we do indeed find a congruence between the differences revealed by our three samples of architects and the differences attributed by Rank to his three stages of the development of individuality.

With respect to the second domain on which I propose to compare our samples with Rank's types, namely, the level of richness or complexity of psychological development, we should be prepared to find increasing richness and complexity as we move from Architects III to Architects II to Architects I. At the same time if our data match or confirm Rank's descriptions, we should not expect to find such clear and sharp distinctions between Architects I and II as between Architects I and III, for, with respect to many traits and attributes, Rank considers the conflicted neurotic type to be close to the creative type since it is only out of such richness, and complexity, and conflict as the former experiences that the creative integrations of the latter are achieved.

On nine scales, each of which in its own way measures some aspect of psychological richness and complexity, Architects I do indeed score significantly higher than Architects III, yet despite the general tendency for Architects II to score slightly lower on these scales than Architects I, on only three of them do they score significantly lower. These measures of psychological richness and complexity are: the Psychological-Mindedness scale (Py), the Flexibility scale (Fx), and the Femininity scale (Fe) of the CPI; the Feminine Interests scale (*Mf*) of the Minnesota Multiphasic Personality Inventory (MMPI; Hathaway & McKinley, 1945); the Barron-Welsh Art scale (Barron & Welsh, 1952) of the Welsh Figure Preference Test (Welsh, 1959); the IPAR Preference for Complexity scale (CS; Barron, 1953a), and the IPAR (0–4) esthetic sensitivity scale (Gough, 1957b); and the perceptiveness and intuitiveness scales of the Myers-Briggs Type Indicator (Myers, 1962).

The next question to which I wish to direct our attention is whether there is any evidence in our data that the psychological richness and complexity, which both Architects II and I experience, is more effectively managed by Architects I than by Architects II. This is what we should expect to find if Architects I exemplify the creative type and Architects II the conflicted neurotic type, and if the characteristics attributed to these types by Rank arc valid.

First we may note that Architects II give evidence of less emotional stability or personal soundness and at the same time manifest more anxiety than either of the other two groups. On the IPAR scale of Personal Soundness (S) they score lower, and on the Taylor (1953) Manifest Anxiety scale they score higher than both Architects I and Architects III. Although the following differences do not reach statistical significance, they all point in the same direction: Architects II score higher than either Architects I or Architects III on the mean of the eight clinical scales of the MMPI, higher on the Welsh Anxiety factor scale of the MMPI, and higher on two IPAR scales developed by Block: Bimodal Ego Control scale (indicative of vacillation between under- and over-control of impulse) and the scale designed to measure psychoneurotic tendencies (PN). On the latter scale Architects II score significantly higher than Architects III.

There is, then, unequivocal evidence as well as some suggestive data that Architects II are more conflicted and more psychologically disturbed than either Architects I or III. We must note, however, that on several of these measures of tension, conflict, and anxiety, Architects I stand very close to Architects II. That being the case, what is it that gives them a greater capacity to handle the psychic turbulence which they also experience? On the two tests in our assessment battery which come closest to being measures of will, as Rank conceives of it as the integrative power of the person as a whole, Architects I earn the highest mean score. These are the Ego Strength (*Es*) scale of the MMPI developed by Barron (1953b), and the IPAR scale of Self-Assertiveness (Hb) developed by Gough, though I am certain that neither of my colleagues in developing these measures had any thought that their scales had anything to do with the Rankian concept of will.

Just as we have found in our test data a considerable degree of confirmation of the Rankian descriptions of the stages of development of individuality and the realization of creative potential, so also in the life-history protocols of our subjects we have obtained supportive evidence for many of the kinds of early interpersonal experiences which Rank would have thought most strengthening of positive will and most conducive to the fullest development of the individual. They may be briefly summarized as follows: an extraordinary respect by the parent for the child, and an early granting to him of an unusual freedom in exploring his universe and in making decisions for himself; an expectation that the child would act independently but reasonably and responsibly; a lack of intense closeness between parent and child so that neither overdependence was fostered nor a feeling of rejection experienced, in other words, the sort of interpersonal relationship between parent and child which had a liberating effect upon the child; a plentiful supply in the child's extended social environment of models for identification and the promotion of ego ideals; the presence within the family of clear standards of conduct and ideas as to what was right and wrong; but at the same time an expectation, if not requirement, of active exploration and internalization of a framework of personal conduct; an emphasis upon the development of one's own ethical code; the experience of frequent moving within single communities, or from community to community, or from country to country which provided an enrichment of experience, both cultural and personal, but which at the same time contributed to experiences of aloneness, shyness, isolation, and solitariness during childhood and adolescence; the possession of skills and abilities which, though encouraged and rewarded, were nevertheless allowed to develop at their own pace; and finally the absence of pressures to establish prematurely one's professional identity (MacKinnon, 1962a).

Though it is clear that I have found Rank's writings a hive of great suggestiveness, and have been impressed by the degree of match of our samples with his types, I would in many instances wish to use a language different from his. I am thinking not only of his frequent use of philosophical and religious terms where the language of psychology would have served him much better in his discussion of psychological problems, but more specifically and concretely of his use of the word "neurotic" to describe his second type.

If I were to apply to Architects II any of the words which Rank used in describing his second stage of psychological development it would be his term, "conflicted," for this at least carries connotations of differentiation, of opposition of forces, of richness and complexity, of psychic turbulence, of possibilities of synthesis and resolution, and of potentiality for further development. These, indeed, were stressed in Rank's discussion of the second stage, for it is clear that Rank thought of it not so much as a state of illness as a condition carrying within it the possibilities of further development.

In my judgment it would be grossly unfair to label Architects II as neurotic, though there is evidence that the neurotic process is more pronounced in them than in either of the other two samples. And I would reject any inference, which might be drawn from my remarks, that one must first be neurotic if one is to become creative. Rather, in agreement with Lawrence Kubie (1961), I believe that both neurotic and creative potential are inherent in the structure of the human psyche. It is a question of which gets emphasized and most developed in any given person.

If I were to draw a summary picture of each of our three groups of architects, I would say that what is most impressive about Architects I is the degree to which they have actualized their creative potentialities. They have become in large measure the persons they were capable of becoming. Since they are not preoccupied with the impression they make on others or the demands that others make on them, they are freer than the other two groups to set their own standards and to achieve them in their own fashion. It is not that they are socially irresponsible, but that their behavior is guided by esthetic values and ethical standards which they have set for themselves and which have been effectively integrated into their images of themselves and of their ideals. They are perhaps the prototype of the person of strong ego, the man of will and deed. Confident of themselves and basically self-accepting, they are to an unusual degree able to recognize and give expression to most aspects of inner experience and character and thus are able more fully to be themselves and to realize their own ideals.

Architects III, on the other hand, appear to have incorporated into their egos, and into their images of the persons they are and the persons they would like to be, the more conventional standards of society and of their profession. More dependent upon the good opinion of others for their own good opinion of themselves, their goals and ideals are to an important degree those of the group rather than uniquely their own.

If I may, for the moment, lapse into the Freudian vernacular, where the egos of Architects I are on more intimate terms with the id, the egos of

Architects III are more at home with their superegos. It is as though Architects I have decided that where id was ego shall be, while Architects III have determined that superego shall be where ego might have been. The egos of Architects I are characterized by effective integration of the id and the development of positive will, while the egos of Architects III are distinguished by a more marked integration of superego and conscience (MacKinnon, 1963).

Architects II, by and large less creative than Architects I but more creative than Architects III, show an overlapping of traits with both of the other groups and consequently appear to experience more conflict than do either of the others.

Finally, I would observe that Rank, a pioneer in the field of ego psychology, was one of the first to note the role of the self-image in determining an individual's behavior and the exercise of his will. Let us look then at the one adjective out of 300 on the Gough Adjective Check List which each of our three groups most often checked as descriptive of the self.

Rank described the adapted man as one who most fully incorporates within himself the norms and dictates of society; 98% of our least creative Architects III check the adjective *conscientious*. He described the creative man, the artist, as one who in large measure creates his own reality; 98% of creative Architects I say they are *imaginative*. In describing the conflicted neurotic type, Rank observed, as many others also have, the relation of neurosis to civilization; the adjective checked most often, by 95% of our intermediate Architects II, is the adjective *civilized*.

References

Barron, F. Complexity-simplicity as a personality dimension. *Journal of Abnormal and Social Psychology,* 1953, **48**, 163–172.   (a)

Barron, F. An ego-strength scale which predicts response to psychotherapy. *Journal of Consulting Psychology,* 1953, **17**, 327–333.   (b)

Barron, F. Some personality correlates of independence of judgment. *Journal of Personality,* 1953, **21**, 287–297.   (c)

Barron, F., & Welsh, G. S. Artistic perception as a possible factor in personality style: Its measurement by a figure preference test. *Journal of Psychology,* 1952, **33**, 199–203.

Gough, H. G. *California Psychological Inventory Manual.* Palo Alto, Calif.: Consulting Psychologists Press, 1957.   (a)

Gough, H. G. Imagination—undeveloped resource. In, *Proceedings, First Conference in Research and Development in Personnel Management.* Los Angeles: University of California, Institute of Industrial Relations, 1957. Pp. 4–10.   (b)

Gough, H. G. *The Adjective Check List.* Palo Alto, Calif.: Consulting Psychologists Press, 1961.

Gough, H. G., & Heilbrun, A. B., Jr. *The Adjective Check List manual.* Palo Alto, Calif.: Consulting Psychologists Press, 1965.

Hathaway, S. R., & McKinley, J. C. *Minnesota Multiphasic Personality Inventory.* New York: Psychological Corporation, 1945.

Kubie, L. S. *The neurotic distortion of the creative process.* New York: Noonday Press, 1961.

MacKinnon, D. W. The nature and nurture of creative talent. *American Psychologist,* 1962, **17,** 484–495.   (a)

MacKinnon, D. W. The personality correlates of creativity: A study of American architects. In G. S. Nielsen (Ed.), *Proceedings of the XIV International Congress of Applied Psychology, Copenhagen, 1961.* Copenhagen: Munksgaard, 1962. Vol. 2. Pp. 11–39.   (b)

MacKinnon, D. W. Creativity and images of the self. In R. W. White (Ed.), *The study of lives.* New York: Atherton Press, 1963. Pp. 251–278.

Munroe, Ruth L. *Schools of psychoanalytic thought.* New York: Dryden Press, 1955.

Murray, H. A. *Explorations in personality.* New York: Oxford Univer. Press, 1938.

Myers, Isabel B. *The Myers-Briggs Type Indicator manual.* Princeton, N.J.: Educational Testing Service, 1962.

Rank, O. *Will therapy* and *Truth and reality.* (Trans. by J. Taft) New York: Knopf, 1945.

Schutz, W. C. *FIRO: A three-dimensional theory of interpersonal behavior.* New York: Rinehart, 1958.

Taylor, Janet A. A personality scale of manifest anxiety. *Journal of Abnormal and Social Psychology,* 1953, **48,** 285–290.

Webster, H., Freedman, M., & Heist, P. Personality changes in college students. In N. Sanford (Ed.), *The American college.* New York: Wiley, 1962. Pp. 805–846.

Welsh, G. S. *Welsh Figure Preference Test: Preliminary manual.* Palo Alto, Calif.: Consulting Psychologists Press, 1959.

FRANK BARRON · The Psychology of Creativity

[*Both Barron and MacKinnon carried out their extensive investi_ 1tions of creative persons at the Institute of Personality Assessment and Research at the University of California at Berkeley. Although Barron has had primary responsibility for studies of creative writers, he has written extensively about the overall research program at the Institute; general orientation, method, and some overall data are summarized in these excerpts. Devoting his entire research career to the study of creativity, Barron has also investigated other types of groups including business administrators in Ireland and, more recently, students at the College of the San Francisco Art Institute* (Artists in the Making, *1972*). *His work has stimulated numerous other investigations, including Helson's research on mathematicians and women excerpted in the next chapter of this book.*]

The problem of psychic creation is a special case of the problem of novelty in all of nature. By what process do new forms come into being? The specification of the conditions under which novelty appears in hu-

SOURCE   From *Creative Person and Creative Process* by Frank Barron. Copyright © 1969 by Holt, Rinehart and Winston, Inc. Reprinted by permission of Holt, Rinehart and Winston. Excerpts from pp. 9–12, 54–55, 63, 65–68, 71–73, 75–78.

man psychical functioning is the task to which the psychology of creativity addresses itself. In doing so, it links itself to the general scientific enterprise of describing the evolution of forms in the natural world.

Such an attempt at a purely naturalistic description of creation is itself relatively new. Creation has long been thought of as a mystery and has been deemed the province of religion or, more broadly, of the supernatural. Supernaturalism includes magic as well as religion, and may be described as an attitude of mind in which the occurrence of the unfamiliar is prone to be interpreted as an interruption of the natural course of events, or as evidence of the existence of another world. The radically novel occurrence thus borders on the uncanny and properly arouses awe.

This sense of the mystery surrounding creation is close to a universal sentiment, and certainly it may be found in the breasts of even the most scientific of psychologists as they approach the phenomenon of psychic creativity. Creativity may be defined, quite simply, as the ability to bring something new into existence. The archetype of the creator is the Divine Being; Aristotle defined the principle of generation of the universe as *nous poiētikos,* the poetic or creative reason. But in the divine creative act something is made to exist where nothing existed before. Since human beings are not able to make something out of nothing, the human act of creation always involves a reshaping of given materials, whether physical or mental. The "something new," then, is a form made by the reconstitution of, or generation from, something old.

To step from the putative divine case to the relatively familiar human case seems at first to remove much of the mystery. It is quickly restored, however, by considering a most common human participation in the creative act: the making of a baby. New flesh is made from old, a new form that has never lived before now comes into being. But the question quickly comes, as indeed it comes to every mother and father, even if fleetingly and darkly, "What on earth had *we* to do with this?" One speaks then of "the miracle of birth," meaning really the miracle of conception and gestation as well as parturition, and the miracle of sexuality, the male and the female principles of generation. The most primitive of emotions participate in the human act of procreation, and the sense of awe and blessedness which the mother and father may feel at the birth of their child derives in part from their recognition that a cosmic process has worked through them in a way they can only dimly understand.

In view of this universal sense of the mystery of creation, we should not be surprised if the techniques of modern psychology can offer only the most modest of beginnings to scientific knowledge in the area of psychic creativity. Indeed, the whole question of mystery may be irrelevant; certainly molecular biology in its unraveling of the genetic code has not diminished the awesomeness of the process of reproduction of living forms, nor have theoretical physics and astronomy in the picture they give us of the magnitude and age and workings, both vast and tiny, of the physical universe diminished our wonder. Quite the contrary; the revelations of science might instead lead all of us, in the back of our minds if not consciously, to be, as an intimate of Franz Kafka's once described him, "constantly amazed."

Psychology cannot as yet promise such amazing revelations concerning the process of creation in the psychic sphere, and it must still follow the older branches of science at a respectful distance. Yet in recent years there has been substantial progress in this area of study, and the vast increase in psychological and educational research has not been without effect on theory as well as practice. Most of the progress can be traced to new efforts at measurement and to new substantive inquiries directed towards the delineation of personality characteristics of notably creative human beings.

As this implies, the psychology of creativity is intimately bound up with the psychology of individual differences. Both deal with the unique, yet both aim at the description of phenomena in terms of general laws. Gordon Allport has accustomed us to think of the difficulties faced by personology as a whole by contrasting the idiographic and the nomothetic approaches to description: the former describes the individual in his unrepeatable, unexampled uniqueness, while the latter describes him in terms of common traits or factors and places him relative to other human beings on hypothesized dimensions of personality.

If this distinction is improperly understood, as indeed it has commonly been in the history of psychology, it leads to much vain argumentation and a wasteful repudiation of one or the other approach to description. The fact is that this opposition is with us constantly in all our thinking and is indeed basic to the nature of perception and thought.

The problem of establishing similarity and discriminating differences is no different in psychology than in any scientific or practical discipline. Setting oneself to the problem when the process that is of special interest is the creative process presents more poignantly, however, the paradox inherent in the classificatory tendency of mind, which is attracted alike to the common and the unique as its means. Creation implies radical novelty, whether making utterly anew or out of nothing. Yet the act of recognition that an act is creative defines in relation to creation a set of principles of classification. This would be a minor professional problem for the psychology of creativity were it not that the paradox is itself central to mind, and the individual mind shows itself creative precisely as it seeks to break out of the bounds of known classifications by raising to the highest level of consciousness the fact and the facets of its constraining conditions.

The study of psychic creation thus requires an attention to both the idiographic and the nomothetic. As psychologists we are interested in understanding a living, and hence changing, form. If our special interest is in the psychology of creativity, we wish especially to understand that form, the particular human person, in terms of its capacity to generate novelty. This means understanding its history, the forces immanent in its present way of being, its conscious and unconscious intentions and motives, its intellectual and temperamental capacities, and its place in the larger stream of events, for all of these are relevant to the creative act.

To this difficult task we must bring rather modest instruments of understanding: our tests and measurements, our interview methods, and finally ourselves both as test analyzers and as intuitive observers and participants in the interview encounter.

. . . .

This method of study [the assessment method] took its name from the "assessment centers" of the U.S. Office of Strategic Services, whose mission was to select men for irregular warfare assignments. It has been described in general terms in [Murray's] *Assessment of Men* [ref. deleted]. Its application in a single, highly detailed case study is exhibited in [Barron's] *Creativity and Psychological Health* [ref. deleted], in a chapter titled "An Odd Fellow."

Each "assessment" in the creativity researches brought together at least five distinguished practitioners in the professions chosen for study. More commonly, 10 such persons participated. The senior staff consisted of six or seven psychologists and usually one or two psychiatrists or analysts who conducted the life history interviews. A single "assessment" generally ran from Friday through Sunday, and took place in a large, comfortably furnished, former fraternity house located on a pleasant tree-lined street of such houses on the edge of the Berkeley campus. In the early days of the Institute the subjects and staff members slept in on Friday and Saturday nights, and of course took all their meals in the house and in general made it a comfortable place of residence for the weekend. A wine cellar and a fireplace added to the amenities, and in as many ways as possible the situation was defined not as test-taking but as a mutually open situation in which staff and subjects could get to know each other.

How the subjects recorded *their* observations, or whether they did at all, is not known (for the most part), but what *the staff* did at the end of the three days was this: each senior staff member wrote down all his impressions of each subject, then used a 300-word adjective checklist to characterize each subject as accurately and tersely as possible, and finally employed a 100-item set of sentences, each of them representing a clinical inference, to describe the subject in somewhat more technical and psychodynamically "deeper" terms. The Gough Adjective Checklist [ref. deleted] was used for this first task, and the Block Clinical Q-sort [ref. deleted] for the second.

These descriptions were given without knowledge of test results and were intended to represent what could be observed from the subject's actions and words during the three days. The full intuitive capacity of the staff observer was thus called into play, and eventually also was brought to bear on each case through the medium of a case conference and final case write-up, with test results and interview data taken into account as well. Finally, when all cases in a given sample had been studied, they were rated relative to one another on a set of 40 personality traits, based largely on the earlier conceptual formulations of Murray and of Gordon Allport [ref. deleted].

. . . .

In all, three groups of eminent individuals were studied by the living-in assessment method: creative writers, mathematicians, and architects. . . .

. . . .

. . . a total of 56 writers participated in the research, out of 101 who were invited. Of these 56 writers, 30 were writers of high reputation whose names had been secured by a similar process to that already described for the architect study. Three professors of English, themselves creative writers, and one editor of a literary review, were asked to suggest names of writers who should be invited to take part, although they were not, as the architect nominators were, asked to suggest a specific number. Their nominations did show considerable agreement among themselves, however, and a list was drawn up consisting of 48 writers who had been suggested by at least two nominators. These writers were accordingly invited, and 26 of them accepted the invitation. Of these 26, only 17 finally did come to Berkeley for the living-in assessments, because of difficulties of scheduling groups; some last minute changes resulted in filling out the groups with three writers who had been nominated by only one nominator. Later, 10 other writers were seen either individually at Berkeley or in their own homes, giving a total of 30 participants in this phase of the research.

A comparison group was chosen from California writers who were members of a writers' association; these writers did not participate in living-in assessment, however. Most of the statistical comparisons to be drawn, therefore, will be based upon test data obtained from the comparison group by mail. The writers' study itself must be considered incomplete at this point and a full report on it will not be attempted here, but it does yield enough interesting data to justify a preliminary report.

The study of mathematicians suffers from a certain lack of symmetry in the design, stemming from practical difficulties. A total of 48 male mathematicians and 44 female mathematicians participated. The men, however, did not take part in living-in assessments, but were administered the test battery individually by the project director, Richard S. Crutchfield. The 44 women were studied by the living-in assessment method under the direction of Ravenna Helson.

Of the male sample, 26 were nominated as unusually creative by a panel of fellow mathematicians, while 22 were considered competent representatives of the profession (all held the Ph.D. in mathematics from reputable universities). The female sample is believed to include virtually every productive woman mathematician in the United States and Canada. Again a nomination technique was used to obtain the list of subjects to be invited; in this case, it consisted of 52 individuals, of whom only eight declined to, or were not able to, participate. The 44 participants were later rated by mathematicians in their own research specialties throughout the United States. From these ratings and accumulated professional opinions it seemed clear that 16 of the women mathematicians stood out from the rest of the sample as the most original and important women mathematicians in this country and Canada; the data analysis therefore concentrates on observed differences between them and the other 28 in terms of performance in living-in assessment. (Incidentally, it should be noted that fully half of the creative women mathematicians, as was true also of the men, are foreign-born. Visher's . . . study of men starred in *American Men of Science* shows that the percentage of eminent men who are foreign-born is higher in mathematics (32 per cent) than in scientific fields as a whole (17 per cent).[1]

We turn now to a sampling of the results of these studies. A comprehensive review of the results must await publication of full reports on each study separately, and some of these are not yet available. Even a thorough first-level correlational analysis based on test measures in relationship to the criterion ratings has not yet appeared in print for the

1. Visher. S. S. *Scientists Starred in* American Men of Science, 1903–1943. Baltimore: The Johns Hopkins Press, 1947.

entire program of research. Nevertheless ... it is possible to pull together a wealth of findings that are of scientific interest even though they have not yet been cross-validated.

Let us begin with staff descriptions of highly creative individuals as contrasted with less creative or merely representative members of the same profession. The assessment of women mathematicians can readily be made to yield such data, since 16 women of unusual creative ability were assessed, together with 28 women undistinguished for creativity. The assessment staff was of course kept in ignorance of the ratings, and, besides, eminent women mathematicians, unlike eminent architects or writers, are rarely known by reputation to anyone outside the profession. None of the psychologists except the project director had any grounds for identifying a given subject as one of the nominated "creatives." Consequently, the staff adjective descriptions and Q sorts obtained from the assessment staff immediately upon conclusion of the three days of assessment were free of bias and preconceptions; the task was simply to give a candid and objective description of each assessee, and the assessee's standing in terms of nominations or criterion ratings was unknown. . . .

. . . .

The emphasis [was] upon genuine unconventionality, high intellectual ability, vividness or even flamboyance of character, moodiness and preoccupation, courage, and self-centeredness. These are people who stand out, and who probably are willing to stand up and strike out if impelled to do so. Creative people have an edge to them, it would seem from these first results.

. . . .

. . . but what do personality and intelligence tests themselves show? What basis is there for thinking that creative individuals have an unusual amount of concern for their own adequacy as persons? What is the psychometric evidence in terms of measures of psychopathology, such as tendencies towards neurosis and psychosis? And what of intelligence? Do the tests of intellectual aptitude used in the research support the notion that creative individuals as a class are of high intellectual ability? How important is measured intelligence in determining originality, and what contribution do motivational and temperamental variables distinct from intelligence make to creativity?

For at least partial answers to these questions, we turn to the results obtained from the use of objective tests. First, there are such questionnaires as the Minnesota Multiphasic Personality Inventory (MMPI) and the California Psychological Inventory (CPI), as well as the Type Indicator based on C. G. Jung's theory of psychological types, to give some idea of the differences between creative individuals and comparison groups from the same professions in terms of personality traits, both normal and abnormal. Consider first the evidence from the MMPI which yields measures on such psychiatric dimensions as Depression, Hypochondriasis, Hysteria, Psychopathic Deviation, Paranoia, Psychasthenia, and Hypomania.

The MMPI comparisons for the samples of mathematicians are among the data not yet available in published form, but we do have such information for both writers and architects. The creative groups consistently emerge as having *more* psychopathology than do the more representative members of the same profession. The *average* creative writer, in fact, is in the upper 15 per cent of the general population on *all* measures of psychopathology furnished by this test! The average creative architect is less markedly deviant, but is still consistently and substantially higher than the average for the general population on these indices of psychopathological dispositions. (See MacKinnon *et al.*,[2] for statistics in the architect sample. . . .)

.   .   .   .

From these data one might be led to conclude that creative writers are, as the common man has long suspected them to be, a bit "dotty." And of course it has always been a matter of pride in self-consciously artistic and intellectual circles to be, at the least, eccentric. "Mad as a hatter" is a term of high praise when applied to a person of marked intellectual endowments. But the "divine madness" that the Greeks considered a gift of the gods and an essential ingredient in the poet was not, like psychosis, something subtracted from normality; rather, it was something added. Genuine psychosis is stifling and imprisoning; the divine madness is a liberation from "the consensus."

If this is so, then we should expect to find evidence of an enhancement of ego strength in our creative individuals, so that greater psychopathology and greater personal effectiveness would exist side by side. Psychometrically, such a pattern would be quite unusual; the Ego-strength scale of the MMPI, for example, correlates −.60 with Schizophrenia in the general population, and −.50 with such other variables as Hysteria, Hypochondriasis, and Psychopathic Deviation.

2. MacKinnon, D. W. *et al.* *Proceedings of the Conference on "The Creative Person,"* University of California Alumni Center, Lake Tahoe, California. Berkeley: University of California Extension, 1961.

Nevertheless, just such an unusual pattern is found, not only in relation to ego strength but in relation to the scales of the California Psychological Inventory, most of which are themselves aspects of ego strength and negatively related to the psychopathological dimensions measured by the MMPI. The average Ego-strength score for the nominated creatives among the writers is 58, and among the creative architects it is 61. In brief, they are almost as superior to the general population in ego strength as they are deviant on such pathological dispositions as Schizophrenia, Depression, Hysteria, and Psychopathic Deviation. This finding is reinforced by evidence from the California Psychological Inventory. . . .

. . . [the] CPI profiles are indicative of a high degree of personal effectiveness. Creative writers are outstanding in terms of flexibility, psychological-mindedness, and the ability to achieve through independent effort as opposed to achievement through conformance; they are high also in self-acceptance, social participativeness, and capacity for gaining high social status. Creative architects are outstanding in rather similar ways: in self-acceptance, in capacity for status, in achievement through independence, in flexibility, in social participativeness, and in personal dominance.

·   ·   ·   ·   ·   ·   ·   ·   ·   ·   ·   ·   ·   ·   ·   ·

Of this unusual patterning of psychopathology and personal effectiveness we have written elsewhere [ref. deleted] as follows:

> If one is to take these tests results seriously, (creative individuals) appear to be both sicker and healthier psychologically than people in general. Or, to put it another way, they are much more troubled psychologically, but they also have far greater resources with which to deal with their troubles. This jibes rather well with their social behavior, as a matter of fact. They are clearly effective people who handle themselves with pride and distinctiveness, but the face they turn to the world is sometimes one of pain, often of protest, sometimes of distance and withdrawal; and certainly they are emotional. All of these are, of course, the intensely normal traits indicated by the peaks on their profile of diagnostic scores. . . .

The CPI profiles reveal also certain consistent differences between the highly creative and less creative members of the two professions. In both writing and architecture, the more creative individuals are more self-accepting and more flexible. Yet they score lower on socialization and on self-control, report less "sense of well-being," and on a scale that was developed to measure "effort to make a good impression" they score significantly lower than the general population. This latter finding probably goes along with their lower scores on "achievement through conformance.". . .

In terms of C. G. Jung's theory of psychological types, there are again consistent differences between the more creative and the less creative members of these two professions. Creative writers and creative architects are markedly "intuitive" as opposed to "sensation" types, and are "perceptual" rather than "judging" in their orientations; in both respects they are different both from the general population and their professional colleagues. These findings are based on the Myers-Briggs Type Indicator, a questionnaire developed from Jung's theories and following quite closely his formulation in his book *Psychological Types*. This questionnaire yields scores on Introversion-Extraversion, Feeling-Thinking, Judging-Perceiving, and Intuition vs. Sensation. Only 25 per cent of the general population is classified as "intuition" types by this test, yet 100 per cent of the creative architects (as opposed to 59 per cent of representative architects) and 92 per cent of creative writers (as opposed to 84 per cent of representative writers) were so classified. In terms of preception vs. judgment, 58 per cent of the creative architects are the former, compared with 17 per cent of representative architects.

MacKinnon discusses these test findings as follows (1962) [see Selected Bibliography, p. 360, *American Psychologist*]:

Employing the language of the test, though in doing so I over-simplify both it and the theory upon which it is based, one might say that whenever a person uses his mind for any purpose, he performs either an act of perception (he becomes aware of something) or an act of judgment (he comes to a conclusion about something). And most persons tend to show a rather consistent preference for and greater pleasure in one or the other of these, preferring either to perceive or to judge, though everyone both perceives and judges.

An habitual preference for the judging attitude may lead to some prejudging and at the very least to the living of a life that is orderly, controlled, and carefully planned. A preference for the perceptive attitude results in a life that is more open to experience both from within and from without, and characterized by flexibility and spontaneity. A judging type places more emphasis upon the control and regulation of experience, while a perceptive type is inclined to be more open and receptive to all experience.

The majority of our creative writers, mathematicians, and architects are perceptive types. Only among research scientists do we find the majority to be judging types, and even in this group it is interesting to note that there is a positive correlation (.25) between a scientist's preference for perception and his rated creativity as a scientific researcher. For architects, preference for perception correlates .41 with rated creativity.

The second preference measured by the Type Indicator is for one of two types of perception: sense perception or sensation, which is a direct becoming aware of things by way of the senses versus intuitive perception or intuition, which is an indirect perception of the deeper meanings and possibilities inherent in things and situations. Again, everyone senses and intuits, but preliminary norms for the test suggest that in the United States three out of four persons show a preference for sense perception, concentrating upon immediate sensory experience and centering their attention upon existing facts. The one out of every four who shows a preference for intuitive perception, on the other hand, looks expectantly for a bridge or link between that which is given and present and that which is not yet thought of, focusing habitually upon possibilities.

One would expect creative persons not to be bound to the stimulus and the object but to be ever alert to the as-yet-not-realized. And that is precisely the way they show themselves to be on the Type Indicator. . . .

Not only outstandingly creative writers but also more representative writers are predominantly intuitive, it should be noted, and the percentage difference is not great enough to be statistically significant. This tendency of professional writers in general to be both more perceptive and more intuitive than the average person probably finds expression in the kinds of inner experiences they report in our interview dealing with "the nonrational." The interview material is difficult to condense in simple statistical terms, and we do not as yet have adequate comparative data. What results are available have been presented in . . . [Barron, 1968; see Selected Bibliography, p. 359]. Their general tendency is to indicate much more intense sensibility in writers: more openness to feelings of awe and of oneness with the universe, as well as the counterface of these, feelings of horror, forsakenness, and desolation; a more vivid dream life, with a notably greater tendency to have dreams in color, and also to have more nightmares; more hunches of an almost precognitive sort, and greater readiness to believe in prophetic dreams; yet, at the same time, skepticism about life after death and, as might be expected, a disinclination to believe in the possibility of communication between the living and the dead.

The generic disposition in these experiences and attitudes is perhaps an openness to experience on the fringes of ordinary consciousness. Many writers have spoken of the unconscious as the source of their important ideas and insights. This goes counter to the psychoanalytic notion of the unconscious as consisting of repressed mental contents. We shall return to this question later, in discussing Lawrence Kubie's theory . . . [see selection here, pp. 143–148] that the creative process is never aided by the unconscious but only hindered by it. Writers seem to feel more friendly to the unconscious than psychoanalysts do, but we must take a closer look at the matter when we come a bit later to consider problems in the facilitation of creative thinking.

J. P. GUILFORD · Factor Analysis, Intellect, and Creativity

[*Guilford's work and influence is usually considered to have been a key stimulus for recent interest in creativity among psychologists. His approach and findings have been incorporated directly into the research of Torrance, Wallach and Kogan, and Khatena. An important part of his overall concern with the structure of the intellect, Guilford's research on creative thinking has been based on the approach known as factor analysis. Seeking for underlying factors in the ability to answer test questions with alternate solutions, Guilford has defined and described the overall factor of "divergent production" as a creative operation. In earlier works, he had emphasized fluency, flexibility, originality, and elaboration in creative thinking and he here organizes those factors into larger categories of function. The selection here contains excerpts from various portions of his book in the following sequence: a description of his factor analytic approach; his concept of the structure of the intellect; a discussion of the factor of divergent production in creative thinking.*]

. . . The multivariate methods most pertinent in this discussion are intercorrelation and factor analysis . . . . The usual application is to samples, each of N individuals, each of whom has taken n tests. The em-

SOURCE   *Excerpted from* The Nature of Human Intelligence *by J. P. Guilford. Copyright* © *1967 by McGraw-Hill, Inc. Used with permission of McGraw-Hill Book Company. Pp. 25, 60–64, 169–170.*

pirical data are in the form of a score matrix composed of N rows and n columns of numbers. Within such a matrix of numbers, we look for an underlying order or system, some lawfulness that should represent something psychologically meaningful regarding the individual differences in scores on the tests. In this general statement lie several differences from the traditional type of psychological experiment.

The capitalizing upon individual differences as the source of variance in the data is the most obvious feature. In the traditional bivariate type of experiment, the experimenter applies "treatments" in the form of varying stimulus conditions, or time conditions, or number of exposures, and so on. As is often pointed out, he is interested in S-R dependencies (response R as some function of stimulus S), whereas the factor analyst deals with R-R dependencies, in which scores from different tests are regarded as response variables. One crucial difference that works to the advantage of the multivariate approach is the fact that the investigator can take his individual subjects very much as they come, within a specified population, with relatively less concern regarding how they got that way.

. . . .

When the writer first faced the problem of organizing the intellectual factors into a system, almost 40 such factors had been demonstrated [ref. deleted]. Several facts based upon experiences in factor analysis of intellectual tests in the United States had cast doubt upon the applicability of a hierarchical structure. Almost no one reported finding a g factor; in fact, the tendency has been for each factor to be limited to a small number of tests in any analysis.

Furthermore, there has been little or no tendency to find a few broader group factors (represented each by a larger number of tests) and a larger number of narrow group factors. The factors appear to be about equally general in this respect, being strongly represented by small numbers, and relatively equal numbers, of tests. In part this may be attributed to the fact that the investigator who approaches analysis problems in a sophisticated manner starts by drawing up a list of hypothesized factors that he expects to find in an area of functioning, and he sees to it that each hypothesized factor is represented by a minimum of three tests. The extra loadings often come out in the analysis because tests designed for one factor so often unintentionally show significant relationships to other factors. The absence of a g factor and the apparently comparable generality of all the factors does not give support to a hierarchical conception of their interrelationships.

A third and most important consideration is that many factors have obviously parallel properties. For example, if one collects a half-dozen verbal factors in one set and an appropriate collection of a half-dozen nonverbal factors in another, it is clear that the factors in the two sets can be paired off in a meaningful manner. The psychological operation is the same in each pair; only the content of the test items is different. Yet the members of each pair come out of an analysis as separate factors. Historically, there seems to have been a belief that a psychological operation is the same whether it is performed with verbal-meaningful information or with visual-figural information, and gestalt psychologists have contributed to fixing this assumption. Extensive factor-analytical results have proved wrong the belief that the same ability is involved regardless of the kind of information with which we deal.

Categories in the Structure of Intellect

Content Categories. The major distinction should not be confined to verbal versus nonverbal, for there is a third category of factors represented by tests composed of numbers or letters that seem completely parallel to factors in the figural and verbal sets, respectively. There is nothing to tie the three sets together except the fact that they are recognized as all being in the general category of intellectual abilities; nor is there a more general factor that would tie together the members of a set of factors. Even if this had been true, a hierarchical model does not take care of parallel members, nor are parallels needed to form a hierarchy, except for the parallel levels of generality; and there are no apparent levels of generality among the factors obtained. Thus it was that three distinct, parallel content categories were recognized and called by the terms *figural, symbolic,* and *semantic.*

As far back as 1933, G. M. Smith did a factor analysis in which he selected tests so that the analysis could cluster the tests either in terms of similar material (space tests, number tests, and verbal tests) or according to formats with similar kinds of items. The results definitely favored factors along the lines of material or content. Over the years since that time, factors of space, number, and verbal abilities have been consistently easy to differentiate.

With the three kinds of content well supported, a fourth kind of content was added.[1] . . . This step was taken on purely logical grounds, for there were no known factors at the time to support the idea. The kind of content called by the term *behavioral* was added to take care of the kind of information involved in cognition and in other operations pertaining to the

1. Thorndike, E. L. "Intelligence and its uses." *Harper's Magazine*, 1920, 140:227–235.

behavior of other people. We know that we know to some extent what the other person is perceiving, attending to, feeling, thinking, and intending to do. We draw inferences from this information and we utilize such information in efforts to control his actions. The addition of this kind of content was also influenced by the proposal of E. L. Thorndike[2] . . . that there is a social intelligence, distinct from the traditional kind of intelligence. Logical support for the other content categories was welcomed from the same direction, for Thorndike and his associates came to recognize a distinction between concrete and abstract intelligence.[3] . . . They failed only to make the further distinction of two kinds of abstract intelligence, as accounted for by the distinction between symbolic and semantic information in the structure-of-intellect model.

Operation Categories. Before these distinctions as to content became evident, there had been some tradition for classifying the intellectual factors in another way, i.e., according to the supposed kind of operations involved. There were recognized perceptual factors, memory factors, and reasoning factors. New investigations in the 1950s pertained to creative-thinking abilities, planning abilities, problem-solving abilities, and judgment or evaluation abilities. New factors were found in each of these heuristic categories. Classification of the same factors, which could be grouped according to kind of information or content, as just indicated, was attempted independently according to operation.

It became obvious that in addition to memory and evaluation, new operation categories were needed. Reasoning proved to be a poor categorical concept because it could not be uniquely defined. Creative-thinking abilities seemed to have properties of their own, involving fluency, flexibility, and elaboration abilities; so a class of factors was given the title of "divergent-thinking" abilities. The representative tests are all of completion form, and the examinee makes a good score for the number and variety of his responses and sometimes for high quality. It was recognized that there were other tests in which the examinee has to generate his own answer to each item but that it must satisfy a unique specification or set of specifications. A set of these abilities, parallel to the divergent-thinking abilities, suggested the title of "convergent thinking"; in accordance with the information given in the item, the examinee must converge upon the one right answer. To avoid the ambiguity of the term *thinking*, the later substitution of the term *production* was made.

2. *Ibid.*
3. Thorndike, E. L. *The measurement of intelligence.* New York: [Columbia University] Teachers College, 1927.

Thus, two operation categories, divergent production and convergent production, were adopted.

With four categories of operation accounted for, including the memory and evaluation abilities, a fifth category was found to take care of the remaining factors: the *cognition* category. Tests of many factors simply determine how much the examinee knows or can readily discover on the basis of what he knows. Such factors of knowing or discovering were recognized as cognitive abilities. In adopting this label for the category, a very apt and descriptive one for the purpose, it was realized that reference has traditionally been made to *cognitive abilities*, a term that is meant to include all intellectual abilities. The use of the term *cognition* in the more limited way seems more appropriate. After all, we do have the term *intellectual* to use for covering the whole range of abilities; there is no point in having two labels for the larger class of abilities.

The Product Categories.   A third way of looking at the abilities and a third way of classifying them came to view more slowly. It came about because of the need for taking into account the parallels that appeared across both the content and the operation categories. That is, if we take a set of factors having in common one of the content properties, say semantic, and also one of the operation categories, say cognition, we have a set of semantic-cognition abilities, not just one. There are parallels to these abilities if we change either to a new content category, say divergent production, or to a new combination of both content and operation, such as figural—divergent-production abilities.

A way was found to integrate all these parallels [ref. deleted] by putting the known intellectual factors in a single, solid model, with the five operation categories arranged along one dimension, the three content categories along a second dimension, and the six product categories along the third dimension. Thus, content, operation, and product became three parameters of a three-dimensional model. The structure-of-intellect model (hereafter often referred to as the SI model), as shown in Figure [1] is the same as when presented in 1958.

The order of the categories along each dimension of the model has some logical reasons behind it but without any great degree of compulsion. Placing the symbolic category between figural and semantic depends upon the relation of symbols to both those two kinds of information. Symbols are basically figural but take on symbolic functions when they are conventionally made to represent something in the semantic category. They do, of course, also represent information in the other categories.

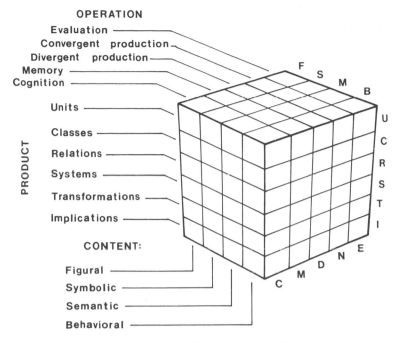

Figure [1]. The structure-of-intellect model, with three parameters (other parameters may need to be added).

As for operations, cognition is basic to all other kinds; hence it appears first. If no cognition, no memory; if no memory, no production, for the things produced come largely from memory storage. If neither cognition nor production, then no evaluation. From front to back of the model, then, there is increasing dependency of one kind of operation upon others.

Of the products, units are regarded as basic; hence they appear at the top. Units enter into classes, relations, systems, and also transformations and implications. There might be some sense in putting implications immediately below units, since implications are the simplest and most general way in which units can be connected. There is reason for putting systems below units and relations, since both enter into systems; but implications do also. The unique character of transformations would be a reason for putting them last, since a transformation involves one item of information (possibly any other kind of product) becoming something else. The transformation of a transformation would not be unthinkable, for transformations, too, can be revised.

The concept of "product" pertains to the way or form in which any information occurs. An appropriate synonym for the term *product* could be the term *conception*, which also pertains to ways of knowing or understanding (see Figure [2] for illustrations of figural products). Information can be conceived in the form of *units*—things, segregated wholes, figures on grounds, or "chunks" [ref. deleted]. Units are things to which nouns are normally applied. *Class*, as a kind of product of information, is near to the common meaning of the term. A class is a set of objects with one or more common properties; but it is more than a set, for a class idea is involved.

A *relation* is some kind of connection between two things, a kind of bridge or connecting link having its own character. Prepositions commonly express relation ideas, alone or with other terms, such as the expressions "married to," "son of," and "harder than." *Systems* are complexes, patterns, or organizations of interdependent or interacting parts, such as a verbally stated arithmetic problem, an outline, a mathematical equation, or a plan or program. *Transformations* are changes, revisions, redefinitions, or modifications, by which any product of information in one state goes over into another state. Although there is an implication of process in this definition, a transformation can be an object

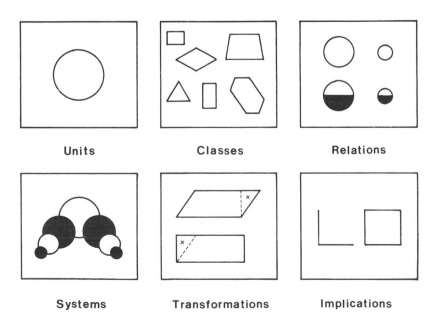

Figure [2]. Illustrations of the six kinds of products, using visual-figural examples.

of cognition or of thought like any other product. The part of speech that we ordinarily apply to a transformation is a participle, a verb in noun form, such as shrinking, inverting, or reddening. It has been impossible thus far to treat transformation as an operation category; that is not the way the factors fall.

Finally, an *implication* is something expected, anticipated, or predicted from given information. Behaviorists who admitted the concept of "expectation" or "anticipation" to their lexicons have been talking about much the same idea. Any information that comes along very promptly suggests something else. One thing suggesting another involves a product of implication. Of all the six kinds of products, implication is closest to the ancient concept of association. But something more is involved in the concept. It is not that one thing merely follows another but that the two have some intimate way of being connected. This does not make an implication the same as a relation, for a relation is more specifiable and verbalizable.

These informal definitions of the category terms of the SI model will have to suffice for now. . . .

.   .   .   .

The conception of divergent-production abilities came about through investigations of certain hypotheses regarding the component abilities most relevant to creative performance. A factor of fluency was expected, and three kinds of fluency were found; a factor of flexibility was expected, and two kinds were found; and an expected factor of originality materialized. Later, in a study of planning abilities, a factor of elaboration was expected and was demonstrated.

But factors of fluency and flexibility have been found in nonverbal tests as well as in verbal tests. Search among nonverbal tests revealed the parallels essentially complete in figural and symbolic areas of information alongside those in the semantic category. In other words, there are factors of fluency, flexibility, originality, and elaboration which fit into the SI model. The three kinds of fluency are concerned with the products of units, relations, and systems; the two kinds of flexibility are concerned with classes and transformation, into which category originality fits; and elaboration has to do with implications.

Tests of DP abilities must call for examinees actually to produce information, in quantity and in variety, and sometimes with alterations in that information. Experimental work with some tests has demonstrated the forms and conditions needed for optimal factor measurement.

Quite a number of studies have lent support to the claim that DP factors and tests have relevance in connection with the measurement of creative potential, but creative potential is very complex and at times and in different ways involves abilities outside the divergent-production and the transformation categories, which are most important in that connection.

Relations between divergent-production-test scores and IQs are generally quite low, but it appears that although a high IQ is not sufficient for doing well in DP tests, being above average in IQ is almost necessary.

MICHAEL A. WALLACH and NATHAN KOGAN · Creativity and Intelligence in Children

[*In this study the authors are more concerned with showing what does not explain creativity, namely intelligence, than they are with describing particular causative factors. Their overall approach to creativity, the tests they use for identifying creative children, however, suggest and imply definite explanations of the phenomenon, and are based on Guilford's factor of divergent production. The testing approach described here has been followed widely by educational and child psychologist investigators.*]

While there has been a great deal of discussion in recent years concerning the importance of fostering "creativity" in our children, there is little solid evidence to support the claim that creativity can be distinguished from the more familiar concept of intelligence. To be sure, the word "creativity" has caught the fancy of the culture — frequent reference is made to creativity in contexts as diverse as education, industry and advertising. Time and time again, however, the "proof" offered to support the existence of a type of cognitive excellence different from general intelligence has proven to be a will-o'-the-wisp.

The logical requirements for such a proof can be put as follows. The psychological concept of *intelligence* defines a network of strongly related abilities concerning the retention, transformation and utilization of verbal and numerical symbols: at issue are a person's memory storage capacities,

SOURCE *From Wallach, M. A., and Kogan, N., "Creativity and Intelligence in Children,"* published by permission of Transaction, Inc. from Human Intelligence, *Hunt, J. McV., Ed. Copyright* © 1972, *by Transaction, Inc. Pp. 165–180.*

his skill in solving problems, his dexterity in manipulating and dealing with concepts. The person high in one of these skills will tend to be high in all; the individual who is low in one will tend to be low in all. But what of the psychological concept of *creativity*? If the behavior judged to be indicative of creativity turns up in the same persons who behave in the ways we call "intelligent," then there is no justification for claiming the existence of any kind of cognitive capacity apart from general intelligence. We would have to assert that the notion of greater or lesser degrees of *creativity* in people simply boils down, upon empirical inspection, to the notion of greater or lesser degrees of general *intelligence*. On the other hand, in order to demonstrate that there are grounds for considering creativity to be a kind of cognitive talent that exists in its own right, another kind of proof would be required. It would be necessary to demonstrate that whatever methods of evaluation are utilized to define variations in creativity from person to person result in classifications that are different from those obtained when the same individuals are categorized as to intelligence.

When we reviewed the quantitative research on creativity, we were forced to conclude that these logical requirements were not met. Despite frequent use of the term "creativity" to define a form of talent that was independent of intelligence, examination of the evidence indicated that the purported measures of creativity tended to have little more in common with each other than they had in common with measures of general intelligence. If one could do about the same thing with an IQ measure as one could with the creativity measures (regarding who should be considered more creative and who should be considered less creative), it was difficult to defend the practice of invoking a new and glamorous term such as "creativity" for describing the kind of talent under study.

While varying conceptions of the meaning of creativity had been embodied in the measures used, they all shared one thing in common: they had been administered to the persons under study as *tests*. From the viewpoint of the person undergoing assessment, the creativity procedures, no less than an intelligence test, carried the aura of school examinations. They were carried out with explicit or implicit time limits in classroom settings where many students underwent the assessment procedures at the same time. Indeed, we even found that the creativity procedures had been described to the students as "tests" by the psychologists who gave them.

We were suspicious that such a test-like context was inimical to the wholehearted display of cognitive characteristics which could be correctly referred to as being involved in creativity. Hence we believed that creativity had not yet been given a fair chance to reveal itself as a different form of excellence than intelligence. . . .

.   .   .   .

With this in mind we formulated a research program that involved the extensive study of 151 fifth-grade children. They were of middle-class socioeconomic status, and boys and girls were about equally represented in our sample. The work, which was supported in part by the Cooperative Research Program of the United States Office of Education, has been described in detail in our book, *Modes of Thinking in Young Children: A Study of the Creativity-Intelligence Distinction.*

.   .   .   .

. . . we mustered every device possible to place the assessment procedures in a context of play rather than in the typical context of testing with which the children were all too familiar. There were no time limits on the procedures. They were administered to one child at a time rather than to groups of children seated at their classroom desks. The adults who worked with the children, moreover, had already established relationships in the context of play activities. We even took pains to avoid the customary vocabulary of tests and testing in connection with the research enterprise as whole — in our talk with the children we described the work as oriented to the study of children's games for purposes of developing new games children would like.

The procedures involved such matters as requesting the child to suggest possible uses for each of several objects, or to describe possible ways in which each of several pairs of objects are similar to each other. For example, in one procedure the child was to suggest all the different ways in which we could use such objects as a newspaper, a cork, a shoe, a chair. "Rip it up if angry" was a unique response for "newspaper," while "make paper hats" was not unique. In another, he was to indicate similarities between, for example, a potato and a carrot, a cat and a mouse, milk and meat. "They are government-inspected" was a unique response for "milk and meat," while "they come from animals" was not unique. In yet another, he was to indicate all the things that each of a number of abstract drawings might be — such as the drawings shown in the illustrations. For the triangle with three circles around it, "three mice eating a piece of cheese" was a unique response, while "three people sitting around a table" was not unique. For the two half-circles over the line, "two haystacks on a flying carpet" was a unique response, while "two igloos" was not unique.

Our interests were in the number of ideas that a child would suggest, and the uniqueness of the suggested ideas—the extent to which a given idea in response to a given task belonged to one child alone rather than being an idea that was suggested by other children as well. In addition, we used a variety of traditional techniques for assessing general intelligence with the same children.

When the results of the creativity assessment procedures were compared with the results of the intelligence measures, a definite divergence was obtained—the kind that had not been found in earlier studies. They had already shown, and so did our study, that a child who scores at the high intelligence end of one intelligence test will tend to score that way in other intelligence tests as well. In addition, however, our research revealed two further facts which tended to be different from earlier studies:

☐ The various measures of creativity that we utilized had a great deal in common with one another: a child who scored at the high creativity end of one of our creativity measures tended to score at the high creativity end of all the rest of these measures.

☐ Of particular importance, the indices of creativity and the indices of intelligence tended to be independent of each other. That is to say, a child who was creative by our measures would just as likely be of low intelligence as of high intelligence. Likewise, a child who was relatively low in creativity by our measures would as likely be of high intelligence as of low intelligence.

In short, the obtained facts *did* support the view that in school children creativity is a different type of cognitive excellence than general intelligence. Such an outcome was especially striking in light of the fact that our procedures for assessing creativity of necessity, called upon the child's

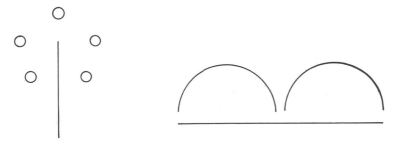

Left: Unique: "Lollipop bursting into pieces"
        Common: "Flower"
Right: Unique: "Two haystacks on a flying carpet"
        Common: "Two igloos"

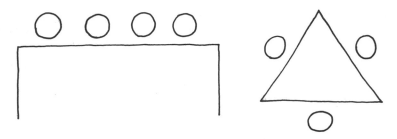

Children's responses to abstract drawings

Left: Unique: "Foot and Toes"
         Common: "Table with things on top"
Right: Unique: "Three mice eating a piece of cheese"
         Common: "Three people sitting around a table"

verbal ability in some degree — and verbal ability is known to contribute substantially to performance on IQ tests. Despite this possible source of commonality, the chances that a child of high intelligence would also display high creativity by our measures were no more than about 50–50.

What are some of the characteristics, then, of children in our four categories: intelligent and creative; neither intelligent nor creative; intelligent but low in creativity; and creative but low in regard to intelligence? The composite pictures that emerged from the experiments and observations that we carried out are composites in the sense that some portions of the evidence upon which they are based were more clear for the boys, while other parts of the evidence were more clear for the girls. However, the general pictures that emerged for the two sexes tended to suggest the same underlying characteristics.

High Creativity — High Intelligence. In many respects these children earn the most superlatives of any of the four groups. For example, when they are observed in the classroom they tend to be particularly high in degree of attention span and concentration upon academic work. At the same time, their academic bent does not put them at a social disadvantage. Quite to the contrary, they are observed to be the most socially "healthy" of the four groups: they have the strongest inclination to be friends with others, and others also have the strongest inclination to be friends with them. (These observations were made during play periods as well as during class sessions.)

These children, in addition, are the least likely of all four groups to behave in ways that suggest disapproval or doubt concerning oneself, one's actions and one's work. However, this isn't merely a question of behaving in a manner most in harmony with the society's expectations, for these children also demonstrate a strong inclination to engage in various sorts of disruptive activities in the classroom. It's as if they are bursting through the typical behavioral molds that the society has constructed.

What are some of the underpinnings of the general behaviors just described for this group? For one thing, they are likely to see possible connections between events that do not have too much in common. The members of this group, in other words, are more willing to posit relationships between events that are in many respects dissimilar. For another thing, these children are particularly good at reading the subtle affective or expressive connotations that can be carried by what goes on in the environment. These two matters are not entirely separate—a sensitive, aesthetic "tuning" to the possible expressive meanings conveyed by human gesture or by abstract design forms involves seeing possible linkages between quite different kinds of objects and events. The children high in both creativity and intelligence seemed to be most capable of all the groups regarding this kind of aesthetic sensitivity.

.   .   .   .

Turning finally to the way these children describe their own feeling states, we find a tendency for them to admit to experiencing some anxiety, some disturbance—neither a great deal nor very little. It may be that experiencing some anxiety serves an energizing function for them: it is not so much anxiety as to cripple them, and not so little anxiety as to leave them dormant. Also, their total mode of adaptation does not minimize the experience of anxiety for them.

Low Creativity—High Intelligence. In what respects are the children who are high with regard to general intelligence but low in creativity different from those who are high in both? Let us return first to behavior observed in classroom and play settings. While the high intelligence–low creativity children resembled the high creativity–high intelligence children in possessing strong capacities for concentration on academic work and a long attention span, in other respects they were quite different. Those of high intelligence but low creativity were least likely of all four groups to engage in disruptive activities in the classroom and tended to hesitate about expressing opinions. In short, these children seemed rather unwilling to take chances.

Parallel behavior was observed in their social relations with other children; while others had a strong inclination to be friends with them, they in turn tended to hold themselves aloof from interaction with other children. The high intelligence–low creativity children, therefore, seemed to be characterized by a coolness or reserve in relations with their peers. Others would seek out the high intelligence–low creativity children for companionship, possibly because of this group's high academic standing. The children in question, however, tended not to seek out others in return. Perhaps this group felt themselves to be on top of the social mountain, as it were—in a position where they could receive homage from others without any need for requital.

The observations regarding a tendency toward caution and reserve on the part of the high intelligence–low creativity children receive further corroboration in other areas of their functioning. For example, when asked to make arrangements and groupings of pictures of everyday objects in whatever ways they considered most suitable, they preferred to make groupings that were more conventional in nature. They tended to avoid making free-wheeling, unconventional arrangements in which there would be greater free play for evolving unique combinations of objects. For instance, a more conventional grouping would be assembling pictures of a lamppost, a door and a hammer, and calling them "hard objects." A more unconventional grouping, on the other hand, would be putting together pictures of a comb, a lipstick, a watch, a pocketbook and a door, and describing them as items that concern "getting ready to go out." It is as if a greater fear of error characterizes these children, so that when left to their own devices, they tend to gravitate toward ways of construing the world that are less open to criticism by others.

　·　·　·　·　·　·　·　·　·　·　·　·　·　·

Since the high intelligence–low creativity children seem to behave in a manner that should maximize correctness and minimize error, we can expect them to be in particularly good standing in their classroom environment. Given their apparent tendency to conform to expectations, their mode of functioning should be maximally rewarding and minimally punishing for them. In short, there should be a high degree of fit between customary environmental expectations and their way of conducting themselves. We find, in fact, that this group admits to little anxiety or disturbance when asked to describe their own feeling states. Their self-descriptions indicate the lowest levels of anxiety reported by any of the four creativity-intelligence groups. Since this group behaves in a manner that should minimize worry or concern for them, their minimal level of reported anxiety probably represents an accurate description of how they feel. But at a cost, as we have noted, of functioning in a constricted manner.

High Creativity — Low Intelligence. Turning to the group characterized by high creativity but relatively low intelligence, we find, first of all, that they tend to exhibit disruptive behavior in the classroom. This is about the only respect, however, in which their observable conduct in the usual school and play settings resembles that of the group high in both creativity and intelligence. Of all four groups, the high creativity–low intelligence children are the least able to concentrate and maintain attention in class, the lowest in self-confidence and the most likely to express the conviction that they are no good. It is as if they are convinced that their case is a hopeless one. Furthermore, they are relatively isolated socially; not only do they avoid contact with other children, but in addition their peers shun them more than any other group. Perhaps, in their social withdrawal, these children are indulging fantasy activities. At any rate, they are relatively alone in the school setting, and in many respects can be characterized as worse off than the group low in both creativity and intelligence.

It should be borne in mind that the high creativity–low intelligence children nevertheless give evidence of the same kind of creative thinking capacities as are found in the high creativity–high intelligence group. Again, for example, we find a greater likelihood of seeing possible connections between events that do not share much in common. The high creativity children, whether high or low regarding intelligence, are more willing to postulate relationships between somewhat dissimilar events.

Apparently, the kinds of evaluational pressures present in the case of intelligence and achievement testing as well as in the typical classroom environment serve to disrupt cognitive powers which can come to the fore when pressure is reduced. An interesting complementarity seems to exist with regard to the psychological situations found for the high creativity–low intelligence group and the low creativity–high intelligence group: while members of the former seem to perform more effectively when evaluational pressures are absent, members of the latter seem to work more adequately when evaluational pressures are present. It is as if the former children tend to go to pieces if questions of personal competence and achievement enter the picture, while the latter children have difficulty if they are denied a framework of standards within which they can evaluate what is required of them if they are to seem competent in the eyes of adults.

Low Creativity — Low Intelligence. While the children in this group show the greatest cognitive deprivation of the four groups under study, they seem to make up for it at least to some degree in the social sphere. From observations of their behavior in school and at play they are found to be more extroverted socially, less hesitant, and more self-confident and self-assured than the children of low intelligence but high creativity. The members of the low-low group are particularly poor regarding the kinds of aesthetic sensitivity that were mentioned earlier — for example, they show the weakest tendencies to respond to the possible expressive meanings that abstract line forms may convey. Despite such deficiencies, however, this group does not seem to be the maximally disadvantaged group in the classroom. Rather, the low-low children seem to have worked out a *modus vivendi* that puts them at greater social ease in the school situation than is the case for their high creativity–low intelligence peers.

Now that we have characterized the four groups of children, let us finally consider the implications of the relative roles played by ability and by motivational factors in a child's thinking. The only group that looks like it is in difficulty with regard to ability — and even in their case we cannot be sure — is the group low in both intelligence and creativity. In the cases of the two groups that are low regarding one cognitive skill and high regarding the other — the low intelligence–high creativity group and the high intelligence–low creativity group — our evidence suggests that, rather than an ability deficiency, the children in question are handicapped by particular motivational dispositions receiving strong environmental support. For the low intelligence–high creativity children, the difficulty seems to concern excessive fear of being evaluated; hence they perform poorly when evaluational standards are a prominent part of the setting. For the high intelligence–low creativity children, on the other hand, the difficulty seems to concern a fear of not knowing whether one is thought well of by significant others. The possibility of making mistakes, therefore, is particularly avoided. Further, if evaluational standards are not a clear part of the setting, so that the child does not know a right way of behaving in order to fulfill the expectations of others, performance will deteriorate because the problem of avoiding error becomes of prime importance.

In theory, at least, these kinds of motivational hindrances could be rectified by appropriate training procedures. If one could induce the low intelligence–high creativity children to be less concerned when evaluational standards are present, and the high intelligence–low creativity children to be less concerned when evaluational standards are absent, their thinking behavior might come to display high levels of both intelligence and creativity.

E. PAUL TORRANCE · Education and Creativity

[*Torrance, an educational psychologist, has carried out an extraordinarily large body of research on creativity and the nurturance of creativity, some of which is summarized here. His design and scoring of tests for identifying creative talent has largely been influenced by Guilford's factor analytic research. The Torrance tests of creativity (previously the Minnesota tests of creativity) are used extensively in his researches and are described briefly here. Torrance and his associates have carried out several experiments with school children and he has constantly emphasized the need for encouragement of unusual and potentially creative children in the classroom.*]

On the basis of an analysis of the diverse ways of defining creativity and what I consider the requirements of a definition for keeping a program of research on factors affecting creative growth in context, I defined creativity as the process of becoming sensitive to problems, deficiencies, gaps in knowledge, missing elements, disharmonies, and so on; identifying the difficulty; searching for solutions, making guesses, or formulating hypotheses about the deficiencies; testing and retesting these hypotheses and possibly modifying and retesting them; and finally communicating the results. This definition describes a natural human process. Strong human needs are involved at each stage. If we sense some incompleteness or disharmony, tension is aroused. We are uncomfortable and want to relieve the tension. Since habitual ways of behaving are inadequate, we begin trying to avoid the commonplace and obvious (but incorrect) solutions by investigating, diagnosing, manipulating, and making guesses or estimates. Until the guesses or hypotheses have been tested, modified, and retested, we are still uncomfortable. The tension is unrelieved, however, until we tell somebody of our discovery.

SOURCE   From Torrance, E. P., "Scientific Views of Creativity and Factors Affecting Its Growth." Reprinted by permission of Dædalus, Journal of the American Academy of Arts and Sciences, Boston, Massachusetts. Summer 1965, Creativity and Learning. Pp. 663–681.

There are many other reasons for favoring this definition. It enables us to begin defining operationally the kinds of abilities, mental functioning, and personality characteristics that facilitate or inhibit the process. It provides an approach for specifying the kinds of products that result from the process, the kinds of persons who can engage most successfully in the process, and the conditions that facilitate the process. . . .

.   .   .   .

If one accepts the definition of creativity that I have offered, it becomes possible to recognize creative behavior, creative thinking abilities, and creative potential both through test and non-test procedures. How it is done will depend in large degree upon the reasons for wanting to recognize creativity, who is attempting to do so, and what professional resources are available. From the standpoint of the teacher and counselor, it would seem important to recognize those kinds of potential that make a difference in the way persons should be taught and guided. A major reason for my interest in developing measures of the creative thinking abilities is that I believe that such instruments can provide one useful basis for making instruction different for different students. Since abilities constitute, at least to some extent, the basis of needs and motivations, knowledge about a person's creative thinking abilities frequently provides clues about differential preferences for ways of learning.

.   .   .   .

[Our] tests represent one rather sharp departure from the factor-type tests developed by Guilford and his associates. We made deliberate attempts to construct test tasks that would be models of the creative process, each involving different kinds of thinking and each contributing something unique to the batteries under development. Test tasks are thus fairly complex and have features that make use of what we know about the nature of the creative thinking processes, the qualities of creative products, and creative personalities.

.   .   .   .

One of the clearest and most straightforward models is found in the Ask-and-Guess Test of which there are several forms. In all forms, subjects are shown a picture (Mother Goose prints for children and certain professional groups, pictures similar to those used in the Thematic Apperception Test for nurses, a picture of boys starting a small business for salesmen, and so forth) and given the following series of instructions:

> The next three tasks will give you a chance to see how good you
> are at asking questions to find out things that you do not know
> and in making guesses about possible causes and consequences

of events. Look at the picture. What is happening? What can you tell for sure? What do you need to know to understand what is happening, what caused it to happen, and what will be the result?

Young children are asked to dictate their responses to an adult and older children and adults are asked to write theirs. In the written version, the following instructions are given for the first of the three tasks:

> On this page, write out all of the questions you can think of about the picture on the page before this one. Ask all of the questions you would need to know for sure what is happening. Do not ask questions that can be answered just by looking at the drawing.

After five minutes, subjects are given the following instructions for the second task (Guessing Causes):

> In the spaces below, list as many possible causes as you can of the action shown in the picture. You may use things that might have happened just before the event in the picture or something that happened a long time ago that made the event happen. Make as many guesses as you can. Do not be afraid to guess.

After another five minutes, the following instructions are given for the third task (Guessing Consequences):

> In the spaces below, list as many possibilities as you can of what might happen as a result of what is taking place in the picture. You may use things that might happen right afterwards or things that might happen as a result long afterwards in the future. Make as many guesses as you can. Do not be afraid to guess.

The first task is designed to reveal the subject's ability to sense what he cannot find out from looking at the picture and to ask questions that will enable him to fill in the gaps in his knowledge. The second and third tasks are designed to reveal the subject's ability to formulate hypotheses concerning cause and effect. The number of relevant responses produced by a subject yields one measure of ideational fluency. The number of shifts in thinking or number of different categories of questions, causes, or consequences gives one measure of flexibility. The statistical infrequency of these questions, causes, or consequences or the extent to which the response represents a mental leap or departure from the obvious and commonplace gives one measure of originality. The detail and specificity incorporated into the questions and hypotheses provide one measure of ability to elaborate.

In another task, subjects are asked to produce unusual or provocative questions about common objects such as tin cans, cardboard boxes, or ice. Subjects are encouraged to ask questions that lead to a variety of different answers and that might arouse interest and curiosity in others concerning the object.

The Product Improvement Task calls for the production of clever, interesting, and unusual ways of changing a toy stuffed animal (for example, a toy dog, monkey, elephant, or kangaroo) so that it will be more interesting for children to play with. The Unusual Uses Test calls for interesting and unusual uses of common objects such as tin cans, cardboard boxes, and books. The Just Suppose Test presents the subject with an improbable situation and asks him to "just suppose" that the situation happened and to think of all of the things that might occur as a result. The improbable situations include such things as:

> Just suppose when it was raining all the rain drops stood still in the air and wouldn't move — and they were solid.
> Just suppose someone got caught in a big soap bubble and couldn't get out.

Each "Just Suppose" is accompanied by an interesting drawing depicting the improbable situation.

The Imaginative Stories Test calls for writing imaginative stories about animals and people having some divergent characteristic. Subjects are asked to select from one of a set of ten titles such as:

> The Flying Monkey.
> The Lion That Won't Roar.
> The Man Who Cries.
> The Woman Who Can But Won't Talk.

The Sounds and Images Test asks the subject to produce imaginative and original images suggested by each of a series of four sound effects, ranging from a familiar and well-organized sound effect to one consisting of six rather strange and relatively unrelated sounds. The four-sound series is presented three times, and each time the subject is asked to stretch his imagination further.

Each of the tasks is based on a rationale developed from some research finding concerning the nature of the creative process, the creative personality, or the conditions necessary for creative achievement. The tasks are designed to involve as many different aspects of verbal creative functioning as possible. Most of the tasks are evaluated for fluency (number of different relevant ideas), flexibility (number of shifts in thinking or different categories of response), originality (number of statistically infrequent responses that show creative intellectual energy), and elaboration (number of different ideas used in working out the details of an idea).

Although a variety of figural test tasks have been developed, the standardized batteries consist of three tasks, each designed to tap a somewhat different aspect of creative functioning. The Picture Construction Test is accompanied by the following instructions:

> At the bottom of this page is a piece of colored paper in the form of a curved shape. Think of a picture or an object in which this form would be an important part. Then lift up the piece of colored paper and stick it wherever you want it on the next page, just like you would a postage stamp. Then add lines with pencil or crayon to make your picture.
>
> Try to think of a picture that no one else will think of. Keep adding new ideas to your first idea to make it tell as interesting and as exciting a story as you can.
>
> When you have completed your picture, think up a name or title for it and write it at the bottom of the page in the space provided. Make your title as clever and unusual as possible. Use it to help tell your story.

This, as well as the other two figural tasks, can be administered at all educational levels from kindergarten to graduate school and to various occupational groups. It is a task to which kindergarteners can respond in groups and one which provides sufficient encouragement to regression to be useful with graduate students and other adults. In each battery a different shape (such as a tear drop or jelly bean) is used as the stimulus object.

The stimulus material for the Figure Completion Test consists of ten incomplete figures and is accompanied by the following instructions:

> By adding lines to figures on this and the next page, you can sketch some interesting objects or pictures. Again, try to think of some picture or object that no one else will think of. Try to make it tell as complete and as interesting a story as you can by adding to and building up your first idea. Make up a title for each of your drawings and write it at the bottom of each block next to the number of the figure.

The Repeated Closed Figures Test consists of two pages of closed figures (circles, squares, triangles, and so on). The instructions for the Circles version of this test are as follows:

> In ten minutes see how many objects or pictures you can make from the circles below and on the next page. The circles should be the main part of whatever you make. With pencil or crayon add lines to the circles to complete your picture. You can place marks inside the circles, on the circles, and outside the circles—wherever you want to in order to make your picture. Try to think of things that no one else will think of. Make as many different pictures or objects as you can and put as many ideas as you can in each one. Make them tell as complete and as interesting a story as you can. Add names or titles in the spaces provided.

This triad of test tasks in a sense represents three different aspects of creativity or three different creative tendencies. The Incomplete Figures task calls into play the tendency toward structuring and integrating. The incomplete figures create tension in the beholder who must control this tension long enough to make the mental leap necessary to get away from the obvious and commonplace. Failure to delay gratification usually results in the premature closure of the incomplete figures and an obvious or commonplace response. The invitation to "make the drawing tell a story" is designed to motivate elaboration and the further filling in of gaps. The Circles Test, as well as other closed figures tasks, brings into play the tendency toward disruption of structure in order to create something new. The repetition of a single stimulus requires an ability to return to the same stimulus again and again and perceive it in a different way. The Picture Construction Test sets in motion the tendency toward finding a purpose for something that has no definite purpose and to elaborate it in such a way that the purpose is achieved. Discoveries and their applications may take place in two major ways: (1) there may be deliberate attempts to discover a creative solution to a problem or (2) some discovery may occur and the discoverer sets out to see what problems the discovery will solve. Theoretically, the Picture Construction Test symbolizes the latter. These tasks tend to discriminate between the good elaborators and the productive original thinkers. Some subjects produce a large number of very original ideas but fail to elaborate any of them very well; some produce very few ideas of any kind but make them very elaborate or "fancy"; still others produce a large number of very commonplace ideas with little elaboration.

Thus, it is seen that we have tried deliberately to base the test stimuli, the test tasks, instructions, and scoring procedures on the best that we know from research about creativity. The same test tasks, in most instances, have been administered at all educational levels. This has made it possible to determine whether or not children and young people identified as "creative" behave in ways similar to the ways in which eminent creative people of the past behaved when they were children and young people. It also enables us to determine whether or not adults identified today as relatively creative on the basis of outside criteria behave in ways that can be called "creative" on the basis of test scores. In general, the evidence has been rather positive in spite of the complexities introduced by problems of motivation, unfavorable conditions, and the difficulties of conducting well-controlled studies. Much of this evidence has been summarized in *Guiding Creative Talent* and in *Rewarding Creative Behavior*.[1] Only the briefest review is possible here.

In observational studies,[2] we found that children scoring high on tests of creative thinking initiated a larger number of ideas, produced more original ideas, and gave more explanations of the workings of unfamiliar science toys than did their less creative peers when placed in five-person groups. When matched for intelligence, sex, race, and teacher, the most creative children in forty-six classrooms from grades one through six more frequently than their controls had reputations for having wild and fantastic ideas, produced drawings and other products judged to be original, and produced work characterized by humor, playfulness, relative lack of rigidity, and relaxation. Weisberg and Springer[3] studied a sample of gifted (high IQ) fourth-grade pupils. In comparison with those who made the lower test scores those who made the higher scores were rated significantly higher on strength of self-image, ease of early recall of life experiences, humor, availability of Oedipal anxiety, and even ego development. On the Rorschach Ink Blots, they showed a tendency toward unconventional responses, unreal percepts, and fanciful and imaginative treatment of the blots. Their performance was described as being both more sensitive and more independent than that of their less creative peers. Among sixth-grade children, Fleming and Weintraub[4] found significant negative relationships between the measures of originality, fluency, and flexibility and measures of rigidity. Yamamoto[5] found correlations of around .50 between creativity test scores and a composite measure of originality based on creative writings.

Studies with adults have also been encouraging. In my own graduate classes, I have found rather consistently that those who achieve high scores on the tests of creative thinking develop original ideas in the content area of the course and make more creative applications of knowledge than do their less creative peers. Hansen and I found that the more creative business education teachers asked more provocative questions, more self-involving questions, and more divergent ones than their less creative peers. Hansen found a number of other significant differences between her high and low creative teachers, showing that the more creative teachers, as identified by the tests, behaved more creatively in the classroom as judged by detailed classroom observations. Blockhus[6] found that the students of the more creative business education teachers showed more growth in originality during a semester than did the pupils of the less creative ones. Sommers[7] found that students carefully identified by college industrial arts instructors as creative scored significantly higher on the tests of creative thinking than did their less creative peers. Wallace[8] found that saleswomen ranking in the upper third on sales in a large department store scored significantly higher on tests of creative thinking than did their peers ranking in the lower third. He also found that the more creative women had tended to gravitate to those departments judged by personnel managers as requiring more creativity. Wallace[9] also found that measures of originality and fluency differentiated the several echelons of personnel in a large national sales organization. The measures of flexibility and elaboration failed to differentiate the highest echelon of sales executives from the lower groups but differentiated within the various lower levels.

Some studies have shown that the measures described herein are positively related to various kinds of school achievement, while others have shown that such measures are unrelated or negatively related to measures of school achievement. A careful examination of these studies suggests that methods of assessing school achievement and methods of instruction may both be important factors in creative growth.

Bentley[10] found the following set of correlation coefficients for four different measures of achievement in a graduate class of 110 students in educational psychology and a composite measure of creative thinking ability based on a battery of the Minnesota tests and the Miller Analogies Test, an instrument commonly used in graduate school admission procedures:

Achievement Measure	Creativity	Miller's
Recognition (multiple-choice test)	.03	.47
Memory (completion and short-answer test)	.11	.41
Productive Thinking (creative applications)	.53	.37
Evaluation and Judgment (decision making)	.38	.27

If one examines closely the research concerning the interaction between different kinds of abilities and different methods of instruction, an interesting picture unfolds.[11] When knowledge is obtained by authority, a measure of mental age or intelligence is a better predictor of achievement than measures of originality, fluency, and the like. When knowledge is obtained in creative ways, for example by discovery or experimentation, the measures of originality, fluency, and the like seem to be better predictors than scores on intelligence tests. . . .

Checklists of activities done on one's own, checklists of creative achievements, biographical or life experience inventories, an inventory of personal-social motivations, a personality checklist, and a variety of other non-aptitude measures also promise to be useful. Other investigators[12] have reported promising results from such well-known instruments as Strong's Vocational Interest Blank, the Allport-Vernon-Lindzey Study of Values, the Myers-Briggs Type Indicator, the California Psychological Inventory, the Barron-Welsh Art Scale, the Thematic Apperception Test, and biographical inventories.

Many complain that we do not yet know enough about the factors affecting creative growth. In my opinion, we have known enough about these factors since the time of Socrates and Plato to do a far better job of creative education than is commonly done. Socrates knew that it was important to ask provocative questions and to encourage natural ways of learning. He knew that it was not enough to ask questions that call only for the reproduction of what has been learned. He knew that thinking is a skill that is developed through practice and that it is important to ask questions that require the learner to do something with what he learns to evaluate it, produce new ideas from it, and recombine it in new ways. Plato knew that "what is honored in a country will be cultivated there." He knew that it was important for educators to be aware of the potentialities of students and that potentialities are rarely discovered under a discipline that is excessively harsh and coercive. He said, "Do not train boys to learning by force or harshness; but direct them to it by what amuses their minds, so that you may be the better able to discover with accuracy the peculiar bent of the genius of each."

Some readers may wonder why I have chosen to place so much emphasis on the identification of creative potentiality and the measurement of what I have called the creative thinking abilities. Scientific studies of factors that affect creative growth require measurement, and the rationale of the test tasks, test task instructions, and methods of assessing or scoring test responses helps to elaborate my definition of creativity and provides a wealth of clues concerning the factors that assess creative growth. More important, however, is the conviction that a teacher must usually recognize creative potentiality in a child or young person before he is willing to permit him to learn in a non-habitual or creative way. On one occasion, I asked a class of two hundred students, including many experienced teachers, to describe some instance in which they had permitted or encouraged a student to learn in a creative way and had then observed that the experience made an important difference in the achievement and behavior of the student. Eighty-two per cent of them were able to recall such an incident, and a content analysis of their responses showed that in eighty-six per cent of the incidents the recognition of a creative potentiality was crucial to the teacher's willingness to permit or encourage such activity.

Although there are certainly many gaps in knowledge concerning the factors that affect creative growth, there is a great variety of research findings that give useful guidance. It would be impossible here even to list these findings. I have collected about thirty related studies conducted by my associates and me in *Rewarding Creative Behavior: Experiments in Classroom Creativity*. These studies help to delineate the roles in creative growth of such factors as ways of rewarding creative behavior (for example, by being respectful of unusual and provocative questions and of unusual ideas), creative motivations or attitudes of the teacher, creative activities and opportunities for practicing skills in creative thinking, differential rewards for boys and girls, differential rewards for originality, competition, unevaluated practice, creative rather than critical peer-evaluated practice, evaluative discussions about creative productions, peer pressures in homogeneous and heterogeneous groups, trouble-shooting evaluation, and helping children and young people value their own ideas. Attention is also given to differences in the ways different cultures encourage and discourage characteristics associated with the creative personality.

I am asked frequently if these and other recent studies advance us any further in the direction of a more creative kind of education than did Progressive Education. Some observers even assert that there is no difference between what I have called creative ways of learning and Progressive Education. Progressive Education aroused so much controversy and still engenders such strong negative reactions that the label of Progressive Education is still used to condemn almost all educational innovations. If one examines what we have learned during the ten years since the dissolution of the Progressive Education Association in 1955, it should become evident that it is possible for us to advance beyond the major precepts of Progressive Education and to come closer to achieving the

American dream of a kind of education that will give every child a chance to grow and to achieve his potentialities.

·   ·   ·   ·   ·   ·   ·   ·   ·   ·   ·   ·

References

1. E. P. Torrance, *Guiding Creative Talent* (Englewood Cliffs N.J., 1962); and *Rewarding Creative Behavior: Experiments in Classroom Creativity* (Englewood Cliffs, N.J., 1965).

2. E. P. Torrance, *Rewarding Creative Behavior, ibid.*

3. P. S. Weisberg and Kayla J. Springer, "Environmental Factors in Creative Function," *Archives in General Psychiatry*, Vol. 5 (1961), pp. 554–564.

4. E. S. Fleming and S. Weintraub, "Attitudinal Rigidity as a Measure of Creativity in Gifted Children," *Journal of Educational Psychology*, Vol. 53 (1962), pp. 81–85.

5. K. Yamamoto, "Creative Writing and School Achievement," *School and Society*, Vol. 91 (October 19, 1963), pp. 307–308.

6. Wanda A. Blockhus, "Creativity and Money Management Understandings," Doctoral dissertation, University of Minnesota, 1961.

7. W. S. Sommers, "The Influence of Selected Teaching Methods on the Development of Creative Thinking," Doctoral dissertation, University of Minnesota, 1963.

8. H. R. Wallace, "Creative Thinking: A Factor in Sales Productivity," *Vocational Guidance Quarterly*, Vol. 9 (1961), pp. 223–226.

9. H. R. Wallace, "Creative Thinking: A Factor in the Performance of Industrial Salesmen," Doctoral dissertation, University of Minnesota, 1964.

10. J. C. Bentley, "The Creative Thinking Abilities and Different Kinds of Achievement," M.A. research paper, University of Minnesota, 1961.

11. See, for example, T. R. McConnell, "Discovery vs. Authoritative Identification in the Learning of Children," *University of Iowa Studies in Education*, Vol. 9, No. 5 (1934), pp. 13–62; L. M. Stolurow, "Social Impact of Programmed Instruction: Aptitudes and Abilities Re visited," Paper presented at the American Psychological Association Annual Convention, St. Louis, Mo., September 2, 1962; L. G. Gotkin and N. Massa, *Programmed Instruction and the Academically Gifted: The Effects of Creativity and Teacher Behavior on Programmed Instruction with Young Learners* (New York, 1963); W. L. Hutchinson, "Creative and Productive Thinking in the Classroom," Doctoral dissertation, University of Utah, 1963; and J. B. MacDonald and J. D. Raths, "Should We Group by Creative Abilities?" *Elementary School Journal*, Vol. 65 (1964), pp. 137–142.

12. D. W. MacKinnon (ed.), *The Creative Person* (Berkeley, Calif., 1961); and C. W. Taylor and J. Holland, "Predictors of Creative Performance," in C. W. Taylor (ed.), *Creativity: Progress and Potential* (New York, 1964), pp. 15–48.

SARNOFF A. MEDNICK · The Associative Basis of the Creative Process

[Mednick is one of the few psychologists in creativity research to start with a definite theory of the creative process and follow it with empirical research. The theory of creation as a bringing together of words and other entities that

SOURCE   From Mednick, S. A. "The Associative Basis of the Creative Process," *Psychological Review*, 1962, *Vol. 69*, pp. 220–227, 232. Copyright 1962 by the American Psychological Association. Reprinted by permission of author and publisher.

are remotely associated or connected with each other has been the basis for a specific creativity test. The Remote Associates Test, which Mednick derived from findings in word association studies, has received wide attention among psychologists and is used very frequently in creativity experiments. As a theory of creativity based on the association model of cognition, Mednick's formulation is related to that of Koestler. As a clearly genetic type of explanation of creating, it is closely related to Skinner's position shown in the next chapter.]

The intent of this paper is the presentation of an associative interpretation of the process of creative thinking. The explanation is not directed to any specific field of application such as art or science but attempts to delineate processes that underlie all creative thought.

.   .   .   .

We will state our basic hypothesis regarding the nature of creative thinking in the form of a definition. . . . the creative thinking process . . . [is] the forming of associative elements into new combinations which either meet specified requirements or are in some way useful. The more mutually remote the elements of the new combination, the more creative the process or solution. An additional criterion of the level of creativeness of a product is described below.

Creative thinking as defined here is distinguished from original thinking by the imposition of requirements on originality. Thus, 7,363,474 is quite an original answer to the problem "How much is 12 + 12?" However, it is only when conditions are such that this answer is useful that we can also call it creative. There are many original ideas expressed in institutions for the mentally ill and mentally retarded; few of these are likely to be creative. There are many fields of creative endeavor in which the usefulness of products would be difficult to measure reliably. While these difficulties must eventually be faced, for the present our research efforts have been concentrated on laboratory situations in which criteria for usefulness can be arbitrarily experimenter-defined and unequivocally explained to the subject. The originality of a response is simply inversely related to its probability in a given population.

It should be pointed out that this definition of creativity is quite similar to basic notions advanced by British associationists from Locke (1690) to Bain (1855), and by those psychologists whose work is based in large measure on their speculations. Freud (1938), Hollingsworth (1928), and Binet (1899) may serve as examples.

.   .   .   .

In terms of associative theory, we may point to three ways of achieving a creative solution. Generally, any condition or state of the organism which will tend to bring the requisite associative elements into ideational contiguity will increase the probability and speed of a creative solution. Therefore, the following three ways of attaining creative solutions are all methods of bringing the requisite associative elements together.

. . . The requisite associative elements may be evoked contiguously by the contiguous environmental appearance (usually an accidental contiguity) of stimuli which elicit these associative elements. This sort of creative solution is often dubbed serendipitous. This is the manner of discovery to which is popularly attributed such inventions as the X ray and such discoveries as penicillin. One physicist has described how he has reduced serendipity to a method by placing in a fishbowl large numbers of slips of paper, each inscribed with a physical fact. He regularly devotes some time to randomly drawing pairs of these facts from the fishbowl, looking for new and useful combinations. His procedure represents the operational embodiment of this method of achieving creative solutions.

. . . The requisite associative elements may be evoked in contiguity as a result of the similarity of the associative elements or the similarity of the stimuli eliciting these associative elements. This mode of creative solution may be encountered in creative writing which exploits homonymity, rhyme, and similarities in the structure and rhythm of words or similarities in the objects which they designate. The contiguous ideational occurrence of such items as alliterative and rhyming associates may be dependent on a factor such as primary stimulus generalization. It seems possible that this means of bringing about contiguity of associational elements may be of considerable importance in those domains of creative effort which are less directly dependent on the manipulation of symbols. Here we might include certain approaches to painting, sculpture, musical composition, and poetry.

. . . The requisite associative elements may be evoked in contiguity through the mediation of common elements. This means of bringing the associative elements into contiguity with each other is of great importance in those areas of endeavor where the use of symbols (verbal, mathematical, chemical, etc.) is mandatory. For example, in psychology, the idea of relating reactive inhibition and cortical satiation may have been mediated by the common associates "tiredness" or "fatigue" (Köhler & Fishback, 1950).

.   .   .   .

From the definition given above, the factors that will make for individual differences in the probability of achieving creative solutions may be deduced. Any ability or tendency which serves to bring otherwise mutually remote ideas into contiguity will facilitate a creative solution; any ability or tendency which serves to keep remote ideas from contiguous evocation will inhibit the creative solution.

Listed below are several illustrative predictions concerning individual differences that one may make from this theoretical orientation.

. . . .

It should be clear that an individual without the requisite elements in his response repertoire will not be able to combine them so as to arrive at a creative solution. An architect who does not know of the existence of a new material can hardly be expected to use it creatively.

. . . .

The organization of an individual's associations will influence the probability and speed of attainment of a creative solution. There is a whole family of predictions that one may draw from this concept of the associative hierarchy. As an initial example, let us take the question of the manner in which the associative strength around ideas is distributed. If we present an individual with the word "table," what sort of associative responses does he make? The individual who tends to be restricted to the stereotyped responses, such as "chair," may be characterized as having an associative hierarchy with a steep slope (see Figure 1). That is, when you get past the first one or two conventional responses to the stimulus, the individual's associative strengths to other words or ideas (lower in the hierarchy) drops rapidly. We can also conceive of a second sort of individual whose associative hierarchy is characterized by a rather flat slope. This is an individual who perhaps also has as his strongest response the conventional chair. But for him this response is not overly dominant and so it is more likely that he will be able to get to the less probable, more

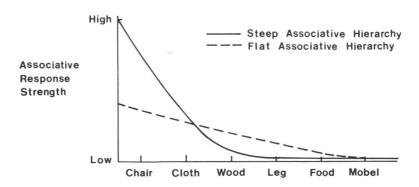

Figure 1. Associative hierarchies around the word "table."

remote kinds of associations to table. It is among these more remote responses that the requisite elements and mediating terms for a creative
solution will be lurking. This slope factor may be related to the mathematical analysis of associative production developed by Bousfield, Sedgewick, and Cohen (1954). It probably is closely approximated by their constant, m, measuring rate of depletion of the associative reservoir. They
found a high negative correlation between rate of association and total
number of associations. It would be predicted from Figure 1 that the high
creative subject (flat hierarchy) would respond relatively slowly and
steadily and emit many responses while the low creative subject (steep
hierarchy) would respond at a higher rate but emit fewer responses.

It would be predicted that the greater the concentration of associative
strength in a small number of stereotyped associative responses (steep
hierarchy) the less probable it is that the individual will attain the creative solution. Thus, the word association behavior of the high creative
individual should be characterized by less stereotypy and commonality.
This last prediction is supported by a study by Mednick, Gough, and
Woodworth (Mednick, 1958). Research scientists rated for creativity were
divided into relatively high ($N = 15$) and relatively low ($N = 15$) groups.
The low creatives gave more stereotyped responses on 80% of a group of
36 test words from the Kent-Rosanoff list. (These test words were chosen
for their tendency to elicit stereotyped responses. Stereotypy was defined
by the Minnesota Kent-Rosanoff Word Association Norms, Russell &
Jenkins, 1954). It should be pointed out that these results lend themselves
to another possible interpretation. The highly creative individual may also
have a steep hierarchy but a deviant one. That is, his most dominant
associative response may be quite strong but quite different from the
popular, dominant associative response. There are different predictions
that can be made for the flat-associative-hierarchy creative and the steep-
deviant associative-hierarchy creative. The latter is more likely to be the
one-shot producer (a not uncommon phenomenon among novelists). If he
does create further products, they will tend to resemble closely the first
product. The former is more likely to be a multiproducer; he is more likely
to produce in a variety of avenues of creative expression.

The prediction suggesting an expectation of less creativity from an individual with a high concentration of associative strength in a few responses leads to another prediction. The greater the number of instances
in which an individual has solved problems with given materials in a certain manner, the less is the likelihood of his attaining a creative solution
using these materials. Such an individual will "know the meaning" of

the elements of the subject matter. That is, he will have a steep associative hierarchy around these elements. An example of the operation of this principle recently occurred to the writer while teaching an honors freshman introductory course in psychology at the University of Michigan. I was giving a well known interpretation of a well known experiment in stimulus generalization when interrupted by a student who calmly stated that the interpretation was in error. After a few minutes of blustering I asked him to explain. His explanation proved him to be correct. I had been dealing with this material for years and "knew" the "correct" interpretation; for him this material was new, he had a low, flat associative hierarchy. Thus, if a newcomer to a field has the requisite information, he is more likely to achieve a creative solution than a long-time worker in the field. This may be the reason that theoretical physicists and master chess players are often said to have passed their prime by the age of 25.

.   .   .   .

The greater the number of associations that an individual has to the requisite elements of a problem, the greater the probability of his reaching a creative solution. This variable is not independent of the preceding one since an individual with a high concentration of associative strength in few associative responses is not likely to have a proliferation of associations. The more associates which are evoked by a requisite element of a problem, the more likely it is that an associate will exist which will serve as a mediating bridge to another requisite element, facilitating combination. It seems likely that this variable will not be related to speed of creative solution since it may take a good deal of time to get to the mediating links.

.   .   .   .

Previously learned or innately predisposed methods of approaching problems will influence the probability of a creative solution. If the requisite associational elements of a new and useful combination are probable associates of the concrete representations of relevant aspects of the problem, an individual with a predominately "perceptual" approach will be more likely to reach a creative solution. If, however, the requisite associational elements are not elicited as responses to these concrete representations or if there is no concrete representation then an individual with a "conceptual" approach will be more likely to reach a creative solution.

Another cognitive style of importance may lie along the "visualizer-verbalizer" dimension. The visualizer is one who tends to call up relatively complete memorial sensory representations of the relevant concrete aspects of problems. If the problem deals with horses, he tends to picture a horse in terms of its sensory qualities. On the other hand, the verbalizer explores the problem by associating with words around the word "horse." If the requisite elements are high in his verbal associative hierarchy to the word horse, the verbalizer will be more likely to attain a creative solution; the visualizer may be thrown off or at least delayed by many false leads. On the other hand, if a requisite verbal associative response to the word horse is very low, or not present in the verbalizer's hierarchy, then the visualizer will be more likely to attain the creative solution. It is therefore clear that some types of problems will be solved more easily by the visualizer and some by the verbalizer.

Factors such as these (admittedly very poorly defined) may be partly responsible for differential aptitudes for creative work in differing fields.

.   .   .   .

The creative combination of elements is only one among the many which may present themselves to the subject. How or why is the creative combination selected? Some speculations regarding this problem follow. The explanation of the process of selection may be related to the nature of the problem. Problems either entail a specific and relatively objective set of testable criteria (Paint a realistic portrait of this individual. Design a refrigerator so that it will be automatically free of frost.) or they do not (The chemist mixes two liquids out of curiosity. The painter dabs hopefully at a fresh canvas waiting for an idea. The psychologist tosses a new test into a correlation matrix). When specific criteria are provided, they form an important part of the stimulus set which is determining which associative elements are being elicited and thus becoming eligible for entering into combination with other elements. Important sets of associations to each of these combinations are the consequents of the combinations. The set of consequents for each combination (If I put x, y, and z together, a and b will happen) is continually compared with the set of requirements of the problem. When the set of consequents of a new combination achieves a close fit with the set of problem requirements, this combination is selected. When there is complete overlap of sets, "search behavior" is terminated. As with the other requisite elements of the problem, individual differences in this case will vary with (among other things) the structure of the associational hierarchies around the requirements of the problem. When the refrigerator-defroster problem was presented to an undergraduate class almost all of the proferred solutions were based on the principle of ridding the refrigerator of already heavily accumulated frost. A couple of individuals (possibly familiar with the defroster principles presently in use) suggested methods which disposed of the frost before it built up to an overly annoying level. In addition to these there were two unique responses, i.e., a "new" method of preventing moisture from condensing in the freezer compartment, and a method of allowing frost to accumulate but limiting the location of accumulation to a small box which could be regularly and conveniently removed and emptied. Thus it may be seen that an individual's associations to the requirements may be characterized as to their stereotypy; the imposed requirements of the problem may be viewed as part of the requisite elements in the situation. The earlier theoretical statements concerning these elements may be seen as being relevant here. The foregoing suggests an explanation of the selection process for the case where the subject must hunt for a combination of elements which will satisfy given criteria. In the case where no criteria are specified, the subject is typically producing random combinations of elements; the task of selection in this case consists in finding relevant criteria for the given partial products.

If we may continue along a bit further with this example of the defroster, we may begin to see some glimmerings of a solution to the most serious problem in research on creative thinking — how may we determine to what degree behavior is creative? We have suggested one criterion in our hypothesis. In the following an additional criterion is developed. To begin with let us examine the requirements as originally stated — "Design a refrigerator so that it is automatically free of frost." The first thing that strikes us is that while some requirements have been stated, there are even more that are strongly implied and essential, many that are desirable, and a number that we would only become aware of after some method of satisfying them had been suggested.

Let us examine some possible solutions:

1. Simply refraining from opening the refrigerator door would solve the problem as stated since this would prevent moisture from entering and condensing as frost. This solution meets many of the implied requirements. It is cheap, convenient, effective, does not require special training, etc. However, it is not an optimal solution since it violates one esssntial, implied requirement — the usefulness of the refrigerator must not be impaired. (This is the cutting-off-your-nose-to-spite-your-face solution.)

2. A primitive solution is the hammer-and-screwdriver method. This is tried and true and meets many of the essential requirements. It falls down in that it is inconvenient, messy, uneconomical (when caked with frost, the refrigerator unit is very inefficient), endangers the mechanism, and is hardly automatic.

3. In a refrigerator we once owned another solution was used. The opening and closing of the refrigerator door operated a counter. At a certain count the refrigerator unit was automatically heated and the melted water evaporated outside the refrigerator. The superiority of this solution is immediately apparent. The source of this superiority lies in the number of requirements which it meets. It is economical, automatic, convenient, peculiarly appropriate (the operation of the heating element is contingent upon the number of door openings. The amount of frost accumulated is also in part dependent on the number of door openings), does not interfere with the normal use of the refrigerator, and does not require special training. Note that the principle behind this highly creative solution (not allowing massive build-ups of frost) was infrequently suggested in the classroom group. However, this solution is not wholly successful at meeting some criteria. The frequent heating and cooling may injure frozen food stored near the heating element. Secondly, since the heating process must be brief and mild, it is inevitable that not all frost is removed. While this solution does effectively curtail the number of defrostings, it does not eliminate them completely. It is clear that a method which would encompass all of the advantages of the "counter" method, but which would, in addition, eliminate defrosting altogether would be even more creative. What is suggested by this discussion is that the creativeness of a product is some function of the number of requirements that the product meets. The most ready application of this definition will be in laboratory research in which tasks, solutions, and requirements may be arbitrarily constructed and varied.

.   .   .   .

The definition of the creative process has suggested a way of testing for individual differences in creativity. The test items are intended to require the testee to perform creatively. That is, he is asked to form associative elements into new combinations by providing mediating connective links. Since the test situation is contrived, the combination must meet specified criteria that are experimenter imposed.

The definition dictates the structure of the test. We must provide stimulus items from two mutually distant realities and ask the subject to "draw a spark from their juxtaposition." To state it more usefully, we must provide stimulus elements from mutually remote associative clusters and have the subject find a criteria-meeting mediating link which combines them. A first problem concerns the type of material of which the stimulus item should be composed. If the test is to be appropriate for all fields of creative endeavor, the material must either be nonsensical so as to avoid bias favoring any specific means of creative expression, or it must be so common in society that familiarity could be assumed to be high across fields of interest. The problems involved in constructing the nonsense materials so as to avoid favoring any interest groups soon proved to be apparently insurmountable. This left us searching for materials with which most individuals in the culture could claim acquaintance; this, in turn, brought us to verbal materials.

While it may be true that certain occupational groups have extensive experience in dealing with words, there are some verbal associative habits that could reasonably be assumed to be familiar to almost all individuals that have been brought up in this (USA) culture. Among such habits are the associative bonds between words like "ham and eggs," "bed-bug," "pool-hall," "hound-dog," "whole-wheat," "chorus-girl," "kill-joy," and "red-hot." These became the materials for the test.

Having decided on the materials, the test almost constructed itself in accordance with the definition. Several words from mutually distant associative clusters must be presented to the subject; his task must be to provide mediating links between them. Further (a factor of extreme importance), the mediating link must be strictly associative rather than being of a sort that follows elaborate rules of logic, concept formation, or problem solving. In their final (or at least present) form, the test items consist of sets of three words drawn from mutually remote associative cluster. One example might be:

Example 1:	rat	blue	cottage

The subject is required to find a fourth word which could serve as a specific kind of associative connective link between these disparate words. The answer to Example 1 is "cheese." "Cheese" is a word which is present in the word pairs "rat-cheese," "blue-cheese," and "cottage-cheese." The subject is presented with several examples so that he has an adequate opportunity to achieve the specific set necessary for the task.

Example 2:	railroad	girl	class
Example 3:	surprise	line	birthday
Example 4:	wheel	electric	high
Example 5:	out	dog	cat[1]

(None of these examples is a test item from any form of the actual test.) The two college level forms of the test (one coauthored by Sharon Halpern

1. Answers to sample RAT items: 2. working; 3. party; 4. chain or wire; 5. house.

and the other by Martha T. Mednick) have 30 items each; the subject is allowed 40 minutes; his score is the number right.

The test, called the Remote Associates Test (RAT), has some interesting correlations with other measures.

.   .   .   .

References

Bain, A. *The senses and the intellect.* 1855.

Binet, A. *The psychology of reasoning.* Chicago: Open Court, 1899.

Bousfield, W. A., Sedgewick, C. H. W., & Cohen, B. H. Certain temporal characteristics of the recall of verbal associates. *Amer. J. Psychol.,* 1954, **57,** 111–118.

Freud, S. Wit and its relation to the unconscious. In, *The basic writings of Sigmund Freud.* New York: Modern Library, 1938.

Hollingsworth, H. L. *Psychology: Its facts and principles.* New York: Appleton, 1928.

Köhler, W., & Fishback, J. The destruction of the Müller-Lyer illusion in repeated trials: II. Satiation patterns and memory traces. *J. exp. Psychol.,* 1950, **40,** 398–410.

Locke, J. *Essay concerning the human understanding.* 1690.

Mednick, S. A. An orientation to research in creativity. (Res. Memo. No. 2) Berkeley, Calif.: University of California, Institute of Personality Assessment and Research, 1958.

Russell, W. A., & Jenkins, J. J. The complete Minnesota norms for responses to 100 words from the Kent-Rosanoff Word Association Test. Technical Report No. 11, 1954, University of Minnesota, Contract N8 onr 66216.

CHAPTER FOUR

EXPLANATIONS 2: SPECIAL TRENDS

Expanding knowledge, ideological and cultural concerns, all leave a stamp on any type of research and inquiry. And the search to explain creativity is no exception. Reflected in the selections to follow is the impact of technological advances and biological discoveries, as well as special types of social concerns of recent decades. Basic approaches here differ little from those in the previous chapter except that, in some cases, they are even more clear-cut and extreme. Skinner, a major contemporary behaviorist, unequivocally states the case for a genetic type of explanation of creativity: creations result from chance events that survive by means of selection. Crovitz proposes a model for computer- or machine-produced creations and his position therefore crystallizes the mechanistic version of genetic explanation.

In separating the selections here, all quite recent, into a special chapter, we are emphasizing both the impact of recent developments and the crystallization of viewpoints and approaches to explanation. Thus, while Skinner has not previously paid a great deal of attention to the creativity question, his statement here represents a type of *obiter dictum* of genetic explanation, the Darwinian conception applied directly to human behavior and to creativity. It is, in essence, an extension of the tradition begun by Galton. For, though Skinner avoids any specification of a hereditary endowment in creative persons, he points to natural selection within the creative process. Similarly, Gordon's position represents a crystallization of a viewpoint and an approach. Gordon's work on creativity spans many decades and, in the recent review included here, he clearly specifies an ideology underlying his own and others' efforts. According to Gordon, all persons are definitely capable of being creative; fostering and nurturing creativity is an important social goal. His is a clear-cut espousal of an egalitarian ideology that is shared by numerous other workers such as Torrance, Taylor, Maslow, Rogers, DeBono, Davis, and Gowan. His synectics approach, teaching the use of metaphor for productive thought, has directly influenced the work of Parnes and Khatena.

Helson's studies also reflect an ideological position, one that derives from some specific cultural concerns. While there has never been an intrinsic or conceptual reason to link creativity to the male or the female sex, there has been increasing attention paid, in recent years, to the legal, social, economic, psychological, and intellectual position of women in society. Creativity of women, a matter connected to all these factors, has therefore become of special research interest. Previous work, such as Greenacre's (1960), focused on biological predispositions and psycho-dynamic structures. Helson, in collaboration with Richard Crutchfield, has used a research methodology similar to that of Barron, Gough, and MacKinnon at the Institute of Personality Assessment and Research of the University of California. She has been interested in identifying personality characteristics of creative women in particular disciplines such as mathematics, and she has followed the previous IPAR researchers closely in her approach to explaining creativity.

Scientific and technological advances have stimulated special trends. In addition to the advances in computer technology and the resulting trend toward computer models of creative thinking such as Crovitz's, there has also been a biological advance that may, as Bogen and Bogen suggest here, have direct pertinence to research in creativity. This is the discovery of the so-called "split" or "bisected" brain. First described by Sperry and his associates (R. W. Sperry, 1959), the "split" or "bisected" brain is produced by removal or severance of the fibers of the structure connecting the two halves or hemispheres of the mammalian brain—the corpus callosum—particularly the posterior portion of this structure. Following such removal or severance, it has been observed that each hemisphere functions independently and each seems to be responsible for different types of human and animal functions and behavior. Although it had been previously known that the left hemisphere of the brain, the side controlling the right side of the body, was also largely responsible for an important aspect of the human language function, little had been known about independent functions of the right hemisphere outside of its control of the other side of the body. Bogen's and Bogen's particular application to creativity of some observations from this type of research follows in the biological tradition of Galton, Lombroso, and Koestler. Also, their concept of an "appositional mind" along with a "propositional

mind" has connections with the view that there are two forms of knowledge—logic and intuition—presented by Croce in the following chapter.
And, as Bogen and Bogen describe, the finding of two seemingly independent but coordinated aspects of the brain crystallizes an intellectual
tradition emphasizing the duality of the mind.

A somewhat different development is the special trend illustrated by
the selection on extrasensory perception by Krippner and Murphy. Research on extrasensory perception has, as these authors indicate, met with
a good deal of opposition in scientific circles from the time of the early
experiments of J. B. Rhine in the 1930s. Over the years, however, the
statistical reliability of a large number of ESP experiments has come to be
recognized as unassailable. Whatever the meaning of these results, the
attempt to connect extrasensory perception to creativity represents an
interesting approach to problems raised by other discussions of creativity,
particularly those emphasizing unconscious factors and those, such as
Plato's, with a supernatural orientation. The events of interest in both
these types of discussions, events seeming to arise outside the creator's
awareness, are, according to the extrasensory perception hypothesis,
explained by lawful, though physically undiscernible and unlocatable,
processes. Moreover, as the ESP investigator is interested in arriving at
explanations, and generally he uses scientific approaches such as extensive documentation and experimentation, this approach to creativity
seems a special attempt at merging the scientific and supernatural traditions.

Related to the focus on extrasensory perception is a current broader
concern with what is called "altered states of consciousness." Phenomena
such as dreams, hypnotic and psychedelic states, meditation, as well as
presumed daily fluctuations in consciousness levels, have all been included in this category. Though there are few intensive studies, theoretical
or experimental, of creativity as an altered state of consciousness, or creativity in relation to altered states of consciousness,[1] the topic has engen-
dered much general interest among psychologists. At the present time
intensive research seems to be hindered by the difficulty in producing
precise and consistent definitions and conceptualizations of the states
and levels of consciousness and the conditions for their emergence. Of
particular note, however, is the connection between creativity conceived
as an altered state of consciousness and the formulations of both Plato

1. Except for Maslow's description of "peak experiences" and creativity (see Chapter Two)
and the studies of psychedelic agents and creativity by Masters and Houston and by Zegans
et al., cited in the bibliography for this chapter.

and Lombroso presented in Chapters One and Two. Though incorporating some of the phenomena described by Lombroso as connecting insanity to genius and creativity, an altered state of consciousness as currently conceived is not necessarily abnormal. Categorized as "paranormal," these states are considered to consist of out-of-the-ordinary but nevertheless potentially productive and valuable experiences. Rather than arising from the type of degenerative illness described by Lombroso, altered states of consciousness are closer to what Plato called "divine madness," being out of one's ordinary mind and senses.

Another special trend, which is related to the focus on altered states of consciousness, is the current interest in "alpha conditioning" and creativity. "Alpha conditioning" refers to a method of artificial control of certain types of electrical waves emitted from the brain, waves emitted especially during relaxed states of mind and, it has been discovered, during trained meditation as well. These rather slow electrical waves, called alpha waves, are ordinarily emitted spontaneously by the brain and are identified by an electroencephalographic device. Through the efforts of a group of investigators, led primarily by Joseph Kamiya (1969), methods have been developed whereby such brain wave emissions and their accompanying states of mind can be induced at will. Because, according to these investigators, creative thinking seems connected to these particular states of mind, some investigation (as yet unreported) of alpha wave emission and creativity has begun. Included in this investigation are attempts at inducing creative thinking through direct alpha wave control and conditioning.

With the selections by Skinner and Crovitz, we conclude these two chapters illustrating explanatory approaches. Both present definitely genetic approaches to explanation, Skinner explicitly and Crovitz implicitly, and these excerpts exemplify the ultimate realization of a trend. Crovitz's model for computer problem-solving is not, however, the only or the earliest attempt in this direction. It is antedated by the groundbreaking work of Newell, Shaw, and Simon in 1962 (see the bibliography for this chapter) in which they proposed a model for a General Problem Solver computer program and related creativity to high-level problemsolving. Moreover, there is a general research effort in the field of "artificial intelligence" which encompasses computer programs that play games, retrieve facts, recognize figural patterns, do high-level mathematics, make decisions, develop experimental procedures, and learn concepts. The model proposed by Crovitz is an example of an "algorithmic" program in distinction to the "heuristic" type of programs designed

by Newell, Shaw, Simon, and others. Heuristic programs are designed
on the basis of known and presumed patterns of human problem-solving
(see also Reitman, 1965) while the algorithmic program is designed to
generate and examine all possible solution combinations in some predetermined order; the algorithmic program therefore does not necessarily
follow human patterns of thought (see Davis, G. A., 1973). The model
proposed by Crovitz is included here as a provocative attempt at applying
an extended series of linguistic structures — derived essentially, of course,
from human patterns of thought and/or linguistic usage — in an algorithmic type of program. As an approach to creativity, the Crovitz presentation
forms a rather sharp contrast to the selections to follow in the final chapter.

RAVENNA HELSON ·Women and Creativity

[*Though focused specifically on women mathematicians, this excerpt is
from one of a series of studies on creativity in women by Helson and her associates. As a researcher at the Institute of Personality Assessment and Research
of the University of California, Helson has used a methodology and a focus on
personality attributes similar to that of Barron and MacKinnon. Her findings
of traits of rebellious independence, flexibility, and strong symbolic interest in
creative women mathematicians are similar to findings about creative men
reported by the former investigators. There is, however, an interesting exception: while creative men were characterized as having high scores on measures
of feminine orientation and interest, Helson's creative women subjects did not
receive comparably high scores on measures of masculine orientation and
interest.*]

Women mathematicians are rare. It has been suggested by both mathematicians and psychologists, informally, that a *creative* woman mathematician would have a brain different from that of other women. A normal
woman, others say, could not so reject the life of feeling and concreteness
without stifling her originality in the process.

Yet creative women mathematicians do exist. It seemed possible that

SOURCE *From Helson, R., "Women Mathematicians and the Creative Personality," Journal
of Consulting and Clinical Psychology, 1971, Vol. 36, pp. 210–211, 217–220. Copyright 1971
by the American Psychological Association. Reprinted by permission.*

these women, if they were not "mutants," might show conspicuously the essential traits of the creative personality, without which they would not have overcome whatever barriers make their numbers so small. A study of these Ss, then, might contribute to our understanding of creativity, regardless of sex, and certainly to the appraisal of creativity in women, and women's potential for scientific accomplishment (Mattfeld & Van Aken, 1965).

This paper describes the personality, research style, and background of some 45 women mathematicians, a sample from an estimated 300 in the United States at the time of the study (Albert, 1957). Of the 45, 18 included virtually all creative women mathematicians in the United States.

The study is one of several which have been conducted by the Institute of Personality Assessment and Research in the area of the creative personality. Particular reference will be made to a companion study of creativity in male mathematicians (Helson, 1967; Helson & Crutchfield, 1970).

Method

Selection of Sample. Names of women who had attended graduate school and obtained the PhD. in mathematics between 1950 and 1960 were furnished by the following institutions: Bryn Mawr College, Cornell University, Stanford University, Yale University, University of California (Berkeley and Los Angeles), University of Oregon, University of Texas, and University of Washington. Mathematicians at these and other institutions also provided additional names, particularly of women they considered creative. Columbia University, Massachusetts Institute of Technology, New York University, Radcliffe, University of Chicago, University of Illinois, and University of Pennsylvania each produced at least two of these Ss.

The Ss were invited to participate by means of a letter which explained the long-term interest of the Institute in studying soundness, achievement, creativity, and other forms of high-level functioning, and its present interest in conducting studies of professional women. A small honorarium was offered. Of 53 invitations extended, 44 (83%) were accepted. Three of these Ss were tested later than the others, and their data are not included in all analyses. Three additional mathematicians, being wives of faculty members at the University of California (Berkeley), were asked to provide data only about their research style. The number of Ss thus varies between 41 and 47.

The creativity of each S was rated by mathematicians in her field of specialization. A 7-point scale was used, a rating of 4.0 signifying that S was about as creative as the author of an average research paper in a mathematical journal. An average of three ratings was obtained for each *S*. Fewer than three were obtained for several older women who had not published beyond their dissertation. Ratings were highly reliable. More than half of the *S*s received ratings with a range of less than two, and only two *S*s received ratings with a range of more than three. The distribution of ratings was as follows: 8 *S*s received average ratings of 3.0 or below, 8 were rated between 3.0 and 4.0, 12 between 4.0 and 5.0, 8 between 5.0 and 6.0, and 8 above 6.0. The *S*s rated above 5.0 were classified as "creative." The creative group thus consisted of women rated as clearly more creative than the author of an average research contribution in mathematics. Subsequent comments from mathematicians lead us to believe that there were no important omissions from the creative group.

In age, *S*s ranged from 24 to 64, the average age being 41. Two-thirds were married. One-third had Jewish parents, and most of the rest were from Protestant backgrounds. Creative and comparison women did not differ in these respects, nor in quality of graduate school. As in the sample of male mathematicians (Helson & Crutchfield, 1970), foreign cultural influence was strong. Half of the creative *S*s were born in Europe or Canada, and almost half of the *S*s born in the United States had at least one parent born in Europe. The difference between creative and comparison *S*s in foreign birth is significant at the .10 level. However, foreign-born and native-born creatives differ not at all in any of the characteristics that we shall report as significantly differentiating the creative from comparison *S*s. The personality of the creative mathematician, among women, seems to cut across national boundaries.

Procedure. Two weekend assessments were held at the Institute of Personality Assessment and Research, and two others in the East, at Bryn Mawr and Swarthmore Colleges. Staff observers and interviewers did not know which *S*s were creative, and indeed the criterion judgments had not yet been obtained. The assessment included a great variety of tests and measures, and the following have been selected for range of coverage and to demonstrate the consistency with which some of the salient findings recur:

1. Intelligence: Concept Mastery Test (Terman, 1956) and Mechanical Comprehension Test (Bennett, 1951); the Wechsler Intelligence Scale was administered after the assessments as part of a larger study by MacKinnon and Hall (1968) of the relation between intelligence and creativity.

2. Overall personality characteristics: California Psychological Inventory (Gough, 1964); Minnesota Multiphasic Personality Inventory (Hatha-

way & McKinley, 1951); Type Indicator (Myers, 1962); staff observations recorded by means of the 100-item Clinical Q Sort (Block, 1961); Adjective Check List (Gough & Heilbrun, 1965).

3. Interests: Strong Vocational Interest Blank (Male Form) (Strong, 1959); Activities Check List (Gough & Hall, 1957).

4. Cognitive and aesthetic tests: Gottschaldt Figures, Street Gestalt, Insight Puzzles, and Masked Word Tests as adapted by Crutchfield (Mac-Kinnon, Crutchfield, Barron, Block, Gough, & Harris, 1958); Unusual Uses and Match Problems Tests (Guilford, Wilson, Christensen, & Lewis, 1951); Art Scale (Barron & Welsh, 1952); Mosaic Construction Test (Hall, 1958).

5. Mathematical style: Mathematicians Q Sort (Helson, 1967).

6. Personal history: Personal history questionnaire and interview. [ftnt. deleted]

7. Professional history: Professional history questionnaire.

.   .   .   .

[Creative women mathematicians were compared with a sample of other women PhDs in mathematics. The two groups differed slightly, if at all, on measures of intelligence, cognition, and masculine traits, but creative Ss had a stronger cathexis of research activity and were highly flexible, original, and rejecting of outside influence. Personality inventories, observations of the assessment staff, and self-descriptions of research style gave consistent results. Half of the creatives were foreign born, and most had professional men as fathers. Interviewers judged that they had identified primarily with their fathers, and that their interest in mathematics had arisen from sublimation or search for autonomy in fantasy rather than from reaction formation or withdrawal. As compared with creative male mathematicians, the creative women had less assurance, published less, and, if they had a job at all, occupied less prestigeful positions.][1]

Discussion

First, the findings offer no support for the idea that creative women mathematicians are "mutants" with cognitive abilities different from those of other women PhDs in mathematics. Neither do the findings show the creative women to be more masculine, if one means by this that they might have been expected to score higher on measures of masculinity–femininity, or dominance, assertiveness, or analytical ability. We

1. Editors' note: The paragraph in brackets here is the abstract of the results of Helson's study, which appears at the beginning of the article. It is inserted here to replace the more detailed explanation of the results in the original.

cannot evaluate the hypothesis that the creative Ss may have had some greater specific talent for higher mathematics (Revész, 1940) which was only slightly reflected in intelligence measures. However, the many large differences between the creative and comparison Ss in background and personality would seem to indicate that personality characteristics are powerful determinants of creativity in women mathematicians.

The traits most characteristic of the creative women would seem to be these: (a) rebellious independence, narcissism, introversion, and a rejection of outside influence; (b) strong symbolic interests and a marked ability to find self-expression and self-gratification in directed research activity; (c) flexibility, or lack of constriction, both in general attitudes and in mathematical work.

These traits have all been ascribed to the creative person, regardless of sex, but they appear more clearly in creative women mathematicians than they do in creative men mathematicians (Helson & Crutchfield, 1970a, 1970b). Among the creative men, some were original, flexible, ambitious, but essentially conventional individuals. One may suppose that a conventional woman would never develop the concentration, the "purity of motive" (Ghiselin, 1952), which seems to be necessary for a new symbolic structure to emerge. A rejection of outside influence and a cathexis of symbolic activity would seem to support, or constitute, purity of motive. Although one would expect to find this complex of traits in creative persons of either sex, it shows more clearly — being more necessary — in the creative women. The third characteristic, flexibility, may be interpreted as a lack of conflict in the person's basic goals. There is cooperation between the ego and the life of impulse; the individual has his own will, and his conditions of life harmonize with his work. That the creative women sought and to a considerable degree attained an integration and simplification of life, despite obstacles, would appear to be one of the important findings of the study. The fact that the creative person can attain a high degree of integration while also manifesting a high level of pathology may perhaps be related to the extreme concentration on the world of symbols. There is a rapprochement between conscious and unconscious, but the separation from people or from society is not overcome, and indeed it may maintain the creative motivation.

It could be argued that the creative women mathematicians manifest the essential characteristics of the creative person. Do their life histories also show us the essential conditions which mold the creative personality? Let us keep this question in mind as we review the main findings about background factors and personal history.

Almost all of the women mathematicians grew up in homes with strong respect for learning and cultural values. Most of them, as little girls, must have been rewarded for intellectual successes. That many Ss grew up outside the United States, or had at least one parent who was European, suggests that they were able to avoid some anti-intellectual influences of the mainstream of American culture.

The comparison Ss grew up in homes they considered secure. Their fathers, described as warm in about half the cases, were usually business-men or skilled workers. The mothers were as well educated as the fathers, and the Ss identified primarily with their mothers. In some cases, a shy, intelligent girl found that mathematics was a subject in which she could excel, and the standards of her family—sometimes the rather narrow standards of the immigrant trying to make good—encouraged her to pursue scholastic excellence in a conventional way. In other cases, the child seemed concerned to defend herself against impulse, and to use mathematics for this purpose. There were, of course, other patterns which attained less statistical prominence.

The background of the creative Ss was different in a number of respects. Financial insecurity was common. The father was a professional man. He was seldom a warm person, and there was a differential in intellectual status between the father and mother. Except in large families, there was usually no brother. The interviewer judged that S identified more with the father than with the mother, and that in coping with her problems she used sublimation and a search for autonomy in fantasy rather than re-pressive techniques.

One forms the picture of a very intelligent child who was attracted by her father's intellectual status, felt alienated from her mother, adopted her father's attitudes toward work and achievement but received rela-tively little attention or affection from him. Isolated from both parents, she developed the strategy of making herself autonomous by nurturing, gratifying, and "growing" herself in symbolic activity. Though such a scheme describes a few creatives well, in many cases it seems to omit important special factors—that this girl had bouts of deafness, that this father was psychotic, that this motherless child resented the fact that she and her sister had to do all the housework while her brothers were a privileged elite.

Nevertheless, the personality and background characteristics reported in this study are similar to those obtained for a very different sample of creative women—college seniors, most of whom were interested in the arts and social sciences (Helson, 1966, 1968). In these studies, data were available from parents and siblings as well as from the creative and comparison women themselves. Ambivalence toward the mother, the need for autonomy, and the development of strong symbolic interests, a father who seems to have modeled the use of intellectual activity for self-expression and for purpose in life—this constellation recurs. Several parts of this pattern of findings have also been reported by Anastasi and Schaefer (1969) in a study of creative adolescent women. The importance of the father, as revealed in autobiographies of several outstanding women mathematicians of the past, has been emphasized by Plank and Plank (1954).

Most boys, of course, undergo an estrangement from the mother as a part of acquiring a masculine identity. This estrangement, termed independence, is eased by considerable social support, and the main obstacle to the development of a creative personality in men seems to be that what the mother represents will be devalued and repressed too much, so that pleasure in imaginative play or attention to feeling is rejected as feminine. Thus one finds among the men mathematicians that the mother is described with more respect and warmth by the creative men than by the comparison Ss. In a sense, it would seem that respect for the mother encourages a cathexis of symbolic activity in the boy, whereas a lack of respect may engender it in the girl. This statement contains some suggestive implications, but it is an oversimplification: a responsible comparison of the development of the creative personality in boys and girls would require a more extended discussion than the scope of the present paper allows. It shall be left as a hypothesis (which owes much to Rank, 1945) that the creative boy or girl experiences an estrangement in the primary milieu, a disadvantageous position from which he (or she) makes an adjustment away from people, seeking to have his own will and provide his own security and emotional satisfaction in intellectual activity, and retaining the hope of bringing about a reconciliation in the symbolic medium.

In the introduction, the question was raised as to how a woman could so suppress her feminine nature to be a mathematician without suppressing her originality also. Part of the answer seems to be that the women mathematicians are introverts, whose "natures" are not the modal American type. Beyond this, the creative women differed from the comparison Ss in their ability to express themselves rather fully and freely in creative activity, with emotional involvement, rather than emotional restriction, and with considerable participation from the unconscious.

The present study does not clarify why so few women in this country go into higher mathematics. The reasons may be deep seated and perhaps innate. However, the extent of foreign birth and parentage in the whole sample, and the degree to which the creative women were found to be rejecting of outside influence — these findings suggest that countervailing social pressures are strong.

Pribram (1963) seems to conceive the question of how women could be creative as that of how women could be made into men "in the best sense of the word." He fears the process would be agonizing if not impossible. However, this difficult approach does not seem necessary. Creative men and women show many similarities in basic personality. It is true that each group has characteristics of its own. Creative men mathematicians are more outgoing, self-accepting, and masterful. It seems very likely that these traits interact with strong symbolic interests, independence, etc., to bring about forceful direct assaults on difficult problems, critical breadth, a high level of productivity, etc. Even under optimal circumstances, creative women might be expected to make a contribution different in type from that of creative men. Of course, it should be noted that among creative men mathematicians, the most creative were not the most outgoing, self-accepting, and efficient. In any event, confidence and effectiveness would seem to be enhanced by success and cultural support. The striking differences between creative men and women in professional status and in productivity after graduate school seem to reflect social roles and institutional arrangements more than fundamental creative traits.

Albert, A. A. (Chm.) A survey of research potential and training in the mathematical sciences. Final report of the Committee on the Survey, Part I. Chicago: University of Chicago, 1957.

Anastasi, A., & Schaefer, C. E. Biographical correlates of artistic and literary creativity in adolescent girls. *Journal of Applied Psychology*, 1969, 53, 267–273.

Barron, F., & Welsh, G. S. Artistic perception as a possible factor in personality style: Its measurement by a figure preference test. *Journal of Psychology*, 1952, 33, 199–203.

Bennett, G. K. *Mechanical Comprehension Test Form BB*, (Rev. ed.) New York: Psychological Corporation, 1951.

Block, J. *The Q-sort method in personality assessment and psychiatric research*. Springfield, Ill.: Charles C Thomas, 1961.

Ghiselin, B. (Ed.) *The creative process*. Los Angeles: University of California Press, 1952.

Gough, H. G. *Manual for the California Psychological Inventory*. (Rev. ed.) Palo Alto: Consulting Psychologists Press, 1964.

Gough, H. G., & Hall, W. B. *The Activities Check List*. Berkeley: University of California, Institute of Personality Assessment and Research, 1957.

Gough, H. G., & Heilbrun, A. B., Jr. *The Adjective Check List manual*. Palo Alto, Calif.: Consulting Psychologists Press, 1965.

Guilford, J. P., Wilson, R. S., Christensen, P. R., & Lewis, D. J. A factor-analytic study of creative thinking: Hypotheses and descriptions of tests. In, *Reports from the Psychological Laboratory, No. 4*. Los Angeles: University of Southern California. April 1951.

Hall, W. B. The development of a technique for assessing aesthetic predispositions and its application to a sample of professional research scientists. Paper presented at the meeting of the Western Psychological Association. Monterey, Calif., April 1958.

Hathaway, S. R., & McKinley, J. C. *Minnesota Multiphasic Personality Inventory manual.* New York: Psychological Corporation, 1951.

Helson, R. Personality of women with imaginative and artistic interests: The role of masculinity, originality, and other characteristics in their creativity. *Journal of Personality*, 1966, **34**, 1–25.

Helson, R. Sex differences in creative style. *Journal of Personality*, 1967, **35**, 214–233.

Helson, R. Effects of sibling characteristics and parental values on creative interests and achievement. *Journal of Personality*, 1968, **36**, 589–607.

Helson, R., & Crutchfield, R. S. Creative types in mathematics. *Journal of Personality*, 1970, **38**, 177–197. (a)

Helson, R., & Crutchfield, R. S. Mathematicians: The creative researcher and the average PhD. *Journal of Consulting and Clinical Psychology*, 1970, **34**, 250–257. (b)

MacKinnon, D. W., Crutchfield, R. S., Barron, F., Block, J., Gough, H. G., & Harris, R. E. *An assessment study of Air Force Officers:* Part I. *Design of the study and description of the variables.* (Tech. Rep. WADC-TR-58-91 (I), ASTIA Document No. AD 151 040) Lackland Air Force Base, Tex.: Wright Air Development Center, Personnel Laboratory, April 1958.

MacKinnon, D. W., & Hall, W. B. Intelligence and creativity. In D. W. MacKinnon (Ed.), *A study of three aspects of creativity, IPAR report to the Carnegie Corporation of New York.* Berkeley, Calif.: Institute of Personality Assessment and Research, 1968.

Mattfeld, J. A., & Van Aken, C. G. *Women and the scientific professions.* Cambridge: M.I.T. Press, 1965.

Myers, I. B. *Manual (1962) for the Myers-Briggs Type Indicator.* Princeton, N.J.: Educational Testing Service, 1962.

Plank, E. H., & Plank, R. Emotional components in arithmetic learning, as seen through autobiographies. *The Psychoanalytic Study of the Child*, 1954, **9**, 274–296.

Pribram, K. H. What is a woman? In S. M. Farber & R. H. L. Wilson (Eds.), *The potential of women.* New York: McGraw-Hill, 1963.

Rank, O. *Will therapy and truth and reality.* (Trans. by J. Taft) New York: Knopf, 1945.

Revész, G. The indivisibility of mathematical talent. *Acta Psychologica*, 1940, **5**(2–3), 1–21.

Strong, E. K., Jr. *Manual for Strong Vocational Interest Blanks for men and women, revised blanks (Forms M and W.)* Palo Alto: Consulting Psychologists Press, 1959.

Terman, L. M. *Concept Mastery Test, manual, Form T.* New York: Psychological Corporation, 1956.

WILLIAM J. J. GORDON · Metaphor and Invention

[The founder of a principle and technique he calls "synectics," Gordon has, as described here, had an impact on management consultation and education. Synectics, the use of metaphorical modes of thinking in constructive and productive ways, is a system relating creativity to a particular cognitive function. In insisting on the capacity for creativity in everyone and the importance of

SOURCE   Gordon, W. J. J., "On Being Explicit About Creative Process," Journal of Creative Behavior, 1972, Vol. 6, pp. 295–300. Copyright 1972 by W. J. J. Gordon. Reprinted by permission of W. J. J. Gordon and the Creative Education Foundation, Inc.

fostering and nurturing this capacity, Gordon has been an unequivocal pro-
ponent of a long-standing and continuing special trend in creativity research.
The distinction he draws between "making the familiar strange" and "making
the strange familiar" relates to issues of the determined and undetermined
aspects of creations raised by other authors in this volume, although Gordon
himself does not make this connection. Things are familiar because they have
some connection to antecedent experiences or antecedent factors; hence, our
experience of familiarity is determined by factors in the past. The experience
of strangeness, on the other hand, depends on a dissimilarity with antecedent
factors and therefore it could be said to arise from discontinuous or undeter-
mined processes. However, Gordon's account, which appears to be fully de-
terministic, relates the strange to factors unknown to an individual in the case
of learning and to factors unknown to society in the case of creations.]

This article presents the argument that being explicit about a previously
implicit process has a profound sociological effect — it changes that process
from an elitist to an egalitarian activity. The article will show how synectics
research (1) destroyed the myth that creativity was the result of factors
completely beyond control; (2) demonstrated an implicit approach to
creativity that yielded inventive results with greater frequency than could
be expected from probability alone; and (3) developed an explicit program
out of the implicit approach.

The traditional view of creativity was completely elitist. It embraced
words such as "inspiration" and "genius" and accepted the fact that "you
had to be born with it." In the face of such militant romanticism, this
author manifested an impious stubbornness when, over twenty-five years
ago, he initiated research directed toward increasing the creative innova-
tion/learning output of individuals and groups. This research resulted
in the *synectics* technique for the conscious use of metaphor in problem-
solving situations requiring innovative viewpoints. Today more than two
hundred businesses and industries in the U.S.A. and abroad have invested over $100,000,000 in the *synectics technique*. Furthermore, materials
developed by Synectics Education Systems have influenced more than
10,000 classrooms.[1] How did all this come about?

Synectics research revealed that the most important element in innovative problem-solving was *making the familiar strange* because break-
throughs depend on "strange" new contexts by which to view a "familiar"
problem. For example, in the 16th century, people thought that blood

1. Gordon, W. J. J. *The metaphorical way of learning and knowing.* Cambridge: Porpoise
Books, 1971.

flowed from heart to body, surging in and out like the tides of the sea. Harvey[2] was *familiar* with this view and believed it until he closely observed a fish's heart that was still beating after the fish had been opened up. Harvey looked for a tidal flow of blood, but the action of the fish's heart reminded him instead of a pump he had seen. The idea of the heart acting like a pump was most *strange* to him and he had to break his ebb and flow connection to make room for his new pump connection. Harvey's discovery, resulting from *making the familiar strange*, has saved countless lives by offering doctors an accurate account of the circulation of blood.

Interdependent with the innovation process is the learning process where one gains an understanding of a new problem or a new idea by *making the strange familiar*. Understanding requires bringing a *strange* concept into a *familiar* context. For example, let's say a student is observing a fish's heart. He knows nothing about physiology and his professor has just explained how the heart acts like a pump. Since the student is ignorant, this concept is *strange* to him and he needs to digest this new fact into the rest of his *familiar* experience.[3] Where Harvey had to break his ebb and flow connection and make his new pump connection, the student only has to make a learning connection. Let's say he is reminded of a swimming pool where the dirty water is pumped through the filter and back into the pool. The student, of course, makes the obvious connection between the heart and the water pump, but he develops other connections as well. He sees how lungs and the liver act as 'filters' when they cleanse the blood. Thus, through an example from his own experience the student creatively contributes to his own learning. He *makes the strange familiar* to himself by means of a highly personal connection process.

Now let's compare the learning process with the innovation process. Both Harvey and the student used creative comparisons. Harvey used his pump connection to *make the familiar strange*, to break the ebb and flow connection. The student used his swimming pool connection to *make the strange familiar* and learn about blood circulation. Harvey's creativity led to an innovative thought that was a benefit to all mankind. The student's creativity, on the other hand, produced the discovery of a connection that only added to his knowledge. Both were creative. Furthermore, the creative connection-making by each of them was highly personal and could have been made only by someone with the particular character, knowledge, and experience of each of them. The learning process, however, led

2. Sullivan, J. W. N. *The limitations of science.* NYC: Viking Press, 1933.
3. Gordon, W. J. J. & Poze, T. *Strange & familiar.* Cambridge: Porpoise Books, 1972.

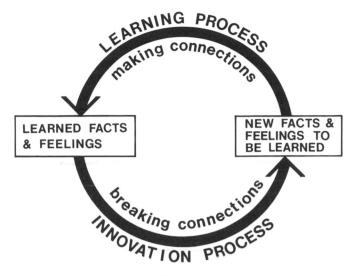

Figure 1

to a private result whereas the innovation process led to a public result. The student was communicating with himself alone. Harvey communicated with himself during his connection-making process, but after he made his brilliant connection he communicated his discovery to the whole world.

So far we have been considering only science. What about art and literature? The student's creative connection of the circulation of blood with a swimming pool led to a result far less general than Harvey's connection. Can that private type of creativity be generalized? Yes. If the blood-circulation/swimming-pool connection were used as the basis of a poem or a painting then it could make a contribution to everyone's aesthetic experience. In fact, that is what <u>aesthetic process is — communicating internal, private connections to the rest of the world</u>. Thus, creative innovation depends on breaking metaphorical connections with "old" facts and feelings and then inventing connections with "new" facts and feelings (see Figure 1). Einstein broke with Euclidean metaphors in order to conceive his relativity theory. Picasso broke with the old metaphors of perception. *Creative* innovation leads to new art and science (external) or to individual, psychological insights (internal). These new facts and feelings feed into the *learning process*.

The <u>creative process depends on developing new</u> contexts for viewing the old, familiar world and metaphors constitute the basis for new contexts. The role of metaphors has been recognized implicitly since antiquity. Aristotle himself said, "The greatest thing by far is to be master of metaphor." When *Synectics*[4] introduced the first explicit scheme for the conscious use of metaphor in creative situations it identified the three basic metaphorical mechanisms that constitute the basis for creative learning and innovation. They are *direct analogy, personal analogy*, and *compressed conflict (symbolic analogy)*.

Direct analogy is the comparison of one thing with another. Shakespeare says, "the tyrant time," and "First, like a trumpet, doth his tongue begin." The telephone was invented from an analogue to the human ear. The theory of evolution came from Darwin's comparing the state of nature with controlled breeding on stock farms.

Personal analogy is empathic identification with something outside oneself. Shakespeare says, "Yet, do thy worst, old time." Dr. Rich, the great General Electric scientist "think(s) like an electron . . . or imagine(s) himself a light beam whose reflection is being measured."

Compressed conflict is a close-coupled phrase where the words fight each other. Shakespeare used expressions like "captive victor" and "unthrifty loveliness." Pasteur based his antitoxin research on the expression "safe attack," and Cajal, the Nobel winner in neurology, was led on in his work by the phrase "protoplasmic kiss."

The pure research that led to being explicit about metaphorical mechanisms was launched in the hope of being able to evoke creative process with more reliability than could be expected on the basis of probability alone. That research showed that you didn't have to wait passively 'till the creative muse struck, that there were definite metaphorical weapons with which you could hunt and track down the muse. These weapons were described explicitly in *Synectics*, but their application was treated implicitly. In fact, the only way to put them into practice was in a group context which left too much to the power and wit of the group leader. Therefore, another research step was initiated and in 1965 work was begun on reducing the implicit elements in *synectics* to an explicit, written, programmed series of workbooks. The motivation for this project went beyond merely making the explicit from the implicit. It implied a sociological step with ethical overtones since it embraced an egalitarian as opposed to an elitist view. For instance, implicit training was inefficient and therefore, expensive. It required an enormous amount of time for study and

4. Gordon, W. J. J. *Synectics.* NYC: Harper, 1961.

travel and its group context necessitated considerable planning. It was clear that an explicit, programmed course for individuals as well as groups would shatter the old *synectics* training elitism and open opportunities for the many, not just the few. The product of this research, *The Basic Course in Synectics (BCS)*,[5] is being used at Buffalo State University College. [ftnt. deleted] In closing, however, the author would like to submit an example of an explicit, egalitarian application of *synectics* that goes far beyond any academic use.

The BCS presently is being considered as a tool for solving the dangerous problem of low morale of people on production lines. Job monotony has become so critical that workers in General Motors' new, showcase plant at Lordstown, Ohio, actually went out on strike because "their jobs were too dull and the job pressure was too intensive."[6]

Many attempts have been made to change workers' attitudes toward their jobs and it is now agreed that the only hope lies in making jobs more interesting. Interest comes from within, however, and efforts to introduce "better" working conditions (music, color-coding, etc.) have failed. What is being planned now is using the Synectics Education Systems *BCS* for the efficient and effective training of thousands of workers in creative problem-solving. Creativity is the highest form of human endeavor and this very epitome of human activity is lacking in job-monotony situations. To counteract this, workers will be trained in the skill of seeing old things in new ways with the goal of inventing better ways to what they are presently doing.

Thus, a worker will begin to view his job as a statement of a problem to be solved, i.e., how to do the job better. He will see a challenge with rewards for him, rather than an inhuman monotony. He will feel honored that he is being trained to be creatively innovative. And he will sense a new dignity about himself that derives from the very process of creative thinking.

The author has tried to show how certain research steps have stripped from the creative process the aura of sheer accidental intuition and how this research led to an increasingly explicit view of creativity. The Lordstown example was selected since it contained the most powerful proof of the sociological importance of the egalitarian effect of being explicit.[7]

5. Gordon, W. J. J. & Poze, T. *The basic course in synectics*. Cambridge: Porpoise Books, 1971.
6. *Business Week*, September 9, 1972, p. 108.
7. For more information about *synectics* please contact: William J. J. Gordon, Synectics Education Systems. Address: 121 Brattle Street, Cambridge, Massachusetts 02138.

JOSEPH E. BOGEN and GLENDA M. BOGEN · Creativity and the Bisected Brain

[*Studies on the bisected brain, severance or removal of the fibers connecting the two hemispheres of the mammalian brain, have yielded a good deal of information about the independent functioning of the hemispheres. Here, in excerpts first from a preliminary article by J. E. Bogen alone and an article by J. E. and G. M. Bogen together, some possible applications to creativity are outlined. The authors suggest that creativity depends on the connecting brain fiber structure called the corpus callosum and on coordination of the distinct functions of the two hemispheres. Emphasizing the more intuitive capacities of the right hemisphere (which also controls the left side of the body), they cite related formulations by psychological investigators and by creative persons.*]

. . . The left hemisphere is better than the right for language and for what has sometimes been called "verbal activity" or "linguistic thought". . . .

. . . Jackson . . . pointed out (1) that the distinguishing feature of the major hemisphere is not its *possession* of words but rather its *use* of them in propositions: "A proposition is not a mere sequence . . . it consists of words referring to one another in a particular manner [so that each] modifies the meaning of the other."

The difficulty in characterizing the ability of the right hemisphere (Table [1]) arises largely from our ignorance—we have barely scratched the surface of a vast unknown. We would do well therefore to choose arbitrarily a word, homologous in structure with the word "propositional" but sufficiently ambiguous to permit provisional use. For example, we can say that the right hemisphere has a highly developed "appositional" capacity. This term implies a capacity for apposing or comparing of perceptions, schemas, engrams, etc., but has in addition the virtue that it implies very little else. If it is correct that the right hemisphere excels in

SOURCE From Bogen, J. E., "The Other Side of the Brain II: An Appositional Mind," Bulletin of the Los Angeles Neurological Societies, 1969, Vol. 34, pp. 146, 147, 149–150, 157–158; Bogen, J. E., and Bogen, G. M., "The Other Side of the Brain III: The Corpus Callosum and Creativity," Bulletin of the Los Angeles Neurological Societies, 1969, Vol. 34, pp, 199, 200–202 204, 217. Copyright 1969 by the Los Angeles Society of Neurology and Psychiatry, and the Southern California Neurological Society. Reprinted by permission.

capacities as yet unknown to us, the full meaning of "appositional" will emerge as these capacities are further studied and understood. The word "appositional" has the essential virtue of suggesting a capacity as important as "propositional," reflecting a belief in the importance of right hemisphere function.

Table [1.] *Dichotomies with Lateralization Suggested*

Jackson (1864)	Expression	Perception
Jackson (1874)	Audito-articular	Retino-ocular
Jackson (1876)	Propositionizing	Visual imagery
Weisenberg & McBride (1935)	Linguistic	Visual or kinesthetic
Anderson (1951)	Storage	Executive
Humphrey & Zangwill (1951)	Symbolic or propositional	Visual or imaginative
McFie & Piercy (1952)	Eduction of relations	Eduction of correlates
Milner (1958)	Verbal	Perceptual or non-verbal
Semmes, Weinstein, Ghent, Teu- ber (1960)	Discrete	Diffuse
Zangwill (1961)	Symbolic	Visuospatial
Hécaen, Ajuriaguerra, Angeler- gues (1963)	Linguistic	Pre-verbal
Bogen & Gazzaniga (1965)	Verbal	Visuospatial
Levy-Agresti and Sperry (1968)	Logical or analytic	Synthetic perceptual
Bogen (1969)	Propositional	Appositional

.   .   .   .

One of the most obvious and fundamental features of the cerebrum is that it is double. Various kinds of evidence, especially from hemispherectomy, have made it clear that one hemisphere is sufficient to sustain a personality or mind. We may then conclude that the individual with two intact hemispheres has the capacity for two distinct minds. This conclusion finds its experimental proof in the split-brain animal whose two hemispheres can be trained to perceive, consider, and act independently. In the human, where *propositional* thought is typically lateralized to one hemisphere, the other hemisphere evidently specializes in a different mode of thought, which may be called *appositional*.

The rules or methods by which propositional thought is elaborated on "this" side of the brain (the side which speaks, reads, and writes) have been subjected to analyses of syntax, semantics, mathematical logic, etc. for many years. The rules by which appositional thought is elaborated on the other side of the brain will need study for many years to come.

.   .   .   .

. . . The observations . . . [derived from "split brain" studies] suggest that integrated use of verbal and visuo-spatial thought may be dependent on interhemispheric communication, including an important contribution from the corpus callosum. . . .

.   .   .   .

Interhemispheric collaboration need not be restricted to verbal-visuospatial interaction; if the right hemisphere has a special capacity for tonal, timbre and other aspects of music, interhemispheric communication could clearly contribute to musical creativity. [ftnt. deleted] Indeed, we can easily entertain the notion that artistic creativity in general benefits from interhemispheric collaboration.

According to Jung, "The experience that furnishes the material for artistic expression is no longer familiar. It is a strange something that derives its existence from the hinterland of man's mind. . . . Every creative person is a duality or a synthesis of contradictory aptitudes. . . ." (2) A compilation of such apposite remarks and opinions could be extended indefinitely. It will suffice to . . . [cite] a revealing quotation from a recent book by Bruner (3).

> The right is order and lawfulness, le droit. . . . Reaching for knowledge with the right hand is science. Yet to say only that much of science is to overlook one of its excitements, for the great hypotheses of science are gifts carried in the left hand. It has been proposed that art students can seduce their proper hand to more expressiveness by drawing first with the left. . . . And should we say that reaching for knowledge with the left hand is art? Again it is not enough, for as surely as the recital of a daydream differs from the well-wrought tale, there is a barrier between undisciplined fantasy and art. To climb the barrier requires a right hand adept at technique and artifice. . . . One thing has become increasingly clear in pursuing the nature of knowing. It is that the conventional apparatus of the psychologist — both his instruments of investigation and the conceptual tools he uses in the interpretation of his data — leaves one approach unexplored. It is an approach whose medium of exchange seems to be the metaphor paid out by the left hand. It is a way that grows happy hunches and 'lucky' guesses, that is stirred into connective activity by the poet and the necromancer looking sidewise rather than directly. Their hunches and intuitions generate a grammar of their own — searching out connections, suggesting similarities, weaving ideas loosely in a trial web. . . . If he is lucky or if he has subtle psychological intuition, he will from time to time come up with hunches, combinatorial products of his metaphoric activity. If he is not fearful of these products of his

own subjectivity, he will go so far as to tame the metaphors that have produced the hunches, tame them in the sense of shifting them from the left hand to the right hand by rendering them into notions that can be tested.

.   .   .   .

If creativity is dependent, in part, on a transcallosal interhemispheric exchange, there are some obvious explanations for its absence. There may be first of all a deficiency in technical competence in a suitable medium; in the case of literary as well as mathematical creativity this is easily seen as a lack of propositional skill. Alajouanine (4) averred, "To conceive is nothing, to express is all." He meant by this that pleasing musical themes and poetical images arise in the minds of many people who have not acquired the means for their expression.

There are many persons possessing technical proficiency in music, drawing or writing whose production is devoid of those innovative and informative values which distinguish an artist from a performer. This may be the result of a genetic deficiency, or a deficiency in the environmental exposure necessary to the development of inherited potential. Wiesel and Hubel (5) and Fifkova (6) among others have demonstrated the lack of structural development consequent on lack of function. As Sperry put it, "Many elements deeper in the brain centers must discharge only in very special activities, and, if these activities are not exercised—especially during maturational stages when the neurons seem to be particularly dependent on use—the neuron types involved may regress, leaving profound functional deficiencies in the integrative machinery" (7). We are accustomed to hear, these days, of the "culturally disadvantaged," those persons whose propositional potential has remained undeveloped for lack of proper schooling. There is likely a parallel lack of appositional development in persons whose only education consists of reading, writing and arithmetic.

Third, there must be a sufficiently free interchange between propositional and appositional modes. Rombauer (8) says of a certain pancake recipe, "Only a strongly intuitive person on speaking terms with his imagination has a chance of success."

Henry Moore opined, "All good art has contained both abstract and surrealist elements, just as it has contained both classical and romantic elements—order and surprise, intellect and imagination, conscious and unconscious."(9) To demonstrate that division of the corpus callosum leads to a loss of creativity, we need some *measure* of creativity which we lack, and a patient whose preoperative creativity is established, which we not only lack but would not likely accept if offered. In the absence of such studies, we must rely on animal experiments, such as those by Bureš and Burešova . . . ; further studies may be expected to show to what extent the "creative" problem solving in the experimental animal is dependent on callosal interaction.

We may further consider that there is not only great variability in the excitatory function of callosal fibers, but that there may be a good deal of inhibitory activity (10, 11, 12). If so, certain kinds of left hemisphere activity may directly suppress certain kinds of right hemisphere action. Or they may prevent access to the left hemisphere of the products of right hemisphere activity. If transcallosal inhibition is indeed a prominent aspect of cerebral function, we can see a physiological basis for the fact that failure to develop fresh insights (in the sense of new understanding of the outside world) is closely related to a failure to gain further sight into one's other self. The possible corollaries suggested by this approach seem nearly limitless. One in particular needs emphasis: it is the inhibitory effect, on the appositional source, of an excess of propositional thinking. There is an inbuilt antagonism between analysis and intuition requiring subtle mediation to attain a common ground. Paul Valéry wrote, "While it is at work, the mind is constantly going and coming from Self to Other; what its innermost being produces is modified by a peculiar awareness of the judgment of others" (13). And Valéry emphasized one of the major obstacles, an excess of analysis: "All that we can define is at once set off from the producing mind, in opposition to it. The mind turns whatever it defines into matter it can work on, or a tool it can work with. Whatever it has clearly defined, the mind places out of its own reach, and in so doing, shows that it knows itself and that it trusts only what is not itself." Steven Spender said, "For there are examples enough to show . . . that the poetic imagination is harmed by absorbing more intellectual knowledge than it can digest" (14). Henry Moore put it bluntly: "It is a mistake for a sculptor or a painter to speak or write very often about his job. It releases tension needed for his work."

It is not merely talking too much that inhibits intuition; it is rather an excessive emphasis on the rational proposition as a criterion of understanding. From his interview with Joan Miro, Fifield (15) concluded that artistic creativity is "the yield of not-think." Fifield quoted Miro:

> The work comes out of the unconscious, that is certain. You recognize if it is good or not. . . . If you have a preconception, any notion of where you are going, you will never get anywhere.

Da Vinci said that. He said you have to go up a tunnel backwards. You do. You mustn't watch yourself.

Creativity has not only made the human race unique in Nature; what is more important for the individual, it gives value and purpose to human existence. Creativity requires more than technical skills and logical thought; it also needs the cultivation and collaboration of the appositional mind. If the constraint of an intellectual ideal can make man a unilateral being, physiologically underdeveloped, a better informed and foresighted community will strive toward a more harmonious development of the organism by assuring an appropriate training and a greater consideration for the other side of the brain.

.   .   .   .

References

1. Jackson, J. H. *Selected Writings of John Hughlings Jackson.* Edited by J. Taylor. New York, Basic Books, 1958. P. 186.

2. Jung, C. G. *Psychology and Literature.* In Ghiselin, B., ed., *The Creative Process: A Symposium.* New York, The New American Library, 1952.

3. Bruner, J. *On Knowing: Essays for the Left Hand.* New York, Atheneum, 1965. P. 74ff.

4. Alajouanine, T. Aphasia and artistic realization. *Brain,* 71:229–241, 1948.

5. Wiesel, T. N., and Hubel, D. H. The effects of visual deprivation on morphology and physiology of cells in the cat's lateral geniculate body. *J. Neurophysiol.,* 26:978–993, 1963.

6. Fifkova, E. The influence of unilateral visual deprivation on optic centers. *Brain Research,* 6:763–766, 1967.

7. Sperry, R. W. *Embryogenesis of Behavioral Nerve Nets.* In Dehaan, R. L., and Ursprung, H., eds., *Organogenesis.* New York, Holt, Rinehart and Winston, 1965.

8. Rombauer, I. S., and Becker, M. R. *The Joy of Cooking.* New York, Bobbs-Merrill, 1953.

9. Moore, H. *Notes on Sculpture.* In Ghiselin, B., ed., *The Creative Process: A Symposium.* New York, The New American Library, 1952.

10. Asanuma, H., and Okuda, O. Effects of transcallosal volleys on pyramidal tract cell activity of cat. *J. Neurophysiol.,* 25:198–208, 1962.

11. Berlucchi, G. (personal communication).

12. Eidelberg, E. Callosal and non-callosal connexions between the sensory-motor cortices in cat and monkey. *EEG Clin. Neurophysiol.,* 26:557–564, 1969.

13. Valéry, P. *The Course in Poetics: First Lesson.* In Ghiselin, B., ed., *The Creative Process: A Symposium.* New York, The New American Library, 1952.

14. Spender, S. *The Imagination in the Modern World.* Washington, D.C., U.S. Govt. Printing Office, 1962. P. 37.

15. Fifield, W. Miro: an interview in Mallorca. *Arts Magazine,* 43:17–19, 1968.

STANLEY KRIPPNER and GARDNER MURPHY · Extra-sensory Perception and Creativity

[*Gardner Murphy, whose work on creativity began with a study of word association responses of literary and scientific types when he was a college undergraduate, has in recent years become interested in research in extrasensory perception and psychic phenomena. Here, with Krippner, a leading researcher in the latter field, he addresses members of the discipline known as humanistic psychology, a movement that began with Abraham Maslow. These excerpts begin with definitions of the forms of parapsychological phenomena —the terms "psi," "extrasensory perception," "telepathy," "precognition," "clairvoyance," and "psychokinesis"—and close with the authors' review of what they believe are suggestive connections between these phenomena and creativity.*]

The subject matter of parapsychology stems from frequently reported experiences which seem to defy an easy explanation. A man may dream of an impending catastrophe before it happens. A woman may experience anxiety about her husband at the moment his car is involved in a collision. A "psychic healer" may be involved in the remarkable recovery of a person from a fatal disease.

All parapsychological phenomena are referred to as "psychic occurrences" or "psi." Psi has both perceptual-cognitive and motor-kinetic aspects. The perceptual-cognitive aspect of psi is designated as "extrasensory perception" or ESP and includes precognition (the ability to foretell future events), telepathy (mind-to-mind communication), and clairvoyance (the knowledge of distant happenings). The motor-kinetic aspect of psi is designated as "psychokinesis" or PK, the ability to influence the movement of objects without the intermediation of any known energy (e.g., psychic healing, thought photography, control of dice from a distance, influence over the growth of plants by paranormal methods).

Most of the experimental data in the parapsychological literature have proceeded in directions unlike those advocated by humanistic psychologists. For example, the pioneering work of J. B. Rhine (1935) involved the development of materials and methods that would permit easy handling and precise measurement. He used a specially designed pack of cards

Source *From Krippner, S., and Murphy, G., "Humanistic Psychology and Parapsychology," Journal of Humanistic Psychology, 1973, Vol. 13, No. 4, pp. 4–5, 13–15, 20–24. Copyright 1973 by the Journal of Humanistic Psychology. Reprinted by permission.*

containing five cards on which there was a cross, five on which there was a circle, five which contained a square, five which contained a star, and five on which there were wavy lines. A series of 25 trials with the ESP cards was called a run; a successful trial was called a hit. Five hits per run is the expected average.

Later, Rhine (Pratt, Rhine, Smith, & Stuart, 1940) conducted similar card tests demonstrating, to his satisfaction, the independent existence of various types of ESP: clairvoyance, telepathy, and precognition. [ftnt. deleted] He then attempted an investigation of PK through various tests with dice. For example, the subjects might concentrate on obtaining a certain number when a pair of dice was thrown. In the first PK experiment (Rhine & Rhine, 1943), 901 runs were completed. The subjects obtained 446 hits more than could be expected by coincidence (the odds against change [sic] being over a million billion to one).

It can be seen that these early experiments in American parapsychology reflected the behavioristic influence which dominated psychology in the United States at that time. Emphasis was placed upon the observed response of the subject, little attention being paid to intervening variables or the "person as a whole" as stressed by humanistic psychologists. Indeed, the few accounts which did attempt to study the whole person were largely clinical reports, many of which displayed a strong psychoanalytic influence (e.g., Devereux, 1953; Eisenbud, 1947).

Rhine (1935) produced some initial information about his eight most outstanding subjects noting that, in general, they were sociable, intelligent, artistic, religious in nonorthodox ways, and free from psychopathology. However, the first sustained effort to study personality variables and ESP was made by Schmeidler (1947). Not only did she explore the psychological variations of ESP subjects with various personality measures (Schmeidler & McConnell, 1958), but she also carried out a number of studies in which believers in ESP fairly consistently made more hits than nonbelievers (e.g., Schmeidler, 1945).

There is controversy in the field as to whether ESP and PK are randomly distributed traits characteristic of all human beings or whether they are gifts possessed by only a few persons. The many experiments which have yielded significant data when large groups have been tested (e.g., Pratt & Woodruff, 1964) strongly suggest that psi is a generic gift. However, there do seem to be individuals who perform at superior levels in laboratory experiments. In recent years, several such persons have appeared who demonstrated a rather consistent ability to obtain statistically significant results in psi research. Their numbers include Malcolm Bessent

(Honorton, 1971), William Erwin (Krippner & Ullman, 1969), Lalsingh Harribance (Roll & Klein, 1972), Ted Serios (Stevenson & Pratt, 1969), and Vladimir Stepanek (Ryzl & Pratt, 1962). With the exception of some psychoanalytic material which has been published concerning Serios (Eisenbud, 1967), nothing about the others has appeared in the literature which would indicate the possible personality matrix in which their psychic ability developed. Therefore, if humanistic psychology can encourage parapsychologists to study psychic sensitives as whole persons, it will have made an important contribution to the understanding of psi phenomena.

.   .   .   .

Creativity, more than any other human behavior, is seen as a manifestation of von Bertalanffy's (1966) theory that the human brain represents an open system with certain freedoms of operation and potentials for change. Parapsychological data also support this notion. Rhine (1935) speaks of the mind's occasional ability to function independently of the physical body. C. D. Broad (1955) discusses the mind's "psi component" which may act independently of its physiological component.

In addition, there are several psi experiments which demonstrate a relationship between psychic ability and creative ability. Utilizing ESP cards, Charles Honorton (1967) found a significant difference in precognition success between high-scoring and low-scoring subjects on a creativity test. The high-scorers did better. Additional studies have been reported by Schmeidler (1964), Henry Pang and Linda Frost (1967), B. M. Humphrey (1949), and others (e.g., Krippner, 1963).

A number of anecdotal reports from the lives of gifted people are often cited to link psi and creativity (e.g., Anderson, 1962). This idea was supported by data produced by Thelma Moss (1966). When she separated artists from nonartists, following an ESP experiment, their scores differed significantly, the artists making higher scores. Moss (1969) obtained similar results in a follow-up study; in this case she predicted that artists would demonstrate higher ESP scores and her prediction was confirmed.

Murphy (1966) has cited three principles which appear to characterize both creativity and psi: positive motivation, relaxation, and dissociation. Positive motivation, a strong, clear need to make contact with objects distant in space and time, makes paranormal perception more likely. It is also needed for creative thought or function. Further, the moments of the richest paranormal experience and the richest creative experience frequently take place under relaxed conditions. One recalls the story of Archimedes leaping out of the bathtub shouting, "I have found it!" because he had solved the problem of determining the amount of gold in Hiero's crown by a sudden inspiration that came to him while relaxing in a warm bath. Helmholtz often remarked that he was in a highly concentrated state as he worked in his physiological laboratory in the morning. However, the solution to his problems more frequently emerged while he was walking in the Heidelberg hills after lunch.

Murphy's third condition, dissociation, serves as a reminder that the person who experiences creative or psychic insights is not relaxed at all levels of awareness. In dissociation, one part of the mind is actively concerned and the rest is capable of only passive, fragmented activity. If part of one's consciousness can be strongly focused while the remainder remains quiet, creativity and psi will be favored. Both abilities may be fostered by selective focusing within a framework of conceptual flexibility (Moriarty & Murphy, 1967). Furthermore, many of the best examples of original and paranormal perception and conceptualization occur when there is a rapid movement from an unmotivated state to a motivated state, from a relaxed to an active state, or from a highly integrated to a very dissociated state (Murphy, 1966). Murphy's observation has been confirmed by a biofeedback experiment (Honorton, Davidson, & Bindler, 1971) in which ESP, as measured by card-guessing scores, appeared to be activated by shifts in consciousness (as measured by generation and suppression of alpha brain wave activity). It should be noted that this type of experiment has great appeal to most humanistic psychologists who do not consider an altered conscious state abnormal per se, but do consider it as one of several valid modes of awareness by which an individual can learn about himself and his world (James, 1961; Krippner & Meacham, 1968; Myers, 1903).

Roy Dreistadt (1971) has presented several instances in which gifted individuals' creative and psychic talents apparently have worked in conjunction. For example, Galois (who lived in the nineteenth century) produced a manuscript that signified a complete transformation of higher algebra. The manuscript projected a full light on what had been only glimpsed thus far by the greatest mathematicians. In a letter Galois wrote to a friend before he died in a duel, he stated a theorem on the "periods" of a certain type of integrals. This theorem could not have been understood by scientists living at the time of Galois as the "periods" acquired meaning only by means of some principles in the theory of certain functions that were found over 20 years after Galois' death. Dreistadt (1971) cites other examples in which a transpersonal experience combined creative and psychic elements; Kepler, Pascal, and Faraday reported these life episodes and ascribed many of their discoveries to sources "beyond the self." The humanistic psychologist would take these reports seriously and would study their possible validity, unlike psychologists with different orientations who would either ignore these experiences or see them as aberrant, rather than as a potentially potent force for personality growth and transformation. Because humanistic psychologists place a high value on creative and transpersonal experience, they might benefit from reading the relevant parapsychological literature and find their understanding aided and illuminated.

. . . .

References

Anderson, M. The relations of psi to creativity. *Journal of Parapsychology*, 1962, **26**, 277–292.

Broad, C. *Human personality and the possibility of its survival.* Berkeley: University of California Press, 1955.

Devereux, G. (Ed.) *Psychoanalysis and the occult.* New York: International University Press, 1953.

Dreistadt, R. The prophetic achievements of geniuses and types of extrasensory perception. *Psychology*, 1971, **8**, 27–40.

Eisenbud, J. The dreams of two patients in analysis interpreted as a telepathic rêve a deux. *Psychoanalytic Quarterly*, 1947, **16**, 39–60.

Eisenbud, J. *The world of Ted Serios.* New York: Morrow, 1967.

Honorton, C. Creativity and precognition scoring level. *Journal of Parapsychology*, 1967. **31**, 29–42.

Honorton, C. Automated forced-choice precognition tests with a "sensitive." *Journal of the American Society for Psychical Research*, 1971, **65**, 476–481.

Honorton, C., Davidson, R., & Bindler, P. Feedback-augmented EEG alpha, shifts in subjective state, and ESP card-guessing performance. *Journal of the American Society of Psychical Research*, 1971, **65**, 308–323.

Humphrey, B. The relation of ESP to mode of drawing. *Journal of Parapsychology*, 1949, **13**, 31–46.

James, W. *The varieties of religious experience.* New York: Collier, 1961. (Originally published, 1902).

Krippner, S. Creativity and psychic phenomena. *Gifted Child Quarterly*, 1963, **7**, 51–63.

Krippner, S., & Meacham, W. Consciousness and the creative process. *Gifted Child Quarterly*, 1968, **12**, 141–157.

Krippner, S., & Ullman, M. Telepathic perception in the dream state: Confirmatory study using EEG–EOG monitoring techniques. *Perceptual and Motor Skills*, 1969, **29**, 915–918.

Moriarty, A., & Murphy, G. An experimental study of ESP potential and its relationship to creativity in a group of normal children. *Journal of the American Society for Psychical Research*, 1967, **61**, 326–338.

Moss, T. A study of experimenter bias through subliminal perception, nonverbal communication, and ESP. Unpublished doctoral dissertation, University of California at Los Angeles, 1966.

Moss, T. ESP effects in "artists" contrasted with "nonartists." *Journal of Parapsychology*, 1969, **33**, 57–69.

Murphy, G. Research in creativeness: What can it tell us about extrasensory perception. *Journal of the American Society for Psychical Research*, 1966, **60**, 8–22.

Myers, F. *Human personality and its survival of bodily death.* London: Longmans, Green, 1903.

Pang, H., & Frost, L. Relatedness of creativity, values, and ESP. *Perceptual and Motor Skills*, 1967, **24**, 650.

Pratt, J., Rhine, J., Smith, M., & Stuart, C. *Extrasensory perception after sixty years.* New York: Holt, 1940.

Pratt, J., & Woodruff, J. Size of stimulus symbols in extrasensory perception. *Journal of Parapsychology*, 1964, **28**, 258–273.

Rhine, J. *Extra-sensory perception*. Boston: Humphries, 1935.

Rhine, L., & Rhine, J. The psychokinetic effect: I. The first experiment. *Journal of Parapsychology*, 1943, **26**, 211–217.

Roll, W., & Klein, J. Further forced-choice ESP experiments with Lalsingh Harribance. *Journal of the American Society for Psychical Research*, 1972, **66**, 103–112.

Ryzl, M., & Pratt, J. Confirmation of ESP performance in a hypnotically prepared subject. *Journal of the American Society for Psychical Research*, 1962, **56**, 237–243.

Schmeidler, G. Separating the sheep from the goats, *Journal of the American Society for Psychical Research*, 1945, **39**, 47–49.

Schmeidler, G. Rorschach variables in relation to ESP scores. *Journal of the American Society for Psychical Research*, 1947, **41**, 35–64.

Schmeidler, G. An experiment on precognitive clairvoyance: IV. Precognition scores related to creativity. *Journal of Parapsychology*, 1964, **28**, 102–108.

Schmeidler, G., & McConnell, R. *ESP and personality patterns*. New Haven: Yale University Press, 1958.

Stevenson, I., & Pratt, J. Further investigations of the psychic photography of Ted Serios. *Journal of the American Society for Psychical Research*, 1969, **63**, 352–364.

von Bertalanffy, L. General systems theory and psychiatry. In S. Arieti (Ed.), *American Handbook of Psychiatry*, Vol. III, 1966.

B. F. SKINNER · A Behavioral Model of Creation

[*Generally considered the leading modern behaviorist, Skinner presents a theoretical model of the act of creation according to strict behaviorist principles. Denying the creator's direct responsibility for creation, Skinner proposes that random changes in structure are selected out because of their consequences, a concept based on Darwin's theory of natural selection.*]

What I am going to say has the curious property of illustrating itself. . . . there is a sense in which having a poem is like having a baby, and in that sense I am in labor; I am having a lecture. In it I intend to raise the question of whether I am responsible for what I am saying, whether I am actually originating anything, and to what extent I deserve credit or blame. . . .

· · · · · · · · · · · · · · ·

. . . I am to compare having a poem with having a baby, and it will do no harm to start with a lower class of living things. Samuel Butler suggested the comparison years ago when he said that a poet writes a poem as a hen lays an egg, and both feel better afterwards.

Source   From "A Lecture on 'Having' a Poem." B. F. Skinner, Cumulative Record: A Selection of Papers, 3rd ed., © 1972, pp. 345, 350–355. Reprinted by permission of Prentice-Hall, Inc., Englewood Cliffs, N.J.

But there are other points of similarity, and on one of them Butler built a whole philosophy of purposive evolution. The statement was current in early post-Darwinism days that "a hen is only an egg's way of making another egg." It is not, of course, a question of which comes first, though that is not entirely irrelevant. The issue is who does what, who acts to produce something and therefore deserves credit. Must we give the hen credit for the egg or the egg for the hen? Possibly it does not matter, since no one is seriously interested in defending the rights of hen or egg, but something of the same sort can be said about a poet, and then it does matter. Does the poet create, originate, initiate the thing called a poem, or is his behavior merely the product of his genetic and environmental histories?

I raised that question a number of years ago with a distinguished poet at a conference at Columbia University. I was just finishing *Verbal Behavior* and could not resist summarizing my position. I thought it was possible to account for verbal behavior in terms of the history of the speaker, without reference to ideas, meanings, propositions, and the like. The poet stopped me at once. He could not agree. "That leaves no place for me as a poet," he said, and he would not discuss the matter further. It was a casual remark which, I am sure, he has long since forgotten, and I should hesitate to identify him if he had not recently published something along the same lines.

When Jerome Weisner was recently inaugurated as President of Massachusetts Institute of Technology, Archibald MacLeish read a poem.[1] He praised Dr. Weisner as:

> A good man in a time when men are
> scarce, when the intelligent foregather,
> follow each other around in the fog like
> sheep, bleat in the rain, complain
> because Godot never comes; because
> all life is a tragic absurdity — Sisyphus
> sweating away at his rock, and the rock
> won't; because freedom and dignity . . .
>
> Oh, weep, they say, for freedom and dignity!
> You're not free: it's your grandfather's itch you're scratching.
> You have no dignity: you're not a man,
> you're a rat in a vat of rewards and punishments,

---

1. Boston *Globe*, October 9, 1971.

you think you've chosen the rewards, you haven't:
the rewards have chosen you.
                            Aye! Weep!

I am just paranoid enough to believe that he is alluding to _Beyond Freedom and Dignity_. In any case, he sums up the main issue rather effectively: "You think you've chosen the rewards; you haven't. The rewards have chosen you." To put it more broadly, a person does not act upon the environment, perceiving it and deciding what to do about it; the environment acts upon him, determining that he will perceive it and act in special ways. George Eliot glimpsed the issue: "Our deeds determine us, as much as we determine our deeds," though she did not understand _how_ we are determined by our deeds. Something does seem to be taken away from the poet when his behavior is traced to his genetic and personal histories. Only a person who truly initiates his behavior can claim that he is free to do so and that he deserves credit for any achievement. If the environment is the initiating force, he is not free, and the environment must get the credit.

The issue will be clearer if we turn to a biological parallel — moving from the oviparous hen to the viviparous human mother. When we say that a woman "bears" a child, we suggest little by way of creative achievement. The verb refers to carrying the fetus to term. The expression "gives birth" goes little further; a bit of a platonic idea, birth, is captured by the mother and given to the baby, which then becomes born. We usually say simply that a woman "has" a baby where "has" means little more than possess. To have a baby is to come into possession of it. The woman who does so is then a mother, and the child is her child. But what is the nature of her contribution? She is not responsible for the skin color, eye color, strength, size, intelligence, talents, or any other feature of her baby. She gave it half its genes, but she got those from _her_ parents. She could, of course, have damaged the baby. She could have aborted it. She could have caught rubella at the wrong time or taken drugs, and as a result the baby would have been defective. _But she made no positive contribution._

A biologist has no difficulty in describing the role of the mother. She is a place, a locus in which a very important biological process takes place. She supplies protection, warmth, and nourishment, but she does not design the baby who profits from them. The poet is also a locus, a place in which certain genetic and environmental causes come together to have a common effect. Unlike a mother, the poet has access to his poem during gestation. He may tinker with it. A poem seldom makes its appearance in a completed form. Bits and pieces *occur* to the poet, who rejects or allows them to stand, and who puts them together to *compose* a poem. But they come from his past history, verbal and otherwise, and he has had to learn how to put them together. The act of composition is no more an act of creation than "having" the bits and pieces composed.

But can this interpretation be correct if a poem is unquestionably new? Certainly the plays of Shakespeare did not exist until he wrote them. Possibly all their parts could be traced by an omniscient scholar to Shakespeare's verbal and nonverbal histories, but he must have served some additional function. How otherwise are we to explain the creation of something new?

The answer is again to be found in biology. A little more than a hundred years ago the act of creation was debated for a very different reason. The living things on the surface of the earth show a fantastic variety — far beyond the variety in the works of Shakespeare — and they had long been attributed to a creative Mind. The anatomy of the hand, for example, was taken as evidence of a prior design. And just as we are told today that a behavioral analysis cannot explain the "potentially infinite" number of sentences composable by a speaker, so it was argued that no physical or biological process could explain the potentially infinite number of living things on the surface of the earth. (Curiously enough the creative behavior invoked by way of explanation was verbal: "In the beginning was the word . . . ," supplemented no doubt by a *generative* grammar.)

The key term in Darwin's title is Origin. Novelty could be explained without appeal to prior design if random changes in structure were selected by their consequences. It was the contingencies of survival which created new forms. Selection is a special kind of causality, much less conspicuous than the push-pull causality of nineteenth-century physics, and Darwin's discovery may have appeared so late in the history of human thought for that reason. The selective action of the consequences of behavior was also overlooked for a long time. It was not until the seventeenth century that any important initiating action by the environment was recognized. People acted upon the world, but the world did not act upon them. The first evidence to the contrary was of the conspicuous push-pull kind. Descartes's . . . theoretical anticipation of the reflex and the reflex physiology of the nineteenth century gave rise to a stimulus-response psychology in which behavior was said to be triggered by the environment. There is no room in such a formulation for a more important function. When a person acts, the consequences may strengthen his tendency to act in the same way again. The Law of Effect, formulated nearly three quarters of a century ago by Edward L. Thorndike, owed a great deal to Darwinian theory, and it raised very similar issues. It is not some prior purpose, intention, or act of will which accounts for novel behavior; it is the "contingencies of reinforcement." (Among the behaviors thus explained are techniques of self-management, once attributed to "higher mental processes," which figure in the gestation of new topographies.)

The poet often knows that some part of his history is contributing to the poem he is writing. He may, for example, reject a phrase because he sees that he has borrowed it from something he has read. But it is quite impossible for him to be aware of all his history, and it is in this sense that he does not know where his behavior comes from. Having a poem, like having a baby, is in large part a matter of exploration and discovery, and both poet and mother are often surprised by what they produce. And because the poet is not aware of the origins of his behavior, he is likely to attribute it to a creative mind, an "unconscious" mind, perhaps, or a mind belonging to someone else — to a muse, for example, whom he has invoked to come and write his poem for him.

A person produces a poem and a woman produces a baby, and we call the person a poet and the woman a mother. Both are essential as loci in which vestiges of the past come together in certain combinations. The process is creative in the sense that the products are new. Writing a poem is the sort of thing men and women do as men and women, having a baby is the sort of thing a woman does as a woman, and laying an egg is the sort of thing a hen does as a hen. To deny a creative contribution does not destroy man qua man or woman qua woman any more than Butler's phrase destroys hen qua hen. There is no threat to the essential humanity of man, the muliebrity of woman, or the gallity of Gallus gallus.

What is threatened, of course, is the autonomy of the poet. The autonomous is the uncaused, and the uncaused is miraculous, and the miraculous is God. For the second time in a little more than a century a theory of selection by consequences is threatening a traditional belief in a creative mind. And is it not rather strange that although we have abandoned that belief with respect to the creation of the world, we fight so desperately to preserve it with respect to the creation of a poem?

But is there anything wrong with a supportive myth? Why not continue to believe in our creative powers if the belief gives us satisfaction? The answer lies in the future of poetry. To accept a wrong explanation because it flatters us is to run the risk of missing a right one — one which in the long run may offer more by way of "satisfaction." Poets know all too well how long a sheet of paper remains a carte blanche. To wait for genius or a genie is to make a virtue of ignorance. If poetry is a good thing, if we want more of it and better, and if writing poems is a rewarding experience, then we should look afresh at its sources.

Perhaps the future of poetry is not that important, but I have been using a poem simply as an example. I could have developed the same theme in art, music, fiction, scholarship, science, invention—in short, wherever we speak of *original* behavior. We say that we "have" ideas and again in the simple sense of coming into possession of them. An idea "occurs to us" or "comes to mind." And if for idea we read "the behavior said to express an idea," we come no closer to an act of creation. We "have" behavior, as the etymology of the word itself makes clear. It "occurs to us" to act in a particular way, and it is not any prior intention, purpose, or plan which disposes us to do so. By analyzing the genetic and individual histories responsible for our behavior, we may learn how to be more original. The task is not to think of new forms of behavior but to create an environment in which they are likely to occur.

Something of the sort has happened in the evolution of cultures. Over the centuries men and women have built a world in which they behave much more effectively than in a natural environment, but they have not done so by deliberate design. A culture evolves when new practices arise which make it more likely to survive. We have reached a stage in which our culture induces some of its members to be concerned for its survival. A kind of deliberate design is then possible, and a scientific analysis is obviously helpful. We can build a world in which men and women will be better poets, better artists, better composers, better novelists, better scholars, better scientists—in a word, better people. We can, in short, "have" a better world.

And that is why I am not much disturbed by the question with which George Kateb concludes his review of *Beyond Freedom and Dignity*. He is attacking my utopianism, and he asks, "Does Skinner not see that only silly geese lay golden eggs?" The question brings us back to the oviparous again, but it does not matter, for the essential issue is raised by all living things. It is characteristic of the evolution of a species, as it is of the acquisition of behavior and of the evolution of a culture, that ineffective forms give rise to effective. Perhaps a goose is silly if, because she lays a golden egg, she gets the ax; but, silly or not, she has laid a golden egg. And what if that egg hatches a golden goose? There, in an eggshell, is the great promise of evolutionary theory. A silly goose, like Butler's hen, is simply the way in which an egg produces a *better* egg.

And now my labor is over. I have had my lecture. I have no sense of fatherhood. If my genetic and personal histories had been different, I should have come into possession of a different lecture. If I deserve any credit at all, it is simply for having served as a place in which certain processes could take place. I shall interpret your polite applause in that light.

HERBERT F. CROVITZ · A Computer Model Approach to Creativity

[*On the basis of the idea of recurrence of thought which Crovitz attributes originally to Galton and describes in some detail in other portions of his book, the following model for creative problem-solving was developed. Providing a means, through a linguistic device, for retrieving and using all possible cognitive operations that might lead to a solution, Crovitz constructs what he has called "the relational algorithm." The "Ogden word-wheel" on which his model is based, was originally developed as a device for presenting Basic English, a vocabulary of the essential words in the English language. The barnstorming type of computer problem-solving described here is somewhat less popular than methods attempting to simulate human problem-solving such as those of workers on "artificial intelligence" and those proposed by the pioneers in this area, Newell, Shaw, and Simon.*]

. . . all there is to discovery and invention is putting a couple of old things in a new relation. An Ogden word-wheel that is stripped for action does it, *exhausting the possibilities* that can be stated in Basic English. The elementary form of a statement of an action is "taking one thing in some relation to another thing." The same elementary sentence is the form of a sentence to describe the statement of a discovery, an invention, or, indeed, an idea. The "things" can be anything you like, as multiple as the things of the world can be, but the relations are small in number, in point of fact, if the elementary form of an action-sentence is "Take one thing dash

SOURCE   *From pp. 99–106, "All there is to discovery and invention . . ."   "Who will find out?" in Galton's Walk by Herbert F. Crovitz. Copyright © 1970 by Herbert F. Crovitz. By permission of Harper & Row, Publishers.*

another thing," there are only 42 words in the set of all Basic English words that can by the wildest stretch of imagination fit where the dash is. The words follow. . . .

about	at	for	of	round	to
across	because	from	off	still	under
after	before	if	on	so	up
against	between	in	opposite	then	when
among	but	near	or	though	where
and	by	not	out	through	while
as	down	now	over	till	with

An old experiment in the psychology of problem-solving is important now. It is the *Umweg* problem. Put some corn on the ground. Put a transparent barrier, like a sheet of glass, in front of the corn. Put a hungry chicken in front of the glass. The barrier is between the chicken and the corn. The chicken acts in a very stupid manner. It tries to get through the barrier that it cannot get through, to go to the corn which it cannot go to, but rather must go away from to go round the barrier to get to the corn. The chicken is wearing a relational-filter before its mind's eye; all it will act on is going straight *to* the corn.

Somebody described an analogous situation. There is a very long line of traffic in the turn-left lane of a highway, but none in the straight-through right lane. Drivers, however, wear their turn-left filters before their mind's eye, seldom doing the "creative, intelligent" thing of going straight across, then going round the block, thence wheeling down the road before any of those twenty cars ahead have got past the stoplight.

Success in problem-solving comes from changing the relational-filter before the mind's eye, tacitly rippling through the set of actions that are possible, and then having the wit to recognize a solution when you see one. Or, if you are very stupid but very quick, like a computer, trying *all* the possible actions till the goal is attained and it is time to stop.

This computer maneuver has been simulated by busy inventive men whose biographers have found their methods out. Perhaps the most instructive case has to do with building a working model of the system you want to change, and then tinkering with it. Tinkering with a model of the thing is harmless; in an undisciplined run through the possible actions you may be lucky enough to come upon a solution. Thomas Edison was a great one for tinkering with models of things, and might be a pattern on which to build a discoverer-computer.

Edison himself was no slowpoke. The glory of his youth was that he had a fast, legible hand, and was capable of writing at a rapid rate. But, according to a son, later on he had little power of abstraction, being always in need of seeing a thing in its concrete form, and tinkering with it. One of the problems that is described well by Josephson[1] is Edison's work on the quadraplex—his putative discovery of how to send four simultaneous messages along a telegraph wire, two in each direction at once. This was important at the time—it would quadruple the power of the telegraph without the need of having to build four times the number of wires. Edison built an "analog" of the electric wire, with pipes and valves and assorted gadgets for affecting the flow of the water in the pipe. Using the gadgets to force water back and forth, in the pattern of wires in the system that was planned, he tinkered and ended with separating the separable features of the flow of current, sending one message controlled by one, and another controlled by another.[2]

Edison also had a workshop that does in space what notebooks do in time, allowing one project to infect a neighboring one, so that moves made here may also be tried out there. His lab was a big barn with work-tables along the room holding separate projects in progress. He would inspect one, then another. Not a bad trick for an ancient to come upon for switching relational-filters. That and working a 20-hour day stood him in good stead indeed. Of course, by his lights he was a failure where inventions were concerned, for he never made any money from them except when he set up commercial ventures to control that practical part of things himself. Yet, when he visited Pasteur once, Edison did not make a very good impression, for Pasteur was horrified at glimpsing the distractions attached to Edison's commercial ventures.

Notice that the switching of relational-filters is hard for problem-solvers to do naturally. The relevant history of intellectual precursors of this small work are reviewed engagingly by Mandler and Mandler,[3] who covered in some detail a history of changing emphasis that evolved from analysis of raw consciousness to inquiries into problem-solving. They detected a growing tendency to probe the processes that intervene between problem and solution.[4] That review ends with Duncker.

Duncker studied this problem: to get rid of an inoperable stomach tumor without harming the healthy tissue of the body, by using rays that can be modulated in intensity; at a high enough intensity, they

1. Josephson, M. *Edison*. New York: McGraw-Hill, 1959. P. 123.
2. *Ibid.*, p. 124.
3. Mandler, J. M., and Mandler, G. *Thinking: From Association to Gestalt*. New York: Wiley, 1964.
4. *Ibid.*, p. 276.

destroy. He gave a protocol, but not a good one. The experimenter kept butting in, giving hints, asking leading questions. Nonetheless, the remarks of the subject—his attempts to solve the problem aloud—are instructive when they are put into relational language. The sequence of comments, so translated, is this:

1. Take the rays *through* the esophagus.
2. Take the sensitivity *from* the tissues.
3. Take tissue *off* the tumor.
4. Take strong rays *after* weak rays.
5. Take a shield *on* stomach walls.
6. Take the tumor *across* the stomach.
7. Take a cannula *through* the stomach wall.
8. Take the power *from* the rays.
9. Take the tumor *to* the exterior.
10. Take strong rays *after* weak rays.
11. Take strong rays *after* weak rays.
12. Take the rays *from* the body, or take the power *from* the rays.
13. Take the tumor *at* the focus of rays.
14. Take one ray *across* another ray.

It is possible to devise an irreverent method for solving "practical" problems with the use of elementary sentences that list the *full* set of possible actions that that form of sentence can cover in the vocabulary of Basic English. . . .

One thing that is wrong with the mind's eye is that it has relational-filters that get stuck. Let us speed up the exchange of filters.

With respect to the x-ray problem as given by Duncker, there are at least two domain-words, "ray" and "stomach-tumor." The Basic English translation of ray is "any of a number of straight lines going out in different directions from a common point." Stomach is "a bag-like expansion of the digestion-pipe." Tumor is "an abnormal mass from normal body materials." Thus the problem might become using lines to get rid of a mass in a bag. In this particular case, the translation into Basic English reduces the problem very quickly to a diagrammatic stark form of it.

I leave the playing of such a diagram to the reader, merely noting that, given a mass in a bag and given lines emanating from a point, there are many possibilities other than framing the question of how to get rid of the mass, i.e., take the mass from the bag. There are words other than *from*.

We can learn a small but very important thing from some protocols we collected on the relational algorithm in Duncker's problems from college students, one of whom was . . . Penelope. . . .

A group of 10 undergraduates was given the x-ray problem and the single sentence, "Take one ray across another ray." Everybody quickly saw the solution. But not Penelope. She rejected the sentence, never having her mind's eye put the tumor at the *intersection* of the two rays. Alas. It is not automatic; success is not assured; there is no royal road nor indeed any commoner's road that is sure to lead to knowledge.

Given the "laws of probability," chances are that a bunch of monkeys at a bunch of typewriters would peck out nonsense, but take the extreme case of their typing out the works in the British Museum. Miller[5] treated this problem with great generality. Even given the sequential probabilities built into the English language, it would take quite a while for the monkeys to come upon anything that made much sense. Miller said that generating sense was *not* the interesting problem. Men or monkeys or machines could be given an algorithm to do it. The problem, said Miller, is that the monkeys would not know the wheat from the chaff.

What one needs are rules for matching output to a standard, the making of such a match being a signal that sense has been made and the typing may stop. However, we may note that the best of us do sometimes miss the significance of what we have before us—indeed, it has commonly been supposed that a rather mystic restructuring of significance underlies the sudden recognition that something is a solution to something that is a problem.

How is the monkey at the typewriter to know to stop? Say we chose to set up a computer to spin out randomness until it came to some, for us, recognizable order. How would we fix the machine to go and then stop? Stopping is the whole of the problem of creative problem-solving if we can run off the set of possible alternatives. We need the wit to recognize a solution—or, in plain talk, we need to stop at the right alternative. How is that to be arranged?

Suppose we know the goal. In the x-ray problem it is most easily stated in two parts: first, the tumor is destroyed; second, the tissue that is not the tumor is unaffected. The second part is always satisfied while the first part is simultaneously satisfied when the goal is transformed into this: tumor is in body; body is around the tumor. The goal is satisfied when we can reach the sentence: the tumor is destroyed; the body around it is unaffected. We draw a figure. On the line AB the energy is constant and

5. Miller, G. In S. S. Stevens, ed., *Handbook of Experimental Psychology*. New York: Wiley, 1951. P. 809.

too low to destroy tissue. On the line *CD* the energy is also constant and too low to destroy tissue. So at *a*,*b*,*c*, and *d*—the body around the tumor—there is no effect. But at the crossing, the energy sums and whatever tissue is there is destroyed. Put the tumor there—the tumor is destroyed; the body around it is unaffected. The sentence representing the goal is matched! Stop!

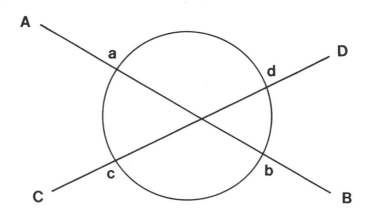

We will plod along through Duncker's problems pairing elements from the domain of the problem through one of the 42 relation words that we took from Basic English. Often coming upon a solution possibility in this way is easy and swift. When one is involved in any problem the number of possible pairs of domain-words is large—it is precisely

(1) $x!$

where $x =$ the number of elements accessible in the domain of the problem. For a single run through the 42 relations in this case one must scan $42x!$ which in the case of a domain with as little as six elements is

(2) $42(6)(5)(4)(3)(2)(1) = 30{,}200$ sentences.

However, in the case in which an accessible element from the domain of the problem is duplicated so it can be related to *itself*, the total number of sentences that need be scanned is

(3) $42(1) = 42$ sentences.

Let us consider the separating of a tangled problem by a clean slice separating the domain to be considered into two identical halves. In the x-ray problem we can leave the esophagus, the throat, the tissues, the stomach wall, the x-ray, and the tumor out in the miasmal fog holding the bag with 30,200 possibilities therein. Instead we choose to take two — two of something: in this case, *fairly* obviously, it must be two rays.

The 42-algorithm is a labored thing except for speedy computers or when the slice is made. After all, in the case of a six-element domain, relating each of the six with another of itself will give as few as

(4) $42(x) = 42(6) = 252$ sentences,

although only the most muddle-headed or the most creative of us will have much choice choosing among relating two esophaguses versus two throats versus two tissues versus two stomach walls versus two x-rays versus two tumors. In the x-ray problem, where one of the relata, the x-ray, is always assumed to be one necessary element, if there are five other elements, the number is still

(5) $42(x) = 42(6) = 252$ sentences.

In terms of the take-two rhythm of this Gordian knot simplification: When each ancient had gone out from preparation into incubation, *re* some invention or discovery, could he have picked his solution out of a list of sentences that numbered 42 in all, when the single element of the problem domain to relate to itself had some special mark of relevance to pick it out? When Mendeleev set out *to arrange the elements* in a good sequence, it was "element dash element" that he needed. When Adams and Leverrier sought *to understand the peculiar orbit* of Uranus, it was "orbit dash orbit" that they needed. Should you seek to solve the problem of weakening the sonic boom, perhaps it is *"noise dash noise"* that you would need to solve that real problem — plus some verificational expertise: taking "a noise under a noise" (the new one under the source of the jet's boom) might deflect the boom or destroy the plane. Who will find out?

CHAPTER FIVE

ALTERNATIVE APPROACHES

The views presented here differ sharply from previous explanatory accounts, both genetic and teleological. Each of the writers here rejects the assumption that creativity can be fully subjected to deterministic explanations, tacit or explicit. According to them, creative activity eludes both regularities (or repeatable sequences of events) and any unbroken complex of necessary connections. In response to the incompatibility of this discontinuity with the regularity required by explanatory principles, each writer suggests an alternative approach to creativity.

The selections are presented so that those writers who are primarily concerned with showing the inadequacies of determinism appear early; those mainly concerned with proposing alternative approaches to understanding creativity follow later. In the excerpts presented here Peirce, Bergson, and Morgan offer arguments against deterministic explanation. Croce, Collingwood, and Rogers, coming later in the chapter, focus on the autonomous mental activities in creating and each affirms a positive interpretation. Both Croce and Collingwood are concerned with preserving distinctions between creative and noncreative mental processes and they discuss the place of creative consciousness within the framework of other mental functions. Rogers acknowledges the unprecedented character of creation, but he proposes a set of hypothetical dispositions for creativity derived from his clinical observations of human behavior. Rogers's work represents a middle position between explanatory approaches and their alternatives because he insists on the uniqueness of the individual, but also displays an interest in identifying general conditions that foster creative acts.

Beardsley attempts to avoid full correlation of creative activities either with antecedents or with factors requiring preestablished direction toward the future. He does not propose an explanation, but a formulation and explication of the spontaneity possible at each moment of the creative process.

Rothenberg, along with all of the other writers in this chapter, rejects the complete reduction of creativity to regularities in nature. He acknowledges that creating may be, at heart, autonomous. Yet he does propose a thesis about certain dynamic conditions that function in the creative act itself and are necessary, though not sufficient, for creative success.

It would be misleading and inaccurate to characterize all of the perspectives represented in this chapter as pointing toward philosophical world views, that is, toward ontology or metaphysics. It is significant, however, that writers who reject the empirical approaches of scientists, or else the empirical and genetic accounts of philosophers, are similar to the teleologist in that they positively lay a groundwork for ontology or metaphysics. World views are clearly developed by Bergson and Croce, world views they believe to be consistent with their insistence on spontaneity and the autonomy of creative acts. Although Peirce does not complete a system, he does write speculative philosophy that is suggestive, as he sees it, of an architectonic. Hausman attempts to explore the philosophical issues peculiar to creativity, and he suggests a basis for developing a way of viewing and speaking about creativity that is appropriate to a world view insisting on discontinuity and spontaneity

These points about ontology and metaphysics highlight one major difference between the aims of the writers included in this chapter and those in the chapters preceding. Philosophical theorizing about creativity is inevitably directed toward broader and more comprehensive discourse. In this section, however, the writers primarily acknowledge fundamental limitations and they do not expect, therefore, to develop completely comprehensive conceptual systems. Rothenberg, as a scientist, explicitly tries to avoid any commitment to a world view. But all the scientists in this book, including Rothenberg, inevitably presuppose an unacknowledged world view: some form of determinism, indeterminism, or self-determinism. In this chapter we see that in the distinctly philosophical writings the authors include in their discussions specific suggestions for world views.

CHARLES SANDERS PEIRCE · A Rejection of Determinism

[*Peirce, along with James and Dewey, is probably best known as one of the major American pragmatists. The following selection comes from a group of Peirce's papers on metaphysics. It presents a portion of his most extensive and most pertinent argument concerning the basis for insisting on an alternative to explanatory accounts of creativity. He shows that the determinist position must involve untenable assumptions when determinism is applied to experience as a world view, or when determinism is taken as sufficient for understanding. Peirce, like Lloyd Morgan, was a scientist who reflected philosophically on issues raised by his scientific concerns.*]

I propose here to examine the common belief that every single fact in the universe is precisely determined by law. . . .

. . . .

The proposition in question is that the state of things existing at any time, together with certain immutable laws, completely determine the state of things at every other time (for a limitation to *future* time is indefensible). Thus, given the state of the universe in the original nebula, and given the laws of mechanics, a sufficiently powerful mind could deduce from these data the precise form of every curlicue of every letter I am now writing.

Whoever holds that every act of the will as well as every idea of the mind is under the rigid governance of a necessity co-ordinated with that of the physical world, will logically be carried to the proposition that minds are part of the physical world in such a sense that the laws of mechanics determine everything that happens according to immutable attractions and repulsions. In that case, that instantaneous state of things from which every other state of things is calculable consists in the positions and velocities of all the particles at any instant. This, the usual and most logical form of necessitarianism, is called the mechanical philosophy.

When I have asked thinking men what reason they had to believe that every fact in the universe is precisely determined by law, the first answer has usually been that the proposition is a "presupposition" or postulate of scientific reasoning. Well, if that is the best that can be said for it, the

SOURCE   From Peirce, C. S., "The Doctrine of Necessity Examined," The Monist, 1892, Vol. 2, pp. 321, 323, 327, 329–334, 336–337. Copyright 1892 by The Open Court Publishing Company, LaSalle, Ill. Reprinted by permission. Also in Hartshorne, C., and Weiss, P. (eds.), Collected Papers of Charles Sanders Peirce, Vol. 6, paragraph 35ff. Cambridge: Harvard University Press, 1935.

belief is doomed. Suppose it be "postulated": that does not make it true, nor so much as afford the slightest rational motive for yielding it any credence. It is as if a man should come to borrow money, and when asked for his security, should reply he "postulated" the loan. To "postulate" a proposition is no more than to hope it is true. . . .

. . . .

I do not think a man who combines a willingness to be convinced with a power of appreciating an argument upon a difficult subject can resist the reasons which have been given to show that the principle of universal necessity cannot be defended as being a postulate of reasoning. But then the question immediately arises whether it is not proved to be true, or at least rendered highly probable, by observation of nature.

. . . .

Those observations which are generally adduced in favor of mechanical causation simply prove that there is an element of regularity in nature, and have no bearing whatever upon the question of whether such regularity is exact and universal, or not. Nay, in regard to this *exactitude*, all observation is directly *opposed* to it; and the most that can be said is that a good deal of this observation can be explained away. Try to verify any law of nature, and you will find that the more precise your observations, the more certain they will be to show irregular departures from the law. We are accustomed to ascribe these, and I do not say wrongly, to errors of observation; yet we cannot usually account for such errors in any antecedently probable way. Trace their causes back far enough, and you will be forced to admit they are always due to arbitrary determination, or chance.

But it may be asked whether if there were an element of real chance in the universe it must not occasionally be productive of signal effects such as could not pass unobserved. In answer to this question, without stopping to point out that there is an abundance of great events which one might be tempted to suppose were of that nature, it will be simplest to remark that physicists hold that the particles of gases are moving about irregularly, substantially as if by real chance, and that by the principles of probabilities there must occasionally happen to be concentrations of heat in the gases contrary to the second law of thermodynamics, and these concentrations, occurring in explosive mixtures, must sometimes have tremendous effects. Here, then, is in substance the very situation supposed; yet no phenomena ever have resulted which we are forced to attribute to such chance concentration of heat, or which anybody, wise or foolish, has ever dreamed of accounting for in that manner.

In view of all these considerations, I do not believe that anybody, not in a state of casehardened ignorance respecting the logic of science, can maintain that the precise and universal conformity of facts to law is clearly proved, or even rendered particularly probable, by any observations hitherto made. In this way, the determined advocate of exact regularity will soon find himself driven to *a priori* reasons to support his thesis. . . .

.   .   .   .

Another *a priori* argument is that chance is unintelligible; that is to say, while it may perhaps be conceivable, it does not disclose to the eye of reason the how or why of things; and since a hypothesis can only be justified so far as it renders some phenomenon intelligible, we never can have any right to suppose absolute chance to enter into the production of anything in nature. This argument may be considered in connection with two others. Namely, instead of going so far as to say that the supposition of chance can *never* properly be used to explain any observed fact, it may be alleged merely that no facts are known which such a supposition could in any way help in explaining. Or again, the allegation being still further weakened, it may be said that since departures from law are not unmistakably observed, chance is not a *vera causa*, and ought not unnecessarily to be introduced into a hypothesis.

These are no mean arguments, and require us to examine the matter a little more closely. Come, my superior opponent, let me learn from your wisdom. It seems to me that every throw of sixes with a pair of dice is a manifest instance of chance.

"While you would hold a throw of deuce-ace to be brought about by necessity?" (The opponent's supposed remarks are placed in quotation marks.)

Clearly one throw is as much chance as another.

"Do you think throws of dice are of a different nature from other events?"

I see that I must say that *all* the diversity and specificalness of events is attributable to chance.

"Would you, then, deny that there is any regularity in the world?"

That is clearly undeniable. I must acknowledge there is an approximate regularity, and that every event is influenced by it. But the diversification, specificalness, and irregularity of things I suppose is chance. A throw of sixes appears to me a case in which this element is particularly obtrusive.

"If you reflect more deeply, you will come to see that *chance* is only a name for a cause that is unknown to us."

Do you mean that we have no idea whatever what kind of causes could bring about a throw of sixes?

"On the contrary, each die moves under the influence of precise mechanical laws."

But it appears to me that it is not these *laws* which made the die turn up sixes; for these laws act just the same when other throws come up. The chance lies in the diversity of throws; and this diversity cannot be due to laws which are immutable.

"The diversity is due to the diverse circumstances under which the laws act. The dice lie differently in the box, and the motion given to the box is different. These are the unknown causes which produce the throws, and to which we give the name of chance; not the mechanical law which regulates the operation of these causes. You see you are already beginning to think more clearly about this subject."

Does the operation of mechanical law not increase the diversity?

"Properly not. You must know that the instantaneous state of a system of particles is defined by six times as many numbers as there are particles, three for the co-ordinates of each particle's position, and three more for the components of its velocity. This number of numbers, which expresses the amount of diversity in the system, remains the same at all times. There may be, to be sure, some kind of relation between the co-ordinates and component velocities of the different particles, by means of which the state of the system might be expressed by a smaller number of numbers. But, if this is the case, a precisely corresponding relationship must exist between the co-ordinates and component velocities at any other time, though it may doubtless be a relation less obvious to us. Thus, the intrinsic complexity of the system is the same at all times."

Very well, my obliging opponent, we have now reached an issue. You think all the arbitrary specifications of the universe were introduced in one dose, in the beginning, if there was a beginning, and that the variety and complication of nature has always been just as much as it is now. But I, for my part, think that the diversification, the specification, has been continually taking place. Should you condescend to ask me why I so think, I should give my reasons as follows:

1) Question any science which deals with the course of time. Consider the life of an individual animal or plant, or of a mind. Glance at the history of states, of institutions, of language, of ideas. Examine the successions of forms shown by paleontology, the history of the globe as set forth in geology, of what the astronomer is able to make out concerning the changes

of stellar systems. Everywhere the main fact is growth and increasing complexity. Death and corruption are mere accidents or secondary phenomena. Among some of the lower organisms, it is a moot point with biologists whether there be anything which ought to be called death. Races, at any rate, do not die out except under unfavorable circumstances. From these broad and ubiquitous facts we may fairly infer, by the most unexceptionable logic, that there is probably in nature some agency by which the complexity and diversity of things can be increased; and that consequently the rule of mechanical necessity meets in some way with interference.

2) By thus admitting pure spontaneity or life as a character of the universe, acting always and everywhere though restrained within narrow bounds by law, producing infinitesimal departures from law continually, and great ones with infinite infrequency, I account for all the variety and diversity of the universe, in the only sense in which the really *sui generis* and new can be said to be accounted for. The ordinary view has to admit the inexhaustible mulitudinous variety of the world, has to admit that its mechanical law cannot account for this in the least, that variety can spring only from spontaneity, and yet denies without any evidence or reason the existence of this spontaneity, or else shoves it back to the beginning of time and supposes it dead ever since. The superior logic of my view appears to me not easily controverted.

3) When I ask the necessitarian how he would explain the diversity and irregularity of the universe, he replies to me out of the treasury of his wisdom that irregularity is something which from the nature of things we must not seek to explain. Abashed at this, I seek to cover my confusion by asking how he would explain the uniformity and regularity of the universe, whereupon he tells me that the laws of nature are immutable and ultimate facts, and no account is to be given of them. But my hypothesis of spontaneity does explain irregularity, in a certain sense; that is, it explains the general fact of irregularity, though not, of course, what each lawless event is to be. At the same time, by thus loosening the bond of necessity, it gives room for the influence of another kind of causation, such as seems to be operative in the mind in the formation of associations, and enables us to understand how the uniformity of nature could have been brought about. That single events should be hard and unintelligible, logic will permit without difficulty: we do not expect to make the shock of a personally experienced earthquake appear natural and reasonable by any amount of cogitation. But logic does expect things *general* to be understandable. To say that there is a universal law, and that it is a hard, ultimate, unintelligible fact, the why and wherefore of which can never be

inquired into, at this a sound logic will revolt; and will pass over at once to a method of philosophising which does not thus barricade the road of discovery.

.   .   .   .

If now I, in my turn, inquire of the necessitarian why he prefers to suppose that all specification goes back to the beginning of things, he will answer me with one of those last three arguments which I left unanswered.

First, he may say that chance is a thing absolutely unintelligible, and therefore that we never can be entitled to make such a supposition. But does not this objection smack of naïve impudence? It is not mine, it is his own conception of the universe which leads abruptly up to hard, ultimate, inexplicable, immutable law, on the one hand, and to inexplicable specification and diversification of circumstances on the other. My view, on the contrary, hypothetises nothing at all, unless it be hypothesis to say that all specification came about in some sense, and is not to be accepted as unaccountable. To undertake to account for anything by saying boldly that it is due to chance would, indeed, be futile. But this I do not do. I make use of chance chiefly to make room for a principle of generalisation, or tendency to form habits, which I hold has produced all regularities. The mechanical philosopher leaves the whole specification of the world utterly unaccounted for, which is pretty nearly as bad as to boldly attribute it to chance. I attribute it altogether to chance, it is true, but to chance in the form of a spontaneity which is to some degree regular. It seems to me clear at any rate that one of these two positions must be taken, or else specification must be supposed due to a spontaneity which develops itself in a certain and not in a chance way, by an objective logic like that of Hegel. This last way I leave as an open possibility, for the present; for it is as much opposed to the necessitarian scheme of existence as my own theory is.

Secondly the necessitarian may say there are, at any rate, no observed phenomena which the hypothesis of chance could aid in explaining. In reply, I point first to the phenomenon of growth and developing complexity, which appears to be universal, and which, though it may possibly be an affair of mechanism perhaps, certainly presents all the appearance of increasing diversification. Then, there is variety itself, beyond comparison the most obtrusive character of the universe: no mechanism can account for this. Then, there is the very fact the necessitarian most insists upon, the regularity of the universe which for him serves only to block the road of inquiry. Then, there are the regular relationships between the laws of nature, — similarities and comparative characters, which appeal to our intelligence as its cousins, and call upon us for a reason. Finally, there is consciousness, feeling, a patent fact enough, but a very inconvenient one to the mechanical philosopher.

Thirdly, the necessitarian may say that chance is not a *vera causa*, that we cannot know positively there is any such element in the universe. But the doctrine of the *vera causa* has nothing to do with elementary conceptions. Pushed to that extreme, it at once cuts off belief in the existence of a material universe; and without that necessitarianism could hardly maintain its ground. Besides, variety is a fact which must be admitted; and the theory of chance merely consists in supposing this diversification does not antedate all time. Moreover, the avoidance of hypotheses involving causes nowhere positively known to act — is only a recommendation of logic, not a positive command. It cannot be formulated in any precise terms without at once betraying its untenable character, — I mean as rigid rule, for as a recommendation it is wholesome enough.

C. LLOYD MORGAN · Emergent Novelty

[*Lloyd Morgan, a biologist, focuses philosophically on scientific interests and assumptions. He concentrates on the problems and issues raised when predictability is posed as a necessary criterion for an adequate scientific understanding of evolution. The clear distinction he makes between recurrent or repeated novelty and primary or original novelty is one that is often overlooked in discussions of creativity. Morgan's general theory of the problem of explaining evolution is found both in the book containing this selection and in* Emergent Evolution.]

At the close of the first lecture on chemistry which I attended, Edward Frankland said to us lads something to this effect: "You have all, I suppose, learnt some grammar. You are here to learn some chemistry. In grammar you have probably been given certain rules and have been told to search for examples which may illustrate them. I shall give you some rules, or laws as we call them, and with the aid of my assistant, Mr. Newth, I shall present to you selected examples of how they work. But in science that is really the wrong way up. So far as it can be managed you will get

SOURCE   *From Morgan, C. L., "Emergent Novelty,"* The Emergence of Novelty, *pp. 30–34. Copyright 1933 by Williams & Norgate, Ltd., London. Reprinted by permission of Ernest Benn, Ltd., London.*

things right way up in the laboratory. There you will start with examples and learn how the laws have grown up out of them. One of the first things you have to grasp is that, in science, observations and experiments in the laboratory, rather than discourse and demonstration in the lecture theatre, put things right way up. First facts; then probable rules or hypotheses; and then more and rather different facts to test the range and validity of these rules. Such is the procedure of science."

When I set to work, I let this simmer in my mind. It seemed to me sound policy. But a further question arose. One discovers and does not invent the facts. Does one invent the laws or discover them? Or are there some laws—those of chemistry, for example—that we invent as hypotheses subject to revision; and others—such as those of mathematics—that are already there, in the very nature of things, for us to discover and nowise invent? I knew not what answer to give. And when I consulted a mathematician of accredited standing, after indicating profitable lines of thought, he said that, after all, it was for each of us to find out—if he could.

Meanwhile, in the laboratory, we were bidden carefully to distinguish mechanical mixtures, say of pulverized charcoal and brimstone, from chemical compounds when, in certain describable circumstances and not others, carbon and sulphur combine in definite proportions and no other. And we were bidden to observe that certain properties of carbon bisulphide were in some sense new in that they differed from those of carbon and sulphur, mixed in approximately the same proportions, prior to their chemical combination.

Five or six years later G. H. Lewes suggested the name 'resultant' for the outcome of mechanical process and the name 'emergent' for the outcome of chemical process with emphasis on something new in the latter which, in the then state of knowledge, could not be predicted before the event of its occurrence. Little then came of his suggestion. The time was not yet ripe for a grasp of the wider significance of a familiar distinction thus merely renamed.

Let us consider first the emphasis on something new, since the word 'new' savours of ambiguity. What is new? If one says that the properties are new, this implies that the compound which 'has' these properties is new; it implies that what I spoke of as the substantial unity of the product of chemical combination is, in some sense, a novelty. Even so, if one says that certain old items of stuff—e.g. atoms of oxygen and hydrogen—so enter into specific relations as to give origin to the new substance, water, it may then be objected that there is here nothing really new; there is only one more instance of what has happened myriads of times.

If, however, I say that it is my belief that in the evolutionary history of our cooling earth there was a time when the new substance, water, *first* appeared; or, more generally, a time before which not one instance of this emergent novelty was anywhere in existence; then the objection takes a different form, because the word 'new' is here used in a more radical sense.

No doubt one is in verbal difficulties. One wants somehow to name a distinction between novelty in accordance with precedent (which may seem a contradiction in terms) and unprecedented novelty (which may be said to be contrary to fact). Otherwise stated, the suggested distinction is that between the novelty which arises on some *first* occasion in the course of evolutionary advance; and novelty which is *repeated* on all subsequent occasions in a like field of relatedness. Or, otherwise stated, is that between primary or original novelty, and secondary or recurrent novelty. I hope that this distinction may at least be comprehensible.

On these terms one may speak of original novelty when one is thinking of the cosmic process as a whole; and of secondary novelty when one is dealing with this or that bit of world-process in which some original novelty reappears as a matter of established routine. It is clear that scientific observation and experiment deal piecemeal with this or that bit of the cosmic process. Hence here only can one seek direct and immediate evidence of evolutionary advance through new products to fresh novelty.

In the technical terms I ask leave to use such novelty, either as original or recurrent, is some new pattern of substantial relatedness. In a sense the 'items' of stuff are not new; and yet, in a sense, at each stage of substantial advance the 'units' of stuff *are* new. In the former sense one refers to the ultimate *items* of stuff, perhaps theoretically 'neutral' stuff; in the latter sense to the proximate *units* of stuff. For stuff and substance advance hand in hand. In the atom, for example, the ultimate items of stuff are electrical somewhats existent within a space-time frame. But, in the atom, these items become *units* of stuff in that mode of substantial relatedness which, since it characterizes an atom, as such, we speak of as 'atomic.' When atoms combine to form a molecule, then, as constituents thereof, they become new units of stuff in a new mode of substantial relatedness which, since it characterizes a molecule, as such, we speak of as 'molecular.' Thereafter the molecule may become a new unit of stuff in another mode of substantial relatedness — say crystalline or colloidal; and so on, up ascending steps of an emergent ladder. To the question, then: What is new at successive stages of evolutionary advance? the reply, in brief, is: Always some new mode of substantial relatedness which entails new units of stuff.

In Lewes's day the kind of novelty he spoke of as emergent seemed to be exemplified chiefly in chemistry, 'inorganic' or 'organic.' To-day in the light of further knowledge the concept of emergent novelty may be extended downwards below the molecule to the atom, and, more conspicuously, upwards beyond molecularity so as to embrace vitality also within the scope of emergence. Thus vitality may be regarded as a new pattern or mode of substantial relatedness which entails new supermolecular units of stuff.

If we speak of 'molecularity' we should do so on the understanding that this word merely names that pattern of process which is found in the molecule. In like manner 'vitality' serves to name that pattern of process which is found in the living organism. Thus used, neither word implies a kind of Activity in terms of which we may seek 'to account for' what we find. If such there be it falls for discussion, not under B, but under A. We thus avoid any such notions as that 'aquosity' which, as invoked to explain the wateriness of water, Huxley held up to ridicule. All such notions Huxley bade us regard as unscientific.

Let us keep strictly to what purports to be scientific treatment and try not to stray beyond its limits. My statement that in each new field of substantial relatedness the constituent units of stuff have new parts to play, purports to be scientific, though its terminology is unusual. . . .

HENRI BERGSON · Creation As Unpredictable

[*Bergson's philosophical thought shows a sharp opposition to traditional philosophical movements that have used the sciences as models and have relied primarily on discursive argument to present their views. In this opposition, Bergson lends support to recent developments in existential philosophy. His position affirming intuition and its role in providing a theory of metaphysics, however, diverges from that of many of the leading figures in existential philosophy. His detailed contributions to understanding creativity can be found in various works, especially* An Introduction to Metaphysics *and* Creative Evolution. *Here, his main concern is showing that the possibilities open to a creator constitute an absence of all precedents or defined potential choices. In the course*

SOURCE From Bergson, H., "The Possible and the Real," The Creative Mind, Andison, M. L. (trans.), pp. 99–105. New York: Philosophical Library, Inc., 1946. Reprinted by permission.

of the argument, he describes the difficulties facing those who attempt to explain creation in terms of antecedent conditions.]

. . . Underlying the doctrines which disregard the radical novelty of each moment of evolution there are many misunderstandings, many errors. But there is especially the idea that the possible is *less* than the real, and that, for this reason, the possibility of things precedes their existence. They would thus be capable of representation beforehand; they could be thought of before being realized. But it is the reverse that is true. If we leave aside the closed systems, subjected to purely mathematical laws, isolable because duration does not act upon them, if we consider the totality of concrete reality or simply the world of life, and still more that of consciousness, we find there is more and not less in the possibility of each of the successive states than in their reality. For the possible is only the real with the addition of an act of mind which throws its image back into the past, once it has been enacted. But that is what our intellectual habits prevent us from seeing.

During the great war certain newspapers and periodicals sometimes turned aside from the terrible worries of the day to think of what would happen later once peace was restored. They were particularly preoccupied with the future of literature. Someone came one day to ask me my ideas on the subject. A little embarrassed, I declared I had none. "Do you not at least perceive," I was asked, "certain possible directions? Let us grant that one cannot foresee things in detail; you as a philosopher have at least an idea of the whole. How do you conceive, for example, the great dramatic work of tomorrow?" I shall always remember my interlocutor's surprise when I answered, "If I knew what was to be the great dramatic work of the future, I should be writing it." I saw distinctly that he conceived the future work as being already stored up in some cupboard reserved for possibles; because of my long-standing relations with philosophy, I should have been able to obtain from it the key to the storehouse. "But," I said, "the work of which you speak is not yet possible." — "But it must be, since it is to take place." — "No, it is not. I grant you, at most, that it *will have been possible.*" "What do you mean by that?" — "It's quite simple. Let a man of talent or genius come forth, let him create a work: it will then be real, and by that very fact it becomes retrospectively or retroactively possible. It would not be possible, it would not have been so, if this man had not come upon the scene. That is why I tell you that it will have been possible today, but that it is not yet so." "You're not serious! You are surely not going to maintain that the future has an effect upon the present, that the present brings something into the past, that action works back over the course of time and imprints its mark afterwards?" — "That depends. That one can put reality into the past and thus work backwards in time is something I have never claimed. But that one can put the possible there, or rather that the possible may put itself there at any moment, is not to be doubted. As reality is created as something unforeseeable and new, its image is reflected behind it into the indefinite past; thus it finds that it has from all time been possible, but it is at this precise moment that it begins to have been always possible, and that is why I said that its possibility, which does not precede its reality, will have preceded it once the reality has appeared. The possible is therefore the mirage of the present in the past; and as we know the future will finally constitute a present and the mirage effect is continually being produced, we are convinced that the image of tomorrow is already contained in our actual present, which will be the past of tomorrow, although we did not manage to grasp it. That is precisely the illusion. It is as though one were to fancy, in seeing his reflection in the mirror in front of him, that he could have touched it had he stayed behind it. Thus in judging that the possible does not presuppose the real, one admits that the realization adds something to the simple possibility: the possible would have been there from all time, a phantom awaiting its hour; it would therefore have become reality by the addition of something, by some transfusion of blood or life. One does not see that the contrary is the case, that the possible implies the corresponding reality with, moreover, something added, since the possible is the combined effect of reality once it has appeared and of a condition which throws it back in time. The idea immanent in most philosophies and natural to the human mind, of possibles which would be realized by an acquisition of existence, is therefore pure illusion. One might as well claim that the man in flesh and blood comes from the materialization of his image seen in the mirror, because in that real man is everything found in this virtual image with, in addition, the solidity which makes it possible to touch it. But the truth is that more is needed here to obtain the virtual than is necessary for the real, more for the image of the man than for the man himself, for the image of the man will not be portrayed if the man is not first produced, and in addition one has to have the mirror."

That is what my interlocutor was forgetting as he questioned me on the theater of tomorrow. Perhaps too he was unconsciously playing on the meaning of the word "possible." *Hamlet* was doubtless possible before being realized, if that means that there was no insurmountable obstacle to its realization. In the particular sense one calls possible what is not im-

possible; and it stands to reason that this non-impossibility of a thing is
the condition of its realization. But the possible thus understood is in no
degree virtual, something ideally pre-existent. If you close the gate you
know no one will cross the road; it does not follow that you can predict
who will cross when you open it. Nevertheless, from the quite negative
sense of the term "impossible" you pass surreptitiously, unconsciously
to the positive sense. Possibility signified "absence of hindrance" a few
minutes ago: now you make of it a "pre-existence under the form of an
idea," which is quite another thing. In the first meaning of the word it
was a truism to say that the possibility of a thing precedes its reality: by
that you meant simply that obstacles, having been surmounted, were sur-
mountable. But in the second meaning it is an absurdity, for it is clear that
a mind in which the *Hamlet* of Shakespeare had taken shape in the form
of possible would by that fact have created its reality: it would thus have
been, by definition, Shakespeare himself. In vain do you imagine at first
that this mind could have appeared before Shakespeare; it is because you
are not thinking then of all the details in the play. As you complete them
the predecessor of Shakespeare finds himself thinking all that Shakespeare
will think, feeling all he will feel, knowing all he will know, perceiving
therefore all he will perceive, and consequently occupying the same point
in space and time, having the same body and the same soul: it is Shakespeare himself.

But I am putting too much stress on what is self-evident. We are forced
to these considerations in discussing a work of art. I believe in the end we
shall consider it evident that the artist in executing his work is creating the
possible as well as the real. Whence comes it then that one might hesitate
to say the same thing for nature? Is not the world a work of art incompa-
rably richer than that of the greatest artist? And is there not as much absurdity, if not more, in supposing, in the work of nature, that the future
is outlined in advance, that possibility existed before reality? Once more
let me say I am perfectly willing to admit that the future states of a closed
system of material points are calculable and hence visible in its present
state. But, and I repeat, this system is extracted, or abstracted, from a whole
which, in addition to inert and unorganized matter, comprises organization. Take the concrete and complete world, with the life and consciousness it encloses; consider nature in its entirety, nature the generator of new
species as novel and original in form as the design of any artist: in these
species concentrate upon individuals, plants or animals, each of which has
its own character—I was going to say its personality (for one blade of
grass does not resemble another blade of grass any more than a Raphael

resembles a Rembrandt); lift your attention above and beyond individual man to societies which disclose actions and situations comparable to those of any drama: how can one still speak of possibles which would precede their own realization? How can we fail to see that if the event can always be explained afterwards by an arbitrary choice of antecedent events, a completely different event could have been equally well explained in the same circumstances by another choice of antecedent—nay, by the same antecedents otherwise cut out, otherwise distributed, otherwise perceived —in short, by our retrospective attention? Backwards over the course of time a constant remodeling of the past by the present, of the cause by the effect, is being carried out.

We do not see it, always for the same reason, always a prey to the same illusion, always because we treat as the more what is the less, as the less what is the more. If we put the possible back into its proper place, evolution becomes something quite different from the realization of a program: the gates of the future open wide; freedom is offered an unlimited field. The fault of those doctrines — rare indeed in the history of philosophy —which have succeeded in leaving room for indetermination and freedom in the world, is to have failed to see what their affirmation implied. When they spoke of indetermination, of freedom, they meant by indetermination a competition between possibles, by freedom a choice between possibles—as if possibility was not created by freedom itself! As if any other hypothesis, by affirming an ideal pre-existence of the possible to the real, did not reduce the new to a mere rearrangement of former elements! As if it were not thus to be led sooner or later to regard that rearrangement as calculable and foreseeable! By accepting the premiss of the contrary theory one was letting the enemy in. We must resign ourselves to the inevitable: it is the real which makes itself possible, and not the possible which becomes real.

But the truth is that philosophy has never frankly admitted this continuous creation of unforeseeable novelty. The ancients already revolted against it because, Platonists to a greater or less degree, they imagined that Being was given once and for all, complete and perfect, in the immutable system of Ideas: the world which unfolds before our eyes could therefore add nothing to it; it was, on the contrary, only diminution or degradation; its successive states measured as it were the increasing or decreasing distance between what is, a shadow projected in time, and what ought to be, Idea set in eternity; they would outline the variations of a deficiency, the changing form of a void. It was Time which, according to them, spoiled everything. The moderns, it is true, take a quite different point of view.

They no longer treat Time as an intruder, a disturber of eternity; but they would very much like to reduce it to a simple appearance. The temporal is, then, only the confused form of the rational. What we perceive as being a succession of states is conceived by our intellect, once the fog has settled, as a system of relations. The real becomes once more the eternal, with this single difference, that it is the eternity of the Laws in which the phenomena are resolved instead of being the eternity of the Ideas which serve them as models. But in each case, we are dealing with theories. Let us stick to the facts. Time is immediately given. That is sufficient for us, and until its inexistence or perversity is proved to us we shall merely register that there is effectively a flow of unforeseeable novelty.

CARL R. ROGERS · Toward a Theory of Creativity

[*Rogers, a noted clinical and research psychologist, developed a form of psychotherapy called "client-centered therapy." He has done extensive research on psychotherapy and his theory of creativity, emphasizing the uniqueness of the individual, is related directly to this work. Rogers also specifies particular factors in individual creativity: openness to experience, locus of evaluation within the individual, and ability to toy with elements and concepts.*]

There are various ways of defining creativity. In order to make more clear the meaning of what is to follow, let me present the elements which, for me, are a part of the creative process, and then attempt a definition.

In the first place, for me as scientist, there must be something observable, some product of creation. Though my fantasies may be extremely novel, they cannot usefully be defined as creative unless they eventuate in some observable product—unless they are symbolized in words, or written in a poem, or translated into a work of art, or fashioned into an invention.

These products must be novel constructions. This novelty grows out of the unique qualities of the individual in his interaction with the materials of experience. Creativity always has the stamp of the individual upon its

Source   Rogers, C. R., "*Toward a Theory of Creativity,*" ETC: A Review of General Semantics, 1954, Vol. 11, pp. 250–258. *Reprinted from ETC, Vol. XI, No. 4 by permission of the International Society for General Semantics.*

product, but the product is not the individual, nor his materials, but partakes of the relationship between the two.

Creativity is not, in my judgment, restricted to some particular content. I am assuming that there is no fundamental difference in the creative process as it is evidenced in painting a picture, composing a symphony, devising new instruments of killing, developing a scientific theory, discovering new procedures in human relationships, or creating new formings of one's own personality as in psychotherapy. (Indeed it is my experience in this last field, rather than in one of the arts, which has given me special interest in creativity and its facilitation. Intimate knowledge of the way in which the individual remolds himself in the therapeutic relationship, with originality and effective skill, gives one confidence in the creative potential of all individuals.)

My definition, then, of the creative process is that it is the emergence in action of a novel relational product, growing out of the uniqueness of the individual on the one hand, and the materials, events, people, or circumstances of his life on the other.

Let me append some negative footnotes to this definition. It makes no distinction between "good" and "bad" creativity. One man may be discovering a way of relieving pain, while another is devising a new and more subtle form of torture for political prisoners. Both these actions seems to me creative, even though their social value is very different. Though I shall comment on these social valuations later, I have avoided putting them in my definition because they are so fluctuating. Galileo and Copernicus made creative discoveries which in their own day were evaluated as blasphemous and wicked, and in our day as basic and constructive. We do not want to cloud our definition with terms which rest in subjectivity.

Another way of looking at this same issue is to note that to be regarded historically as representing creativity, the product must be acceptable to some group at some point of time. This fact is not helpful to our definition, however, both because of the fluctuating valuations already mentioned, and also because many creative products have undoubtedly never been socially noticed, but have disappeared without ever having been evaluated. So this concept of group acceptance is also omitted from our definition.

In addition, it should be pointed out that our definition makes no distinction regarding the degree of creativity, since this too is a value judgment extremely variable in nature. The action of the child inventing a new game with his playmates; Einstein formulating a theory of relativity; the housewife devising a new sauce for the meat; a young author writing his first novel; all of these are, in terms of our definition, creative, and there is no attempt to set them in some order of more or less creative.

. . . .

The mainspring of creativity appears to be the same tendency which we discover so deeply as the curative force in psychotherapy — *man's tendency to actualize himself, to become his potentialities*. By this I mean the directional trend which is evident in all organic and human life — the urge to expand, extend, develop, mature — the tendency to express and activate all the capacities of the organism, to the extent that such activation enhances the organism or the self. This tendency may become deeply buried under layer after layer of encrusted psychological defenses; it may be hidden behind elaborate facades which deny its existence; it is my belief however, based on my experience, that it exists in every individual, and awaits only the proper conditions to be released and expressed. It is this tendency which is the primary motivation for creativity as the organism forms new relationships to the environment in its endeavor most fully to be itself.

Let us now attempt to deal directly with this puzzling issue of the social value of a creative act. Presumably few of us are interested in facilitating creativity which is socially destructive. We do not wish, knowingly, to lend our efforts to developing individuals whose creative genius works itself out in new and better ways of robbing, exploiting, torturing, killing, other individuals; or developing forms of political organization or art forms which lead humanity into paths of physical or psychological self-destruction. Yet how is it possible to make the necessary discriminations such that we may encourage a constructive creativity and not a destructive?

The distinction cannot be made by examining the product. The very essence of the creative is its novelty, and hence we have no standard by which to judge it. Indeed history points up the fact that the more original the product, and the more far-reaching its implications, the more likely it is to be judged by contemporaries as evil. The genuinely significant creation, whether an idea, or a work of art, or a scientific discovery, is most likely to be seen at first as erroneous, bad, or foolish. Later it may be seen as obvious, something self-evident to all. Only still later does it receive its final evaluation as a creative contribution. It seems clear that no contemporary mortal can satisfactorily evaluate a creative product at the time that it is formed, and this statement is increasingly true the greater the novelty of the creation.

Nor is it of any help to examine the purposes of the individual participating in the creative process. Many, perhaps most, of the creations and

discoveries which have proved to have great social value, have been motivated by purposes having more to do with personal interest than with
social value, while on the other hand history records a somewhat sorry
outcome for many of those creations (various Utopias, Prohibition, etc.)
which had as their avowed purpose the achievement of the social good.
No, we must face the fact that the individual creates primarily because it
is satisfying to him, because this behavior is felt to be self-actualizing,
and we get nowhere by trying to differentiate "good" and "bad" purposes
in the creative process.

Must we then give over any attempt to discriminate between creativity
which is potentially constructive, and that which is potentially destructive? I do not believe this pessimistic conclusion is justified. It is here that
recent clinical findings from the field of psychotherapy give us hope. It
has been found that when the individual is "open" to all of his experience
(a phrase which will be defined more fully), then his behavior will be creative, and his creativity may be trusted to be essentially constructive.

The differentiation may be put very briefly as follows. To the extent that
the individual is denying to awareness (or repressing, if you prefer that
term) large areas of his experience, then his creative formings may be
pathological, or socially evil, or both. To the degree that the individual is
open to all aspects of his experience, and has available to his awareness
all the varied sensings and perceivings which are going on within his
organism, then the novel products of his interaction with his environment
will tend to be constructive both for himself and others. To illustrate, an
individual with paranoid tendencies may creatively develop a most novel
theory of the relationship between himself and his environment, seeing
evidence for his theory in all sorts of minute clues. His theory has little
social value, perhaps because there is an enormous range of experience
which this individual cannot permit in his awareness. Socrates, on the
other hand, while also regarded as "crazy" by his contemporaries, developed novel ideas which have proven to be socially constructive. Very
possibly this was because he was notably nondefensive and open to his
experience.

.   .   .   .

What are the conditions within the individual which are most closely
associated with a potentially constructive creative act? I see these as
possibilities.

[A.] *Openness to Experience: Extensionality.* This is the opposite of psychological defensiveness, when to protect the organization of the self,
certain experiences are prevented from coming into awareness except in

distorted fashion. In a person who is open to experience each stimulus is freely relayed through the nervous system, without being distorted by any process of defensiveness. Whether the stimulus originates in the environment, in the impact of form, color, or sound, on the sensory nerves, or whether it originates in the viscera, or as a memory trace in the central nervous system, it is available to awareness. This means that instead of perceiving in predetermined categories ("trees are green," "college education is good," "modern art is silly") the individual is aware of this existential moment as *it* is, thus being alive to many experiences which fall outside the usual categories (*this* tree is lavender; *this* college education is damaging; *this* modern sculpture has a powerful effect on me).

This last suggests another way of describing openness to experience. It means lack of rigidity and permeability of boundaries in concepts, beliefs, perceptions, and hypotheses. It means a tolerance for ambiguity where ambiguity exists. It means the ability to receive much conflicting information without forcing closure upon the situation. It means what the general semanticist calls the "extensional orientation."

This complete openness of awareness to what exists at this moment is, I believe, an important condition of constructive creativity. In an equally intense but more narrowly limited fashion it is no doubt present in all creativity. The deeply maladjusted artist who cannot recognize or be aware of the sources of unhappiness in himself, may nevertheless be sharply and sensitively aware of form and color in his experience. The tyrant (whether on a petty or grand scale) who cannot face the weaknesses in himself may nevertheless be completely alive to and aware of the chinks in the psychological armor of those with whom he deals. Because there is the openness to one phase of experience, creativity is possible; because the openness is *only* to one phase of experience, the product of this creativity may be potentially destructive of social values. The more the individual has available to himself a sensitive awareness of all phases of his experience, the more sure we can be that his creativity will be personally and socially constructive.

B. *An Internal Locus of Evaluation.* Perhaps the most fundamental condition of creativity is that the source or locus of evaluative judgment is internal. The value of his product is, for the creative person, established not by the praise or criticism of others, but by himself. Have I created something satisfying to *me*? Does it express a part of me—my feeling or my thought, my pain or my ecstasy? These are the only questions which really matter to the creative person, or to any person when he is being creative.

This does not mean that he is oblivious to, or unwilling to be aware of, the judgments of others. It is simply that the basis of evaluation lies within himself, in his own organismic reaction to and appraisal of his product. If to the person it has the "feel" of being "me in action," of being an actualization of potentialities in himself which heretofore have not existed and are now emerging into existence, then it is satisfying and creative, and no outside evaluation can change that fundamental fact.

C. *The Ability to Toy with Elements and Concepts*. Though this is probably less important than A or B, it seems to be a condition of creativity. Associated with the openness and lack of rigidity described under A is the ability to play spontaneously with ideas, colors, shapes, relationships — to juggle elements into impossible juxtapositions, to shape wild hypotheses, to make the given problematic, to express the ridiculous, to translate from one form to another, to transform into improbable equivalents. It is from this spontaneous toying and exploration that there arises the hunch, the creative seeing of life in a new and significant way. It is as though out of the wasteful spawning of thousands of possibilities there emerges one or two evolutionary forms with the qualities which give them a more permanent value.

.   .   .   .

When these three conditions obtain, constructive creativity will occur. But we cannot expect an accurate description of the creative act, for by its very nature it is indescribable. This is the unknown which we must recognize as unknowable until it occurs. This is the improbable that becomes probable. Only in a very general way can we say that a creative act is the natural behavior of an organism which has a tendency to arise when that organism is open to all of its inner and outer experiencing, and when it is free to try out in flexible fashion all manner of relationships. Out of this multitude of half-formed possibilities the organism, like a great computing machine, selects this one which most effectively meets an inner need, or that one which forms a more effective relationship with the environment, or this other one which discovers a more simple and satisfying order in which life may be perceived.

There is one quality of the creative act which may, however, be described. In almost all the products of creation we note a selectivity, or emphasis, an evidence of discipline, an attempt to bring out the essence. The artist paints surfaces or textures in simplified form, ignoring the minute variations which exist in reality. The scientist formulates a basic law of relationships, brushing aside all the particular events or circumstances which might conceal its naked beauty. The writer selects those words and phrases which give unity to his expression. We may say that

esthetic quality

this is the influence of the specific person, of the "I." Reality exists in a multiplicity of confusing facts, but "I" bring a structure to my relationship to reality; I have "my" way of perceiving reality, and it is this (unconsciously?) disciplined personal selectivity or abstraction which gives to creative products their esthetic quality.

Though this is as far as we can go in describing any aspect of the creative act, there are certain of its concomitants in the individual which may be mentioned. The first is what we may call the Eureka feeling—"This is *it!*" "I have discovered!" "This is what I wanted to express!"

alone doubt.

Another concomitant is the anxiety of separateness.[1] I do not believe that many significantly creative products are formed without the feeling, "I am alone. No one has ever done just this before. I have ventured into territory where no one has been. Perhaps I am foolish, or wrong, or lost, or abnormal."

journal.

Still another experience which usually accompanies creativity is the desire to communicate. It is doubtful whether a human being can create, without wishing to share his creation. It is the only way he can assuage the anxiety of separateness and assure himself that he belongs to the group. He may confide his theories only to his private diary. He may put his discoveries in some cryptic code. He may conceal his poems in a locked drawer. He may put away his paintings in a closet. Yet he desires to communicate with a group which will understand him, even if he must imagine such a group. He does not create in order to communicate, but once having created he desires to share this new aspect of himself-in-relation-to-his-environment with others.

·   ·   ·   ·   ·   ·   ·   ·   ·   ·   ·   ·   ·   ·   ·

Thus far I have tried to describe the nature of creativity, to indicate that quality of individual experience which increases the likelihood that creativity will be constructive, to set forth the necessary conditions for the creative act and to state some of its concomitants. But if we are to make progress in meeting the social need which was presented initially, we must know whether constructive creativity can be fostered, and if so, how.

From the very nature of the inner conditions of creativity it is clear that they cannot be forced, but must be permitted to emerge. The farmer cannot make the germ develop and sprout from the seed; he can only supply the nurturing conditions which will permit the seed to develop its own potentialities. So it is with creativity. How can we establish the external conditions which will foster and nourish the internal conditions described

1. For this and the idea in the following paragraph I am specifically indebted to my student and colleague, Mr. Robert Lipgar.

above? My experience in psychotherapy leads me to believe that by setting up conditions of psychological safety and freedom, we maximize the likelihood of an emergence of constructive creativity. Let me spell out these conditions in some detail, labelling them as X and Y.

X. *Psychological Safety*. This may be established by three associated processes.

1. *Accepting the individual as of unconditional worth*. Whenever a teacher, parent, therapist, or other person with a facilitating function feels basically that this individual is of worth in his own right and in his own unfolding, no matter what his present condition or behavior, he is fostering creativity. This attitude can probably be genuine only when the teacher, parent, etc., senses the potentialities of the individual and thus is able to have an unconditional faith in him, no matter what his present state.

The effect on the individual as he apprehends this attitude, is to sense a climate of safety. He gradually learns that he can be whatever he is, without sham or facade, since he seems to be regarded as of worth no matter what he does. Hence he has less need of rigidity, can discover what it means to be himself, can try to actualize himself in new and spontaneous ways. He is, in other words, moving toward creativity. *Andrew/julie.*

2. *Providing a climate in which external evaluation is absent*. When we cease to form judgments of the other individual from our own locus of evaluation, we are fostering creativity. For the individual to find himself in an atmosphere where he is not being evaluated, not being measured by some external standard, is enormously freeing. Evaluation is always a threat, always creates a need for defensiveness, always means that some portion of experience must be denied to awareness. If this product is evaluated as good by external standards, then I must not admit my own dislike of it. If what I am doing is bad by external standards, then I must not be aware of the fact that it seems to be me, to be part of myself. But if judgments based on external standards are not being made then I can be more open to my experience, can recognize my own likings and dislikings, the nature of the materials and of my reaction to them, more sharply and more sensitively. I can begin to recognize the locus of evaluation within myself. Hence I am moving toward creativity.

To allay some possible doubts and fears in the reader, it should be pointed out that to cease evaluating another is not to cease having reactions. It may, as a matter of fact, free one to react. "I don't like your idea" (or painting, or invention, or writing), is not an evaluation, but a reaction.

It is subtly but sharply different from a judgment which says, "What you are doing is bad (or good), and this quality is assigned to you from some external source." The first statement permits the individual to maintain his own locus of evaluation. It holds the possibility that I am unable to appreciate something which is actually very good. The second statement, whether it praises or condemns, tends to put the person at the mercy of outside forces. He is being told that he cannot simply ask himself whether this product is a valid expression of himself; he must be concerned with what others think. He is being led away from creativity.

3. Understanding empathically. It is this which provides the ultimate in psychological safety, when added to the other two. If I say that I "accept" you, but know nothing of you, this is a shallow acceptance indeed, and you realize that it may change if I actually come to know you. But if I understand you empathically, see you and what you are feeling and doing from your point of view, enter your private world and see it as it appears to you—and still accept you—then this is safety indeed. In this climate you can permit your real self to emerge, and to express itself in varied and novel formings as it relates itself to the world. This is a basic fostering of creativity.

Y. Psychological Freedom. When a teacher, parent, therapist, or other facilitating person permits the individual a complete freedom of symbolic expression, creativity is fostered. This permissiveness gives the individual complete freedom to think, to feel, to be, whatever is most inward within himself. It fosters the openness, and the playful and spontaneous juggling of percepts, concepts, and meanings, which is a part of creativity.

Note that it is complete freedom of *symbolic* expression which is described. To express in behavior all feelings, impulses, and formings may not in all instances be freeing. Behavior may in some instances be limited by society, and this is as it should be. But symbolic expression need not be limited. Thus to destroy a hated object (whether one's mother or a rococo building) by destroying a symbol of it, is freeing. To attack it in reality may create guilt and narrow the psychological freedom which is experienced. (I feel unsure of this paragraph, but it is the best formulation I can give at the moment which seems to square with my experience.)

The permissiveness which is being described is not softness or indulgence or encouragement. It is permission to be *free,* which also means that one is responsible. The individual is as free to be afraid of a new venture as to be eager for it; free to bear the consequences of his mistakes as well as of his achievements. It is this type of freedom responsibly to be oneself which fosters the development of a secure locus of evaluation within oneself, and hence tends to bring about the inner conditions of constructive creativity.

MONROE C. BEARDSLEY · On the Creation of Art

[*Monroe Beardsley is best known for his work in aesthetics and general philosophy of language. His paper, "The Intentional Fallacy," written in collaboration with William K. Wimsatt, has been greatly influential in the rigorous textual analysis of modern literary criticism and aesthetics.[1] Arguing here for an autonomous generating factor within the creative process itself, Beardsley takes a compromise position between antecedent and teleological types of determinism, which he calls the "propulsion" and "finalistic" theories respectively.*]

What I mean by the creative process is that stretch of mental and physical activity between the incept and the final touch — between the thought "I may be on to something here" and the thought "It is finished." My problem is about what goes on in this interval — how the work of art itself comes into existence and takes on its character through the stages or phases of this process.

·   ·   ·   ·   ·   ·   ·   ·   ·   ·   ·   ·   ·   ·   ·   ·

Philosophic reflection on the available empirical data has given us two widely-held accounts of the creative process. When we consider any artistic work of major proportions, whose creation we know something about, we are often struck by the gap between the final achievement and its humble incept. Clearly, the process between can be said to have moved in a desirable direction. Now in the usual case, although lucky accidents may make an important contribution, this process appears to be at least partly controlled. The problem for the aesthetician is, then: What is the nature of this control?

The earliest people who raised this question — Homer, Hesiod, and

SOURCE   *From Beardsley, M. C. "On the Creation of Art,"* Journal of Aesthetics and Art Criticism, *Spring 1965, No. 23, pp. 291, 293–294, 297–303. Copyright 1965 by the* Journal of Aesthetics and Art Criticism. *Reprinted by permission of publisher and author.*
    1. Wimsatt, W. K., Jr., and Beardsley, M. C. *"The Intentional Fallacy."* Sewanee Review, 1946, 54:468–488.

Pindar—were inclined to give it a supernatural answer, attributing their own feats to the intervention of the Muses. And the theory of divine inspiration, often in a pantheistic version, remains with us. But if we insist upon a naturalistic theory of artistic creation, we find two main ones. And these are distinguished in a way familiar to other branches of philosophy.

According to what I shall call the Propulsive Theory, the controlling agent is something that exists prior to the creative process, and presides over it throughout. According to the Finalistic Theory, the controlling agent is the final goal toward which the process aims. No doubt the two theories run into each other in the minds of some philosophers, and perhaps we need not strain to keep them wholly distinct. . . .

.   .   .   .

[Both views contain errors; however, the] real nature of the artist's control over the creative process will elude anyone who looks for a single guiding factor, whether a need or an end. It is internal to the process itself. I do not plan to argue for a single creative pattern, but to show how, in the absence of any such general pattern, each individual process that eventuates in a work of art *generates* its own direction and momentum. For the crucial controlling power at every point is the particular stage or condition of the unfinished work itself, the possibilities it presents, and the developments it permits. There are three things to discuss here, and I will say something about each—the incept, the development, and the completion of the work.

The first control over the artistic process is set up by the incept itself. And I want to emphasize, as I have said before, that the incept may be any sort of thing: the first sentence of a story or the last, a simple plot situation, a character, theme, scene, figure of speech, or tone or style. . . .

.   .   .   .

One of the most important questions about the role of the incept in the creative process is this: Does it exercise a pervasive influence throughout? If the Propulsive Theory is correct, one would expect to find the incept dominating the whole process, for whatever appears first would presumably be closely related to the original emotion. On second thought, I am not sure this really follows. . . . Again, if the Finalist Theory is correct, one would also expect the incept to dominate, for it would presumably embody the original problem or goal which directs the process to the end.

Now, one thing is evident: once an element is chosen, it sets up demands and suggestions as to what may come next, and also places limits upon it. Draw a single line on a piece of paper. If you do not think what you have there is worth much attention, the question is what you can do next to improve upon it. You can balance it, cross or oppose it by other lines, thicken and emphasize it, transform it into a more complex line or a shape, etc. Or, of course, you can erase it—but then you are rejecting it as an incept, and putting an end to that particular creative process. That every stage of the process powerfully affects the succeeding stage is plain; but our present question is whether the first stage is somehow dominant over all. Artists have spoken rather differently about this. For instance, Picasso once said that "Basically a picture doesn't change, that the first 'vision' remains almost intact, in spite of appearances." [ftnt. deleted] But he also said that a picture cannot be thought out ahead of time, and "changes as one's thoughts change." The sketches for *Guernica* do have a notable continuity despite all the changes. The bull and the horse were there in the first sketch, and a woman appeared in one of the later sketches done the same day.

Another example is provided by Beethoven's long series of sketches for the spacious melody that he used for the variations in the slow movement of his string quartet in E flat, *Op. 127*. These have been studied by Victor Zuckerkandl.[1] When they are placed side by side, they illustrate the force of the incept very clearly. . . . But this is by no means true of all of Beethoven's work; Allen Forte, a careful student of the piano sonata, *Op. 109*, has remarked that "in many instances one can hardly recognize the final version from the initial sketches."[2]

Indeed, an incept that initiates a successful creative process may become almost lost in it. Of course there must be some continuity from incept to final work, otherwise we could not say that the incept was the start of that particular work. But there is a wide range of deviation from the straight line of development. An ingredient that has one quality as it first appears to the artist may later find a context that alters its quality completely. . . .

Once the work is under way, with a tentative commitment to some incept, the creative process is kept going by tensions between what has been done and what might have been done. At each stage there must be a perception of deficiencies in what now exists, plus the sense of unrealized possibilities of improvement. . . . In other words, as the poet moves from stage to stage, it is not that he is looking to see whether he is saying what he already meant, but that he is looking to see whether he

1. I am referring to a lecture given in the spring of 1963 at Swarthmore College.
2. *The Compositional Matrix* (Baldwin, N.Y., Music Teachers National Association Monographs, 1961), p. 4. . . .

wants to mean what he is saying. Thus, according to Valéry, "Every true poet is necessarily a first rate critic" — not necessarily of others' work, but of his own.[3]

Each time the artist — whether poet, or painter, or composer — takes a step, he adds something to what is already there (A), and makes another and different object (B). If he judges B worse than A, he must go back. If B is better than A, the question is whether it is good enough to stand alone as a work of art. If not, the question is whether B can be transformed into still another and better object, C. If this is impossible, if every attempt to improve it only makes it worse, then the whole project is left unfinished, for it is unfinishable.

One of the most puzzling questions about the creative process is how the artist knows when to stop. If the Propulsion Theory is correct, the answer is that he stops when his original impulse has exhausted itself. If the Finalistic Theory is correct, then the artist compares his work at every stage with the intact memory of his original vision of his goal, and when they match the work is done. But without these theories, it becomes more difficult to explain what it means to come to an end of a creative process.[4]

There are really two questions here: how the artist knows when *he* is finished, and how he knows when the *work* is finished. The first question is no doubt the easier. The artist comes to a point when he can no longer think of any way to improve his work. This becomes more and more difficult as the work progresses. In the early stages, lines and colors, stanzas and melodic fragments, can be added quite freely to see whether they can be assimilated. But in the later stages, as the work becomes more complex, the effect of every addition or alteration is more serious; a wrong line or color, a wrong word or melodic figure, can throw the whole thing badly off. Of course, the artist can never be certain he has done all he can. . . .

. . . .

. . . Though there are no universal *stages* of the creative process, there are two clearly marked *phases*, which constantly alternate throughout. They involve an interplay between conscious and preconscious activities. There is the *inventive* phase, traditionally called *inspiration*, in which new

3. "Poetry and Abstract Thought," [*The Art of Poetry*, trans. Denise Folliot (New York, 1961)], p. 76. This is echoed by Richard Wilbur in *The Nature of Creative Thinking*, p. 59, and by Ben Shahn, in *The Shape of Content* (see selection in Tomas [ed., *Creativity in the Arts* (Englewood Cliffs, N.J., 1964)], p. 20).
4. I. A. Richards, "How Does a Poem Know When It Is Finished?" in Daniel Lerner, ed., *Parts and Wholes* (New York, 1963).

ideas are formed in the preconscious and appear in consciousness. And there is the *selective* phase, which is nothing more than criticism, in which the conscious chooses or rejects the new idea after perceiving its relationships to what has already tentatively been adopted.

The problem of what goes on in the preconscious is apparently still unsolved. We would like to know how it is that a composer, having sung two bars to himself, suddenly thinks of a way to continue it—or that a painter, having outlined a figure, thinks of certain colors that might be added—or that a poet may look at a line he has just written and think of possible substitute words. To take a few examples from R. P. Blackmur,[5] suppose the poet has written "breathless tiptoeing," and it occurs to him that "flowering tiptoeing" might be better; or suppose he has written "chance deepening to choice" and substitutes "chance flowering to choice." Whether the new words are better than the old is the question to be decided by his conscious mind; but why one set of words rather than another comes to consciousness is the more mysterious question.

.   .   .   .

It is no doubt high time to face up to the question that is bound to arise after all these reflections and speculations about the creative process: what is the point of them? Or, in other words: what difference does it make to our relationship with the arts that we understand the creative process in one way or another? And here my answer is brief and unequivocal. It makes no difference at all. I think it is interesting in itself to know, if we can, how the artist's mind works, but I do not see that this has any bearing upon the value of what he produces. For that value is independent of the manner of production, even of whether the work was produced by an animal or by a computer or by a volcano or by a falling slopbucket.[6]

.   .   .   .

Is this our final conclusion, then—that questions about creativity are irrelevant to questions about actual works of art? Somehow it does not seem enough. From the beginning of thought about art, though in many different forms, the creativity of art has been noted and pondered. Associationists, intuitionists, romantics, and idealists have offered explanations. In the making of such works, something very special seems to be happening; something fresh is added to the world; something like a miracle occurs. All this is true. There is such a thing as creativity in art,

5. *Poets at Work* [New York, 1948], p. 48.
6. For a decisive argument along this line, see John Hospers, "The Concept of Artistic Expression," *Proceedings of the Aristotelian Society*, LV (1955), 313–344.

and it is a very important thing. What I want to say is that the true locus of creativity is not the genetic process prior to the work but the work itself as it lives in the experience of the beholder. Let me explain — all too briefly and puzzlingly, no doubt — what I mean.

To begin with, what is a melody? It is, as we all know, a gestalt, something distinct from the notes that make it up, yet dependent upon them for its existence. And it has its own quality, which cannot be a quality of any particular note or little set of notes. Recall that melody from Beethoven's E flat Quartet — grave, serene, soaring, affirmative, yet in a way resigned. Now when we hear a melody, however simple, we hear two levels of things at once: the individual notes and the regionally qualified melody that emerges from them. We hear the melody being born out of the elements that sustain it; or we hear the elements, the tones and intervals, coming together in an order that calls into existence an entity distinct from them, and superior to them. In the experience of a melody, creation occurs before our very ears. And the more intense the created qualities, the more complex the sets of cooperating elements, the tighter their mutual relations, the more fully we can participate in that basic aesthetic experience.

I need not argue in detail that the same holds for works of fine art. The essential feature of such a work — I am tempted to say, but recognizing that I am likely to sound dogmatic — the essential feature is not merely that certain visual elements (lines, shapes, colors) are assembled together, but that as we concentrate on their natures and relations, we become aware, suddenly or gradually, of what they add up to as a whole. For what they add up to is not an addition at all, but the projection of a new pattern, a new quality of grace or power.

When we consider a poem in this perspective, we see again that the important creativity is in the operation of the work itself. . . .

.   .   .   .

It may seem that this way of looking at artistic creativity demeans the artist by making not him, but the work itself, the creative thing. But I do not think so. I do not forget that man is the maker — of nearly all the great works we have, or are likely to have. But the finest qualities of a work of art cannot be imposed on it directly and by fiat; the artist can, after all, only manipulate the elements of the medium so that *they* will make the quality emerge. He can only create a solemn melody by finding a sequence of notes that will have that quality. The powers he works with are, in the end, not his own but those of nature. And the miracle he makes is a miracle that celebrates the creative potentialities inherent in nature itself.

But when in this way the artist makes plain to us over and over the marvellous richness of nature's potentialities, he also presents us with a model of man's hope for control over nature, and over himself. Artistic creation is nothing more than the production of a self-creative object. It is in our intelligent use of what we are given to work with, both in the laws of the universe and in the psychological propensities of man, that we show our mastery, and our worthiness to inhabit the earth. In this broad sense, we are all elected, or perhaps condemned, to be artists. And what keeps us going in the roughest times is the reminder that not all the forms and qualities and meanings that are to emerge in the fullness of time have already appeared under the sun — that we do not know the limits of what the universe can provide or of what can be accomplished with its materials.

ALBERT ROTHENBERG · The Process of Janusian Thinking in Creativity

[*Rothenberg is one of the few psychiatrists carrying out both clinical and experimental research on creativity. This excerpt includes conclusions based on numerous interviews with poets and novelists as well as experiments with creative persons and control groups and is the first published use of the term "Janusian thinking." Janusian thinking is a specific form of cognition that usually appears early in diverse types of creative processes, in art as well as in science. More recently, Rothenberg has defined another thought process in creativity called "Homospatial thinking." This second thought process is described extensively in the work cited in the Selected Bibliography for this chapter and it consists of* actively conceiving two or more discrete entities occupying the same space, a conception leading to the articulation of new identities.]

A difficult problem besetting all scientific research in creativity pertains to the essential definition of the phenomenon itself. Creativity is not synonymous with originality, productivity, spontaneity, good problem-solving, or craftsmanship although the term is often used interchangeably

SOURCE *Rothenberg, A., "The Process of Janusian Thinking in Creativity,"* Archives of General Psychiatry, 1971, *Vol. 24, pp. 195–205. Reprinted by permission.*

with all of these. Creations are products which are *both* new and valuable and creativity is the capacity or state which brings forth creations. A painter may be original but uncreative; a literary scholar may be productive, even prolific, but notably uncreative; a spontaneous person may produce conventional poems spontaneously; computers as well as scientists provide good but uncreative solutions to problems; and the skilled craftsman may replicate great works of art over and over again but never be able to create one of his own. Many scientific explorations into creativity have ignored or shown confusion about these distinctions and much laborious and meticulous research has yielded results which have little if any direct pertinence to the phenomenon. But the basic problem lies deeper than that—even if we restrict the definition of creations to products which are both new and valuable, it is difficult for a scientific psychology to attempt to explain the appearance of such products; it is difficult, if not impossible, to explain the act of creation. Value judgments are anathema to objective scientists and the value judgment that designates a new product as true creation is subject to extensive variation depending on time, place, and person. Even more difficult for the scientist, particularly the determinist scientist, is the criterial attribute of newness or novelty. As Hausman[1] and Morgan[2] have pointed out, if the concept of novelty in creation is taken literally, ie, a creation is truly new and therefore radically different from its antecedents, it is impossible to account for all the factors leading to its production and it is impossible to predict what it will be before it actually appears. I will return to this problem again later. At this point, I would simply like to make clear that I am going to define a previously undescribed thought process operating in the act of creation, a process which accounts for a limited aspect of creativity although it by no means explains the phenomenon. In defining this process, I will assume that creations are products which *appear* new and are considered valuable by *consensus,* ie, experts have considered them creations over extended periods of time.

The thought process I will describe is based in part on the notion of structural opposition. Although Jung has emphasized the importance of opposition in all of psychic life[3] and philosophers, poets, and critics have, at various times, recognized the importance of opposition in works of art, the thought process I will describe pertains specifically to the act of creation. It does not, like Jung's opposition principle, necessarily pervade the psychic life of everyone or the entire psychic life of the creative person, but functions particularly when the creative person is engaged in creating. Furthermore, it involves *simultaneity* of opposition. Although opposition is often present in a completed work of art, a point I will soon corroborate, it has not previously been suggested that a specific thought process involving simultaneity of opposition could account for its presence.

·   ·   ·   ·   ·   ·   ·   ·   ·   ·   ·   ·   ·   ·   ·   ·   ·   ·   ·

I call this process "Janusian thinking." I first described or discovered this thought mechanism several years ago in connection with an intensive study of the revision process in Eugene O'Neill's play, *The Iceman Cometh*.[4] At that time I called the process "oppositional thinking"—the capacity to conceive and utilize two or more opposite or contradictory ideas, concepts, or images *simultaneously*. I have substituted the term "Janusian" for "oppositional" because it more accurately conveys the simultaneity of opposition and because, as a metaphor, it embodies the process it denotes. Janus, of course, was the Roman god with two faces, the god who looked and apprehended in opposite directions simultaneously. He was the god of all doorways and his two faces (*Janus bifrons*) allowed him to observe both the exterior and interior of a house and the entrance and exit of all buildings. It is perhaps not generally known that he was a very important god, appearing at the head of religious ceremonies and, on the Roman list, he came even before Jupiter. He was the god of "beginnings," presiding over daybreak, and was considered to be the promoter of all initiative. His role as beginner is commemorated in the name January, the month which begins our year. In fact, he had an essential role in the creation of the world itself and was also known as *Janus Pater*, the god of gods. Of particular interest for this exposition of Janusian thinking, especially in relation to artistic creation, is the fact that Janus was also considered to be the god of all communication, an extension of his function as god of departure and return.

In the original exposition of the thought process, I presented evidence (derived from extensive study of revisions in the play, life history information, and extensive interviews with O'Neill's widow, Mrs. Carlotta Monterrey O'Neill) that the central iceman symbol in the play *The Iceman Cometh* had at least three different connotations: (1) the iceman was death (this is stipulated in the play itself); (2) the iceman was Christ (the phrase "the iceman cometh" refers to the biblical phrase "the bridegroom cometh" and the play is structured as a modern parable of the Last Supper); and (3) the iceman was a sexually potent adulterer (based on an old joke known to O'Neill which goes as follows: a husband comes home from work and calls upstairs, "Dear, has the iceman come yet?" His wife calls back down, "No, but he's breathing hard!"). Substituting these meanings into the central creation of the play, the notion of the iceman coming, produces four or more logically opposite ideas: (1) Christ's coming or deliverance is the opposite of bleak death; (2) sexual potency is the biological and, according to Freud and others, the psychological antithesis of death; (3) a bridegroom and an adulterer are polar extremes; and (4) infidelity is opposed to the ultimate tenet of Christian faithfulness, Christ's coming. A potential fifth and probably more implicit opposition is the celebration and elevation of sexuality, particularly illicit sexuality, in conjunction with Christ himself. Christ was not only the opponent of illicit sex, especially adultery, but his teaching could be considered to be generally antisexual or antihedonistic. In the unconscious, of course, many of these oppositions can be significantly equivalent and one of the sources of the awful strength and beauty of the iceman symbol is its ability to connote logical contradiction and basic truth simultaneously—in other words, the integration of opposites.

In this same study, I also presented evidence that suggested that O'Neill arrived at a central idea in the play, an idea which led in part to his creation of the iceman symbol, by means of a *simultaneous* conceptualization of opposites. This idea pertained to the suicide of the man who was O'Neill's roommate during the year 1912, a man upon whom the 1939 play was based in large part and who was represented in the play by a character named "Jimmy Tomorrow." O'Neill came to realize that this roommate committed suicide because, as the man had said, he was upset about his wife's infidelity with another man, but also because of an opposite feeling—he had unwittingly wanted his wife to be unfaithful to him. All his life, O'Neill had been plagued by the memory of this man's suicide and plagued by the man's assertion shortly before he died that his wife's infidelity had brought him to his state of deep depression. It appears that only in his later life did O'Neill come to realize that the man had also wanted his wife to be unfaithful and that this was a motivating factor in the suicide. This insight was incorporated into *The Iceman Cometh* and the evidence indicates that it had a good deal of influence on the structure of the play and O'Neill's motivation to write it.

As exemplified in O'Neill's creation of *The Iceman Cometh*, Janusian thinking is a type of thought process used by a creator while engaged in a creative act. It primarily occurs early in the creative process, the so-called inspiration phase (eg, O'Neill's discovery early in the conception of *The Iceman Cometh* play that his roommate both wanted and did not want his wife to be unfaithful) and is often, therefore, frequently hidden although its effects may be manifest in the final product, ie, the simultaneous oppositions in the iceman symbol. Janusian thinking may enter into basic plot ideas, specific early metaphors, or early formulations of the overall structure of a work of art; it may not be apparent or remembered by the artist himself and it may or may not lead to clear oppositions in the completed work. Moreover, within the psychoanalytic model of thought, the process of Janusian thinking must be considered to be a secondary process mechanism. The evidence indicates that O'Neill arrived at these insights by a simultaneous conceptualization of opposites on a conscious ego level. He was completely aware of the contradiction in his roommate's simultaneous wishes for fidelity and infidelity and he must have been aware of some if not all of the contradictions embodied in the symbol of the iceman in the play. Furthermore, he did not unearth his own unconscious by slavishly employing the freudian formula that unconscious motivations are often opposite conscious ones, nor did he engage in any process of making his own unconscious conscious. There is evidence that he did not apply the insight about his roommate, for example, to his own thoughts about infidelity and that the notions remained embedded as emotionally isolated issues in the play itself. In fact, one of the general characteristics of such creative insights is that an author often actually denies that they have any relation to his own feelings or conflicts. They are considered to be relevant only to the work of art; a common assertion of novelists and playwrights is that such ideas are only insights into the feelings, thoughts, and conflicts of the characters in the work itself.

It is important to stress the secondary process nature of Janusian thinking because primary process thinking has previously been considered to be a crucial aspect of the creative process. As a secondary process mechanism, however, Janusian thinking helps account for the seeming ubiquity of primary process thought in works of art. . . . Kris and others had long been interested in the apparent ability of the artist to render unconscious material manifest in art. Since the artist, unlike the schizophrenic, does not seem to be overwhelmed by primary-process-like thinking, Kris postulated his concept, "regression in the service of the ego," to emphasize the phenomenon of ego control. At the time he presented this concept, Kris quoted Freud's comment that "one would like to know more about how, precisely, the ego achieves this."[5] One important aspect of the concept of Janusian thinking is that it offers a partial answer to this question in that it describes a specific ego process which allows primary-process-like material to appear in consciousness. This form of thinking, the simultaneous conceptualization of opposites, produces artistic products which appear to embody unconscious material because opposites are equal in the unconscious. O'Neill, for example, was not aware that he was very likely unearthing his own unconscious sexual and aggressive fantasies in equating sex and death in the iceman symbol, but he was aware of the conflict and opposition between the notion of a sexual coming and the coming of death. Ambiguity, tension, and paradox very frequently are manifest goals in an aesthetic creative act. The iceman symbol was not created by means of the type of primary process symbolization found in dreams. It was created, in part, by a secondary process mechanism which allowed unconscious material to appear in consciousness but did not overcome repression. The ego defense which allows such a phenomenon to occur, the defense associated with Janusian thinking, is *negation*. Freud long ago pointed out that the process of saying something was not so could be an effective means of sidestepping repression without overcoming it.[6] Thinking of the opposite, the least likely alternate, simultaneously, is a way of utilizing negation as a defense. In the example of O'Neill's iceman symbol, again, the negation defense operates as follows: sex overtly negates death and vice versa but the simultaneous negation could indicate and indirectly express O'Neill's repressed castration fear. As I have pointed out in some detail elsewhere [see ftnt. 4], creative artists use the negation defense in other aspects of the creative act beside the Janusian process and defensive negation may very well be one of the hallmarks of creativity.

.   .   .   .

There is reason to believe that Janusian thinking operates widely in diverse types of creative processes. In Eastern culture, the concepts of Yin and Yang, Mazda and Ahriman, Nirvana and Samsara, are creations of the mind of man which convey simultaneous oppositions. In Western culture, pre-Socratic conceptions of Being and Becoming, religious conceptions of God and the Devil, Nietzsche's formulation of Dionysian and Apollonian, Freud's concept of the id containing a sexual and aggressive instinct or the Eros and Thanatos idea, all convey an integration of opposites. These concepts, like the iceman metaphor, are final products of creative thought and their mere existence does not prove that Janusian thinking, a relatively early phenomenon in the creative process, accounted for their formulation. As mentioned before, however, there is evidence that O'Neill's original idea for *The Iceman Cometh* play was based on a simultaneous conception of opposites and we can infer that the oppositional iceman symbol, a later formulation related to the original idea, also resulted from such a process. Concepts such as Yin and Yang may have been formulated all at once and only later developed into a metaphysical system on the basis of exegesis of the implications of the metaphor.

In literary creation, the fact that paradox or opposition plays a role in the construction and aesthetic appeal of various types of literature seems to have been recognized for some time. Aristotle was probably the first thinker to emphasize the role of paradox or reversal in tragedy particularly.[7] Modern critics such as Alan Tate, I. A. Richards, and, more recently, R. P. Warren (unpublished observations) have implicitly and explicitly indicated the importance of opposition in all of fiction. Cleanth Brooks[8] has attempted to support a strong assertion that the basic feature of all of poetry is paradox. Even more pertinent to the issue of simultaneous opposition in the Janusian process, Monroe Beardsley,[9] the noted aesthetician, has expounded a detailed theory that all metaphor is based on verbal opposition. Metaphor is a very specific and crucial entity in all forms of literature and many have considered the creation of metaphor to be the paradigm for all of literary creation. Furthermore, a metaphor is a unity referring simultaneously to disparate aspects of experience. If Beardsley is right and metaphor is based specifically on verbal opposition, Janusian thinking would clearly play a large role in the creation of metaphor. The importance of metaphor and the general importance of opposition in all of literature suggests that Janusian thinking plays a crucial role in the entire process of literary creation.

In aesthetic fields other than literature, integrated opposition and, by implication, Janusian thinking can be seen to have an important role. In architecture, the Janus metaphor is particularly appropriate since it is necessary for the creative architect to conceptualize the inside and outside of a building simultaneously. For example, convex outer shapes produce concave inner shapes and the architect must reconcile these contradictory spatial characteristics with the overall conception of a building to be built. Furthermore, the best buildings do not convey a quality of spaciousness on the outside which is contradicted once one is inside. Since external shapes conveying spaciousness often deceptively require a great deal of internal buttressing structure and consequent cramping, it is necessary for the creative architect to overcome this. He does this, I believe, by formulating designs which accomplish spaciousness in opposite spatial orientations simultaneously. Frank Lloyd Wright, the great creative architect, has described the operation of Janusian thinking on an even wider scale than this in his description of the development of Organic Architecture, the type of architecture he created. He referred to the Organic Architecture idea as an "affirmative negation,"[10] meaning that it negated the three-dimensional concept in architecture and affirmed it simultaneously. In the visual arts, the capacity to attend to the ground (in Gestalt terms) without loss of figure perception and the painter's freedom to reverse figure and ground to a degree that is not characteristic of ordinary perception seems to represent an ability to maintain opposite orientations simultaneously. The visual effect of moving back and forth while standing still, which has been achieved by artists of the "Op" school, is an example of an art product which may have involved Janusian thinking at some stage.

An interesting example of Janusian thinking in music comes from Arnold Schoenberg's creation of the twelve-tone scale, an important development leading to the so-called atonal movement in modern music. Schoenberg reported that he had arrived at a notion that consonance and dissonance were equivalent. "Dissonances are only the remote consonances,"[11] he said—a highly revolutionary integration of opposites.

Scientific and mathematical creators also seem to use Janusian thought. Poincaré, the great and clearly creative mathematician, referred explicitly to a process of combining elements "drawn from domains which are far apart" and "as disparate as possible" in his discoveries.[12] The recent discovery of the "double helix" structure of DNA, the basic factor in genetic replication, shows a dramatic example of the operation of Janusian thinking in creative scientific thought. The double helix structure discovered by Watson contains two similar but opposed spatial forms. In his fascinating book describing the discovery of this structure, Dr. Watson makes clear that the notion of identical chains running in opposite directions occurred to him all at once. After describing a long period of struggle consisting of numerous observations by x-ray crystallography combined with careful, logical assessment of alternate possibilities, Watson indicates that the actual discovery occurred as follows:

> When I got to our still empty office the following morning, I quickly cleared away the papers from my desk top so that I would have a large flat surface on which to form pairs of bases held together by hydrogen bonds. Though I initially went back to my like-with-like prejudices, I saw all too well that they led nowhere. When Jerry Donohue came in I looked up, saw that it was not Francis [Crick], and began shifting the bases in and out of various other pairing possibilities. Suddenly I became aware that an adenine-thymine pair held together by two hydrogen bonds was identical in shape to a guanine-cytosine pair held together by at least two hydrogen bonds. All the hydrogen bonds seemed to form naturally; no fudging was required to make the two types of base pairs identical in shape. . . .

The hydrogen bonding requirement meant that adenine would always pair with thymine, while guanine could pair only with cytosine. Chargaff's rules [adenine equals thymine, guanine equals cytosine] then suddenly stood out as a consequence of a double-helical structure for DNA. Even more exciting, this type of double helix suggested a replication scheme much more satisfactory than my briefly considered like-with-like pairing. Always pairing adenine with thymine and guanine with cytosine meant that the base sequences of the two intertwined chains were complementary to each other. Given the base sequence of one chain, that of its partner was automatically determined. Conceptually, it was thus very easy to visualize how a single chain could be the template for the synthesis of a chain with the complementary sequence.

Upon his arrival Francis did not get more than halfway through the door before I let loose that the answer to everything was in our hands. Though as a matter of principle he maintained skepticism for a few moments, the similarly shaped A-T and G-C pairs had their expected impact. His quickly pushing the bases together in a number of different ways did not reveal any other way to satisfy Chargaff's rules. A few minutes later he spotted the fact that the two glycosidic bonds (joining base and sugar) of each base pair were systematically related by a dead axis perpendicular to the helical axis. *Thus, both pairs could be flipflopped over and still have their glycosidic bonds facing in the same direction. This had the important consequence that a given chain could contain both purines and pyrimidines. At the same time, it strongly suggested that the backbones of the two chains run in opposite directions.* [italics mine]

The question then became whether the A-T and G-C base pairs would easily fit the backbone configuration devised during the previous two weeks. . . . We both knew that we would not be home until a complete model was built in which all the stereo-chemical contacts were satisfactory. There was also the obvious fact that the implications of its existence were far too important to risk crying wolf. Thus I felt slightly queasy when at lunch Francis winged into the Eagle [restaurant] to tell everyone within hearing distance that we had found the secret of life.[13]

Watson's description makes clear that the actual breakthrough consisted of conceiving simultaneously of identical but spatially opposed forms. Also, he indicates that this breakthrough was not the complete answer, not the total creation, so to speak, but that a whole system of reactions had to be worked out to give it coherence and validity.

A relatively recent and influential creation in the realm of social thought is the work of Marshall McLuhan. Here, McLuhan's early and central idea is a clear representation of Janusian thinking.[14] In the development of his theory about the modern ethos based on technological communication, McLuhan initially formulated the idea, "the medium is the message." The sentence meaning and syntax turns back on itself in simultaneous opposition. Preserving the form of a previously held general belief and assumption about messages, ie, "the content is the message," McLuhan substituted the word which was the antithesis of "content" in this context, "medium." In doing so, he has it both ways: he conveys a sense of content to the medium. Although some may question whether McLuhan has actually developed a new or creative philosophical system or whether he has actually applied notions developed by previous thinkers about the relationship of form and content to a new context, there is little doubt that the phrase itself was new at the time it was formulated and that it did spark a relatively new approach to art and modern experience.

·   ·

Clinical Evidence. Later, I will discuss some of the reasons that McLuhan's sentence and similar formulations are experienced as creations. Now, I will briefly specify some further evidence for Janusian thinking as a process in creation which has come out of clinical and experimental studies currently in progress. For the past seven years, I have conducted intensive interview studies of prominent and novice creative writers, studies which focus on the writing process itself. These inverviews are carried out on a regular weekly or biweekly basis over extended periods of time, from months to several years in some cases, but they focus on the literary work in progress and are not contracted to be therapeutically oriented or to be personality explorations per se. Although I can not reveal the identity of the subjects, the prominent writers have been poets and novelists who have been winners of Pulitzer Prizes, National Book Awards, Bollingen Poetry Prizes, and members of the American Academy of Arts and Letters. Novice writers have been persons of varying ages who are serious about a writing career and who have been identified as talented by prominent literary critics and teachers. In addition to these criteria, subjects in both these groups are consistently rated as highly creative by their writer peers. In order to establish a comparison baseline for the results of these interview studies with creative writers, I have also conducted similar intensive interviews with "noncreative" persons engaging in an attempt to produce a work of fiction or poetry for financial reimbursement. These noncreative persons are similar to both the prominent and novice writer subjects in age, sex, socioeconomic characteristics, and ethnic background, but differ in that they have never been interested in literature, have never engaged in serious creative writing on their own, and are not considered creative or creatively oriented by peers or superiors. To be specific, they have not shown evidence or inclination for literary creativity.

During these interview series, I have seen many examples of the process of Janusian thinking in operation in the prominent and novice writer subjects but never in the noncreative persons. In order to indicate the nature of the evidence I have collected and to clarify the specific operation of Janusian thinking in the literary creative process, I will cite some specific examples.

In the course of discussing the circumstances surrounding the genesis of a particular poem, a poet subject told me that he got an idea for a particular poem while walking on a beach. He came upon some rocks and thought that they were heavy and were weapons but that, *at the same time,* they felt like human skin. The poetic ideas that followed this inspiration and the final poem itself were a comment on the relationship between sex and violence in the world. Indeed, the idea that sex and violence had many things in common was an early realization in this poet's mind as he wrote the poem.

In another instance, a poet was cooking cream of celery soup and began to think of arguments she had heard as a child at school that things had no form unless they had boundaries or were in a container. She thought of the fact that cream of celery soup had no form outside the pot and simultaneously thought of the first line of a poem which went as follows: "Cream of celery soup has a soul of its own." In this case, using the term "soul," she was thinking of an entity which was both formed and formless. The total poem went on to become a vibrant statement of conflict between herself as a child and as an adult.

The two examples cited indicate the way in which Janusian thinking enters into the formation of poetic content. A third example relates to the operation of Janusian thinking in relation to alliteration, a formal property (not, of course, divorced from content) of the poem. A poet with a Southern background created a line, the best in the poem he felt, which contained the words "price" and "praise" in an alliterative sequence. Spontaneously, the poet informed me that he had thought of these words together and, in the South, they would be pronounced almost identically.

After some questioning, the poet readily acknowledged that, in the context of the poem, the words "price" and "praise" denoted oppositions, referring to paying a price, a punishment, and being praised, a reward.

In numerous instances throughout these interviews, single phrases, images, and metaphors which were embodiments of simultaneous opposition were the starting points for poems. Because of the necessity of preserving the anonymity of my subjects I cannot quote actual poems or significant lines and the examples I have given necessarily lack some richness. Richer examples taken from final versions of poems by poets I have not worked with are Hart Crane's "penniless rich palms,"[15] Keats' "all his men looked at each with a wild surmise/Silent upon a peak in Darien,"[16] Hopkins' "all life death does end"[17] and "Elected silence, sing to me,"[18] as well as Emerson's[19] section from the poem, "Brahma":

> Far or forget to me is near
> Shadow and sunlight are the same
> The vanished gods to me appear
> And one to me is shame and fame.

This is an explicit series of poetic statements embodying Janusian thought.

Novels also, in their early stages, have been powered by Janusian thinking. In one instance, a revolutionary hero was conceived as being responsible for the deaths of hundreds of people but only killing one person with his own hand; this person was someone who was kind to him and whom he loved. This idea occurred early during the germination of the plot and much of the subsequent novel became an elaboration of it.

The examples cited pertain to concrete manifestations of form or content that demonstrate Janusian thought. I would like to make clear, however, that such thinking can operate to dictate formal aspects of cognition as well as to account for actual words and contents. The artist's capacity to integrate abstract ideas with concrete forms, a capacity which Arnheim[20] suggests is the hallmark of aesthetic creation, can be considered to be a capacity to maintain opposite cognitive orientations simultaneously. The notion of "regression in the service of the ego" connotes a cognitive orientation in which past and future are manipulated simultaneously and, indeed, my subjects consistently show me as we explore the experiential roots of their work that their literary themes come out of their past and are concomitant projections into the future.

Experimental Evidence. In addition to the clinical evidence for the existence of Janusian thinking in creation, preliminary results of some experiments I have carried out tend to confirm the hypothesis. In one experiment (Rothenberg, unpublished data),* carried out in similar fashion to the study by Carroll et al[21] on opposite responding to the Kent-Rosanoff (K-R) word-association test, a high tendency to rapid opposite responding was found in a creatively oriented group of male college students. The standard K-R word-association test procedure (including measurement of response time) was administered to a population of 114 male college students. On the basis of a detailed questionnaire designed to assess creative orientation and performance in the arts and in science, the subjects were divided into two groups: high creative orientation and low creative orientation. Proportion of opposite responses to the K-R stimulus words (eg, "white" as a response to stimulus word "black," "health" as a response to stimulus word "sickness") and the mean difference of time response between these opposite responses and all other responses were computed for both groups. Analysis of results indicates that the high group gave a significantly greater proportion of opposite and contrast responses in a significantly *shorter period of time* (latency of response) than the low group. The results of the experiment by Carroll et al had previously indicated that certain groups of subjects responded to the K-R test preferentially with opposite and contrast words, but that experiment had not identified such subjects as potentially creative (no identification of salient subject characteristics was made; also, response times were not recorded). Although associating in opposites to the K-R test is not equivalent to directed or creative thinking, the results suggest a proclivity toward verbal opposition in persons with a high creative orientation. Furthermore, the rapidity of opposite responding in the high creative orientation group suggests that opposite associations could occur simultaneously in creative work.

Other experimental procedures have been carried out to clarify and test hypotheses about opposite and contrast word associations versus word associations which are merely different (Rothenberg, unpublished data). Again, rapid opposite and contrast associations rather than merely different ones were characteristic of aesthetic and creative groups. Special association tasks as well as the K-R word-association test have also been administered to prominent and novice creative writers, the subjects of the interview studies described above. Preliminary assessment of the results of these latter studies indicates a high propensity to rapid oppositional association in these highly creative subjects as well. Further studies as-

---

* Editors' note: Now published. See Selected Bibliography, p. 365, "Word Association and Creativity."

sessing the role of Janusian thinking as a function of directed thought as well as a function of associative processes are in progress.

.   .   .   .

I began this exposition of Janusian thinking by raising the problem of the definition of creations and of creativity and the notion of novelty in that definition. I also suggested that a complete explanation of the act of creation may be intrinsically and logically impossible. I will not withdraw that suggestion at this point but will try to spell out the significance of Janusian thinking in creation. As one of the thought processes employed by creators during the act of creation, Janusian thinking does not contradict the view that the nature of creations may be intrinsically unpredictable and that creation is an undetermined event.

In a strictly deterministic view of the universe, there is nothing truly new under the sun or suns. Not only have all thoughts and productions (particularly human thoughts and productions) been anticipated in the thoughts and productions of the past, but all apparently new events are simply recombinations of factors previously in existence. According to this view, newness or novelty is basically a phenomenon experienced in the eye of the beholder and the creation of the world is simply an unknown event, not an unknowable one. Leaving aside, for the moment, the possible fallacious metaphysical implications of such a position, let me say that Janusian thinking goes a long way toward explaining the appearance of creations in this extreme determinist context. In its purest form, Janusian thinking consists of conceiving a notion, belief, or "fact" which is generally taken to be absolutely true and formulating its opposite or contradiction simultaneously. An example of such a pure Janusian thought which has so far not led to a creation (as far as I know) is, "The sun will rise tomorrow" simultaneously accompanied by "The sun will not rise tomorrow." The product of such a thought, an integration of these contradictory ideas, would be experienced as new in the eye of a beholder because no one had ever before considered the possibility that the sun could both rise and not rise tomorrow. So, too, any time that an opposite or contradiction is posited as of equal value or truth as a previously held notion, belief, or fact, it would be experienced as new and, by the laws of chance, occasionally of value. In art, such equating of opposites could account for a good deal of the sense of surprise and novelty which is intrinsic to artistic creations. If scientific creations are simply important and valuable discoveries which are surprising and appear novel in the eye of a beholder, the integration of opposition and contradiction can explain a good deal of scientific creation as well.

I think it is incorrect to espouse this extreme determinist view although it would clearly give Janusian thinking a very critical role in creation. Nevertheless, I think it is untenable to assert that creation exists only in the eye of the beholder and that nothing is truly new. There are many events which have been truly radical departures from anything preceding and are in no sense contradictions of the past, even integrated contradictions. (The notion of truth of any kind existing only in the eye of the beholder also raises the whole Idealism-Realism philosophical controversy. The position of Idealism has been rejected by modern philosophy many times over and the determinist argument cited is rendered further untenable by its implying such a position.) The creation of the universe and of life are models for such radical creation and human creations have often followed such models in kind if not in degree. I will not pursue this argument further here because I think it is self-evident that neither strict determinism nor Janusian thinking by itself is up to explaining such events as Shakespeare's *Hamlet*, Beethoven's *Ninth Symphony*, or Einstein's Theory of Relativity. The determinist position can simply account for one of the effects of Janusian thinking as a factor in the creative process.

Janusian thinking is a factor in the creative process but it must be accompanied by many other cognitive, affective, and synthetic processes before an actual creation is produced. Opposition is a complicated phenomenon and it can often be so idiosyncratic that it has no communicative value and, hence, no value in artistic type of creation and probably other types as well. There is a wide variety of types of opposition, ranging from strong opposition containing logical antithesis or contradiction to mild opposition consisting of simple contrast. To return to the Janus metaphor, the god simply *faces* in two distinct directions simultaneously. When the Janusian thought embodies strong opposition or logical antithesis it has the greatest shock or surprise value; it conveys the greatest sense of novelty and may also convey the greatest truths. In artistic creation, for example, many integrations of opposites do not convey this sense of surprise and novelty because they are integrations of contrasts rather than contradictions. Most metaphors are really manifestations of the integration of mild oppositions or contrasts. Although Beardsley's verbal opposition theory of metaphor, referred to previously, is basically sound, he does not take this multilevel nature of opposition adequately into account in his analysis.

Actually, when taken literally, the conception of true opposite depends a good deal on the level of sophistication of the conceiver. For example, many people take red and green or blue and yellow to be opposites. In certain contexts, say in the use of a palette, this may be true but in terms of the physical spectrum, red and blue are actually polar extremes and, therefore, opposites. Given these limitations and variations, how then does opposition actually function in creative thought?

I think it functions specifically in relation to sophistication and other factors which allow the creator to know and sense the most salient oppositions in the human and physical world at a particular point in time or, sometimes, throughout human history. The truly creative person knows his field well and also knows which widely held notions, beliefs, and "facts" are important and susceptible to opposition or contradiction on some level. It is this type of knowledge, a knowledge which may come into play after the creator hits on an integrated opposition by chance, unconscious determination, or other factors, which makes the Janusian thought meaningful and, in fact, valuable. Many oppositions, or disparate elements, as Poincaré stated in another part of the same statement cited earlier, are useless and without any value whatsoever [see ftnt. 12].

With respect to value, I have said little of the many other processes including psychological dynamisms which actually integrate oppositions as well as capacities and facilities with words, plastic materials, and conceptual symbols. These and myriad other factors go into the creative process and have a good deal to do with imparting value to a created product, but they cannot be elaborated here. Moreover, I do not intend to claim that Janusian thinking is the only or even the primary type of process accounting for inspirations or creative ideas, as I think I have made clear. Many of the other factors are so far not only unknown but undefined in any sense, and, as I have suggested, possibly unknowable. Janusian thinking is, however, a factor in the creative process and it is the first *specific* thought process in creativity to be defined.

References

1. Hausman, C. R.: The role of form, value, and novelty in [creative activity], in Vaught, C. (ed.): *Essays in Metaphysics*. University Park, Pa., Pennsylvania State University Press, [1970, pp. 79–103].

2. Morgan, [C.] L: *The Emergence of Novelty*. London, Williams & Norgate Ltd., 1933.

3. Jung, C. G.: The psychology of the unconscious, in Hull, F. C. (trans): *Two Essays on Analytical Psychology*. New York, Pantheon Books Inc., 1953.

4. Rothenberg, A.: The iceman changeth: Toward an empirical approach to creativity. *J. Amer. Psychoanal. Assoc.* 17:549–607, 1969.

5. Kris, F.: Spontaneous artistic creations by psychotics, in Kris, E.: *Psychoanalytic Explorations in Art*. New York, International Universities Press Inc., 1952, p. 116.

6. Freud, S.: Negation (1925), in Strachey, J. (trans-ed): *Complete Psychological Works*. London, Hogarth Press Ltd., 1961, vol. 19, pp. 235–242.

7. Aristotle: *Poetics*. S. H. Butcher (trans). New York, Macmillan Co. Publishers, 1911.

8. Brooks, C.: The language of paradox, in Tate, A. (ed): *The Language of Poetry*. Princeton, N.J., Princeton University Press, 1942.

9. Beardsley, M.: The metaphorical twist. *Philosophy & Phenomenological Res.* 22:293–307, 1962.

10. Wright, F. L.: Organic architecture looks at modern architecture, in Puma, F. (ed): *Seven Arts*. New York, Doubleday & Co. Inc., 1953.

11. Schoenberg, A.: *Style and Idea*. New York, Philosophical Library Inc., 1950, p. 104.

12. Poincaré, H.: Mathematical creation, in Ghiselin, B. (ed): *The Creative Process: A Symposium*. New York, New American Library Inc., 1955.

13. Watson, J.: *The Double Helix*. New York, New American Library Inc., 1968.

14. McLuhan, M.: *Understanding Media: The Extensions of Man*. New York, McGraw-Hill Book Co. Inc., 1964.

15. Crane, H.: "Voyages II," in Weber, B. (ed): *The Complete Poems and Selected Letters and Prose of Hart Crane*. Garden City, N.Y., Doubleday & Co. Inc., 1966.

16. Keats, J.: "On First Looking Into Chapman's Homer," in Thorpe, C. D. (ed): *John Keats: Complete Poems and Selected Letters*. New York, Odyssey Press Inc., 1935.

17. Hopkins, G. M.: "No worst there is none. pitched past pitch of grief," in Williams, O. (ed): *A Little Treasury of Modern Poetry*. New York, Charles Scribner's Sons, 1947.

18. Hopkins, G. M.: "The Habit of Perfection," in Williams, O. (ed): *A Little Treasury of Great Poetry*. New York, Charles Scribner's Sons, 1947.

19. Emerson, R. W.: "Brahma," in Williams, O. (ed): *A Little Treasury of Great Poetry*. New York, Charles Scribner's Sons, 1947.

20. Arnheim, R.: Psychological notes on the poetical process, in Arnheim, R., et al (eds): *Poets at Work*. New York, Harcourt Brace & World Inc., 1948.

21. Carroll, J. B., Kjeldegaard, P. M., Carton, A. S.: Number of opposites versus number of primaries as a response measure in free association test. *J. Verbal Learning Verbal Behav.* 1:22–30, 1962.

BENEDETTO CROCE · Intuition and Expression in Art

[*Croce is one of the most important philosophers of art in this century. His work on aesthetic theory as well as on literary criticism has been a key influence in the development of contemporary aesthetics and art criticism. In insisting on the autonomy of art and the art process, he set the stage both for concordant and for strongly opposing positions following him. Because of his view of the autonomy of art, his aesthetic theory as a whole may be thought of as a theory of creativity in art. In these excerpts from various sections of the Æsthetic, Croce argues that the creative act gives form to impressions (precognitive experiences) in such a way that the ensuing creation is a new, individual articulation of experience. This creation "exists" only in the mind, and it is intelligible to the mind because it is an internalized expression — in Croce's terms, an intuition. If the artist creator wishes to communicate his*

Source *From Croce, B., Æsthetic: as Science of Expression and General Linguistic, Ainslie, D. (trans.), pp. 1–6, 8–11, 14–15, 50–51. London: Macmillan and Co., Ltd., 1909. Reprinted by permission of Macmillan, London and Basingstoke.*

intuitions, he may will to externalize his internal expression. Such externalizing is not an aesthetic fact, but a moral act in the service of knowledge or moral persuasion.]

Knowledge has two forms: it is either *intuitive* knowledge or *logical* knowledge; knowledge obtained through the *imagination* or knowledge obtained through the *intellect*; knowledge of the *individual* or knowledge of the *universal*; of *individual things* or of the *relations* between them: it is, in fact, productive either of *images* or of *concepts*.

In ordinary life, constant appeal is made to intuitive knowledge. It is said that we cannot give definitions of certain truths; that they are not demonstrable by syllogisms; that they must be learnt intuitively. The politician finds fault with the abstract reasoner, who possesses no lively intuition of actual conditions; the educational theorist insists upon the necessity of developing the intuitive faculty in the pupil before everything else; the critic in judging a work of art makes it a point of honour to set aside theory and abstractions, and to judge it by direct intuition; the practical man professes to live rather by intuition than by reason.

But this ample acknowledgment granted to intuitive knowledge in ordinary life, does not correspond to an equal and adequate acknowledgment in the field of theory and of philosophy. There exists a very ancient science of intellectual knowledge, admitted by all without discussion, namely, Logic; but a science of intuitive knowledge is timidly and with difficulty asserted by but a few. Logical knowledge has appropriated the lion's share; and if she does not slay and devour her companion outright, yet yields to her but grudgingly the humble place of maid-servant or doorkeeper. — What can intuitive knowledge be without the light of intellectual knowledge? It is a servant without a master; and though a master find a servant useful, the master is a necessity to the servant, since he enables him to gain his livelihood. Intuition is blind; intellect lends her eyes.

Now, the first point to be firmly fixed in the mind is that intuitive knowledge has no need of a master, nor to lean upon any one; she does not need to borrow the eyes of others, for she has excellent eyes of her own. Doubtless it is possible to find concepts mingled with intuitions. But in many other intuitions there is no trace of such a mixture, which proves that it is not necessary. The impression of a moonlight scene by a painter; the outline of a country drawn by a cartographer; a musical motive, tender or energetic; the words of a sighing lyric, or those with which we ask, command and lament in ordinary life, may well all be intuitive facts without a shadow of intellectual relation. But, think what one may of these instances, and admitting further the contention that the greater part of the intuitions of civilized man are impregnated with concepts, there yet remains to be observed something more important and more conclusive. Those concepts which are found mingled and fused with the intuitions are no longer concepts, in so far as they are really mingled and fused, for they have lost all independence and autonomy. They have been concepts, but have now become simple elements of intuition. The philosophical maxims placed in the mouth of a personage of tragedy or of comedy, perform there the function, not of concepts, but of characteristics of such personage; in the same way as the red in a painted face does not there represent the red colour of the physicists, but is a characteristic element of the portrait. The whole is that which determines the quality of the parts. A work of art may be full of philosophical concepts; it may contain them in greater abundance and they may there be even more profound than in a philosophical dissertation, which in its turn may be rich to overflowing with descriptions and intuitions. But notwithstanding all these concepts the total effect of the work of art is an intuition; and notwithstanding all those intuitions, the total effect of the philosophical dissertation is a concept. The *Promessi Sposi* contains copious ethical observations and distinctions, but does not for that reason lose as a whole its character of simple story or intuition. In like manner the anecdotes and satirical effusions to be found in the works of a philosopher like Schopenhauer do not deprive those works of their character of intellectual treatises. The difference between a scientific work and a work of art, that is, between an intellectual fact and an intuitive fact, lies in the difference of the total effect aimed at by their respective authors. This it is that determines and rules over the several parts of each, not these parts separated and considered abstractly in themselves.

But to admit the independence of intuition as regards concept does not suffice to give a true and precise idea of intuition. Another error arises among those who recognize this, or who at any rate do not explicitly make intuition dependent upon the intellect, to obscure and confuse the real nature of intuition. By intuition is frequently understood *perception*, or the knowledge of actual reality, the apprehension of something as *real*.

Certainly perception is intuition: the perceptions of the room in which I am writing, of the ink-bottle and paper that are before me, of the pen I am using, of the objects that I touch and make use of as instruments of my person, which, if it write, therefore exists;—these are all intuitions. But the image that is now passing through my brain of a me writing in another room, in another town, with different paper, pen and ink, is also an intuition. This means that the distinction between reality and non-reality is extraneous, secondary, to the true nature of intuition. If we imagine a human mind having intuitions for the first time, it would seem that it could have intuitions of actual reality only, that is to say, that it could have perceptions of nothing but the real. But since knowledge of reality is based upon the distinction between real images and unreal images, and since this distinction does not at the first moment exist, these intuitions would in truth not be intuitions either of the real or of the unreal, not perceptions, but pure intuitions. Where all is real, nothing is real. The child, with its difficulty of distinguishing true from false, history from fable, which are all one to childhood, can furnish us with a sort of very vague and only remotely approximate idea of this ingenuous state. Intuition is the undifferentiated unity of the perception of the real and of the simple image of the possible. In our intuitions we do not oppose ourselves as empirical beings to external reality, but we simply objectify our impressions, whatever they be.

.   .   .   .

Having thus freed intuitive knowledge from any suggestion of intellec-tualism and from every later and external addition, we must now explain it and determine its limits from another side and defend it from a different kind of invasion and confusion. On the hither side of the lower limit is sensation, formless matter, which the spirit can never apprehend in itself as simple matter. This it can only possess with form and in form, but postulates the notion of it as a mere limit. Matter, in its abstraction, is mechanism, passivity; it is what the spirit of man suffers, but does not produce. . . .

.   .   .   .

And yet there is a sure method of distinguishing true intuition, true representation, from that which is inferior to it: the spiritual fact from the mechanical, passive, natural fact. Every true intuition or representation is also *expression*. That which does not objectify itself in expression is not intuition or representation, but sensation and mere natural fact. The spirit only intuites in making, forming, expressing. He who separates intuition from expression never succeeds in reuniting them.

Intuitive activity *possesses intuitions to the extent that it expresses them.* Should this proposition sound paradoxical, that is partly because, as a general rule, a too restricted meaning is given to the word "expression." It is generally restricted to what are called verbal expressions alone. But there exist also non-verbal expressions, such as those of line, colour and sound, and to all of these must be extended our affirmation, which embraces therefore every sort of manifestation of the man, as orator, musician, painter, or anything else. But be it pictorial, or verbal, or musical, or in whatever other form it appear, to no intuition can expression in one of its forms be wanting; it is, in fact, an inseparable part of intuition. . . .

The principal reason which makes our view appear paradoxical as we maintain it, is the illusion or prejudice that we possess a more complete intuition of reality than we really do. One often hears people say that they have many great thoughts in their minds, but that they are not able to express them. But if they really had them, they would have coined them into just so many beautiful, sounding words, and thus have expressed them. If these thoughts seem to vanish or to become few and meagre in the act of expressing them, the reason is that they did not exist or really were few and meagre. People think that all of us ordinary men imagine and intuite countries, figures and scenes like painters, and bodies like sculptors; save that painters and sculptors know how to paint and carve such images, while we bear them unexpressed in our souls. They believe that any one could have imagined a Madonna of Raphael; but that Raphael was Raphael owing to his technical ability in putting the Madonna upon canvas. Nothing can be more false than this view. The world which as a rule we intuite is a small thing. It consists of little expressions, which gradually become greater and wider with the increasing spiritual concentration of certain moments. They are the words we say to ourselves, our silent judgments: "Here is a man, here is a horse, this is heavy, this is sharp, this pleases me," etc. It is a medley of light and colour, with no greater pictorial value than would be expressed by a haphazard splash of colours, from among which one could barely make out a few special, distinctive traits. This and nothing else is what we possess in our ordinary life; this is the basis of our ordinary action. It is the index of a book. The labels tied to things (it has been said) take the place of the things themselves. This index and these labels (themselves expressions) suffice for small needs and small actions. From time to time we pass from the index to the book, from the label to the thing, or from the slight to the greater intuitions, and from these to the greatest and most lofty. This passage is sometimes far from easy. It has been observed by those who have best studied the psychology of artists that when, after having given a rapid glance at any one, they attempt to obtain a real intuition of him, in order, for example, to paint his portrait, then this ordinary vision, that seemed so precise, so lively, reveals itself as little better than nothing. What remains is found to be at the most some superficial trait, which would not even suffice for a caricature. The person to be painted stands before the artist like a world to discover. Michael Angelo said, "One paints, not with the hands, but with the brain." Leonardo shocked the prior of the Convent of the Graces by standing for days together gazing at the "Last Supper," without touching it with the brush. He remarked of this attitude: "The minds of men of lofty genius are most active in invention when they are doing the least external work." The painter is a painter, because he sees what others only feel or catch a glimpse of, but do not see. We think we see a smile, but in reality we have only a vague impression of it, we do not perceive all the characteristic traits of which it is the sum, as the painter discovers them after he has worked upon them and is thus able to fix them on the canvas. We do not intuitively possess more even of our intimate friend, who is with us every day and at all hours, than at most certain traits of physiognomy which enable us to distinguish him from others. The illusion is less easy as regards musical expression; because it would seem strange to every one to say that the composer had added or attached notes to a motive which was already in the mind of him who is not the composer; as if Beethoven's Ninth Symphony were not his own intuition and his intuition the Ninth Symphony. Now, just as one who is deluded as to the amount of his material wealth is confuted by arithmetic, which states its exact amount, so he who nourishes delusions as to the wealth of his own thoughts and images is brought back to reality, when he is obliged to cross the *Pons Asinorum* of expression. Let us say to the former, count; to the latter, speak; or, here is a pencil, draw, express yourself.

Each of us, as a matter of fact, has in him a little of the poet, of the sculptor, of the musician, of the painter, of the prose writer: but how little, as compared with those who bear those names, just because they possess the most universal dispositions and energies of human nature in so lofty a degree! . . .

. . . .

Nor can we admit that the word *genius* or artistic genius, as distinct from the non-genius of the ordinary man, possesses more than a quantitative signification. Great artists are said to reveal us to ourselves. But how could this be possible, unless there were identity of nature between their imagination and ours, and unless the difference were only one of quantity? . . . The cult of the genius with all its attendant superstitions has arisen from this quantitative difference having been taken as a difference of quality. It has been forgotten that genius is not something that has fallen from heaven, but humanity itself. The man of genius who poses or is represented as remote from humanity finds his punishment in becoming or appearing somewhat ridiculous. Examples of this are the *genius* of the romantic period and the *superman* of our time.

But it is well to note here, that those who claim unconsciousness as the chief quality of an artistic genius, hurl him from an eminence far above humanity to a position far below it. Intuitive or artistic genius, like every form of human activity, is always conscious; otherwise it would be blind mechanism. The only thing that can be wanting to artistic genius is the *reflective* consciousness, the superadded consciousness of the historian or critic, which is not essential to it.

.   .   .   .

... we must condemn as erroneous every theory which annexes the æsthetic activity to the practical, or introduces the laws of the second into the first. That science is theory and art practice has been many times affirmed. Those who make this statement, and look upon the æsthetic fact as a practical fact, do not do so capriciously or because they are groping in the void; but because they have their eye on something which is really practical. But the practical [at] which they aim is not Æsthetic, nor within Æsthetic; it is *outside and beside it*; and although often found united, they are not united necessarily or by the bond of identity of nature.

The æsthetic fact is altogether completed in the expressive elaboration of impressions. When we have achieved the word within us, conceived definitely and vividly a figure or a statue, or found a musical motive, expression is born and is complete; there is no need for anything else. If after this we should open our mouths—*will* to open them to speak, or our throats to sing, that is to say, utter by word of mouth and audible melody what we have completely said or sung to ourselves; or if we should stretch out—*will* to stretch out our hands to touch the notes of the piano, or to take up the brush and chisel, thus making on a large scale movements which we have already made in little and rapidly, in a material in which we leave more or less durable traces; this is all an addition, a fact which obeys quite different laws from the former, with which we are not concerned for the moment, although we recognize henceforth that this second movement is a production of things, a *practical* fact, or fact of *will*. It is usual to distinguish the internal from the external work of art: the terminology seems to us infelicitous, for the work of art (the æsthetic work) is always *internal*; and what is called *external* is no longer a work of art. Others distinguish between *æsthetic* fact and *artistic* fact, meaning by the second the external or practical stage, which may follow and generally does follow the first. But in this case, it is simply a question of a linguistic usage, doubtless permissible, though perhaps not advisable.

R. G. COLLINGWOOD · Consciousness and Attention in Art

[*The English philosopher Collingwood followed after Croce and he developed an originally Crocean view into an approach that is in some ways more empirical. This is particularly evident in his emphasis on the importance of the externalization of imagination (æsthetic and creative experience) in his theory of art. Collingwood's account of the way an active, spontaneous consciousness clarifies precognitive experience is both an explanation of, and a development beyond, Croce's theory of intuition-expression. Further accounts of imagination are included in Collingwood's philosophy of history. These accounts complement the present one and suggest a theory of imagination as a re-creative as well as a creative activity of consciousness. Historical imagination depends upon an interpretive appropriation of contextual factors through which the historian reconstructs past thought.*]

With the entry of consciousness into experience, a new principle has established itself. Attention is focused upon one thing to the exclusion of the rest. The mere fact that something is present to sense does not give it a claim on attention. Even what is most vividly present to sense can do no more than solicit attention; it cannot secure it. Thus, the focus of attention is by no means necessarily identical with the focus of vision. I can fix my eyes in one direction, and my attention upon what lies at a considerable angle away from it. I can deliberately refuse attention to the loudest of the noises I am hearing, and concentrate upon a much less conspicuous one. Often, no doubt, we idly allow our attention to be attracted by whatever is most prominent in sensation and emotion; the brightest light, the loudest noise, the pain or anger or fear that comes most strongly upon us; but there is no reason for this in principle, and it only happens so long as our consciousness is a faint and confused one.

Thus attention is in no sense a response to stimulus. It takes no orders from sensation. Consciousness, master in its own house, dominates feeling. Now feeling as so dominated, feeling as compelled to accept whatever place consciousness gives it, focal or peripheral, in the field of attention, is no longer impression, it is idea. Consciousness is absolutely autonomous: its decision alone determines whether a given sensum or emotion shall be attended to or not. A conscious being is not thereby free to decide

SOURCE *From Collingwood, R. G.,* The Principles of Art, *pp. 207–208, 213, 216, 221–224, 281–284, 300, 302, 306–308. Oxford: Oxford University Press, 1938. Reprinted by permission of the Oxford University Press, Oxford.*

what feelings he shall have; but he is free to decide what feeling he shall place in the focus of his consciousness.

Yet he is not free to choose whether he shall exercise this power of decision or not. In so far as he is conscious, he is obliged to decide; for that decision is consciousness itself. Further: in so far as he is simply conscious, he does not review his various feelings and then decide which of them he shall attend to. Such a review would be a successive attention to these various feelings. In order to choose, in the strict sense of that word, which feeling he shall attend to, he must first have attended to them all. The freedom of consciousness is thus not a freedom of choice between alternatives; that is a further kind of freedom, which arises only when experience reaches the level of intellect.

. . . We have in effect distinguished three stages in the life of a feeling. (1) First, as bare feeling, below the level of consciousness. (2) Secondly, as a feeling of which we have become conscious. (3) Thirdly, as a feeling which, in addition to becoming conscious of it, we have placed in its relation to others. Whether these three stages are sometimes or always separated in time, we need not ask. Their essential relation is not temporal, but logical. Where A is logically presupposed by B, A need not have existed by itself before B came into existence; the logical relation may stand, even though they came into existence at the same time.

. . . [With respect to the second stage, consciousness] is the activity of thought without which we should have no terms between which intellect in its primary form could detect or construct relations. Thus consciousness is thought in its absolutely fundamental and original shape.

As thought, it must have that bipolarity which belongs to thought as such. It is an activity which may be well or ill done; what it thinks may be true or false. But this seems paradoxical; for since it is not concerned with the relations between things, and hence does not think in terms of concepts or generalizations, it cannot err, as intellect can, by referring things to the wrong concepts. It cannot, for instance, think 'This is a dog', when the object before it is a cat. If, as we said above, the kind of phrase which expresses what it thinks is something like 'This is how I feel', such a statement might seem incapable of being false, in which case consciousness would have the peculiar privilege of being a kind of thought not liable to error, and this would amount to saying that it was not a kind of thought at all.

But the statement 'This is how I feel' does imply bipolarity. It has an opposite: 'This is not how I feel'; and to assert it is to deny this opposite. Even if consciousness never actually erred, it would still have this in common with all forms of thought, that it lives by rejecting error. A true consciousness is the confession to ourselves of our feelings; a false consciousness would be disowning them, i.e. thinking about one of them 'That feeling is not mine'.

. . . .

We have now reached a point where the results of the argument can be summarized into a general theory of imagination. All thought presupposes feeling; and all the propositions which express the results of our thought belong to one of two types: they are either statements about feelings, in which case they are called empirical, or statements about the procedure of thought itself, in which case they are called a priori. 'Thought', here, means intellect; 'feeling' means not feeling proper, but imagination.

Feeling proper, or psychical experience, has a double character: it is sensation and emotion. We may attend chiefly or exclusively to one or the other aspect, but in the experience of feeling as it actually comes to us the two are firmly united. Every feeling is both sensuous and emotional. Now, feeling proper is an experience in which what we now feel monopolizes the whole field of our view. What we have felt in the past, or shall feel in the future, or might feel on a different kind of occasion, is not present to us at all, and has no meaning for us. Actually, of course, these things have a meaning for us, and we can form some idea of them, sometimes no doubt a fairly correct one; but that is because we are able to do other things besides merely feeling.

If I assert any relation between what I feel now and what I have felt in the past, or what I should expect to feel in different circumstances, my assertion cannot be based on mere feeling; for mere feeling, even if it can tell me what I now feel, cannot acquaint me with the other term of the relation. Hence the so-called sense-data which are described as organized into families or the like are not feelings as they actually come to us, sensa with their own emotional charges; they are not even the sensuous element in these feelings sterilized of its emotional charge; they are something quite different. But further: mere feeling cannot even tell me what I now feel. If I try to fasten my attention on this present feeling, so as to give myself some account of its character, it has already changed before I can do so. If, to take the other alternative, I succeed in doing so (and it is clear that we do succeed, otherwise we could never know the things about feeling which have already been stated), the feeling to which I attend must be somehow stabilized or perpetuated in order that I may study it, which means that it must cease to be mere feeling and enter upon a new stage of its existence.

This new stage is reached not by some process antecedent to the act of attention, but by that act itself. Attention or awareness is a kind of activity different from mere feeling, and presupposing it. The essence of it is that instead of having our field of view wholly occupied by the sensations and emotions of the moment, we also become aware of ourselves, as the activity of feeling these things. Theoretically considered, this new activity is an enlargement of our field of view, which now takes in the act of feeling as well as the thing felt. Practically considered, it is the assertion of ourselves as the owners of our feelings. By this self-assertion we dominate our feelings: they become no longer experiences forcing themselves upon us unawares, but experiences in which we experience our own activity. Their brute power over us is thus replaced by our power over them: we become able on the one hand to stand up to them so that they no longer unconditionally determine our conduct, and, on the other, to prolong and evoke them at will. From being impressions of sense, they thus become ideas of imagination.

In this new capacity, as losing their power over us and becoming subject to our will, they are still feelings, and feelings of the same kind as before; but they have ceased to be mere sensations and have become what we call imaginations. From one point of view, imagination does not differ from sensation: what we imagine is the very same kinds of things (colours, &c.) which present themselves to us in mere sensation. From another point of view, it is very different through being, in the way above described, tamed or domesticated. That which tames it is the activity of consciousness, and this is a kind of thought.

Specifically, it is the kind of thought which stands closest to sensation or mere feeling. Every further development of thought is based upon it, and deals not with feeling in its crude form but with feeling as thus transformed into imagination. [ftnt. deleted] In order to consider likenesses and differences between feelings, classify them or group them in other kinds of arrangement than classes, envisage them as arranged in a time-series, and so forth, it is necessary first that each one of the feelings thus reflected upon should be attended to and held before the mind as something with a character of its own; and this converts it into imagination.

Consciousness itself does not do any of these things. It only prepares the ground for them. In itself, it does nothing but attend to some feeling which I have here and now. In attending to a present feeling, it perpetuates that feeling, though at the cost of turning it into something new, no longer sheer or crude feeling (impression) but domesticated feeling or imagination (idea). But it does not compare one idea with another. If, while I am thus enjoying one idea, I proceed to summon up another, the new idea is not held alongside the old, as two distinct experiences, between which I can detect relations. The two ideas fuse into one, the new one presenting itself as a peculiar colouring or modification of the old. Thus imagination resembles feeling in this, that its object is never a plurality of terms with relations between them, but a single indivisible unity: a sheer here-and-now. The conceptions of past, future, the possible, the hypothetical, are as meaningless for imagination as they are for feeling itself. They are conceptions which appear only with a further development of thought.

When, therefore, it is said that imagination can summon up feelings at will, this does not mean that when I imagine I first form some idea of a feeling and then, as it were, summon it into my presence as a real feeling; still less, that I can review in fancy the various feelings which I might enjoy, and choose to evoke in myself the one which I prefer. To form an idea of a feeling is already to feel it in imagination. Thus imagination is 'blind', i.e. cannot anticipate its own results by conceiving them as purposes in advance of executing them. The freedom which it enjoys is not the freedom to carry out a plan, or to choose between alternative possible plans. These are developments belonging to a later stage.

To the same later stage belongs the distinction between truth and error, regarded as the distinction between true and false accounts of the relations between things. But there is a special way in which that distinction applies to consciousness, and therefore to imagination. Consciousness can never attend to more than a part of the total sensuous-emotional field; but either it may recognize this as belonging to itself, or it may refuse so to recognize it. In the latter case, certain feelings are not ignored, they are disowned; the conscious self disclaims responsibility for them, and thus tries to escape being dominated by them without the trouble of dominating them. This is the 'corrupt consciousness', which is the source of what psychologists call repression. Its imaginations share in its corruption; they are 'fantasies', sentimentalized or bowdlerized pictures of experience, Spinoza's 'inadequate ideas of affections'; and the mind that takes refuge in them from the facts of experience delivers itself into the power of the feelings it has refused to face.

.   .   .   .

Any theory of art should be required to show, if it wishes to be taken seriously, how an artist, in pursuing his artistic labour, is able to tell whether he is pursuing it successfully or unsuccessfully: how, for example, it is possible for him to say, 'I am not satisfied with that line; let us try it this way . . . and this way . . . and this way . . . there! that will do.' A theory which pushes the artistic experience too far down the scale, to a point below the region where experience has the character of knowledge, is unable to meet this demand. It can only evade it by pretending that the artist in such cases is acting not as an artist, but as a critic and even (if criticism of art is identified with philosophy of art) as a philosopher. But this pretence should deceive nobody. The watching of his own work with a vigilant and discriminating eye, which decides at every moment of the process whether it is being successful or not, is not a critical activity subsequent to, and reflective upon, the artistic work, it is an integral part of that work itself. A person who can doubt this, if he has any grounds at all for his doubt, is presumably confusing the way an artist works with the way an incompetent student in an art-school works; painting blindly, and waiting for the master to show him what it is that he has been doing. In point of fact, what a student learns in an art-school is not so much to paint as to watch himself painting: to raise the psycho-physical activity of painting to the level of art by becoming conscious of it, and so converting it from a psychical experience into an imaginative one.

What the artist is trying to do is to express a given emotion. To express it, and to express it well, are the same thing. To express it badly is not one way of expressing it (not, for example, expressing it, but not *selon les règles*), it is failing to express it. A bad work of art is an activity in which the agent tries to express a given emotion, but fails. This is the difference between bad art and art falsely so called. . . . In art falsely so called there is no failure to express, because there is no attempt at expression; there is only an attempt (whether successful or not) to do something else.

But expressing an emotion is the same thing as becoming conscious of it. A bad work of art is the unsuccessful attempt to become conscious of a given emotion: it is what Spinoza calls an inadequate idea of an affection. Now, a consciousness which thus fails to grasp its own emotions is a corrupt or untruthful consciousness. For its failure (like any other failure) is not a mere blankness; it is not a doing nothing; it is a misdoing something; it is activity, but blundering or frustrated activity. A person who tries to become conscious of a given emotion, and fails, is no longer in a state of sheer unconsciousness or innocence about that emotion; he has done something about it, but that something is not to express it. What he has done is either to shirk it or dodge it: to disguise it from himself by pretending either that the emotion he feels is not that one but a different one, or that the person who feels it is not himself, but some one else: two alternatives which are so far from being mutually exclusive that in fact they are always concurrent and correlative.

If we ask whether this pretence is conscious or unconscious, the answer is, neither. It is a process which occurs not in the region below consciousness (where it could not, of course, take place, since consciousness is involved in the process itself), not yet in the region of consciousness (where equally it could not take place, because a man cannot literally tell himself a lie; in so far as he is conscious of the truth he cannot literally deceive himself about it); it occurs on the threshold that divides the psychical level of experience from the conscious level. It is the malperformance of the act which converts what is merely psychic (impression) into what is conscious (idea).

The corruption of consciousness in virtue of which a man fails to express a given emotion makes him at the same time unable to know whether he has expressed it or not. He is, therefore, for one and the same reason, a bad artist and a bad judge of his own art. A person who is capable of producing bad art cannot, so far as he is capable of producing it, recognize it for what it is. He cannot, on the other hand, really think it good art; he cannot think that he has expressed himself when he has not. To mistake bad art for good art would imply having in one's mind an idea of what good art is, and one has such an idea only so far as one knows what it is to have an uncorrupt consciousness; but no one can know this except a person who possesses one. An insincere mind, so far as it is insincere, has no conception of sincerity.

But nobody's consciousness can be wholly corrupt. If it were, he would be in a condition as much worse than the most complete insanity we can discover or imagine, as that is worse than the most complete sanity we can conceive. He would suffer simultaneously every possible kind of mental derangement, and every bodily disease that such derangements can bring in their train. Corruptions of consciousness are always partial and temporary lapses in an activity which, on the whole, is successful in doing what it tries to do. A person who on one occasion fails to express himself is a person quite accustomed to express himself successfully on other occasions, and to know that he is doing it. Through comparison of this occasion with his memory of these others, therefore, he ought to be able to see that he has failed, this time, to express himself. And this is precisely what every artist is doing when he says, 'This line won't do'. He remembers what the experience of expressing himself is like, and in the light of that memory he realizes that the attempt embodied in this particular line has been a failure. Corruption of consciousness is not a recondite sin or a remote calamity which overcomes only an unfortunate or accursed few; it is a constant experience in the life of every artist, and his life is a constant and, on the whole, a successful warfare against it. But this warfare always involves a very present possibility of defeat; and then a certain corruption becomes inveterate.

What we recognize as definite kinds of bad art are such inveterate corruptions of consciousness. Bad art is never the result of expressing what is in itself evil, or what is innocent perhaps in itself, but in a given society a thing inexpedient to be publicly said. Every one of us feels emotions which, if his neighbours became aware of them, would make them shrink from him with horror: emotions which, if he became aware of them, would make him horrified at himself. It is not the expression of these emotions that is bad art. Nor is it the expression of the horror they excite. On the contrary, bad art arises when instead of expressing these emotions we disown them, wishing to think ourselves innocent of the emotions that horrify us, or wishing to think ourselves too broad-minded to be horrified by them.

. . . .

The work of art, as we have seen, is not a bodily or perceptible thing, but an activity of the artist; and not an activity of his 'body' or sensuous nature, but an activity of his consciousness. A problem arises out of this statement, concerning the artist's relation to his audience.

It seems to be a normal part of the artist's work that he should communicate his experience to other people. In order to do that, he must have means of communication with them; and these means are something bodily and perceptible, a painted canvass, a carved stone, a written paper, and so forth.

. . . .

. . . We must ask: what is the relation between the artist's aesthetic experience and the painted canvasses, carved stones, and so forth, in which, according to the view I have stated and criticized, he 'externalizes' it?

. . . .

. . . Wherever there is an idea, or imaginative experience, there are also the following elements: (1) an impression, or sensuous experience, corresponding with it; (2) an act of consciousness converting that impression into an idea. When the impression is said to correspond with the idea, what is meant is that it is the impression which an act of consciousness would convert into that idea and no other.

We get, therefore, this result. Every imaginative experience is a sensuous experience raised to the imaginative level by an act of consciousness; or, every imaginative experience is a sensuous experience together with consciousness of the same. Now the aesthetic experience is an imaginative experience. It is wholly and entirely imaginative; it contains no elements that are not imaginative, and the only power which can generate it is the power of the experient's consciousness. But it is not generated out of nothing. Being an imaginative experience, it presupposes a corresponding sensuous experience; where to say that it presupposes this does not mean that it arises subsequently to this, but that it is generated by the act which converts this into it. The sensuous experience need not exist by itself first. It may come into being under the very eyes, so to speak, of consciousness, so that it no sooner comes into being than it is transmuted into imagination. Nevertheless, there is always a distinction between what transmutes (consciousness), what is transmuted (sensation), and what it is transmuted into (imagination).

The transmuted or sensuous element in the aesthetic experience is the so-called outward element: in the case under examination, the artist's psycho-physical activity of painting; his visual sensation of the colours and shapes of his subject, his felt gestures as he manipulates his brush, the seen shapes of paint patches that these gestures leave on his canvass: in short, the total sensuous (or rather, sensuous-emotional) experience of a man at work before his easel. Unless this sensuous experience were actually present, there would be nothing out of which consciousness could generate the aesthetic experience which is 'externalized' or 're-corded' or 'expressed' by the painted picture. But this sensuous experience, although it is actually present, is never present by itself. Every element in it comes into existence under the eyes of the painter's consciousness; or rather, this happens in so far as he is a good painter; it is only bad painters who paint without knowing what they are doing; and every element in it is therefore converted into imaginative experience at birth. Nevertheless, reflection distinguishes between the imaginative experience and the sensuous experience out of which it is thus made, and discovers that 'nihil est in imaginatione quod non fuerit in sensu'.

What of the case where a man looks at the subject without painting? He, too, has an aesthetic experience in so far as his impressions are transmuted into ideas by the activity of his imagination. But our artist was right to claim that there is far less in that experience than in the experience of a man who has painted the subject; for the sensuous elements involved in merely looking, even where looking is accompanied by a smile of pleasure, gestures, and so forth, are necessarily much scantier and poorer, and also much less highly organized in their totality, than the sensuous elements involved in painting. If you want to get more out of an experience, you must put more into it. The painter puts a great deal more into his experience of the subject than a man who merely looks at it; he puts into it, in addition, the whole consciously performed activity of painting it; what he gets out of it, therefore, is proportionately more. And this increment is an essential part of what he 'externalizes' or 'records' in his picture: he records there not the experience of looking at the subject without painting it, but the far richer and in some ways very different experience of looking at it and painting it together.

CARL R. HAUSMAN · Creativity and Rationality

[*What is said here about the problems encountered in attempting to understand creative acts and the proposal for metaphorical discourse suggests the basic outlines of an ontology that is open to the presence of radical creativity in the world. The creative act, like the outcome or the creation, is paradoxical and it defies all varieties of rational explanation that attempt to trace such acts to antecedent factors and principles. This excerpt is from one of a series of arguments and proposals for an alternative approach to creativity, references to which appear in the Selected Bibliography for this chapter.*]

There are at least two reasons why a theory of reality can be considered inadequate. On the one hand, the theory may either contain incompatible principles or fail to imply the data which it purports to explain. On the other hand, the data may be such that they resist rational interpretation. In this paper, I should like to examine the extent to which spontaneity or creativity is the kind of phenomenon that resists rational explanation.

It is necessary at the outset to indicate the way in which the terms "novelty" and "creativity" or "spontaneity" will be used throughout the discussion. "Creativity" and "spontaneity" will be taken to refer to that kind of activity which issues in genuine novelty. That is to say, each appearance of genuine novelty is a sign of creative activity. "Genuine

SOURCE   From Hausman, C. R., "*Spontaneity: Its Arationality and Its Reality,*" International Philosophical Quarterly, 1964, *Vol. 4, pp. 20–21, 30–35, 38–39, 44–47. Reprinted with permission of* International Philosophical Quarterly.

novelty" will refer to that character of the result of a creative process which marks the result as different in kind or type from any form available to the process before it began. Thus the novelty that issues from spontaneity must be distinguished from particularity in time. A first experience such as my first observation of a friend's library is in a sense a new experience. It is new in that it never happened before — it is unique. But all experiences are in that sense novel. As Paul Henle suggests, the sense of "novelty" which is of interest is the sense in which a form is new in its first occurrence in the world.[1]

It is also necessary to observe here that the presence of novelty in a created result is to be taken as fact — as that which is at least phenomenally given. I see no way of "proving" this point. It is based upon an immediate and direct confrontation of certain objects that appear to consciousness. If the appearance is denied, the denial must construe the consciousness in question as somehow deluded. The problem of accounting for novelty as an illusion will be treated later.

. . . .

. . . [After examining the way creativity eludes rationality in the theories of Whitehead, Husserl, and Nicholai Hartmann,] it is necessary to consider the implications of those approaches which deny the reality of novelty; for it might be claimed that if spontaneity is arational, and if the world is rational, the notion of spontaneity must be excluded from our thought about the world. While I shall not try to "prove" conclusively that spontaneity and novelty are real, I shall attempt to show that the contradictory view encounters difficulties which point to an arational remainder.

It must be emphasized once more that the kind of newness in question is not that which is attributable to a first occurrence of an experience. No one but a Parmenidean, perhaps, would deny this kind of novelty. As was indicated at the outset, the kind of novelty in question is that which appears in such a way as to be the mark of something different in type or kind. The novelty-characteristic presents itself as a new form, not a new thing with an old form.

. . . .

Before considering the approach that flatly denies novelty, some attention must be given to a view that does not totally reject, but rather excludes spontaneity from its sights. This view is the positivistic interpretation of natural science.[2] Strictly speaking, positivism ignores the existence

---

1. "The Status of Emergence," *The Journal of Philosophy*, XXXIX (1942), 487.
2. The label "positivistic" is used in the broadest sense, to include any view that insists on the use of "empirical methods" — the adherence to publicly verifiable data, predictability, etc., as necessary criteria of knowledge — and the "meaninglessness" of assertions that do not abide by its strictures.

of spontaneity. It does so by insisting upon the primacy of observability and predictability as criteria for empirical knowledge. . . .

The conclusion that the positivistic approach ignores spontaneity and its product, novelty, is explicitly indicated by Russell's account of causality and its relation to the predictability of human behavior. Russell points out that the determinist in science need only foresee the *kind* of act he hopes to predict. He has little "practical interest" in predicting the "fine shades which cannot be foreseen."[3] Thus one could argue, for example, that predicting an explosion of a nuclear weapon in Russia at a given time and given place would not require foreknowledge of specific qualities of the explosion. The explosion might very well have unique and novel characteristics, but foreknowledge of these characteristics is more than can or should be expected of the prediction. But to disclaim the need for foreseeing individuality in a predicted event is to disclaim an interest in features of the world that may very well disclose novelty. And it is just those features that are of utmost importance in the kind of events in which novelty and spontaneity occur in their most obvious manifestations, works of art. Indeed, the "fine shades" of an occurrence which is an aesthetic object are often of such importance as to be the marks of an event that is different in kind or type from any other prior event. As Croce points out, for example, Don Quixote is a type who possesses characteristics common to others; yet the Don Quixote type is singular, and, as Don Quixote, is like nothing else in the world.

Thus if the positivist's approach is willing to grant that there is novelty in the world, it is hard to see how novelty could be subjected to the positivistic program for rational understanding. For positive knowledge must look for repeated and repeatable patterns in observations. Its methods call for treating the world in terms of kinds and classes of previously known observable events.

. . . .

. . . the positivist interpretation of the world either must deny by ignoring the phenomenon in question, or it must presuppose the predictability of all characteristics of reality. On the former alternative, its approach is not relevant to the question whether spontaneity is arational. On the latter alternative, positivism is a version of the second approach to be considered: the view that denies the reality of novelty by interpreting the appearance of novelty as illusory or deceptive.

. . . .

Theories of this kind may follow from a determinism directed toward the nature of consciousness or toward the nature of the object of con-

3. *Our Knowledge of the External World* (London: Allen & Unwin, 1952), p. 234.

sciousness. That is to say, consciousness may be called "mistaken" in every instance in which it is aware of a phenomenon as novel; or the object of consciousness may be called "unreal," or in some way deficient in being.

. . . .

One of the plainest examples of the psychological approach is that of Freudian psychoanalytic theory.[4] . . .

Within the framework of Freudian theory, a phenomenon which is interpreted as illusory presumably can be traced to its origin in the personal or private dynamism of the psyche. Thus hallucinations experienced in a case of hysteria are interpreted as illusory because they are products of some form of mental conflict that manifests itself in a way peculiar to the person. That an hallucination appears is not denied. But the appearance is characterizable as illusory because it can be described as causally related to other antecedent experiences. And when felt and described by the person suffering from it, it ceases to appear. Thus knowledge of the origin of the hallucination not only "corrects" the initial interpretation of the appearance as externally caused but it also leads to the extinguishing of the phenomenon entirely. Can an appearance of novelty, then, be described in terms of antecedent experiences so that the appearance vanishes?

In considering this question, it is important to notice that novelty, unlike hallucinations, appears for a kind of consciousness which, though perhaps abnormal in its sensitivity and freedom from stereotyped, hardened patterns of activity, is not pathological.

Thus novelty in general (not specific cases of pathological delusions) need not vanish before the knowing eye of the psychoanalyst. For if novelty is a "normal" illusion (common to nonpathological consciousness), it may continue to appear as always, even though it is recognized for what it is—a phenomenon the conditions for which are fully known. Thus a "normal" illusion such as a mirage may be called "illusory" insofar as it is inadequately or mistakenly interpreted. It remains illusory only for the unenlightened. For the enlightened, the phenomenon, though it still appears in its original guise, is not an illusion, since it is not misinterpreted; it is known for what it is. Hence, a mirage of an oasis, if understood, is not sought as a source of comfort.

However, whether novelty is construed as abnormal or normal, it has a

4. Granted that there are other forms of psychoanalytic psychology, so varied as to include "existential psychoanalysis," the concern in this paper is with the kind of determinism that calls for interpreting novelty in terms of pre-existing mental contents and drives.

peculiarity not present in other illusory appearances. Other phenomena called "illusory" appear as like what they are not. They are (with a possible exception that will be separately dealt with) characterized by resemblances to the phenomena of which they are illusions. Thus ordinary illusions appear as images of things, or as composite images of qualities, antecedently known. For example: a mirage presents itself as that which it is not; and it is a deception by virtue of qualities that it has in common with that which it is not and thus with that which is already known. A distorted mirror image in a "fun house" (whether or not mistakenly interpreted) is a composite of the exaggeration of qualities already known. And a hallucination such as a specter is a composite or combination of qualities — vapor and flame, or a deceased body and light, for instance — that are otherwise known.

Appearances of novelty on the other hand, are unlike rather than like what is. They cannot, as initially given, be characterized by resemblances to antecedent phenomena. If they could be, they would not even be appearances of novelty; they would not present themselves as instances of novelty.

Now, to interpret newness as illusory in the way other appearances are illusory is to construe all appearances of newness as like what they are not. But since there is nothing which they appear to be like but are not, they must be either illusions of nothing or pretenses for nothing but themselves. Hence, if they are illusions of nothing, they are not illusions, or, if they are deceptions of themselves, they continue to insist on being what they are — appearances of newness.

. . . the implication of the deterministic approach to spontaneity can be suggested by an analogy in which the determinist is pictured with a book of knowledge in which each event is described in terms of fixed laws and is given within a total network of all events, past, present, and future. The determinist finds himself as well as all other consciousnesses described in the book. He sees that his existential consciousness is confronted with "novelty-presentations." And his transcendent consciousness understands why these appearances occur within the world as they do and why his existential consciousness grasps them as appearances of novelty. But his transcendent understanding does not change by one iota either the novelty-presentation or existential consciousness. They occur independently of his knowledge. If they did not, if transcendent consciousness intervened, the deterministic chain would be broken. If the determinist could change the book, the book would be wrong. That is, the book would not exhaustively treat all factors operative in the causal chain. For if transcendent consciousness can change the book just once, the book cannot guarantee that what it says now may not be different according to the whim — the spontaneous whim — of the determinist in his position of transcendence. But if deterministic understanding sees novelty-presentations as given within necessary continuities in the world, there remains a radical gap between the transcendent, deterministic consciousness and the existential, determined consciousness. And spontaneity as an ingredient of the world is denied for the sake of accepting an arationality in the relation between infinite mind and finite mind, between transcendent being and existential contingency.

.   .   .   .

In conclusion, I should like first to repeat that, given what is regarded as rationality, the theoretical approaches that assume the reality of spontaneity encounter an element of paradox or arationality which seems to be inherent within the nature of spontaneity. The reason explanation cannot avoid this irrational increment is that the phenomenon of spontaneity is peculiar in that it eludes categories and principles which, in their capacity as being rational, insist upon having unity. They necessarily impose repeatability or continuity on the phenomena which they successfully interpret. Other kinds of change which do not disclose novelty but rather conform to antecedent patterns may not resist continuities. But spontaneity, since it yields newness, does resist.

It was also argued that theories which deny the reality of spontaneity must come to grips with the appearance of novelty. They must show that the appearance of novelty is in some sense illusory. And the way in which a theory can show this leads, in its own way, once again to perplexities that indicate a paradox inherent in the world.

It is of utmost importance, however, to insist that the arationality for which I have argued appears for understanding in terms of rationality as it has traditionally been interpreted. Whether or not spontaneity is unintelligible as well as non-rational depends upon whether rationality as traditionally conceived is to be identified with intelligibility. In this connection, I should like to indicate a way of approaching the problem of making spontaneity intelligible.

.   .   .   .

If the problem is broadened and formulated as a question concerning how "the supra-rational" may be made intelligible, suggestions, of course, can be found in the philosophical tradition — in Plato, Aristotle,

Plotinus, Spinoza, etc. However, some contemporary movements have brought the issue into sharp focus, treating it as a major problem requiring resolution or at least clarification as a step toward a reconstituted view of the function and method of philosophy. More specifically, it can be said that the proper way to bring lucidity to a mode or level of reality not amenable to conceptual thought has recently been a crucial concern for personalists, existentialists, and certain representatives of Thomistic philosophy, as well as others such as Bergson and perhaps even Wittgenstein. It would be inappropriate at this point, however, to attempt a list of names, for my purpose here is not to survey the literature but simply, first, to emphasize that the issue is alive and then to mention some of the directions possible for a study of the problem. . . .

I should like to suggest, then, that philosophic discourse . . . may join with poetic expression to yield a quasi-conceptual form of language, a language which can move toward an illumination of the arational being of spontaneity. This suggestion, of course, is not new. Much philosophical writing has traditionally employed a kind of poetic-conceptual way of speaking. Plato's use of myth illustrates a juxtaposition of rationally directed dialectic with poetic language — a poetry intended to transcend conceptual thought. But within conceptual argument, philosophers have made use of metaphorical expressions which have later been absorbed into philosophical vocabulary: the use of the term "light" which now occurs frequently in expressions such as "throw light on the subject," is one case in point; another is the word "substance" suggesting something more than simply that which stands under. . . . They can function in this two-fold way to the extent that they are taken as a fusion of conceptual and poetic — or, more specifically, metaphorical — meaning. This point will be considered further below.

. . . [It should be emphasized, however, that] I have tried to show that rationality directed toward spontaneity reaches its limits in the recognition of a phenomenon that is structured as rationally absurd. For this reason, I want to insist that spontaneity as it lies beyond the reach of rational understanding is paradoxical as well as supra-rational. Thus the intelligibility of spontaneity must be found in a kind of apprehension and a kind of language which reflects this structure.

As a final suggestion concerning the intelligibility of spontaneity, I should like to propose a way of viewing poetic expression which may

indicate how the apprehension of spontaneity may be clarified and communicated. The suggestion is in no way intended as a definitive statement,
for it is in need of much further investigation than I can give it here.

Although poetic expression cannot be defined as metaphorical language,
the use of metaphors plays a dominant if not essential role in poetry. In
any case, it is the metaphorical aspect of poetry which I should like to
emphasize. There are, of course, different kinds of metaphors and many
theories of metaphor. However, one characteristic of metaphorical expressions, and perhaps, at bottom, of all such expressions is: suggested
relation through difference.[5] A metaphor which functions creatively or
which contributes to a creative work is generative of new meaning rather
than simply a comparison or directing of attention to unnoticed similarities already in existence. Hamlet's expression, "And thus the native hue
of resolution is sicklied o'er with the pale cast of thought," does not
simply refer the reader to possible similarities between hues and resolutions or paleness and thought; the reader is forced to recognize a unique
meaning appropriate to the way of being of Hamlet's consciousness as it is
revealed in the metaphorical expression and the total context of the drama.
This meaning is called to attention by virtue of the difference between
thought and paleness, between hues and resolutions, between sickness
and thoughtfulness. Thus metaphorical expression functions so as to
disclose disruptions in the strands of commonly recognized continuities.
Beardsley speaks of metaphor as grounded in a form of "logical absurdity."
The characteristics or qualities brought into relation are, taken literally,
thought of as unreal. Thus the reader is forced beyond literal significance
by a conflict or disruption — of his rational view of the world — by recognizing a break in previously known patterns by virtue of which the world
was made intelligible in terms of conceptual thought.

If this interpretation of metaphor is accepted, the suggestion follows
that metaphorical language expresses directly non-rational limits of conceptual thought. It strains concepts and creates meanings. Thus every
metaphorical utterance presents an instance of spontaneity and thereby
reveals to consciousness a non-rational feature of being. To the extent,
then, that poetic language is creative, it presents consciousness with
spontaneity. And to the extent that its creative achievements can be
apprehended by an audience, it communicates that which is non-rational.

5. Recent independent thinking I have done on this subject has led to an interpretation of
metaphor which is similar to one presented by Monroe C. Beardsley in *Aesthetics, Problems
in the Philosophy of Criticism* (New York: Harcourt, Brace and Company, 1958). See especially
pp. 134–147.

Thus one might regard poetic language, joining and enhancing philo-sophical language, as a mirror reflecting spontaneities. But the mirror is peculiar. And, because poetic expression reflects spontaneity in a peculiar way, the suggestion I have made is not without its difficulties. For, as an instance of creativity, a poetic utterance generates its own light and pre-sents its own image. To the extent that it succeeds as poetry which is creative, it discloses not something else, but rather its own newness. It cannot be an image of another spontaneity without losing its own spon-taneity. Nevertheless, I should like to suggest, a poetic expression may reflect other spontaneities in the sense that it can cooperate with other expressions, all of which, in the service of philosophical language, circum-scribe and focus attention on the non-rational reality with which they are concerned. The non-rational being of spontaneity, then, can be made intelligible only indirectly, but indirectly through a direct presentation of an instance of the non-rational being in question. For poetic language is a self-illuminating and self-reflecting mirror.

SELECTED BIBLIOGRAPHY

CHAPTER ONE · SEMINAL ACCOUNTS

Philosophical Background

Aristotle. *Physics*, Bk. 2, Chaps. 5–6, in McKeon, R. (ed.), *The Basic Works of Aristotle.* Oxford: Clarendon Press, 1928, pp. 244–247. Also in Wicksteed, P. H., and Cornford, F. M. (trans.), *Aristotle: The Physics*, Vol. 1. Cambridge, Mass.: Harvard University Press, 1957. (Loeb Classical Library; first published 1929.)

Aristotle. *Poetics*, in McKeon, R. (ed.) *The Basic Works of Aristotle.* Oxford: Clarendon Press, 1928. Also in Fyfe, W. H. (trans.), *Aristotle: The Poetics.* Cambridge, Mass.: Harvard University Press, 1932. (Loeb Classical Library; first published 1927.)

Heraclitus. *Fragments*, in Kirk, G. S., and Raven, J. E. (eds.), *The Presocratic Philosophers: A Critical History with a Selection of Texts.* Cambridge: Cambridge University Press, 1957, pp. 182–215. Also in Diels, H. *Die Fragmente der Vorsokratiker*, Kranz, W. (ed.). Berlin: Weidmann, 1951–1952.

Heraclitus is not included here because of his general influence on Plato and Aristotle. He is included because, in his attempt to understand nature, he specifically articulates the need to acknowledge radical change as well as stable structure. Without this emphasis, creative change would be either overlooked or treated as unreal.

Kant, I. *The Critique of Practical Reason*, Abbot, T. K. (trans.), 6th ed. London: Longmans, Green, 1923.

Kant, I. *Groundwork of the Metaphysic of Morals*, Paton, H. J. (trans.). London: Hutchinson's University Library, 3rd ed., 1956 (1st ed., 1948).

This relatively short work is important not only for Kant's ethical theory, but also for the basic outlines of Kant's defense of freedom in human action. In light of the view that creative acts are autonomous and in some sense self-determined, the arguments pertaining to freedom are important for the kind of approach Kant takes to the topic of genius or creativity.

Parmenides. *Fragments:* "The Proem" and "The Way of Truth," in Kirk, G. S., and Raven, J. E. (eds.), *The Presocratic Philosophers: A Critical History with a Selection of Texts.* Cambridge: Cambridge University Press, 1957, pp. 263–278. Also in Diels, H. *Die Fragmente der Vorsokratiker*, Kranz, W. (ed.). Berlin: Weidmann, 1951–1952.

Parmenides, in contrast to Heraclitus, takes a world view that openly and vigorously affirms the need to subject change (and thus creative activity) to unchanging structures.

Plato. *Phaedrus*, in Jowett, B. (trans.), *The Dialogues of Plato*, Vol. 1. Oxford: Clarendon Press, 1889.

Plato. *Republic*, in Jowett, B. (trans.), *The Dialogues of Plato*, Vol. 2. Oxford: Clarendon Press, 1889.

Plato. *Symposium*, in Jowett, B. (trans.), *The Dialogues of Plato*, Vol. 1. Oxford: Clarendon Press, 1889.

Plato. *Timaeus*, in Jowett, B. (trans.), *The Dialogues of Plato*, Vol. 2. Oxford: Clarendon Press, 1889.

This dialogue is important for a general world view that takes into account the possibility of creative activity within the world, as well as the conditions for creative generation of the world as a whole. Plato's suggestions about how a divine agency (the demiurge) might have created the world out of chaos— but in accord with preestablished ideals—has influenced the traditions of thought about both divine and human creativity.

Heredity and Genius

Barron, F. "Heritability of Factors in Creative Thinking and Aesthetic Judgment," *Acta Geneticae Medicae et Gemellologie*, 1970, 19:294–298.

Cattell, J. McK. "Families of American Men of Science," *Popular Science Monthly*, 1915, 86:504–515.

Terman, L. M. (ed.). *Genetic Studies of Genius*. Stanford, Calif.: Stanford University Press, 5 Vols., 1925–1959.

The following series of reports describes the only longitudinal study of children with exceptionally high IQs ever attempted:

Terman, L. M. *Mental and Physical Traits of a Thousand Gifted Children*. (*Genetic Studies of Genius*, Terman, L. M. (ed.), Vol. 1. Stanford, Calif.: Stanford University Press, 1925.)

Cox, C. *The Early Mental Traits of Three Hundred Geniuses*. (*Genetic Studies of Genius*, Terman, L. M. (ed.), Vol. 2. Stanford, Calif.: Stanford University Press, 1926.)

Burks, B. S.; Jensen, D. W.; and Terman, L. M. *The Promise of Youth: Follow-up Studies of a Thousand Gifted Children*. (*Genetic Studies of Genius*, Terman, L. M. (ed.), Vol. 3. Stanford, Calif.: Stanford University Press, 1930.)

Terman, L. M. and Oden, M. H. *The Gifted Child Grows Up: Twenty-five Years' Follow-up of a Superior Group* (*Genetic Studies of Genius*, Terman, L. M. (ed.), Vol. 4. Stanford University Press, 1947.)

Terman, L. M., and Oden, M. H. *The Gifted Group at Mid-Life. Thirty-Five Years' Follow-up of the Superior Child*. (*Genetic Studies of Genius*, Terman, L. M. (ed.), Vol. 5. Stanford, Calif.: Stanford University Press, 1959.)

Voronoff, S. *From Cretin to Genius*. New York: Alliance Book Corporation, 1941.

Freud on Creativity

Freud, S. "Dostoevsky and Parricide" (1928), in Strachey, J. (ed.), *The Standard Edition of the Complete Psychological Works of Sigmund Freud*, Vol. 21. London: Hogarth Press, 1961, pp. 175–198.

Freud, S. *Formulations on the Two Principles of Mental Functioning* (1911), in Strachey, J. (ed.), *The Standard Edition of the Complete Psychological Works of Sigmund Freud*, Vol. 12. London: Hogarth Press, 1958, pp. 213–226.

Freud, S. *The Interpretation of Dreams* (1900–1901), in Strachey, J. (ed.), *The Standard Edition of the Complete Psychological Works of Sigmund Freud*, Vols. 4 and 5. London: Hogarth Press, 1953.

   Although this work does not directly pertain to creativity (except for some cursory remarks about the genesis of Shakespeare's *Hamlet* on pp. 264–266 of Vol. 4), it contains Freud's basic exposition of primary and secondary process thinking, the foundation for most psychoanalytic formulations about creativity.

Freud, S. "Introductory Lectures on Psychoanalysis" (1916–1917), in Strachey, J. (ed.), *The Standard Edition of the Complete Psychological Works of Sigmund Freud*, Vol. 16. London: Hogarth Press, 1963, pp. 375–377.

   Freud here refers briefly to personality processes in the artist and the motivations for artistic creation.

Freud, S. *Jokes and their Relation to the Unconscious* (1905), in Strachey, J. (ed.), *The Standard Edition of the Complete Psychological Works of Sigmund Freud*, Vol. 8. London: Hogarth Press, 1964.

   Like *The Interpretation of Dreams*, this work does not pertain directly to creativity but the formulations about the psychodynamics of wit and humor contained here are indirectly pertinent. These formulations have influenced most psychoanalytic theories about art and creativity.

Freud, S. "Preface to Marie Bonaparte's *The Life and Works of Edgar Allan Poe: A Psychoanalytic Interpretation*" (1933), in Strachey, J. (ed.), *The Standard Edition of the Complete Psychological Works of Sigmund Freud*, Vol. 22. London: Hogarth Press, 1964, p. 254.

   Freud states the limitations of psychoanalytic psychography.

Chapter Two · DESCRIPTIVE ACCOUNTS

The Creative Process

Arnheim, R. *Picasso's Guernica: The Genesis of a Painting.* Berkeley: University of California Press, 1962.

Arnheim, R., et al. *Poets at Work.* New York: Harcourt, Brace, 1948.

   This is a psychological and literary evaluation of the poetry manuscript collection at State University of New York at Buffalo.

Benham, E. "The Creative Activity: Introspective Experiments in Musical Composition," *British Journal of Psychology*, 1929, 20:59–65.

   A rare description of the creative process in music. See also Vaughan and Myers below.

Eindhoven, J. E., and Vinacke, W. E. "Creative Processes in Painting," *Journal of General Psychology*, 1952, 47:139–164.

Ficke, G. B. "A Technique for the Study of the Process of Painting in Children," *Journal of Nervous and Mental Disease*, 1964, 139:153–160.

This is a description of an unusual technique for observing the creative process systematically.

Hutchinson, E. D. *How to Think Creatively*. New York: Abingdon-Cokesbury Press, 1949.

Morgan, D. N. "Creativity Today," *Journal of Aesthetics and Art Criticism*, 1953, 12: 1–24.

This article is a philosopher's assessment of studies of explanatory as well as descriptive accounts. Morgan discusses the various problems and foci of interest that are found in the literature.

Patrick, C. "Creative Thought in Poets," *Archives of Psychology*, 1935, No. 178. 74 pp.

Patrick, C. "Scientific Thought," *Journal of Psychology*, 1938, 5:55–83.

Perkins, D. "Probing Artistic Process: A Progress Report from Harvard Project Zero," *Journal of Aesthetic Education*, 1974, 8:33–57.

A recent attempt at systematic observation of the creative process in art.

Reitman, W. R. "Creative Problem Solving: Notes from the Autobiography of a Fugue," in Reitman, W. R., *Cognition and Thought*. New York: Wiley, 1966, pp. 166–180.

Vaughan, M., and Myers, R. E. "An Examination of Musical Process as Related to Creative Thinking," *Journal of Research in Music Education*, 1971, 19:337–341.

Vinacke, W. E. *The Psychology of Thinking*. New York: McGraw-Hill, 1952.

The Creative Person

Stark, S. "An Essay in Rorschach Revisionism, with Special Reference to the Maslowian Self-Actualizer: I. Innovation Versus Imagination, Idealism, Mysticism, Romanticism," *Perceptual and Motor Skills*, 1971, 33:343–357.

Taylor, C. W., and Ellison, R. L. "Predictors and Criteria of Creativity," in Taylor, C. W. (ed.), *Climate for Creativity*, Report of the 7th National Research Conference on Creativity, Greensboro, N.C., 1966. New York: Pergamon Press, 1972, pp. 149–165.

Taylor has been one of the most active proponents of creativity research in the United States for many years. This article summarizes some of the work done at Utah on the identifying characteristics of creative persons and on the development of a "Biographical Inventory."

Trilling, L. *The Liberal Imagination*. New York: Viking Press, 1950.

In this volume a literary critic discusses Freud's implication in the Introductory Lectures that the artist is neurotic.

van den Haag, E. "Creativity, Health and Art," *American Journal of Psychoanalysis*, 1963, 23:144–156.

Wilson, E. *The Wound and the Bow*. New York: Oxford University Press, 1941.

A literary critic maintains that artistic creativity is related to disability.

Subjective Reports

Allen, W. E. (ed.). *Writers on Writing*. Boston: The Writer, 1948.

Brooks, V. W. (ed.). *Writers at Work II*. New York: Viking Press, 1963.

Buckler, W. E. *Novels in the Making.* Boston: Houghton Mifflin, 1961.

Cane, M. *Making a Poem.* New York: Harcourt, Brace, 1953.

Cole, T. (ed.). *Playwrights on Playwriting.* New York: Hill and Wang, 1961.

Coleridge, S. T. *Kubla Khan: A Vision.* London: Printed for John Murray by William Bulmer, 1816.

Cook, J. W., and Klotz, H. *Conversations with Architects.* New York: Praeger, 1973.

Cowley, M. (ed.). *Writers at Work I.* New York: Viking Press, 1958.

Ghiselin, B. (ed.). *The Creative Process.* New York: New American Library, 1952.

Herbert, R. L. (ed.). *Modern Artists on Art.* Englewood Cliffs, N.J.: Prentice-Hall, 1965.

Kazin, A. (ed.). *Writers at Work III.* New York: Viking Press, 1967.

Morgenstern, S. (ed.). *Composers on Music.* New York: Pantheon Books, 1956.

Newquist, R. (ed.). *Counterpoint.* Chicago: Rand McNally, 1964.

Puma, F. (ed.). *Seven Arts.* New York: Doubleday, 1953.

Rosner, S., and Abt, L. E. (eds.). *The Creative Experience.* New York: Grossman, 1970.

Chapter Three · Explanations 1: FORMS AND SCOPE

Philosophical and Literary Accounts

Berdeyaev, N. *The Meaning of the Creative Act,* Lowrie, D. A. (trans.). London: Gollancz, 1955.
    Berdeyaev provides a theistic explanation of creativity.

Blanshard, B. *The Nature of Thought.* 2 vols. New York: Humanities Press, 1964 (first published 1939).

Burnshaw, S. *The Seamless Web. Language-Thinking, Creature-Knowledge, Art-Experience.* New York: Braziller, 1970.

Hegel, G. W. F. *Philosophy of Fine Art,* Osmaston, F. P. B. (trans.). London: Bell, 1920.

Maritain, J. *Art and Scholasticism,* Scanlan, J. F. (trans.). New York: Scribner's, 1930.

Tomas, V. "Creativity in Art," *Philosophical Review,* 1958, 67:1–15.

Psychoanalytic and Clinical Studies

Arieti, S. *The Intrapsychic Self. Feeling, Cognition, and Creativity in Health and Mental Illness.* New York: Basic Books, 1967.

Bellak, L. "Creativity: Some Random Notes to a Systematic Consideration," *Journal of Projective Techniques,* 1958, 22:363–380.

Beres, D. "Communication in Psychoanalysis and in the Creative Process: A Parallel," *Journal of the American Psychoanalytic Association,* 1957, 5:408–423.

Beres, D. "The Psychoanalytic Psychology of Imagination," *Journal of the American Psychoanalytic Association,* 1960, 8:252–269.

Bergler, E. *The Writer and Psychoanalysis*. Garden City, N.Y.: Doubleday, 1950.
This is a highly controversial study by a psychoanalyst who has written copiously about literary creativity.

Brill, A. A. "Poetry as an Oral Outlet," *Psychoanalytic Review*, 1931, 18:357–378.

Bychowski, G. "Metapsychology of Artistic Creation," *Psychoanalytic Quarterly*, 1951, 20:592–602.

Ehrenzweig, A. *The Psycho-analysis of Artistic Vision and Hearing: An Introduction to a Theory of Unconscious Perception*. New York: Julian Press, 1953.

Gardner, H. *The Arts and Human Development: A Psychological Study of the Artistic Process*. New York: Wiley, 1973.

Gedo, J. E. "On the Psychology of Genius," *International Journal of Psychoanalysis*, 1972, 53:199–203.

Giovacchini, P. L. "Characterological Factors and the Creative Personality," *Journal of the American Psychoanalytic Association*, 1971, 19:524–542.

Giovacchini, P. L. "On Scientific Creativity," *Journal of the American Psychoanalytic Association*, 1960, 8.407–426.

Gowan, J. C. *Development of the Creative Individual*. San Diego, Calif.: Knapp, 1972.

Greenacre, P. "The Childhood of the Artist," *The Psychoanalytic Study of the Child*, 1957, 12:47–72.

Greenacre, P. "Discussion and Comments on the Psychology of Creativity," *Journal of Child Psychiatry*, 1962, 1:129–137.

Greenacre, P. "Play in Relation to Creative Imagination," *The Psychoanalytic Study of the Child*, 1959, 14:61–80.

Hatterer, L. J. *The Artist in Society*. New York: Grove Press, 1965.
This is a discussion of the psychotherapy of artists based on the author's clinical experience.

Jung, C. G. "General Description of Types," in *Psychological Types*. New York: Harcourt, Brace, 1946, pp. 412–517.

Jung, C. G. "Psychology and Literature," in *Modern Man in Search of a Soul*, Dell, W. S., and Baynes, C. F. (trans.). New York: Harcourt, Brace, 1933, pp. 175–199.

Lee, H. B. "The Creative Imagination," *Psychoanalytic Quarterly*, 1949, 18:351–360.

Lee, H. B. "A Critique of the Theory of Sublimation," *Psychiatry*, 1939, 2:239–270.

Lee, H. B. "On the Esthetic States of the Mind," *Psychiatry*, 1947, 10:281–306.

Lee, H. B. "Poetry Production as a Supplemental Emergency Defense Against Anxiety," *Psychoanalytic Quarterly*, 1938, 7:232–242.

Lee, H. B. "Spirituality and Beauty in Artistic Experience," *Psychoanalytic Quarterly*, 1948, 17:507–523.

Lowenfeld, V. *Creative and Mental Growth*. New York: Macmillan, 1947.
Lowenfeld's theories about haptic and visual types of artists are based on his extensive experience in art education.

Lowenfeld, V. *The Nature of Creative Activity*, Oeser, O. A. (trans.). New York: Harcourt, Brace, 1939.

Muensterberger, W. "The Creative Process: Its Relation to Object Loss and Fetishism," in *Psychoanalytic Study of Society*, 1962, Vol. 2. New York: International Universities Press, 1962, pp. 161–185.

Murray, H. A. "Personality and Creative Imagination," in *English Institute Annual* — 1942. New York: Columbia University Press, 1943, pp. 139–162.

   Murray's work on personality and his interest in creativity has influenced the work of a generation of clinical psychologists and psychiatrists including MacKinnon, Bellak, Stein, Barron, and Rothenberg.

Murray, H. A. "Vicissitudes of Creativity," in Anderson, H. H. (ed.), *Creativity and Its Cultivation*. New York: Harper, 1959, pp. 96–118.

Neumann, E. *Art and the Creative Unconscious*, Mannheim, R. (trans.). New York: Pantheon Books (Bollingen Series 61), 1959.

Niederland, W. G. "Clinical Aspects of Creativity," *American Imago*, 1967, 24:6–34.

Noy, P. "About Art and Artistic Talent," *International Journal of Psychoanalysis*, 1972, 53:243–249.

Noy, P. "A Theory of Art and Aesthetic Experience," *Psychoanalytic Review*, 1968, 55:623–645.

Rank, O. "Der Doppelgänger," *Imago*, 1914, 3:7–164. Also in Rank, O. "The Double," *Psychoanalytic Review* (abstract), 1919, 6:450–460; and Rank, O. *The Double: A Psychoanalytic Study*, Tucker, H. E., Jr. (trans.), Chapel Hill: University of North Carolina Press, 1971.

Rank, O. *Der Künstler*. Vienna: Heller, 1907.

Rank, O. *The Myth of the Birth of the Hero: A Psychological Interpretation of Mythology*, Robbins, F., and Jelliffe, S. E. (trans.). New York: Journal of Nervous and Mental Disease Publishing Co., 1914.

Rank, O. *The Trauma of Birth*. New York: Harcourt, Brace, 1929.

Rank, O. *Will Therapy* and *Truth and Reality*, Taft, J. (trans.). New York: Knopf, 1936.

Rickman, J. "On the Nature of Ugliness and the Creative Impulse," *International Journal of Psychoanalysis*, 1940, 21:294–313.

   This is an account by a follower of the Melanie Klein school of psychoanalysis.

Rose, G. J. "Body Ego and Creative Imagination," *Journal of the American Psychoanalytic Association*, 1963, 11:775–789.

Rose, G. J. "Creative Imagination in Terms of Ego 'Core' and Boundaries," *International Journal of Psychoanalysis*, 1964, 45:75–84.

Rose, G. J. "Narcissistic Fusion States and Creativity," in Kanzer, M. (ed.), *The Unconscious Today, Essays in Honor of Max Schur*. New York: International Universities Press, 1971, pp. 495–505.

Rosen, V. H. "Some Effects of Artistic Talent on Character Style," *Psychoanalytic Quarterly*, 1964, 33:1–24.

Sachs, H. *The Creative Unconscious*. Cambridge, Mass.: Sci-Art Publishers, 1942.

Schafer, R. "Regression in the Service of the Ego: the Relevance of a Psychoanalytic Concept in Personality Assessment," in Lindzey, G., and Hall, C. (eds.). *Assessment of Human Motives*. New York: Rinehart, 1958, pp. 119–148.

Schneider, D. E. *The Psychoanalyst and the Artist*. New York: Farrar, Straus, 1950.

Storr, A. *The Dynamics of Creation*. New York: Atheneum, 1972.

Watts, V. N. "Effect of Therapy on the Creativity of a Writer," *The American Journal of Orthopsychiatry*, 1962, 32:186–192.

Weissman, P. "Theoretical Considerations of Ego Regression and Ego Functions in Creativity," *Psychoanalytic Quarterly*, 1967, 36:37–50.

Weissman, a psychoanalyst, criticizes Kris's notion, "regression in the service of the ego."

Experimental and Psychological Studies

Arnheim, R. *Art and Visual Perception: A Psychology of the Creative Eye*. Berkeley: University of California Press, 1974 (first published 1954).
    This is an outstanding Gestalt psychologist's formulation of the artistic creative process.
Arnheim, R. *Visual Thinking*. London: Faber and Faber, 1969.
Barron, F. *Artists in the Making*. New York: Seminar Press, 1972.
Barron, F. *Creativity and Personal Freedom*. Princeton, N.J.: Van Nostrand, 1968 (first published 1963).
Barron, F. "The Disposition Toward Originality," *Journal of Abnormal and Social Psychology*, 1955, 51:478–485.
Barron, F. "The Psychology of Creativity," in Newcomb, T. M. (ed.), *New Directions in Psychology II*. New York: Holt, Rinehart and Winston, 1965, pp. 1–134.
Barron, F., and Welsh, G. S. "Artistic Perception as a Possible Factor in Personality Style: Its Measurement by a Figure Preference Test," *Journal of Psychology*, 1952, 33:199–203.
    This article describes the Barron-Welsh figure preference test, a test used frequently in creativity assessment studies.
Brogden, H. E., and Sprecher, T. B. "Criteria of Creativity," in Taylor, C. W. (ed.), *Creativity: Progress and Potential*. New York: McGraw-Hill, 1964, pp. 155–176.
Chambers, J. A. "Relating Personality and Biographical Factors to Scientific Creativity," *Psychological Monographs*, 1964, 78: Whole No. 584.
Cropley, A. J. "A Five-Year Longitudinal Study of the Validity of Creativity Tests," *Developmental Psychology*, 1972, 6:119–124.
Csikszentmihalyi, M., and Getzels, J. W. "The Personality of Young Artists: An Empirical and Theoretical Exploration," *British Journal of Psychology*, 1973, 64:91–104.
Eiduson, B. T. "Artist and Non-Artist: A Comparative Study," *Journal of Personality*, 1958, 26:13–28.
Eiduson, B. T. *Scientists: Their Psychological World*. New York: Basic Books, 1962.
Getzels, J. W., and Csikszentmihalyi, M. *Creative Thinking in Art Students: The Process of Discovery*. Chicago: University of Chicago (C.R.P. No. E-008), 1964.
Getzels, J. W., and Csikszentmihalyi, M. "Scientific Creativity," *Science Journal*, 1967, 3:80–84.
Getzels, J. W., and Jackson, P. W. *Creativity and Intelligence*. New York: Wiley, 1962.
Getzels, J. W., and Jackson, P. W. "Family Environment and Cognitive Style: A Study of the Sources of Highly Intelligent and of Highly Creative Adolescents," *American Sociological Review*, 1961, 26:351–359.
Getzels, J. W., and Jackson, P. W. "Occupational Choice and Cognitive Functioning, Career Aspirations of Highly Intelligent and of Highly Creative Adolescents," *Journal of Abnormal and Social Psychology*, 1960, 61:119–123.

Gough, H. G. "Techniques for Identifying the Creative Research Scientist," in MacKinnon, D. W. (ed.), *The Creative Person*. Berkeley: University of California Extension, 1961.

    Gough has collaborated with Barron and MacKinnon on the studies of creative persons at the Institute for Personality Assessment and Research at Berkeley.

Guilford, J. P. "Creative Abilities in the Arts," *Psychological Review*, 1957, 64:110–118.

Guilford, J. P. "Creativity," *American Psychologist*, 1950, 5:444–454.

Guilford, J. P. "Creativity: Retrospect and Prospect," *Journal of Creative Behavior*, 1970, 4:149–168.

Guilford, J. P. "Creativity: Yesterday, Today, and Tomorrow," *Journal of Creative Behavior*, 1967, 1:3–14.

Guilford, J. P. "Executive Functions and a Model of Behavior," *Journal of General Psychology*, 1972, 86:279–287.

Guilford, J. P. "An Informational Theory of Creative Thinking," *U.S. Air Force Instructor's Journal*, 1963, 1:28–33.

Guilford, J. P. "Some Misconceptions Regarding Measurement of Creative Talents," *Journal of Creative Behavior*, 1971, 5:77–87.

Guilford, J. P., and Christensen, P. R. "The One-way Relation Between Creative Potential and IQ," *Journal of Creative Behavior*, 1973, 7:247–252.

Guilford, J. P., and Hoepfner, R. "Abilities in Creative Thinking and Planning," in Guilford, J. P., and Hoepfner, R. *The Analysis of Intelligence*. New York: McGraw-Hill, 1971, pp. 123–188.

Hammer, E. F. *Creativity*. New York: Random House, 1961.

    This is a clinical psychologist's study of a group of creative adolescents.

Havelka, J. *The Nature of the Creative Process in Art*. The Hague: Nijhoff, 1968.

Humphrey, G. *Directed Thinking*. New York: Dodd, Mead, 1948.

Khatena, J. "Note on Reliability and Validity of Onomatopoeia and Images," *Perceptual and Motor Skills*, 1970, 31:86.

Khatena, J. "Repeated Presentation of Stimuli and Production of Original Responses," *Perceptual and Motor Skills*, 1970, 30:91–94.

Kogan, N. "Creativity and Cognitive Style: A Life Span Perspective," in Goulet, L. R., and Baltes, P. B. (eds.), *Life-Span Developmental Psychology*. New York: Academic Press, 1973, pp. 145–178.

Levin, J., and Brody, N. "Information-Deprivation and Creativity," *Psychological Reports*, 1974, 35:231–237.

MacKinnon, D. W. "The Nature and Nurture of Creative Talent," *American Psychologist*, 1962, 17:484–495.

MacKinnon, D. W. "The Personality Correlates of Creativity: A Study of American Architects," in Nielsen, G. S. (ed.), *Proceedings of the XIV International Congress of Applied Psychology*, Vol. 2. Copenhagen: Munksgaard, 1962, pp. 11–39.

Maier, N. R. F. *Problem Solving and Creativity in Individuals and Groups*. Belmont, Calif.: Brooks/Cole, 1970.

Noller, R. B., and Parnes, S. J. "Applied Creativity: The Creative Studies Project Part III — The Curriculum," *Journal of Creative Behavior*, 1972, 6:275–294.

Parnes, S. J. "Effects of Extended Effort in Creative Problem Solving," *Journal of Educational Psychology*, 1961, 52:117–122.

S. J. Parnes has done extensive work on brainstorming and the nurturance of creative talent.

Parnes, S. J., and Meadow, A. "Development of Individual Creative Talent," in Taylor, C. W., and Barron, F. (eds.), *Scientific Creativity: Its Recognition and Development.* New York: Wiley, 1963, pp. 311–320.

Parnes, S. J., and Noller, R. B. "Applied Creativity: The Creative Studies Project: Part I—The Development," *Journal of Creative Behavior,* 1972, 6:11–22.

Parnes, S. J., and Noller, R. B. "Applied Creativity: The Creative Studies Project: Part II—Results of the Two-Year Program." *Journal of Creative Behavior,* 1972, 6:164–186.

Parnes, S. J., and Noller, R. B. "Applied Creativity; The Creative Studies Project: Part IV—Personality Findings and Conclusions," *Journal of Creative Behavior,* 1973, 7:15–36.

Parnes, S. J., and Noller, R. B. "The Creative Studies Project: Raison d'etre and Introduction," *Journal of Research and Development in Education,* 1971, 4:62–66.

Pine, F., and Holt, R. R. "Creativity and Primary Process: A Study of Adaptive Regression," *Journal of Abnormal and Social Psychology,* 1960, 61:370–379.
This is an empirical investigation of Kris's concept of "regression in the service of the ego."

Roe, A. "Artists and their Work," *Journal of Personality,* 1946, 15:1–40.

Roe, A. *The Making of a Scientist.* New York: Dodd, Mead, 1952.

Rothenberg, A.; Johnson, J. C.; and Brooks, M. B. "An Approach to Teaching Gifted Emotionally Disturbed Adolescents," *Gifted Child Quarterly,* 1966, 10:90–100.

Shouksmith, G. *Intelligence, Creativity and Cognitive Style.* Sydney: Angus and Robertson, 1973.

Spearman, C. *The Abilities of Man.* New York: Macmillan, 1927.

Spearman, C. *Creative Mind.* London: Nisbet, 1930.

Sprecher, T. B. "A Proposal for Identifying the Meaning of Creativity," in Taylor, C. W., and Barron, F. (eds.), *Scientific Creativity: Its Recognition and Development.* New York: Wiley, 1963, pp. 77–88.

Stein, M. I. "Creativity and Culture," *Journal of Psychology,* 1953, 36:311–322.

Stein, M. I. "A Transactional Approach to Creativity," in Taylor, C. W., and Barron, F. (eds.), *Scientific Creativity: Its Recognition and Development.* New York: Wiley, 1963, pp. 217–227.

Taylor, C. W. (ed.). *Climate for Creativity.* New York: Pergamon Press, 1972.

Taylor, C. W., and Ellison, R. L. "Predicting Creative Performances from Multiple Measures," in Taylor, C. W. (ed.), *Widening Horizons in Creativity.* New York: Wiley, 1964, pp. 227–260.

Taylor, C. W., and Parnes, S. J. "Humanizing Educational Systems: A Report of the Eighth International Creativity Research Conference, June 1970," *Journal of Creative Behavior,* 1970, 4:169–182.

Taylor, D. W.; Berry, P. C.; and Block, C. H. "Does Group Participation When Using Brainstorming Facilitate or Inhibit Creative Thinking?" *Administrative Science Quarterly,* 1958, 3:23–47.

Torrance, E. P. "Creativity and Infinity," *Journal of Research and Development in Education,* 1971, 4:35–41.

Torrance, E. P. *Education and the Creative Potential.* Minneapolis: The University of Minnesota Press, 1963.

Torrance, E. P. *Rewarding Creative Behavior.* Englewood Cliffs, N.J.: Prentice-Hall, 1965.

Torrance, E. P., and Myers, R. E. *Creative Learning and Teaching.* New York: Dodd, Mead, 1973.

Torrance, E. P., and Torrance, J. P. *Is Creativity Teachable?* Bloomington, Ind.: Phi Delta Kappa Educational Foundation, 1973.

Wallach, M. A., and Kogan, N. *Modes of Thinking in Young Children.* New York: Holt, Rinehart and Winston, 1965.

Wallach, M. A., and Kogan, N. "A New Look at the Creativity-Intelligence Distinction," *Journal of Personality*, 1965, 33:348–369.

Wallach, M. A., and Wing, C. W., Jr. *The Talented Student. A Validation of the Creativity-Intelligence Distinction.* New York: Holt, Rinehart and Winston, 1969.

Wertheimer, M. *Productive Thinking.* New York: Harper, 1945.

   This is a classic presentation of the Gestalt psychology theory of thought.

Wild, C. "Creativity and Adaptive Regression," *Journal of Personality and Social Psychology*, 1965, 2:161–169.

   This is an empirical investigation of Kris's concept of "regression in the service of the ego" in art students and teachers.

Wolfle, D. (ed.) *The Discovery of Talent.* Cambridge, Mass.: Harvard University Press, 1969.

Yamamoto, K. "Do Creativity Tests Really Measure Creativity?" *Theory Into Practice*, 1966, 5:194–197.

   Yamamoto is an educational psychologist who has done a good deal of work on creativity.

Yamamoto, K. "Validation of Tests of Creative Thinking: A Review of Some Studies," *Exceptional Children*, 1965, 31:281–290.

Chapter Four · EXPLANATIONS 2: SPECIAL TRENDS

Angoff, A., and Shapin, B. (eds.). *Psi Factors in Creativity.* New York: Parapsychology Foundation, 1970.

Davis, G. A. *Psychology of Problem Solving.* New York: Basic Books, 1973. See especially Chap. 5 on "Computer Problem Solving Models."

Davis, G. A., and Scott, J. A. *Training Creative Thinking.* New York: Holt, Rinehart and Winston, 1971.

DeBono, E. *About Think.* London: Cape, 1972.

DeBono, E. "Information Processing and New Ideas — Lateral and Vertical Thinking," *Journal of Creative Behavior*, 1969, 3:159–171.

DeBono, E. *Lateral Thinking: A Textbook of Creativity.* London: Ward Lock Educational, 1970.

DeBono, E. *Po: A Device for Successful Thinking.* New York: Simon and Schuster, 1972.

Eisenman, R., and Brownstein, G. M. "Restriction of Emotional Release and Creativity," *Perceptual and Motor Skills*, 1970, 31:647–650.

Eisenman, R., and Schussel, N. R. "Creativity, Birth Order and Preference for Symmetry," *Journal of Consulting and Clinical Psychology*, 1970, 34:275–280.

Gazzaniga, M. S. *The Bisected Brain*. New York: Appleton-Century-Crofts, 1970.

Gowan, J. C. *Development of the Creative Individual*. San Diego, Calif.: Knapp, 1972.

Greenacre, P. "Woman As Artist," *Psychoanalytic Quarterly*, 1960, 29:208–227.

Helson, R. "Childhood Interest Clusters Related to Creativity in Women," *Journal of Consulting Psychology*, 1965, 29:352–361.

Helson, R. "Generality of Sex Differences in Creative Style," *Journal of Personality*, 1968, 36:33–48.

Helson, R. "Narrowness in Creative Women," *Psychological Reports*, 1966, 19:618.

Helson, R. "Personality Characteristics and Developmental History of Creative College Women," *Genetic Psychology Monographs*, 1967, 76:205–256.

Helson, R. "Personality of Women with Imaginative and Artistic Interests: The Role of Masculinity, Originality, and Other Characteristics in Their Creativity," *Journal of Personality*, 1966, 34:1–25.

Helson, R. "Sex Differences in Creative Style," *Journal of Personality*, 1967, 35: 214–233.

Helson, R. "Sex-Specific Patterns in Creative Literary Fantasy," *Journal of Personality*, 1970, 38:344–363.

Helson, R., and Crutchfield, R. S. "Creative Types in Mathematics," *Journal of Personality*, 1970, 38:177–197.

Helson, R., and Crutchfield, R. S. "Mathematicians: The Creative Researcher and the Average PhD" *Journal of Consulting and Clinical Psychology*, 1970, 34:250–257.

Honorton, C. "Creativity and Precognition Scoring Level," *Journal of Parapsychology*, 1967, 31:29–42.

Kamiya, J. "Operant Control of the EEG Alpha Rhythm and Some of Its Reported Effects on Consciousness," in Tart, C. T. (ed.), *Altered States of Consciousness*. New York: Wiley, 1969, pp. 507–517.

Khatena, J. "The Use of Analogy in the Production of Original Verbal Images," *Journal of Creative Behavior*, 1972, 6:209–213.

Krippner, S. "Consciousness and the Creative Process," *Gifted Child Quarterly*, 1968, 12:141–157.

Krippner, S. "The Psychedelic State, the Hypnotic Trance, and the Creative Act," *Journal of Humanistic Psychology*, 1968, 8:49–67.

Lidz, T., and Rothenberg, A. "Psychedelism: Dionysus Reborn," *Psychiatry*, 1968, 31:116–125.

Ludwig, A. M. "Altered States of Consciousness," *Archives of General Psychiatry*, 1966, 15:225–234.

Masters, R. E. L., and Houston, J. (eds.). *Psychedelic Art*. New York: Grove Press, 1968.

Murphy, G. *Personality*. New York: Harper, 1947.

Murphy, G. "Research in Creativeness: What it Tells Us About Extrasensory Perception," *Journal of the American Society for Psychical Research*, 1966, 60:8–22.

Murphy, G., and Moriarty, A. E. "Some Thoughts About Prerequisite Conditions or States in Creativity," *Journal of the American Society for Psychical Research,* 1967, 61:203–218.

Newell, A.; Shaw, J. C.; and Simon, H. A. "The Processes of Creative Thinking," in Gruber, H. E.; Terrell, G.; and Wertheimer, M. (eds.), *Contemporary Approaches to Creative Thinking.* New York: Atherton Press, 1964.

   The first attempt at relating computer problem-solving to creativity.

Newell, A., and Simon, H. A. *Human Problem Solving.* Englewood Cliffs, N.J.: Prentice-Hall, 1972.

Ornstein, R. E. (ed.) *The Nature of Human Consciousness.* San Francisco: Freeman, 1973.

Reitman, W. R. *Cognition and Thought: An Information-Processing Approach.* New York: Wiley, 1965.

   A heuristic approach to computer problem-solving.

Rothbart, H. A. *Cybernetic Creativity.* New York: Speller, 1972.

Schmeidler, G. (ed.). *Extra Sensory Perception.* New York: Atherton Press, 1969.

Skinner, B. F. *Beyond Freedom and Dignity.* New York: Knopf, 1971.

Sperry, R. W. "Preservation of High-Order Function in Isolated Somatic Cortex in Callosum-Sectioned Cat," *Journal of Neurophysiology,* 1959, 22:78–87.

Tart, C. T. (ed.). *Altered States of Consciousness.* New York: Wiley, 1969.

Zegans, L. S.; Pollard, J. C.; and Brown, D. "The Effects of LSD-25 on Creativity and Tolerance to Regression," *Archives of General Psychiatry,* 1967, 16:740–749.

Chapter Five · ALTERNATIVE APPROACHES

Alexander, S. *Art and Instinct.* Oxford: Clarendon Press, 1927.

Alexander, S. *Beauty and Other Forms of Value.* London: Macmillan, 1933.

Bergson, H. *Creative Evolution,* Mitchell, A. (trans.). New York: Holt, 1911.

Bergson, H. *An Introduction to Metaphysics,* Hulme, T. E. (trans.). New York: Macmillan, 1913.

Bradley, A. C. *Oxford Lectures on Poetry.* London: Macmillan, 1909.

Collingwood, R. G. *The Idea of History.* Oxford: Clarendon Press, 1946.

Collingwood, R. G. *Outlines of a Philosophy of Art.* London: Oxford University Press, 1925.

Croce, B. "Aesthetics," *Encyclopædia Britannica,* 14th ed., Vol. 1, pp. 263–271.

Croce, B. "Criticism and Aesthetics," *Encyclopædia Britannica,* 14th ed., Vol. 6, p. 781.

Croce, B. *The Essence of Aesthetic,* Ainslie, D. (trans.). London: Macmillan, 1921.

Dewey, J. *Art as Experience.* New York: Minton, Balch, 1934.

Gruber, H. E., and Barrett, P. H. *Darwin on Man: A Psychological Study of Scientific Creativity.* New York: Dutton, 1974.

   An excellent description of Darwin's thinking, emphasizing that creation is the result of a free, intention-directed process rather than a single act.

Hartmann, N. *Ethics.,* Vol. 3, Coit, S. (trans.). New York: Macmillan, 1932.

   This volume from Hartmann's extended work on ethics provides a careful and rigorous argument in defense of human freedom. Although the general context of the discussion is ethics, the arguments and conclusions are particularly relevant to creativity because of the inseparability of issues concerning free activity and the creative process.

Hausman, C. R. *A Discourse on Novelty and Creation*. The Hague: Nijhoff, 1975.

Hausman, C. R. "The Existence of Novelty," *Pacific Philosophy Forum*, 1966, 4, No. 3:3–60.

Hausman, C. R. "Form, Value and Novelty in Creative Activity," in Vaught, C. G. (ed.), *Essays in Metaphysics*. University Park: Pennsylvania State University Press, 1970, pp. 79–103.

Hausman, C. R. "Mechanism or Teleology in the Creative Process," *Journal of Philosophy*, 1961, 58:577–584.

Hausman, C. R. "Mystery, Paradox, and the Creative Act," *Southern Journal of Philosophy*, 1969, 7:289–296.

Hausman, C. R. "Understanding and the Act of Creation," *Review of Metaphysics*, 1966, 20:88–112.

Langer, S. K. *Feeling and Form*. New York: Scribner's, 1953.

Morgan, C. L. *Emergent Evolution*. New York: Holt, 1923.

Nahm, M. C. *The Artist as Creator: An Essay on Human Freedom*. Baltimore: Johns Hopkins Press, 1956.

Peirce, C. S. "The Law of Mind," *The Monist*, 1892, 2:533–559. Also in Hartshorne, C., and Weiss, P. (eds.), *Collected Papers of Charles Sanders Peirce*, Vol. 6, Chap. 5, paragraphs 102–163, Cambridge, Mass.: Harvard University Press, 1935.

This paper introduces the hypothesis that an understanding of the creative growth of personality requires explanation in terms of a developmental teleology, or a teleology that includes the self-determination by specific agents of their own intelligible goals—goals that are not conditioned by a preestablished system or scheme guaranteeing the value and effectiveness of these goals.

Rothenberg, A. "Cognitive Processes in Creation," in Krausz, M. (ed.), *The Idea of Creativity*. Berkeley: University of California Press, in press.

Rothenberg, A. "Homospatial Thinking in Creativity," *Archives of General Psychiatry*, 1976, 33:17–26.

Rothenberg, A. "The Iceman Changeth: Toward an Empirical Approach to Creativity," *Journal of the American Psychoanalytic Association*, 1969, 17:549–607.

Rothenberg, A. "Janusian Thinking and Creativity," in Muensterberger, W. (ed.), *Psychoanalytic Study of Society*. New Haven, Conn.: Yale University Press, in press.

Rothenberg, A. "Opposite Responding as a Measure of Creativity," *Psychological Reports*, 1973, 33:15–18.

Rothenberg, A. "Poetic Process and Psychotherapy," *Psychiatry*, 1972, 35:238–254.

Rothenberg, A. "Poetry and Psychotherapy: Kinships and Contrasts," in Leedy, J. (ed.) *Poetry, the Healer*. Philadelphia: Lippincott, 1973, pp. 351–366.

Rothenberg, A. "Word Association and Creativity," *Psychological Reports*, 1973, 33:3–12.

Sartre, J. P. *Psychology of the Imagination* (trans. anon.). New York: Philosophical Library, 1948.

Sartre, J. P. *What is Literature?*, Frechtman, B. (trans.). New York: Philosophical Library, 1948. (Also, New York: Citadel Press, 1961.)

Vivas, E. *Creation and Discovery*. New York: Noonday Press, 1955.

Westland, G. "The Investigation of Creativity," *Journal of Aesthetics and Art Criticism*, 1969, 28:127–131.

Whitehead, A. N. *Process and Reality: An Essay in Cosmology*. New York: Macmillan, 1929.

This work sets forth a general metaphysical view based upon the acknowledgment that radical creativity must serve as a fundamental component of a world view. Whitehead's characterization of creativity provides a principle for building an alternative approach to explaining creativity.

Wieman, H. N. *The Source of Human Good*. Chicago: University of Chicago Press, 1946. (Also, Carbondale: Southern Illinois University Press, 1964.)

Wieman was influenced by Whitehead. However, Wieman focuses on the creativity in concrete experience rather than on the role of a transcendent God.